Italian as a foreign language
Teaching and acquisition in higher education

Edited by
Alberto Regagliolo
UKSW University

Series in Language and Linguistics

Copyright © 2024 by the Authors.

All rights reserved. No part of this publication may be reproduced, stored in a retrieval system, or transmitted in any form or by any means, electronic, mechanical, photocopying, recording, or otherwise, without the prior permission of Vernon Art and Science Inc.

www.vernonpress.com

In the Americas:
Vernon Press
1000 N West Street, Suite 1200
Wilmington, Delaware, 19801
United States

In the rest of the world:
Vernon Press
C/Sancti Espiritu 17,
Malaga, 29006
Spain

Series in Language and Linguistics

Library of Congress Control Number: 2023938926

ISBN: 978-1-64889-912-6

Also available: 978-1-64889-678-1 [Hardback]; 978-1-64889-786-3 [PDF, E-Book]

Cover design by Alberto Regagliolo using elements designed by Freepik.

Product and company names mentioned in this work are the trademarks of their respective owners. While every care has been taken in preparing this work, neither the authors nor Vernon Art and Science Inc. may be held responsible for any loss or damage caused or alleged to be caused directly or indirectly by the information contained in it.

Every effort has been made to trace all copyright holders, but if any have been inadvertently overlooked the publisher will be pleased to include any necessary credits in any subsequent reprint or edition.

Table of contents

List of figures and tables	ix
Abbreviations	xi
Contributors	xv
Introduction	xxi
Part I. Pedagogical approaches & methodological proposals	1

Chapter 1 **Teaching L2 Italian phonetics and pronunciation in academic courses**   3
Olga Broniś
Cardinal Stefan Wyszyński University in Warsaw
   1. Introduction
   2. Different approaches towards teaching L2 Italian phonetics at the university
   3. The rationale for teaching L2 Italian phonetics at the university
   4. Conclusions
   References

Chapter 2 **Historical linguistics and Italian at university**   15
Josh Brown
The University of Western Australia
   1. Introduction
   2. Historical linguistics in particular courses
   3. Pedagogy and pedagogical issues
   4. Conclusion
   References

Chapter 3 **Telecollaborating in Italian**   37
Stefania Chiapello and Carmen González Royo
University of Alicante
   1. Introduction

        2. Methodology
        3. Results
        4. Conclusions
        References
        Appendix

Chapter 4   **Teaching Italian (with) comics**   59
Sara Dallavalle
University of Chicago

    1. Introduction
    2. Terms and definitions
    3. Pedagogical approach
    4. Pedagogical applications
    5. Further readings
    References

Chapter 5   **Teaching and understanding Italian through the language of the press**   87
Marta Kaliska
Nicolaus Copernicus University in Toruń

    1. Introduction
    2. Theoretical assumptions
    3. Italian language teaching: methodological proposals
    4. Conclusion
    References

Chapter 6   **Teaching and learning Italian word-formation patterns**   105
Irene Lami
Lund University

    1. Introduction
    2. Morphology and word-formation theory
    3. Derivation and compounding (but not inflection)
    4. Word-formation in Italian
    5. Conclusion
    References

Chapter 7	**Teaching Italian Dialectology**	129

Adam Ledgeway
University of Cambridge

    1. Introduction
    2. Why teach Italian dialectology?
    3. Teaching Italian dialectology
    4. Linguistic theory
    5. Conclusion
    References
    Appendix A: selective sources for the study of the dialects
    Appendix B: selective sources for the study of regional Italian

Chapter 8	**Teaching and learning Italian indecent language**	165

Alberto Regagliolo
UKSW University

    1. Introduction
    2. Part one: theoretical foundation
    3. Part two: educational proposals
    4. Conclusion
    References

        Part II. Italian through projects and case-studies   213

Chapter 9	**Teaching specialist language skills in Italian through History of Art**	215

Cinzia Bacilieri
University of York

    1. Introduction
    2. Teaching Italian through History of Art
    3. Curricula design: embedding general language skills in a specialist language course
    4. Applied teaching methodology
    5. Examples of classroom activities
    6. Conclusions
    References

Chapter 10 **For an interdisciplinary approach in language learning: exploring the use of subtitling in the Italian language classroom** 233

Rosalba Biasini
University of Liverpool

Francesca Raffi
University of Macerata

    1. Introduction
    2. FL teaching and learning through interlingual subtitling
    3. The project
    4. Preliminary results
    5. Conclusion
    References
    Appendix: an example of subtitling task for summative assessment

Chapter 11 **Embodied and experiential immersion into transculturality: learning Italian through ethnography and translation** 251

Eliana Maestri
University of Exeter

    1. Introduction
    2. Translation and ethnography: a composite, long-standing interrelationship
    3. Translation and ethnography: teaching and learning migratory contexts
    4. Translation and ethnography: towards an embodied and experiential immersion in language acquisition
    5. Translation and ethnography in the classroom as the Third Space
    6. Conclusion
    Acknowledgement
    References

Chapter 12 **Learning Italian with cartoons** 271

Stefano Maranzana
Emory University

    1. Introduction
    2. Captioned video
    3. Animated Cartoons in L2 Instruction: *Peppa Pig*
    4. The Role of Humour to Stimulate L2 Learning

5. *Peppa Pig* for 1st and 2nd semester university-level Italian classes

6. Conclusion

References

| Chapter 13 | **Italian through geography at university level** | 291 |

Leonardo Masi
Cardinal Stefan Wyszyński University in Warsaw

1. Introduction
2. Resources
3. Geography and Language Learning
4. An approach for beginners
5. Conclusion

References

| Chapter 14 | **The teaching of Italian through *Process Drama*** | 305 |

Ilaria Salonna
University of Warsaw

1. Introduction
2. Process Drama *in Glottodidactics*
3. The importance of atmosphere and the balance between risk and safety in the dimension of playing
4. Playing with the stereotypical theatricality of the Italian language: Improvisation and Diction
5. Practical indications for a Theatre-Italian laboratory
6. Conclusion

References

| Chapter 15 | **Learning from the essay** | 319 |

Valentina Tibaldo
University of Oxford

1. Introduction
2. Developing self-awareness through the essay
3. Emotions and intercultural competence
4. Essay classes. Two pedagogical applications
5. Conclusion

References

Index   331

List of figures and tables

List of figures

Figure 4. 1. On the left, an example of a cartoon or single-panel comics (It. Vignetta). On the right, an example of comic strip (It. Striscia) — 64

Figure 4. 2. This is a comics page with its main elements: gutter (It. lo spazio bianco), caption (It. la didascalia), balloon (It. la nuvoletta or il balloon), onomatopoeia (It. l'onomatopea), emanata (It. la metafora visualizzata), and panel (It. la vignetta). In the bottom tier, you see three types of balloons: a bubble-shaped balloon for normal speech a balloon with a jagged outline for screams; a cloud-shaped balloon for thoughts. — 65

Figure 8. 1. Registers — 172

Figure 8. 2. Metaphor — 204

Figure 9. 1. The split between class time spent on the development of specialist and non-specialist language skills in the first half of the course — 223

Figure 9. 2. Split between class time spent on development of specialist and non-specialist skills in the second part of the course — 224

Figure 9. 3. Example of exercises — 225

Figure 9. 4. Examples of History of Art-related exercises for students to practice numbers and dates. — 227

Figure 9. 5. Vocabulary used to prepare students for role-plays focusing on asking for a ticket or booking a guided tour in a museum in Italy — 228

Figure 9. 6. Example of speaking practice — 230

List of tables

Table 2. 1. Example of 'questions and answers' embedded into the body of the chapter from Alkire and Rosen (2010: 96) — 26

Table 2. 2. Features of Vulgar Latin — 30

Table 6. 1. Deverbal suffixes — 110

Table 6. 2. Agentive, instrumental, locative suffixes — 114

Table 6. 3. Abstract concept suffixes — 116

Table 6. 4.	Verb suffixes	119
Table 7. 1.	Integration of learnèd and foreign loans in Italian	139
Table 7. 2.	Translate the following forms into Italian (note that a single dialect form might correspond to several forms in Italian)	140
Table 7. 3.	Translate the following Italian forms into Neapolitan (the only relevant differences of interest are unstressed vowels)	140
Table 7. 4.	Translate the following Sicilian forms into Italian (note that a single dialect form might correspond to several forms in Italian)	140
Table 7. 5.	Basic day-based divisions	145
Table 7. 6.	Lexicalizations of '2 / 3 days ago'	146
Table 7. 7.	Lexicalizations of 'in 2 / 3 / 4 / 5 days time'	147
Table 8. 1.	The linguistic function	171

Abbreviations

*	ungrammatical or not attested
¿	doubt
=	cliticised to
A level	Advanced Level qualification
AS level	Advanced Subsidiary level
CALL	Computer-Assisted Language Learning
CEFR	Common European Framework of Reference
CEFRL	Common European Framework of Reference for Languages
CLA	Centro Linguistico di Ateneo
DOM	differential object marker
EFL	English as a foreign language
F	feminine
FL	foreign language
FUT	future
GCSE	General Certificate of Secondary Education
GER	gerund
HoA	Department of History of Art
ICT	information communications technology
IFL	Italian as a foreign language
IMP	imperative
INF	infinitive
Infl	(verbal) inflection
IPFV	imperfect(ive)
IRR	irrealis
It	Italian
L&LS	Department of Language and Linguistic Science
L1	mother tongue
L2	second language

LFA	Languages for all
lit.	literally
LSP	Languages for Specific Purposes
LU	learning unit
M	masculine
MALL	Mobile-Assisted Language Learning
Mod.	Modern
N	native speaker
N	northern
NEG	negator
NN	non-native speaker
O	old
OBL	oblique
PFV	perfect(ive)
PL	plural
PRO	null pronoun
PST	past
PTCP	participle
SCL	subject clitic
SG	singular
SLA	second language acquisition
SVO	Subject – verb – object
V2	verb-second (syntax)
W	western

Varieties

Abr.	Abruzzese
Bas.	Basilicatese
Bol.	Bolognese
BS	province of Brescia
Cal.	Calabrian
CE	province of Cuneo

Abbroviations

Cmp.	Campanian
Cos.	Cosentino
Crs.	Corsican
CS	province of Cosenza
Eml.	Emilian
FG	province of Foggia
Fr.	French
Gen.	Genoese
It.	Italian
Lat.	Latin
Laz.	Laziale
LE	province of Lecce
Lig.	Ligurian
Lmb.	Lombard
Mac.	Maceratese
Mol.	Molisano
MT	province of Matera
NA	province of Naples
Nap.	Neapolitan
Pdm.	Piedmontese
Pgl.	Pugliese
PZ	province of Potenza
RC	province of Reggio di Calabria
Rml.	Romagnol
Ro.	Romanian
Sal.	Salentino
Sic.	Sicilian
Tsc.	Tuscan
Umb.	Umbrian
Ven.	Venetan

Contributors

Cinzia Bacilieri. After completing her studies in Conservation and Heritage studies (Laurea Specialistica Magistrale) at the University of Bologna in Italy with a Specialization in Classical Archaeology, Cinzia Bacilieri later pursued a career in Aerial Archaeology in the UK (University of Cambridge, English Heritage, WYAS, ARS ltd.). Bacilieri joined the Department of Language and Linguistic Science (University of York) in 2011. As a Lecturer in Italian, she specialises in teaching the Italian language through the History of Art and has developed courses such as *Italian for Art Historians* (for the BA in History of Art) and *The Role of Art in Italian Society* (for the BA in Italian).

Rosalba Biasini is a Lecturer in Italian at the University of Liverpool (UK), where she teaches the Italian language and culture at all levels. She graduated in *Lettere Classiche* (L'Aquila, Italy, 2004) and completed an MA in Translation Studies (Manchester, UK, 2005) and a Master in ITALS (Ca' Foscari, Venezia, Italy, 2013). She holds a PhD/D.Phil. in Italian literature (Oxford, UK, 2010). Her research interests and publications span from the works of partisan writer Beppe Fenoglio (1922-1963) to the didactics of Italian as a foreign language, with a focus on the use of translation in foreign language learning.

Olga Broniś is an assistant professor at the Faculty of Humanities, Cardinal Stefan Wyszyński University in Warsaw. Her research is focused on the synchronic analysis of standard Italian. In particular, she is interested in the phonetic and phonological adaptation of foreign words borrowed into Italian and in other phonological issues related to cross-linguistic similarities and differences. She also takes part in group research on multilingualism and cross-linguistic influences in the acquisition of Italian as L3.

Joshua Brown is a senior lecturer in Italian Studies at The University of Western Australia. After his PhD, he completed a postdoctoral fellowship at Stockholm University before returning to Australia. His main areas of interest are historical sociolinguistics, philology, language contact and digital humanities. He also has interests in Italian as a second language, language policies, and the teaching of Italian. Recent publications include a co-edited volume entitled *Languages and Cross-Cultural Exchanges in Renaissance Italy* (Brepols), "Towards the elaboration of a diastratic model in historical analyses of Koineization" (*Sociolinguistic Studies* 2020) and "Language History from Below. Standardization and Koineization in Renaissance Italy" (*Journal of Historical Sociolinguistics* 2020).

Stefania Chiapello, BA/MA in Modern Languages and Literatures at the University of Genova, MA in Japanese Studies at the Sophia University of Tokyo and Diploma of Advanced Studies in Translation Studies at the University of Alicante. She collaborates at the University of Alicante (Dept. Translation and Interpretation), and she teaches Italian as a Foreign Language at the University of Dhaka in Bangladesh. Her working languages are Spanish, English and Italian. Her research mainly focuses on contrastive analysis, TICs as an innovation on didactics, politeness in the political discourse and humanism. She participates in the following research groups: ORSA (action-research and new technologies in the collaborative teaching-learning at the University of Salerno); HUMANISMO EUROPA (human sciences and universalism at the University of Alicante) and Research Networks in EHEA (ICE, University of Alicante) in addition to being engaged in the Teletándem-CORINÉI project. She is a sworn translator of English, French and Spanish in Italy and an Examiner of IFL at the University of Perugia (CELI).

Sara Dallavalle is an Assistant Instructional Professor at the University of Chicago, where she teaches all levels of Italian and coordinates the first-year sequence. She has a laurea magistrale in Specialized Translation (IULM University, Milan) and a PhD in Italian Studies (Indiana University-Bloomington). She specializes in comics studies, and her research includes popular culture, media industry studies, publishing studies, digital humanities, and translation studies. Her doctoral dissertation, titled "Italian Auteur Comics Magazines: the case of Orient Express (1982-1985)," explored the culture of auteur comics in Italy and the phenomenon of auteur comics magazines (1960-1980). In combining traditional and digital methods, including close readings, text analysis, and data visualization, her work proposes an innovative method for studying comic magazines that can be effectively applied to other forms of periodical products. Other projects consider comics, their positioning in the publishing industry, and their impact on Italian society. Sara is also interested in exploring original pedagogical applications of comics in foreign language courses and is currently developing a course on the translation of Italian comics.

Carmen González Royo has obtained a Degree in Romance Philology and a PhD in Philology at the University of Valencia. Senior lecturer at the

Department of Translation and Interpreting Studies at the University of Alicante, formerly of Italian Philology. She is currently teaching both in graduate and postgraduate programmes. Her research focuses on contrastive analysis of Spanish/Italian but also on methodology, phraseology and translation. She participates in multiple research groups: FRASYTRAM, BITRA (Bibliography of Interpreting and Translation), CLIL (Content and Language Integrated Learning) and ORSA (action-research and TICs in teaching and learning) at the University of Salerno. She has coordinated several Research Networks in EHEA (ICE, UA) on TICs and innovation in didactics, and she is engaged in Teletándem-CORINÉI and Tel.Int:Lab projects.

Marta Kaliska is an associate professor at the Nicolaus Copernicus University in Toruń, where she is involved in language education and language teacher education. She obtained a PhD in the humanities in 2007 and a postdoctoral degree (termed a 'national scientific habilitation') in 2019. Her research mostly focuses on Italian language teaching, textbooks, and the development of teaching materials. She is also a co-author of the three-volume series of Italian foreign language textbooks *Va bene! A1, A2, A2+* (B1) and *Va benissimo! 1, 2, 3* intended for primary school learners.

Irene Lami is a PhD candidate at the Centre for Languages and Literature at Lund University, Sweden. Her research project focuses on the role of compounding in word-formation processes, with an attention on the morphosyntactic behaviour of specific types of compounds. She is also interested in multimodal linguistics and worked as a research assistant at Lund University on several projects dedicated to the role of gestures in human cognition and communication.

Adam Ledgeway is a Professor of Italian and Romance Linguistics in the Faculty of Modern and Medieval Languages and Linguistics of the University of Cambridge, and Professorial Fellow of Downing College, and Fellow of the British Academy and a Member of the Academia Europaea. His research is channelled towards bringing together traditional Romance philological scholarship with the insights of recent syntactic theory. He is the author of 5 monographs, 17 co-edited books, some 40 journal articles, and over 70 book chapters. He is the founding co-editor of the OUP book series *Oxford Studies in Diachronic and Historical Linguistics* and *The Oxford Guides to the World's Languages* and is co-editor of the *Journal of Linguistics*.

Eliana Maestri obtained her PhD from the University of Bath in 2012. She is now Senior Lecturer in Translation Studies and Director of Postgraduate Research in the Department of Languages, Cultures and Visual Studies, University of Exeter. Her research focuses on the interplay between translation, mobility and visual culture. She was the recipient of a British Academy Rising Star Engagement Award to co-organise the 2019 Exeter Translation Festival and of a 2019 Europe Network Grant (Global Partnerships, Exeter) with KU Leuven, Belgium, to study street art. Previous awards include a EUOSSIC Erasmus Mundus Post-Doctoral Fellowship in European Studies, University of Sydney and University of Bath (2011-12), and a MEEUC Research Fellowship, Monash University, Melbourne (2014). Together with colleagues from KU Leuven, Exeter University and IUAV University of Venice, Maestri is one of the main faculty members of the Venice International University Summer School: Linguistic Landscapes: Using Signs and Symbols to Translate Cities. Maestri has published on visions of Europe among migrants in Australia, on translations of mobile traditions into Italian Australian folk music (with Rita Wilson), on street art in anti-mafia contexts (with Inge Lanslots and Paul Sambre) and translations of languages and cityscapes into the visual, with particular attention to prominent artist Jon Cattapan. Her monograph *Translating the Female Self across Cultures* appeared in the 2018 John Benjamins Translation Library.

Stefano Maranzana is an Assistant Teaching Professor of Italian at the Department of French & Italian at Emory University. His research interests focus on the acquisition of Italian grammatical gender, captioned video in listening comprehension, virtual reality in language learning and Italian American ethnicity and immigration. His latest research centres on the use of French language variations (argot and verlan) in contemporary TV shows and its implications for learners of the French language.

Leonardo Masi studied Polish language and literature at the Universities of Florence and Milan and Music at the Conservatory of Florence. He currently works at the Cardinal Stefan Wyszyński University in Warsaw, where he directed the Department of Italian Studies for several years. His main research fields are the relationships between literature and music, Italian-Polish relations and translation practices. He has published works, among others, on Szymanowski, Brzozowski, Fellini, Fortini, contemporary poetry and popular music. He translates into Italian some of the most important contemporary Polish authors.

Francesca Raffi is a Senior Research Fellow in English language and translation at the University of Macerata (Italy), where she has been teaching

English language and translation at undergraduate and postgraduate levels since 2015. She holds a PhD in English for Special Purposes and Audiovisual Translation from the University of Naples Federico II (Italy), and she is a Chartered Linguist at the Chartered Institute of Linguists (UK). Since 2019, she has been an Honorary Fellow at the Department of Modern Languages and Cultures, University of Liverpool (UK).

Alberto Regagliolo is an Assistant Professor of Italian Linguistics at UKSW University, a translator, a CELI Instructor and a graphic designer. He holds a Post-Doc in Italian Linguistics with a specialization in vulgarity (Universidade de Lisboa) and is qualified to teach Italian, Latin and Spanish. He holds an MBA in Business Executive; He is an expert in commerce and trade and specialises in Montessori Pedagogy. He collaborates with the Spanish Ministry of Education, Cefire, for the planning of courses for teaching Latin and with the Teledántem-CORINÉI Research Group on the acquisition of the Italian language. His main research interests are teaching and acquisition of the Italian and the Latin language, vulgarity, business Italian, play in education and the creation of language teaching materials. He has published four manuals in the Italian language for advanced university students and one for teaching Latin. He has worked at various centres, including Oxford University, Universidad de Alicante, Italian Cultural Institute in Krakow, Adam Mickiewicz University, High School of Philology in Wroclaw, and different schools in Spain and Morocco. He also carried out research at the Universidade de Lisboa and St. Andrews University.

Ilaria Salonna is currently a PhD student in Cultural Studies at the Faculty of 'Artes Liberales', University of Warsaw (Poland). She holds a Master's degree in Philosophy with a specialization in Aesthetics from the University of Milan (Italy) and a Diploma as an actor from the Accademia dei Filodrammatici di Milano. Ilaria worked as an actor from 2003 until 2014 and trained with Anatoli Vassiliev in his theatre laboratory at the Grotowski Institute in Wroclaw (Poland) between 2011 and 2013. Ilaria's field of interest lies in the aesthetics and anthropology of theatre, with a particular focus on the relationship between performance practice and philosophy. She is a member of the working group "Performance, Religion and Spirituality" within the International Federation of Theatre Research. She has been a lecturer of 'Practice and knowledge of the Italian language' at the University of Cardinal Stefan Wyszynski in Warsaw. Ilaria's doctoral thesis is about the notion of atmosphere in aesthetics and in the history of acting techniques.

Valentina Tibaldo is a DPhil Candidate in Medieval and Modern Languages at the University of Oxford, where she teaches Italian language and literature, translation, and French theory. Her doctoral thesis focuses on the poetry of Vittorio Sereni and Giorgio Caproni and explores, through a comparative framework, a possible way in which literature can know: that of afterthoughts. Before joining Oxford University, she studied at the Università degli Studi di Padova, Université Paris-Sorbonne (Paris IV), and Freie Universität Berlin. She is co-founder of the Image and Thought Network (TORCH), an interdisciplinary network which considers the porous boundaries between image and thought.

Introduction

Starting a university course represents a choice in response to specific motivations; indeed, going to university should not be seen as a mandatory step for a student. Therefore, it is expected that deciding on the degree course to follow should be done in a mindful manner, even if young people between the ages of seventeen and eighteen sometimes do not yet have clear ideas about what they would like to do in their future.

However, this is not a problem if one pursues his/her own interests. On the one hand, motivations could be related to personal development, such as studying new subjects, opening up to new horizons, or becoming more independent, among others. On the other hand, one could enrol in a university to increase the chances of finding a good job and, therefore, having greater prospects in this area, together with a better economic and social position.

The programs offered within the various universities are different from each other, based on the curriculum chosen, on the faculty, and also on the basis of the country. Therefore, those who want to study Italian will be able to compare the different educational offers proposed by the numerous universities and choose the one that is most suited to their own perspectives and inclinations; thus, diversity manifests richness because each program will be unique of its kind and will be able to respond to the individual needs of students who have a particular interest in certain subjects rather than others.

In fact, some degree courses are more focused on the literary aspect, and others on linguistic or didactic. Sometimes, a foreign language is embedded within a specific study curriculum (such as, for example, Business, Law, and Psychology) and, therefore, the language is an additional element to the course itself.

The student who begins a course in Foreign Languages, Italian Studies, Italian Philology, or Linguistics will, therefore, in most cases, find a rich and varied curriculum. The latter will provide the basis for acquiring the Italian language while equipping the student with further knowledge and practical elements to understand the language itself, to know it more deeply, as well as analyzing the historical, literary, and artistic aspects that characterize it along with its cultural heritage. This happens because the latter and the linguistic field are strongly linked and feed each other. In consequence, in many cases, the Italian language is accompanied by other courses which - although not strictly related to it (grammar, listening, conversation, etc.) - integrate with the subject. Take, for example, the case of Dialectology, Phonetics, and History of

Art or Geography, to name just a few disciplines; these provide the student with a complete view of the Italian language and culture.

Italian as a Foreign Language: Teaching and acquisition in Higher Education aims to focus on teaching and learning the Italian language - in its broadest sense - in the university setting.

The idea for this book comes from personal reflections that have surfaced in recent years, as in the studies of language teaching, we often focus on the Italian language; however, these studies on Higher Education are still very diffident, and it is not completely clear how to propose, teach and acquire the university subjects present in the Italian curriculum abroad. One might think that one's university career, scientific research and experience in the field could also lead to knowledge of language teaching and a certain educational quality. However, university education for foreigners requires rethinking the subject in question and understanding how it should be adequate for the times and easily acquirable, all while considering the language itself as a medium for conveying new knowledge.

This book thus places emphasis on the teaching methodology, and on the tools and resources available, with the aim of prompting professionals and students to reflect on alternative teaching disciplines and proposals within the university. In fact, in the panorama of the study of foreign languages, through the research of language teaching in particular, extreme attention has been noted toward training, innovation, and the systems used to offer teaching that is in step with the times and, above all, valid.

This volume, therefore, seeks to be a point of reference for both teachers and students who deal with Linguistics, Philology, Didactics and Pedagogy in order to understand better how to present a specific discipline and what are the characteristics, the benefits, difficulties, activities, materials, and projects to facilitate teaching, understanding and acquisition.

The volume, for practical reasons, is divided into two parts: the first, Pedagogical Approaches and Methodological proposals, presents some theoretical studies with the relative proposals for their implementation. In the second part, Italian through Projects and Case-Studies, a series of insights are highlighted through different projects and the teaching and learning of the Italian language in universities through specific case studies.

Important contributions have been used in each section of the manual; in the first, Pedagogical Approaches and Methodological proposals, we have: Teaching L2 Italian phonetics and pronunciation in academic courses (Olga Broniś); Historical linguistics and Italian at university (Josh Brown); Telecollaborating in Italian (Chiapello Stefania and González Royo Carmen); Teaching Italian (with) comics (Sara Dallavalle); Teaching and understanding

Italian through the language of the press (Marta Kaliska); Teaching and learning Italian word-formation patterns (Irene Lami); Teaching Italian Dialectology (Adam Ledgeway); and Teaching and learning Italian indecent language (Alberto Regagliolo);

In the second, Italian through Projects and Case-Studies there are: Teaching specialist language skills in Italian through History of Art (Cinzia Bacilieri); For an interdisciplinary approach in language learning: Exploring the use of subtitling in the Italian language classroom (Rosalba Biasini and Francesca Raffi); Embodied and experiential immersion into transculturality: learning Italian thorough ethnography and translation (Eliana Maestri); Learning Italian with cartoons (Maranzana Stefano); Italian through geography at university level (Leonardo Masi); The teaching of Italian through Process Drama (Ilaria Salonna) and Learning from the essay (Valentina Tibaldo).

As a result, the contributions included in this work are varied and reflect the different university curricular realities. In fact, the courses offered in higher education in the specialized courses of the Italian language, as already mentioned, range considerably and embrace different areas and disciplines: historical, geographical, literary, philological, artistic, translatological and linguistic, without omitting the technology, multimedia and the actuality itself, positioning themselves both as theoretical studies, but also as practical ones, because, in a globalized and digitized world, the teaching and acquisition of foreign languages and related subjects at university are essential for proposing informed, valid teaching that is functional, practical, adapted and organized.

Part I.
Pedagogical approaches & methodological proposals

Chapter 1

Teaching L2 Italian phonetics and pronunciation in academic courses

Olga Broniś
Cardinal Stefan Wyszyński University in Warsaw

Abstract: The goal of the present chapter is to discuss the importance of teaching phonetics in L2 Italian Studies academic programmes. The chapter also aims to overview different approaches towards teaching Italian pronunciation and phonetics, pointing out that raising the metalinguistic knowledge of the students, also by teaching them pronunciation in an instructed, phonetics-based manner, offers better opportunities for the learners to improve their pronunciation skills. The paper outlines the recent research in the domain of explicit vs non-instructed learning and, based on that, offers a compact pronunciation and phonetics course as one unit.

Keywords: Phonetics, Pronunciation, Teaching phonetics, Italian

***

1. Introduction

Pronunciation has often been considered a secondary issue in broader language performance skills (Brown, 1991, *inter alia*). In L2 education, grammar and vocabulary learning, as well as speaking and listening trainings, are typically given far more attention than the L2 pronunciation practice. Still, the correctness of the speech sounds and the proper perception of L2 structures are undeniably part of a language acquisition process. As noted by Barrera Pardo (2004), most of the research shows that pronunciation practice should be present in L2 training, and, more importantly, it should be based on explicit instructions grounded in phonetics.

Phonetics is a branch of linguistics investigating the production and perception of human speech sounds (Ladefoged, 1975). It focuses on the physical properties of speech, such as the description of articulation mechanisms, speech segmentation, or transcription. Crucially, phonetics does not study abstract interactions between segments or sound changes. This is the domain of phonology (Trubetzkoy, 1939). According to traditional parlance, phonetics is divided into three major sub-fields: articulatory, auditive and acoustic phonetics. Articulatory phonetics investigates how human sounds are produced, which organs of speech are involved, and what types of movements are performed in the production of various speech sounds. On the other hand, auditory phonetics studies the hearing, the perception, and the conversion of human speech, while acoustic phonetics deals with the physical properties of speech signals, such as the duration and the amplitude of a waveform (Ladefoged, 1975). Typically, L2 university programmes aspiring to teach not only pronunciation but also theoretical phonetics, which gives a solid background for pronunciation training, are designed around the basic notions of articulatory phonetics. A classic example of such an approach is Peter Roach's textbook *English Phonetics and Phonology* (1983). In this ground-breaking book, Roach talks about L2 English phonetics and pronunciation with thorough reference to articulatory phonetics. This view is now widespread, and although more and more universities offer their students courses in experimental phonetics, the typical approach it to provide the L2 students with articulatory preliminaries and, if possible, use them also in pronunciation classes.

2. Different approaches towards teaching L2 Italian phonetics at the university

Nowadays, it can be observed that an increasing number of Italian Studies programmes are designed around the study of L2 Italian, Italian culture and literature. An overview of different universities' websites indicates that many universities seem to ground their Italian Studies programmes on the idea that the potential students want to study the Italian language and learn about the country's culture, cuisine and literature. Hence, many university programmes of Italian Studies focus on the cultural and literary background of Italy. In such programmes, courses in linguistics are often either limited in a programme time span or not mandatory. Within such an approach, a course in phonetics is also not included in the obligatory set of courses. However, this does not necessarily mean that such programmes neglect teaching the pronunciation of Italian. Typically, some elements of pronunciation are covered in the courses of Italian L2 language, but with no reference to the theoretical knowledge of articulation, as the students are not mandatorily provided with theoretical knowledge in phonetics. This model of the university programme, focused on developing practical language skills and the knowledge of culture and literature, is quite common in the US, in the UK, and in some West European countries. If the students of such programmes want to learn about linguistics, they can do so by taking part in facultative linguistics courses, whose content is usually quite varied and rich. For example, the University of Bologna offers a course in acoustic and articulatory phonetics, which also explores some notions of experimental phonetics. However, the course is intended for the students of Speech and Language Therapy students. However, the basic idea seems to be not overloading the students with complex linguistic concepts but rather providing them with practical knowledge of the Italian language, culture and literature.

So, the general trend seems to be focused on cutting down on the number of obligatory linguistic courses. However, some European universities still look at Italian Studies programmes from the angle of old-school traditional philological studies. For instance, at many German and Polish universities, such as LMU in Munich, Humboldt-Universität in Berlin, or the University of Warsaw, theoretical linguistics still belongs to the obligatory core courses. Typically, a course in phonetics is part of the mandatory descriptive grammar course, and it is included in the first year of the undergraduate programme. The classical approach is to start the descriptive grammar course at the very beginning of the first year of the undergraduate programme with classes in phonetics, designed as a one-semester course (30 hours/semester) together with the phonology of a given language. The programme is typically constructed around the notions of articulatory phonetics and transcription, which are considered the absolute must-have knowledge for students. This leaves a very limited space for phonology, which is a rather complex branch of linguistics, and requires many hours of presentation and processing by the students, be it taught in the framework of the Rule-Based Theory (Chomsky and Halle, 1968) or the Optimality Theory (Prince and Smolensky, 1991; McCarthy and Prince, 1993), or in any other framework.

To present the reader with an alternative approach towards teaching phonetics, phonology, and pronunciation of an L2, let me briefly discuss the programme of English L2 Studies at the Institute of English Studies at the University of Warsaw. Here phonetics, phonology and pronunciation are taught in three separate courses. This programme gives the students much time and opportunity to understand and acquire all the target concepts of phonetics, phonology, and English pronunciation. At this institution, the course in phonetics (30 hours/semester) aims to provide the students with the basic concepts of articulatory phonetics and transcription. This course is taught in the first semester of the first year of the undergraduate programme. Following that, the second semester of the first year of the undergraduate programme comprises a lecture in phonology (30 hours/semester) and a phonology group course (30 hours/semester), both couched in the framework of the generative Rule-Based Phonology. Additionally, the students in the first year of the undergraduate English Studies programme are required to complete two semesters of pronunciation classes, which are part of the Practical English course. Such a design of an L2 studies programme guarantees a thorough and multifaceted education for its students. It also ensures a better understanding of a language, which raises their language awareness, thus facilitating the acquisition of the target L2 e.g. of its desired pronunciation.

3. The rationale for teaching L2 Italian phonetics at the university

As discussed above, it looks like there is a preference towards simplifying the university programmes of Italian Studies and of making them practical and culture-oriented. Many universities seem to be increasingly open towards the idea of minimizing the number of obligatory linguistic courses. Undeniably, this type of updated Italian Studies programme has its advantages, the major one being the encouragement of simplicity. In order to increase the enrolment rates, many universities worldwide adjust the overall structure of their undergraduate programs and university requirements, thus making their programs, among others, the program of Italian Studies courses, as simple and attractive as possible, without impractical and over-challenging courses.

However, one should also take into account the possible drawbacks of this approach. First, eliminating or minimizing the number of theoretical linguistics courses from the list of compulsory subjects deprives students of opportunities to broaden their horizons in terms of general philological knowledge. Second, if the linguistics courses are facultative, the students do not get a chance to expand their metalinguistic awareness,[1] which according to Gombert (1992), is known to facilitate foreign language acquisition, and is a crucial component of language proficiency. This observation is supported by a robust body of research. For example, Sorace (1985) notices that students with more advanced explicit knowledge had better results in Italian L2 production tasks than the students with lower knowledge about the explicit components of the language. Sorace also highlights the importance of metalinguistic knowledge in "acquisition-poor environments" (Sorace, 1985), that is, when the L2 training is conducted in a country where it is not a native language, and the students' exposure to the target language is limited to the classroom.

Raising learners' metalinguistic awareness has also been investigated from the perspective of L2 pronunciation training. Importantly, the evidence points to the significant role of explicit phonetic instruction in L2 pronunciation

---

[1] According to Bialystok (2001), metalinguistic awareness is the capability of one's focusing attention 'on the domain of knowledge that describes the explicit properties of language'.

training.[2] For example, Saito (2011) carried out a study which showed that explicit phonetic instruction raises the students' comprehensibility skills. By the same token, Arteaga (2000) stresses the importance of pronunciation training in the second language (L2) acquisition, observing that explicit phonetic instruction should be part of the pronunciation training.

Given the facts mentioned above, articulatory phonetics seems to have the potential of a highly practical use to the academic students of L2 Italian Studies. Explicit phonetic training is very likely to enhance the effectiveness of teaching pronunciation in a foreign language. However, without any background knowledge in the domain of articulatory phonetics, Italian pronunciation can be taught without resorting to any terms and notions related to articulatory phonetics. So, it must be organized around automatic repetition exercises and drills or left to the uninstructed acquisition by natural immersion. If the L2 learners live in the country where the target language is used on the daily basis, the uninstructed learning linked together with the natural immersion might actually serve the goal (Sorace, 1985). However, as pointed out by Sorace (1985), in monolingual environments, where the L2 learners are exposed to the target language only in the classroom, instructed learning and raising the metalinguistic knowledge do increase the effectiveness of L2 pronunciation acquisition.

In sum, articulatory phonetics gives the teacher all the required theoretical background which can be very helpful in teaching L2 Italian pronunciation in academic programmes. However, without an obligatory course in articulatory phonetics, pronunciation can only be taught by means of drills and repetitions, which is typically insufficient (recall Sorace, 1985). In other words, it looks like obliging the students to take part in linguistics courses, such as articulatory phonetics, gives them the opportunity to increase their proficiency in the target L2 pronunciation.

In order to show the effectiveness of explicit articulatory instruction in the acquisition of Italian L2 pronunciation, let me consider two practical issues related to the pronunciation of L2 Italian. First, one of the most challenging speech sounds of Italian is the palatal lateral approximant /ʎ/,[3] which is not present in many modern European languages, such as English, German, French, or Polish. In most of the Italian courses, students are told that the palatal lateral consonant /ʎ/, as in *famiglia*, is similar to the alveolar lateral

---

[2] Still, some researchers notice that instructed pronunciation training requires further empirical and methodological studies (Lee, Jang and Plonsky, 2015, inter alia).
[3] The author of the present paper is a trained Italian L2 teacher working in Poland and teaching Italian mostly to the native speakers of Polish. Thus, the examples cited in the present paper are based on working with L1 Polish learners.

consonant /l/, as in *Livorno*. This is correct, as the two consonants share the same, that is, lateral, manner of articulation. Both /ʎ/ and /l/ are produced with the centre of the tongue raised and pressed against the passive articulator[4] at the roof of the mouth and the sides of the tongue lowered. The air passes over the lowered tongue sides. While in the case of /l/, this gesture is performed naturally by the speakers of languages such as English, German, or Polish, the production of /ʎ/ usually poses a challenge for most L2 Italian learners. Typically, the learners are told that /ʎ/ is similar to /l/. However, it appears to be hardly possible to successfully transpose the lateral gesture from the tip of the tongue and the alveolar ridge for /l/ to the hard palate and the middle of the tongue for /ʎ/. Students uninstructed in articulatory phonetics are simply unable to make use of the comparison of /l/ to /ʎ/, as they are unaware of the articulation mechanism for /l/ as such. Actually, my observations show that this typical Italian language courses lateral comparison of /ʎ/ to /l/ is not sufficient also for the students who obtain the explicitly instructed training in phonetics. Even the phonetically aware students need additional articulatory instructions as to how to position the tongue in order to produce the target consonant /ʎ/. In the case of /ʎ/, one can resort to the similarity of this consonant to other Italian consonants in terms of the place of articulation. Recall that the speech sound /ʎ/ is palatal, similar to the other two Italian segments, /j/ and /ɲ/ (Bertinetto and Loporcaro, 2005). Given the fact that the approximant /j/ is present in Polish, and its similar realizations can be found in diphthongs in, e.g. English and German, one could exploit this similarity of the place of articulation as a starting point for teaching the intended pronunciation of the target consonant /ʎ/. Being aware of the similarities between the /ʎ/ and /j/, the learners can be trained to pronounce words with the /ʎ/ sound as if it was a /ʎ/. For example, the students can be instructed to pronounce the word *famiglia* as /faˈmijja/ instead of the unreachable at this stage of training /faˈmiʎʎa/.[5] When the students learn to position the tongue at the correct target position, which is the hard palate, the teacher can push their phonetic instruction even further by explaining to the phonetically aware students how to change the manner of articulation of the non-lateral approximant /j/ to the lateral position for /ʎ/. My experience shows that this type of phonetically-based training is very productive. However, this type of instructed pronunciation practice is hardly possible without resorting to the basic knowledge of articulatory phonetics of Italian.

---

[4] The passive articulator for /ʎ/ is the hard palate, and for /l/ the alveolar ridge.
[5] In Italian, all the palatal consonants and the palato-alveolar consonants /ʃ ʒ/ are assumed to be inherently long consonants.

Another Italian pronunciation challenge, quite prevalent among Polish learners of L2 Italian, is the erroneous pronunciation of Italian "soft"[6] consonants, i.e. the alveolo-palatal segments /ʃ tʃ ʒ dʒ/, and the palatal consonants /j ɲ ʎ/. Interestingly, most of the segments in question are intrinsically long in Italian (except for /tʃ/ and /dʒ/). To illustrate the typical pronunciation errors in the production of the consonants in question, consider the following examples:

1) Examples of typical errors in the production of Italian soft consonants made by L1 Polish learners of L2 Italian.

Italian word	target pronunciation (IT)[7]	common pronunciation errors (PL)[8]
a. *Bologna*	/boˈloɲɲa/	/boˈloɲja/
b. *prosciutto*	/proʃʃutto/	/proˈšjutto/[9, 10]
c. *parmigiano*	/parmiˈdʒano/	/parmiˈdžjano/

All the Italian words cited above contain soft consonants /ɲ/, /ʃ/, and /dʒ/, respectively. In (1a), one can observe a discrepancy between the word's target representation /boˈloɲɲa/ and its common Polish erroneous rendition /boˈloɲja/. The difference between the two forms consists of the realization of the long nasal consonant /ɲɲ/,[11] which in Polish is often pronounced as a sequence of /ɲ/ and /j/. In Polish, the nasal consonant /ɲ/ is part of the

---

[6] With reference to the traditional SPE features, Rubach (2019) notes that "secondary articulations of velarization and palatalization are characterized in terms of the feature [±back]: hard consonants carry the feature [+back] while soft consonants carry the feature [-back]."

[7] The transcription of all the Italian words cited in the present paper is based on Canepari's Dizionario di pronuncia italiana (1999/2009).

[8] For transparency, I ignore all the vocalic discrepancies between Polish and Italian. I also follow Canepari in not including the vocalic length in stressed penultimate syllables in the phonemic transcription of the examples presented in the text.

[9] The word prosciutto is also often mispronounced by the speakers of Polish as /prosˈtšjutto/.

[10] The transcription uses the IPA symbols as well as two symbols from the Slavic traditional phonetic alphabets, used to denote the Polish consonants /š/ and /ž/. Following Rubach (1977), I assume that the two Polish consonants are phonetically substantially different from their English and Italian correspondents /ʃ/ and /ʒ/, thus they require the introduction of the two non-IPA symbols.

[11] Italian geminates can be alternatively transcribed as e.g. /ɲːl/.

phonemic inventory, but it is not pronounced as a geminate. My experience shows that the students who are aware of the fact that the Italian consonant /ɲ/ is inherently long, they obtain more lasting results in their pronunciation course. Also, the fact that /ɲ/ and /j/ have the same place of articulation makes it more comprehensible for the students to understand the nature of this negative pronunciation transfer. Interestingly, Polish learners of L2 Italian often pronounce the word *Bologna* in almost the same way as they pronounce the Italian word *Polonia* "Poland", with the only difference (ignoring the vocalic discrepancies) in the voicing of the word-initial segments /b/: /p/. According to Canepari (1999/2009), this is incorrect, as the word *Polonia* is pronounced in Italian with a sequence of /n/ and /j/, that is, as *Polo*[nj]*a*, while many Polish learners of Italian L2 mispronounce it as *Polo*[ɲj]*a*. To clarify the difference, the correct Italian realization is not subject to total place assimilation of the nasal consonant, while the Polish seem to apply it across the board. What is more, the incorrect Polish rendition is very similar to the incorrect realization of the word *Bologna*, cited in (1a). Undeniably, it is a formidable task to explain these subtle differences to a student untrained in phonetics.

Similarly, the word *prosciutto* "ham" cited in (1b) is often pronounced by the Polish learners of L2 Italian with a sequence of a consonant and the glide /j/ instead of the desired "soft", palato-alveolar geminate /ʃʃ/. In other words, the soft geminate /ʃʃ/ in /proʃˈʃutto/ is substituted with a single /ʃ/-like consonant and the glide /j/. However, the lack of the geminate is not the only difference between the desired Italian pronunciation and its Polish version. What transpires from the transcription of the word /proˈšjutto/ is additionally a change in the quality of the consonant, from the alveo-palatal /ʃ/ to the post-alveolar /š/.[12] This means that the two consonants are different in terms of the place of articulation.

Dealing with this mispronunciation is much more effective when the lecturer can resort to the phonetic and phonological knowledge of the learners. Uninstructed training would be based on repetitions and drills, which would require a lot of time-consuming practice, which, as noticed by Sorace (1985), is much less effective in monolinguals. On the other hand, learners who are trained in articulatory phonetics and in basic structural phonology can be offered a metalinguistic explanation of the process and, consequently, obtain explicit training. The phonetically aware students can be

---

[12] For the information on the places of articulation of Italian and Polish consonants, see e.g. Broniś (2019).

shown that there are two separate discrepancies between the target form and its incorrect realization and then analysed them separately.[13]

The discrepancy related to the place of articulation can also be noticed in the example in (1c). In the case of the Italian word *parmigiano* 'parmesan', the Italian target pronunciation /parmiˈʤano/ happens to be changed by the Polish Learners of L2 Italian into /parmiˈdžjano/. As in (1b), the Italian palato-alveolar consonant, in this case, the affricate /ʤ/, is reproduced by the Polish learners as a sequence of the post-alveolar affricate /dž/, and the palatal approximant /j/. Just as in the examples *prosciutto* in (1b), the place of articulation of the affricate is changed from the soft palato-alveolar into the hard post-alveolar. For some reason, the Polish postalveolar affricates /š ž/ in the Polish output forms are accompanied by the palatal /j/. Although the phonological analysis does not lie within the scope of the present work, it looks like the realizations of the soft consonants might be an instance of segmental decomposition. However, this is a separate issue which requires thorough phonological investigation[14].

The pronunciation conundrums outlined above are just a few examples of what crops up in L2 Italian pronunciation courses. Moreover, they are typically encountered by native speakers of Polish. Students speaking other languages might experience other difficulties, such as lack of aspiration in voiceless stops for the native speakers of English or no vowel reduction to schwa for both German and English. All these issues can be addressed in class with or without resolving the explicit phonetic instructions. However, given their complex phonetic nature, it is much easier to address with reference to explicit articulatory knowledge. An additional rationale for teaching articulatory phonetics and transcription in an obligatory course of phonetics is the fact that it helps the learners expand their cross-linguistic awareness and language skills, such as the pronunciation of other foreign languages, L3, L4, and so on. To see the point, consider an illustrative example of an exercise used in the Italian phonetics and pronunciation course at Cardinal Stefan Wyszynski University in Warsaw. Notice that all the words used in the exercise come from the languages Polish learners are likely to have studied in high school.

---

[13] For a more detailed phonetic analysis of consonantal discrepancies between Italian and Polish, see Broniś (2019).
[14] For an example of a phonological analysis of decomposition, among others, in Polish, see Rubach (2008).

2) An exercise introducing the IPA transcription symbols[15].

Look at the words given below. They are grouped into three separate columns. The words come from different languages, but despite the fact the words, when pronounced, contain one identical consonant. Try determining which languages these words come from and find the speech sound they have in common.

I	II	III
Hania	ship	bell
lasagne	brioche	Школа
español	Schuh	Ratusz Arsenał
....	....	....

To deal with this task, the students work in pairs or in small groups. After about 5 minutes of group work, the teacher elicits the answers and discusses them frontally. As for column I, the words *Hania* "Hannah, a name (dimin.)", *lasagne*, a pasta type, and *español* 'Spanish' come from Polish, Italian, and Spanish, respectively. The consonant these words have in common in /ɲ/, a palatal nasal sound spelt differently in all three languages. Column II contains words from English, French/Italian, and German, that is, **ship**, **brioche**, a sweet roll, and **Schuh** 'shoe', respectively. Here, the consonant shared by all three words is the palato-alveolar fricative /ʃ/, also spelt diversely in the three words and languages. Finally, column III contains the English word *bell*, the Russian word *Школа* 'school', and the Polish name of one of the Warsaw's underground train stations *Ratusz Arsenał*.[16] In the case of column III, the shared speech sound is /ɫ/, the so-called "dark /l/", which is a velarized alveolar lateral consonant. This exercise raises the students' metalinguistic awareness by showing them that even unrelated languages contain similar or identical speech sounds. The exercise is used as a lead-in practice for introducing the International Phonetic Alphabet for Italian consonants and

---

[15] The exercise was created by the author of the present paper.
[16] In modern standard Polish, the Polish name of the Warsaw underground train station Ratusz Arsenał is pronounced with a clear /l/ at the end of the word arsenał. However, older and educated speakers of Polish, such as the actor reading out this name on Warsaw underground trains, pronounce it with a velarized, so-called dark /ɫ/. Most of the students from Warsaw are familiar with this particular train voice recording.

vowels, but it also draws the learners' attention to cross-linguistic similarities. The most recent studies on multilingualism show that all languages known to the learner can influence one another. According to Jarvis and Pavlenko (2008), "the influence of a person's knowledge of one language on that person's knowledge or use of another language". Thus, presenting the students with explicit information about one language may also contribute to raising their proficiency in other languages.

4. Conclusions

The arguments presented above show the advantages of providing the students of university Italian Studies with both practical pronunciation classes and a theory-based course in articulatory phonetics. However, given the fact that many higher education institutions around the world cut down on the courses in theoretical linguistics, it might be difficult to add to the Italian Studies programs a separate course in theoretical phonetics. Thus, we suggest including in the Italian Studies programs a 30-hour course in Italian phonetics and pronunciation. Such a course should focus on introducing only these topics of transcription and articulatory phonetics that are indispensable in meta-linguistically aware pronunciation practice. Crucially, every theoretical issue presented in class should be followed by instructed pronunciation training related to the discussed topic. Additionally, such a course can be complemented by a facultative phonology and/or advanced pronunciation class offered to the students in the subsequent semester.

References

Arteaga, D. (2000). Articulatory phonetics in the first-year Spanish classroom. *Modern Language Journal*, 84, 339–354.

Barrera Pardo, D. (2004). Can pronunciation be taught?: A review of research and implications for teaching. *Revista Alicantina de Estudios Ingleses [Alicante Journal of English Studies]*, 17, 6–38.

Bertinetto, P. M., & Loporcaro, M. (2005). The sound pattern of Standard Italian, as compared with the varieties spoken in Florence, Milan and Rome. *Journal of the International Phonetic Association*, 35(2), 131–151.

Bialystok, E. (2001). *Bilingualism in development: Language, literacy, and cognition*. Cambridge University Press.

Broniś, O. (2019). Inventari consonantici dell'italiano e del polacco a confronto. *Forum Filologiczne Ateneum* 7(1), 27–41.

Brown, A. (1991). *Pronunciation Models*. Singapore: Singapore University Press.

Canepari, L. (1999/2009). *Dizionario di pronuncia italiana*. Bologna: Zanichelli.

Chomsky, N., & Halle, M. (1968). *The Sound Pattern of English*. New York: Harper & Row.

Gombert, J. E. (1992). *Metalinguistic Development*. New York: Harvester Wheatsheaf.

Jarvis, S., & Pavlenko, A. (2008). *Crosslinguistic Influence in Language and Cognition*. London: Routledge.

Ladefoged, P. (1975). *A course in phonetics*. New York: Harcourt Brace Jovanovich.

Lee J., Jang J., & Plonsky, L. (2014). The Effectiveness of Second Language Pronunciation Instruction: A Meta-Analysis. *Applied Linguistics*, 36(3), 345–366.

McCarthy, J., & Prince, A. (1993). *Prosodic Morphology I: Constraint Interaction and Satisfaction*. Rutgers University Center for Cognitive Science.

Prince, A., & Smolensky, P. (1993/2004). *Optimality Theory: Constraint Interaction in Generative Grammar*. Blackwell, Oxford.

Roach, P. (1983). *English Phonetics and Phonology: A Practical Course*. Cambridge University Press.

Rubach, J. (1977). *Changes of consonants in English and Polish. A generative account*. Wrocław: Wydawnictwo Polska Akademia Nauk.

Rubach, J. (2008). Palatal Nasal Decomposition in Slovene, Upper Sorbian and Polish. *Journal of Linguistics*, 44(1), 169–204.

Rubach, J. (2019). Three Arguments for Underspecified Representations. *Studies in Polish Linguistics*, 14(4), 191–217.

Saito, K. (2011). Examining the role of explicit phonetic instruction in native-like and comprehensible pronunciation development: an instructed SLA approach to L2 phonology. *Language Awareness*, 20(1), 45–59.

Sorace, A. (1985). Metalinguistic knowledge and language use in acquisition-poor environments. *Applied Linguistics*, 6, 239–254.

Trubetzkoy, N. S. (1939). *Grundzüge der Phonologie*. Göttingen: Vandenhoeck & Ruprecht.

Chapter 2

Historical linguistics and Italian at university

Josh Brown
The University of Western Australia

Abstract: This chapter discusses various aspects of the teaching of historical linguistics in Italian Studies curricula. A brief introduction discusses the position of linguistics in Italian departments in general and the sustained interest in linguistics from scholars in Italian Studies. Since historical linguistics is rarely taught as a subject in itself, the chapter describes three different courses where knowledge of historical linguistics may be taught or be useful for students: (1) history of the Italian language; (2) Italian dialectology; (3) Romance linguistics. In each section, potential topics for inclusion in a possible curriculum are canvassed before discussing the most useful references and bibliography when teaching such courses. Some comments on pedagogical aspects are included, such as possible assessment items and the language of instruction, before the conclusion. Overall, the chapter reports that while historical linguistics can be seen to be a traditional discipline in many respects, the linguistic variety characteristic of Italy's past and present remains a source of fascination for students.

Keywords: Historical linguistics, Linguistic variety, Romance linguistics, Italian

***

1. Introduction

The aim of this chapter is to survey some of the ways in which historical linguistics finds itself being taught in various courses traditionally housed in Italian Studies at the university level. Historical linguistics has a long history in Italian departments. In part, this is due to the strong traditions of the disciplines *linguistica storica, dialettologia* and *filologia* in Italy. Now, courses with a linguistic focus have been taught in Italian departments in universities in the English-speaking world for several decades. In recent years, the 'broadening out' of language departments to cognate areas of study and a renewed emphasis on 'interdisciplinarity' has seen Italian Studies become even more connected to linguistics in different ways. Part of this diversification has seen linguistics become part of the broad curricula offered. This chapter focuses on one type of linguistics in particular, historical linguistics. It looks at the different types of topics which are taught in university courses, with a focus on the author's particular experience in Australia.

As a discipline in its own right, historical linguistics "is currently undergoing something of a renaissance" (Bowern and Evans, 2014: 1); for an overview of even more recent developments, see Boas and Pierce, (2020). The offering of linguistics in Italian departments often waxes and wanes, according to the staff profile of departments themselves, as well as the teaching and research strengths of individuals in those programmes. In this context, it is important to recognise that linguistics is now competing with a plethora of thematic or 'elective' courses in Italian Studies, as the discipline itself has become more interdisciplinary (Caruso and Brown, 2022; Brook, Mussgnug and Pieri, 2017; Glynn, Keen, and Pieri, 2020; Ceravolo and Finozzi, 2022) and broadened out to new areas of teaching and research. The popularity of linguistics seems to have increased only since the mid-twentieth century – in other words, after the foundation of linguistics as a discipline itself as an academic discipline. In his survey of articles published in the first half of the period since the appearance in 1937 of the journal *Italian Studies*, for example, Robey (2012) notes that only two are on linguistics. Although it is not the intention here to discuss the more general question of linguistics in Italian departments, Kinder (1996) provides an excellent overview, with comments that can still be seen as valid today. He notes how "linguistics has made a rather uncertain entry into departments of Italian" (p. 516) and that "the boundary lines between linguistic studies of Italian and literary studies of Italian need not become barricades" (p. 527). The growing presence of linguistics in Italian departments as a worldwide phenomenon can be dated, in the words of the former president of the Accademia della Crusca, Francesco Sabatini, to sometime before 1990:

> Si è affermata e si va diffondendo in varie parti del mondo la figura dell'italianista linguista, mentre fino a qualche decennio fa campeggiava dappertutto isolata la figura dell'italianista "letterato" (per lo più dantista o rinascimentalista). Si tratta dunque di un vero e proprio "nuovo corso" per la nostra lingua all'estero, un evento che si spiega solo guardando all'intera realtà sociale e culturale dell'Italia odierna e all'intensità e varietà dei suoi rapporti col mondo.
>
> (Sabatini, 1990: 260)

Given the many subdisciplines of linguistics as a social science in its own right and the varied interests of linguists (both Italian and not) who teach in such departments, all I can offer below are but a few examples of some courses which use the tools and methods from historical linguistics and show ways in which these might be helpful for whoever is considering approaching such courses in their own teaching. I have tried as much as possible to avoid using the term *filologia* and its English translation *philology*, since both terms (arguably) do not correspond to each other's present or historical reality. Confusion continues to characterise both terms, even when treated in their own linguistic traditions, whether in an Italian or Anglophone context. Nevertheless, I have referred to certain Italian publications which do adopt the term *filologia* in their title when this is taken to refer to methodologies and subjects that are clearly historical in nature. While not wishing to enter into a detailed discussion of the various ways this term (and others, such as *linguistica storica*, for example) are used across the literature, may it suffice to say that, in this chapter, I use the term 'historical linguistics' in a broad sense to refer to any course taught with a focus on the diachronic evolutions of language. Where possible, the chapter makes use of examples from recent publications (often 'manuali') that I have adopted in my own courses. I have attempted to provide details of publications in English as much as possible. However, since resources published in English are not as abundant as those published in Italian and given the nature of this particular volume for an English-speaking audience, I have referred the reader to what I believe are indispensable references also in Italian. I have also included references to the major grammars and electronic corpora, which can be used for didactic purposes. Much work has been done in recent years, and there now exist excellent teaching materials for subdisciplines of linguistics that deal with historical Italian and the 'dialects of Italy'. I have placed emphasis on those works which are seen as useful pedagogical tools for the teacher, but also introductions to historical linguistic phenomena for the student; to this end, I have made mention of some of the more general reference works on Italian and also Romance, but have deliberately avoided the most recent, research-driven monographs or theoretical treatments of particular phenomena.

The rest of the chapter is structured as follows. Section 2 narrows to look at particular courses where methodologies and approaches from historical linguistics are often adopted: (1) history of the Italian language; (2) Italian dialectology; (3) Romance linguistics. In each section, potential topics for inclusion in a possible curriculum are canvassed before discussing the most useful references and bibliography when teaching such courses. I also provide a series of general reference tools and a bibliography useful for teaching and student research projects in Italian linguistics. Section 3 makes some comments surrounding pedagogical issues, including the language of instruction and potential assessment items. Final comments about the future of historical linguistics and Italian Studies, and the appeal of historical linguistics for students, are made in the conclusion.

2. Historical linguistics in particular courses

Different types of courses exist where a general approach to historical linguistics can be introduced in Italian Studies at the university level. To my knowledge, there is no course housed in an Italian department anywhere which has as its explicit focus the general discipline of historical linguistics *per se*. Monographic courses which do focus on the broader question of language change over time are often simply termed *historical linguistics, language change, language across time* or similar, and are traditionally housed in departments of linguistics proper. What follows below are historical approaches to language that *are* taught by Italianists and which refer to the specific context of Italy or use Italian data.

2.1. History of the Italian Language

Courses on the history of the Italian language are taught around the world, often mirroring the traditional *Storia della lingua italiana* stalwart in universities in Italy. Such courses may adopt a so-called 'external' approach (with a focus on social, political, economic etc.) to issues surrounding the development of the language. Alternatively, they can adopt an 'internal' perspective (with a focus on the linguistic description and evolution of determiners, pronouns, adjectives, and so on). Typically, courses combine both approaches. In the case of the latter, excellent resources are available which help show the successive stages in the development from Latin to Italian. Courses on *History of the Italian Language* may take either a thematic or chronological approach. In Australia, teaching periods are often fixed at twelve weeks of instruction, and therefore, a one-semester course can be articulated into the following topics. I have included the subtitles and focus for each topic used in my own courses. These generalist topics can be adapted according to the particular interests of the teacher and students:

1) The languages of pre-Roman Italy
2) Antica Roma: Classical and Vulgar Latin
3) Dal Latino al Romanzo: the first documents
4) Alto Medioevo: Carlo Magno
5) il Due e Trecento: Dante, Boccaccio, Petrarch
6) il Quattrocento: Humanism, Latin, vernacular

7) il Rinascimento: the invention of dialects

8) il Seicento: language of a new reality

9) il Settecento: purists and anti-purists

10) l'Ottocento: language for a new country

11) il Novecento: Italians learn Italian

12) Italy today: contemporary Italy

While there are few textbooks or guides available in English, Kinder and Scotellaro's recently published *A Linguistic History of Italy* (2020) serves as an excellent introductory resource. Completely available online, it provides a history which tells over 2000 years of linguistic development through a range of multimedia, providing a cutting-edge option for teachers and students. It is also unique in that the whole volume is entirely bilingual, with all material available in both English and Italian. One particular characteristic of this volume is its focus on the linguistic history *of Italy* rather than *of Italian*, thus adopting an open approach to the multiplicity of linguistic varieties used throughout the history of 'Italy', broadly defined. This history is divided according to both thematic and chronological criteria, allowing the teacher to select the topics and time periods which they wish to focus on and thereby providing a tailored experience. An additional advantage is the in-built student activities: at the end of certain modules, one finds a series of questions and answers which use the traditional methods of historical linguistics. These activities allow students to test their knowledge based on the reading they have just completed. For example, in the case of the first module on Ancient Rome, one of the activities involves describing the evolution from spoken Latin to Italian by looking at the interaction between phonology, morphology, and syntax that lie at the foundation of the grammar of modern Italian. After an example of the phonological tendency to drop word-final consonants in Latin, students are asked to perform the same operations on a set of practice sentences. A solution key is also provided, so students can check they have understood correctly as they go (example 1.):

1) Ora esegui gli stessi passaggi:

Ordine delle parole SVO

Caduta di consonanti in fin di parola

Inserzione delle prime forme degli articoli e della preposizione *de* sulle seguenti frasi latine:

1. canem filius dominae videt
2. librum filii legit domina
3. canis librum dominae manducat
4. filium canis videt dominae filius
5. pastam dominae manducat canis

Example 1: An example exercise showing the evolution from spoken Latin to Italian (Kinder and Scotellaro, 2020)

While this is a particularly novel publication, there exist more traditional resources available for whoever is involved in planning and teaching a course on the history of Italian. In English, Martin's *A Linguistic History of Italian* (1995) provides an excellent 'internal' history and further explanations for students and scholars alike who are looking for historical explanations of linguistic developments. In Italian, a particularly useful volume is Patota's *Nuovi lineamenti di grammatica storica dell'italiano* (2007), designed for university students in Italy. Patota explains in his Introduction that the volume "ambisce a spiegare in modo facile una materia difficile". The aim is to introduce the student to those notions of historical linguistics that are indispensable for a course of 30-32 hours on *Storia della lingua italiana*. An attractive characteristic of this volume is its ability to be wide in scope but provide the essential accounts that are necessary for further reading (similar in nature, but more dated, is Serianni, 1998). Patota's volume includes simple and effective explanations of the main phenomena at all linguistics levels (phonology, morphology, syntax, lexis). It also includes a selection of representative texts from the Middle Ages and an accompanying philological description. Each chapter is followed by a set of activities for the student, and an answer-key is provided at the end of the book. By way of example, Chapter 3 entitled *Dal latino all'italiano: i mutamenti fonetici* contains multiple-choice questions such as the following:

Perché nella parola *domani* (< DE MANE) la [e] del latino volgare è passata ad [o]?

1. a causa dell'anafonesi
2. perché è protonica
3. perché, in posizione protonica, è seguita da una consonante labiale
4. perché è una labiovelare

Patota (2007: 112)

Not only do these activities provide a gentle introduction to fundamental concepts in historical linguistics, such as anaphonesis, pretonic vowels etc., but the addition of sample texts means that students can begin to explore the importance of these concepts in actual data, and then also across languages more generally. From this understanding, they can learn to see how the specific-to-general nature of their learning can be of service to those embarking on linguistic research at the graduate level.

Courses on history of the Italian language can also benefit from a recent proliferation of publications that have appeared in Italian during the past twenty years or so. Although there exist too many to mention here, we can list the series *Storia dell'italiano scritto* edited by Antonelli, Motolese, and Tomasin (6 volumes, published 2014-2021), Serianni and Pizzoli's *Storia illustrata della lingua italiana* (2017) and Serianni's *Prima lezione della lingua italiana* (2015), De Mauro's *Storia linguistica dell'Italia repubblicana dal 1946 ai nostri giorni* (2016), Cella's *Storia dell'italiano* (2015), Morgana's *Capitoli di storia linguistica italiana* (2003), and Tesi's *Storia dell'italiano: la formazione della lingua comune dalle origini al Rinascimento* (2001). This is not to mention the more traditional and classic studies on the subject, among which I recall only a few (e.g. Migliorini, 1960, Durante, 1981, Gensini, 1982, Coletti, 1993, De Mauro, 1963, Serianni and Trifone, 1993, Marazzini, 1994), as well as the *Storia della lingua* series published by il Mulino and edited by Bruni (1990-2003). Electronic resources and corpora useful for studying history of the Italian language are provided in section 2.4 below, under general resources.

2. 2. Dialectology

Courses on the dialects of Italy adopting either a historical or contemporary perspective also make use of historical linguistics. The position of dialectology in the Italian curriculum has previously been argued for by Repetti (1996), and many of these arguments stand as strong reasoning today. Not least of which, Repetti mentions that "without a thorough understanding of how dialects work, we will miss out on some of the most brilliant writers Italy has produced" (1996: 511, see also Ledgeway, 2011). Repetti's article provides a still useful outline for a course on Italian dialectology or, better still, the Dialects of Italy. It may be useful here to summarise the iteration of the course explained in further detail in Repetti (1996):

1. What is dialectology?
2. Early linguistic history of Italy

3. Linguistic resources: Pellegrini's *Carta dei dialetti d'Italia*, dialect families

4. Dialects in depth (varies according to student interests) – phonology, morphology, syntax, lexicon; particular phenomena of interest: metaphony, *raddoppiamento sintattico*, subject clitic pronouns

5. Bibliography: Professional journals in the field (*Rivista italiana di dialettologia, Rivista di linguistica* etc.). Linguistic Atlases (*Atlante italo-svizzero*). Dialect dictionaries

6. linguistic minorities

7. dialects outside of Italy

8. Italian sociolinguistics (diglossia, bilingualism, code-switching)

Points (6-8) above can be altered in line with the particular context, country, and student backgrounds. These final three topics can be considered flexible offerings in this regard. Repetti makes the point, however, that varieties of 'Italian' and dialects generate much excitement on the part of Italian-American students who are already familiar with an American variety of Italian dialects. Much the same is true of students also in Australia and (I imagine) around the world. This range of topics can be extended further, depending on the focus of the course and its length, to consider the use of dialect also in electronic media, such as on the internet or on Twitter, for example. Alternative topics include the use of dialect in particular domains of Italian society, such as politics, in the home, or in youth speak. A recent and particularly interesting example is Duberti and Tosco (2021), who report on their efforts at teaching Piedmontese at the University of Turin. Since the appearance of Repetti's article, more recent publications have made the teaching of Italian dialectology much easier for an English audience (see also Repetti, 2014).

While the topics listed above still serve, in my view, as an excellent introductory structure to a course on Italian dialectology, updated resources in English are now available which facilitate their teaching to new generations of students. This is the case, for example, with the volume by Clivio, Danesi and Maida-Nicol (2011). In their Introduction, the authors specify that the book has been designed for non-specialists and non-Italian scholars, thereby making the content easily digestible while not coming across as intimidating for the beginner. The liberal adoption of maps to indicate the location of particular dialect phenomena and regions is very helpful for students who may have little familiarity with Italian geography. The examples provided are clear and contain glosses for those unsure of the meaning of certain data. Another benefit is that the final two chapters provide an overview of contemporary phenomena which can often be overlooked: diglossia, contact phenomena and the social value of the Italian dialects, and Italian and the dialects today. One desideratum of the volume is an accompanying set of exercises for the student to work through, as well as a section for additional readings and online resources.

Given this available structure, what follows below updates some bibliographical references and makes further suggestions for use in class. Excellent resources remain for overviews of Italian dialects in general, such as Loporcaro's *Profilo linguistico dei dialetti italiani* (2009), Maiden and Parry's *The Dialects of Italy* (1997), Grassi, Sobrero and Telmon's *Fondamenti di dialettologia italiana* (1997), Cortelazzo et al.'s *I dialetti italiani: storia, strutture, uso* (2002) but also the relevant sections in handbooks of dialectology, such as Telmon's (2018) overview of Italian dialects and regions, as well as the section "the scientific tools of dialectology" in Clivio, Danesi and Maida-Nicol (2011: 21-37). Today, digital approaches are breaking new ground in measuring dialect groupings and other phenomena which use dialect data, such as Tamburelli and Brasca (2018), who offer a reclassification of Gallo-Italic.

New datasets available online, as well as the online publication of traditional volumes, also mean a plethora of resources are readily accessible for teaching dialectology and historical linguistics. Examples include the *Lessico Etimologico Italiano digitale* (www.lei-digitale.org), the *Atlante Linguistico Italiano* (www.atlantelinguistico.it), and the *Atlante lessicale toscano*[1]. One innovative resource, entitled *Atlante sonoro delle lingue e dei dialetti d'Italia*[2], allows the user to access a sample of dialect recordings from around the whole of Italy. Transcriptions of recordings also appear at the bottom of the online map accompanying this website. This database also contains an option to search for a particular *comune*, in order to verify whether data are available from that particular location or not. Dialect dictionaries are also available online. To cite but one example, ArchiWals is a digital archive designed to protect the linguistic and cultural heritage of the Walser in Piedmont and Valle d'Aosta (www.archiwals.org). A more complete list of dialect dictionaries and linguistic atlases online can be found at the website of *Korpus im Text: Innovatives Publizieren im Umfeld der Korpuslinguistik*[3]. A recent volume, entitled *Historical Dialectology in the Digital Age*, has been published by

---

[1] Parole di Toscana. Retrieved 24 April 2022 from http://serverdbt.ilc.cnr.it/altweb
[2] Atlante sonoro delle lingue e dei dialetti d'Italia. Retrieved 24 April 2022 from https://atlas.limsi.fr/?tab=it
[3] Korpus im Text. Retrieved 24 April 2022 from www.kit.gwi.uni-muenchen.de/?p=12110

Alcorn et al. (2020), albeit with a focus on English. Nevertheless, similar methodological approaches are being applied to historical Italian as new corpora are built. It is barely worth mentioning that YouTube and many other social media sites mean that a range of audio and video samples of dialect data are readily accessible.

2. 3. Romance linguistics

Compared to the two courses discussed above, Romance linguistics is somewhat removed from departments of Italian Studies proper. Nevertheless, it represents a thriving field of research, and it is not uncommon for staff in Italian to teach in such an area. Courses on Romance linguistics are more likely to be taught in US and European universities, as well as some universities in Asia, rather than in Australasia. Students who are interested in historical linguistics and the internal and external properties of Italian will likely find a wealth of recent publications and resources available. The benefit to students of enrolling in courses with a broader focus on the whole Romance family can be immense. Recently, the importance of using Romance data in studies for questions in general linguistics has been brought to the fore (see Maiden 2004, for example). On this point, Sornicola makes the following important observation:

> Romance linguistics has rather more to offer general linguistics in its thinking on the synchrony-diachrony relationship and the problem of language change than contemporary general linguistics has to offer Romance linguistics.
>
> Sornicola (2011: 1)

The field of Romance linguistics is broad in scope. Any introductory course on the subject will likely vary according to the particular research interests of the instructor and the passions of the students. One benefit of offering a course in Romance linguistics is that the teaching can often be shared among colleagues from different disciplines (Latin, linguistics, and the various Romance languages). Since many students are often enrolled in one or more of these subjects throughout their degree programmes, they are often curious about a subject whose structure is comparative by nature. Romance linguistics may assume some or no background knowledge of Latin prior to enrolment (even if some is often recommended). Courses can begin with an Introduction to what the discipline of Romance linguistics is and what Romance linguists do before considering the external history and Latin. While there exist many examples of different curricula available, one option for a general structure can be articulated into the following topics:

1. Introduction to the Romance Languages
2. External history
3. Latin and the Romance languages
4. Sound changes I
5. Sound changes II
6. Morphological changes I
7. Morphological changes II
8. Syntax: current issues I
9. Syntax: current issues II
10. Sociolinguistics of the Romance Languages I
11. Sociolinguistics of the Romance Languages II
12. Final review and presentations

Other offerings might also involve non-standard languages, such as Occitan, Sardinian, Catalan, Breton, Sicilian, Friulian etc., language contact in the history of one or more Romance languages, as well as the so-called Romance-based creoles. Given the diverse nature of the many topics which can be potentially taught in a course on Romance linguistics, it can be useful to assign readings from select journal articles or chapters if the objective of the course is not a general introduction. The field itself has benefited from many excellent handbooks and recent histories. Some of these volumes also include introductory sections explaining the fundamental concepts in historical linguistics. One particularly welcome, successful, and recent overview is Alkire and Rosen's (2010) *Romance languages: a historical introduction.* This volume sets the material out in a clear and concise way, introducing students to the fundamental questions in the discipline. The benefits for both teachers and students include a glossary of linguistic terms, suggestions for further reading, but also practice questions and answers that are embedded within the body of the text itself. For example, chapter 6, entitled *Verb Morphology: the present indicative*, begins with a brief overview of the different conjugation classes in Latin, Italian, Spanish, and French; it then provides a series of questions based on material which the reader has just encountered, or has come across in previous chapters:

6.1.1 The conjugation classes

Latin had four classes:

Latin conjugation			Italian	Spanish	French
I	LAVĀRE	'wash'	lavare	lavar	laver
	PENSĀRE	'think'	pensare	pensar	penser
II	HABĒRE	'have'	a<u>ve</u>re	ha<u>ber</u>	a<u>voir</u>
	DEBĒRE	'owe'	do<u>ve</u>re	de<u>ber</u>	de<u>voir</u>
III[1]	PERDĚRE	'lose'	<u>per</u>dere	<u>per</u>der	<u>perdre</u>
	VENDĚRE	'sell'	<u>ven</u>dere	<u>ven</u>der	<u>vendre</u>
IV	DORMĪRE	'sleep'	dormire	dormir	dormir
	PARTĪRE	'depart'	partire	partir	partir

Question: Based on the Penultimate Rule (§ 1.1.4), which Latin infinitives are rhizotonic (stressed on the root)?

Answer: Only class III

Question: In which of these languages were the rhizotonic infinitives retained?

Answer: In Italian and French: *perdere, vendere* and *perdre, vendre* with syncope.

Table 2. 1. Example of 'questions and answers' embedded into the body of the chapter from Alkire and Rosen (2010: 96)

A final benefit is that, through the book's companion website accessible through Cambridge Core, additional resources such as practice tests, final exam questions, and answers to exercises can be downloaded for free (with an institutional subscription). More generally, there exist many other recent contributions to the field which contain valuable overviews of particular Romance standards, varieties, and structures, such as *Cambridge History of the Romance Languages. Volume 1: Structures* (Maiden, Smith and Ledgeway, 2011) and *Volume 2: Contexts* (Maiden, Smith and Ledgeway, 2013), as well as

The Oxford Guide to the Romance Languages (Ledgeway and Maiden, 2016). In Italian, excellent treatments are provided by Barbato (2017) and Schlösser (2005). Specific topics and approaches to the study of Romance data have benefited from the publication of recent manuals, such as *Manual of Standardization in the Romance Languages* (Lebsanft and Tacke, 2020) and *Manual of Romance Sociolinguistics* (Ayres-Bennett and Carruthers, 2018). Other volumes remain a stalwart for their comprehensive and lucid explanations of particular phenomena, including Harris and Vincent (1988), Posner (1996), Lausberg (1965-1969), and Elcock (1975).

Online resources for Romance linguistics specifically created for didactic purposes or the sharing of data are not as plentiful as one might wish. Nevertheless, useful are the *Oxford Online Database of Romance Verb Morphology*[4] and *CRL: Clitics of Romance Languages*[5], a searchable database that allows the user to perform refined searches across a variety of syntactic categories, speakers, regions, and other fields. Other useful websites include *Orbis Latinus*[6] and the large range of links and resources provided by the Department of Linguistics, Faculty of Arts and Letters at Tohoku University[7].

2. 4. General Resources

Regardless of the particular course being taught, I list here more general reference works and electronic corpora from Italian linguistics which can be usefully exploited when taking a historical approach. In certain cases, explanations of the historical evolution of Italian can be found in general reference works. Given the nature of the subject at hand, the majority of these are in Italian. I list only the most relevant here for those new to the field and who wish to explore further.

Rohlfs *Grammatica storica* (1966-1969) is encyclopaedic in its nature by providing standard and dialect data from many individual *comuni* around Italy. The three volumes cover all linguistic levels of phonology, morphology, and lexical variation and are articulated into the various historical changes from Latin to Italian. Similarly, Castellani's *Grammatica storica della lingua italiana e dei suoi dialetti* (2000) provides extraordinary detail of some of the earliest variations in Italian, as does Tekavčić's historical grammar (1980). A

---

[4] Oxford Online Database of Romance Verb Morphology. Retrieved 24 April 2022 from http://romverbmorph.clp.ox.ac.uk

[5] CRL: Clitics of Romance Languages. Retrieved 24 April 2022 from https://crl-database.herokuapp.com

[6] OL, Orbis Latinus. Retrieved 24 April 2022 from www.orbilat.com/index.html

[7] Romance Linguistics and Related Fields. Retrieved 24 April 2022 from www2.sal.tohoku.ac.jp/~gothit/romance.html

useful resource is the *Manuale di linguistica italiana* (2016), edited by Lubello, which provides a state-of-the-art overview of some major fields in Italian linguistics. This volume presents 30 different chapters articulated into various subsections including *L'italiano nella storia; L'italiano contemporaneo: strutture e varietà*, and; *I luoghi della codificazione / le questioni / gli sviluppi recenti della ricerca*. For historical linguistics in general, Lyle's *Historical Linguistics: An Introduction* (1999) remains a much-used guidebook. There exist numerous introductions to historical linguistics in Italian (for example, Luraghi, 2016; Magni, 2014).

With regard to online resources, readings, and corpora, a useful overview is provided by Formentin's entry on *grammatica storica* (2010) in Treccani online. The entry begins with an introduction to historical grammar between diachrony and synchrony before discussing the relationship between *grammatica storica* and *filologia*. It then provides an overview of some of the major developments in the history of Italian at the broad linguistic levels and structures. In terms of online databases and corpora, a range of different resources exist for historical linguistic research in Italian. The database of the *Opera del vocabolario italiano* (OVI)[8] continues to remain one of the major resources. Updated quarterly, at the time of writing, it contained 2,978 texts from the origins up until around 1525. The *Tesoro della lingua italiana delle Origini (TLIO)*[9] is an easily accessible dictionary of old Italian. A more recent database, designed specifically for research in historical Italian over a range of text types, genres, and time periods, is *MIDIA: Morfologia dell'Italiano in DIAcronia* (www.corpusmidia.unito.it). This corpus begins from the early thirteenth century until the first half of the twentieth century. It contains around 800 texts, for a total number of 7.5 million forms. A specific database for research on nineteenth-century Italian is the *Corpus Epistolare Ottocentesco Digitale*, known as *CEOD*, (ceod.unistrasi.it). This database allows for both simple and advanced searches for linguistic items. It is currently made up of approximately 1,350 letters by 75 different writers for a total of over 600,000 different linguistic forms. Of course, the website of the *Accademia della Crusca* (accademiadellacrusca.it), available in both English and Italian, provides access to a wealth of material. A list of available online resources can be found on the website of Accademia by navigating to *collegamenti utili > banche date, corpora e archivi testuali*.

While most research in historical linguistics relies on textual data, spoken corpora can also be usefully exploited in historical linguistic research (for a list

---

[8] Corpus OVI dell'Italiano antico. Retrieved 24 April 2022 from http://gattoweb.ovi.cnr.it
[9] TLIO, Tesoro della Lingua Italiana delle Origini. Retrieved 24 April 2022 from http://tlio.ovi.cnr.it/TLIO

of some of these in various languages, including Italian, see the LISA online page[10]. One option is to search for particular variants and the number of tokens to see how issues of historical variation have 'sorted themselves out' in contemporary language (for example, the polymorphy of 1sg. verbs such as *dovere: debbo / devo / deggio*, doublets such as *disco / desco*, or so-called geo-synonyms, for example, the corresponding lexemes for 'cloth for use in housework' like *straccio* (north), *cencio* (centre), *pezza* (south) (for a list of some of these, Kinder and Savini, 2004: 11). In terms of historical linguistics, many handbooks are available. Recent guides include *The Handbook of Historical Linguistics. Volume II* (Joseph, Janda and Vance, 2020), *The Routledge Handbook of Historical Linguistics* (Bowern and Evans, 2014), and others.

3. Pedagogy and pedagogical issues

The introductory notes to this chapter have already commented on the place of linguistics in the Italian Studies curriculum generally. In this author's view, the main pedagogical issues at hand in the teaching of historical linguistics can often include a hesitation on the part of the student to enrol in a course which is linguistic in nature, given that they may have had little to no previous instruction in linguistics, or even understanding of what linguistics is. These fears are often quickly allayed as students discover the wonders of the historical evolution of Italian and how it can reveal the mysteries of its evolving present. Once the appetite is whet, students are often intrigued by the fascinating linguistic variety that characterises Italy's past and present. This variety can be studied from a wide variety of perspectives, not just from the example courses described above. Online tools and recent publications of textbooks and other introductory materials attest to the vitality of linguistics as a prime area of interest for researchers and their desire to make them known to their students as well. This is not to speak of other subdisciplines which can also pique students' interests and are also worthy of study in the Italian context, such as sociolinguistics, sociophonetics, second language acquisition, dialect syntax, historical sociolinguistics, to name just a few.

In general, historical linguistics, as integrated into the above courses, presents few obstacles. Given the flexibility of topics and possible approaches, the level of depth and difficulty can be adjusted according to the particular cohort of students. The same goes for deciding the language of instruction. In some cases, students may have Italian language skills deemed sufficiently strong to engage with the material in a meaningful way. However, these topics can also be delivered entirely in English, thereby making them attractive options for

---

[10] LISA. Retrieved 24 April 2022 from www.lilec.it/lisa/category/strumenti-linguistici/corpora-online

students who have little to no previous knowledge of Italian. In my experience, a mixture of both languages can be helpful in introducing the subjects to beginner students, while Italian is preferable at more advanced levels, especially at the MA and PhD levels. In this sense, the courses described above can be pitched at any level of instruction. When it comes to the history of the Italian language and dialectology, students who are majoring in linguistics may see these courses as particular avenues of parallel interest and therefore enrol if the course is taught in English; in the case of Romance linguistics, students who are majoring in one or more Romance languages will be able to gain a deeper appreciation of the family as a whole, as well as the general properties of language change.

Assessment is also likely to vary according to the particular requirements of university programmes and the methods which teachers feel are appropriate for their students. I have found it best to offer weekly tests, as well as a mid-term paper and/or a final exam. For the linguistic history of Italy, typical questions I have set for practice tests include the following, usually delivered after four or five weeks of instruction:

Question 1

Describe the features of Vulgar Latin which can be deduced from the above items from the Appendix Probi, AND say what further changes have taken place from Vulgar Latin to modern Italian.

4	masculus *non* masclus	[Mod. It. = maschio]
20	columna *non* colomna	[Mod. It. = colonna]
54	frigida *non* frigda	[Mod. It. = fredda]
83	auris *non* oricla	[Mod. It. = orecchia]

Table 2. 2. Features of Vulgar Latin

By this point, students will have become familiar with some of the major vicissitudes in the early linguistic history of Italy, such as the concepts of Classical and Vulgar Latin and their sociolinguistic contexts. They will also have spent some time during seminars investigating and describing major textual evidence, such as *Appendix Probi*. Students are able to describe the social and historical context of various documents, as well as some of their linguistic features, using the appropriate terminology from historical linguistics. These features include syncope in unstressed syllables, lowering of /ŭ/, monophthongization, loss of word-final consonants, loss of /h/, changes to vowels in hiatus, etc. Students are also encouraged to think more broadly about how changes at the phonological level are connected to the broader developments occurring at so-called 'higher' levels of linguistic abstraction, such as morphology and syntax. For the mid-term paper, questions generally tend to address broader topics and take the form of a traditional research essay. This format allows students to explore the rich tradition of scholarship that lies behind some of the major preoccupations that still characterise the field of Italian language history. At the same time, students are able to acquire familiarity with some of the fundamental aspects of linguistic and general history from Italy's past, which they have not often had the opportunity to explore. Example questions include:

1) Discuss the reasons for the rise and success of the vernaculars during the Low Middle Ages and for the predominance of Sicilian and Tuscan vernaculars at that time.

2) Describe and discuss the presence of a popular and a learned tradition in the history of the Italian language. Give examples.

Similarly, dialectology can be assessed through tests and mid-term papers. Questions can range from focussing on the specific, such as describing metaphony and its effects in particular dialects; in other cases, students might describe the features of a particular dialect or dialect group based on a piece of dialect writing, such as a poem or short text. Assessment for a course on Romance linguistics can also follow a similar format but ask students to compare or contrast particular phenomena across two (or more) Romance varieties. In any case, this final note aims to serve as a reminder for the instructor that questions of selection should be made carefully. It is vital that the introduction of technical terms from historical linguistics be delivered in a digestible and approachable way, especially at lower levels, so as not to scare students off the path before they even begin the journey.

4. Conclusion

Historical linguistics has much to offer Italian departments and, more importantly, to interest our students in Italian Studies. Not only do such topics provide an important background to the historical development of language in Italy, but they complement a now vast array of courses in literature, cinema, arts, visual studies, and many other traditional and emerging fields of study. This chapter has surveyed just one subdiscipline of linguistics, but courses from related or cognate areas, for example, sociolinguistics, equally provide important and fascinating areas of student interest. Feedback on linguistic courses that I have taught has been consistently positive. The encouraging reaction provoked in students confirms the utility of offering such topics in the curriculum. In part, this may be because the question of the historical development of Italian dialects and the sociolinguistic landscape of contemporary Italy can be a difficult reality to grasp for non-native students. Further, these are courses which students are unlikely to encounter during the course of a traditionally structured degree in 'linguistics' at an Anglophone university. Conversely, it is not unusual for them to be part of a traditional *laurea* in an Italian university; in this way, they allow students to have a 'taste' of the kind of subjects which students in Italy are able to pursue.

Offering linguistics and linguistic-related courses can also be one way to diversify the curriculum in Italian Studies. Traditional approaches to historical linguistics can be supplemented by the new methodologies and tools that are emerging for linguistic research, including a plethora of online material and corpora. I have attempted to survey only the most useful and well-known resources in this chapter. In such a short space, the selection is, of course, made harder by the many different types of academic publications, online material, journals, and handbooks that are now available across fields that have large bibliographies. The aim here has been not to focus on the most ground-breaking research innovations in any one particular field but to suggest some basic tools that can be helpful in a didactic sense and provide a possible structure for those embarking on teaching historical linguistics for the first time. I have attempted to focus on English-language rather than Italian publications, but given the nature of the topic, Italian resources are, of course, more plentiful. This is not to speak of the resources available in other Romance languages and other languages still, including the abundant material available in German. The reader will be able to find for themselves another bibliography that is most relevant to their interests and will undoubtedly (and quickly) discover other dictionaries, websites, and volumes that are of most use for their particular needs.

The development of new research fields, such as historical sociolinguistics, has also allowed new research questions (and new histories) to emerge. The popularity of such courses may also be due to the range of linguistic varieties in Italy, which students are often unaware of, but also the complex way in which these varieties have evolved throughout the history of Italy and are still present today. It is worth recalling that linguistics is itself a relatively new discipline in universities. In this context, it has provided a fertile testing ground for new research questions to be applied to Italian data; in turn, it is the data which have driven new questions and methodologies to come to the fore. Teaching in an English-speaking university, where English is the *de facto* national language, and in a context with a 'monolingual mindset' (Clyne, 2008), has further corollaries; not least of all, it makes the linguistic diversity characteristic of Italy even more enticing as an object of study for students, as they encounter a reality that is so different from the Anglophone one. In short, in this but in many things, Italy once again provides an example of fascinating diversity in both a historical and contemporary sense, as well as a source of constant cultural enrichment.

References

Antonelli, G., Motolese, M., & Tomasin, L. (Eds.), (2014-2021). *Storia dell'italiano scritto*. Rome: Carocci.

Alcorn, R., Kopaczyk, J., Los, B., & Molineaux, B. (Eds.), (2020). *Historical Dialectology in the Digital Age*. Edinburgh: Edinburgh University Press.

Alkire, T., & Rosen, C. (2010). *Romance languages: a historical introduction*. New York: Cambridge University Press.

Ayres-Bennett, W., & Carruthers, J. (Eds.), (2018). *Manual of Romance Sociolinguistics*, Berlin: De Gruyter.

Barbato, M. (2017). *Le lingue romanze. Profilo storico-comparativo*. Rome: Laterza.

Boas, H. C., & Pierce, M. (Eds.), (2020). *New directions for historical linguistics*. Leiden: Brill.

Bowern, C., & Evans, B. (2014). Editors' introduction: foundations of the new historical linguistics. In Bowern, C., & Evans, B. (Eds.). *The Routledge Handbook of Historical Linguistics* (pp. 1–42). Routledge.

Bowern, C., & Evans, B. (Eds.), (2014). *The Routledge Handbook of Historical Linguistics*. Routledge.

Brook, C., Mussgnug, F., & Pieri, G. (2017). Italian Studies: An Interdisciplinary Perspective. *Italian Studies*, 72(4), 380–392.

Bruni, F. (Ed.), *Storia della lingua italiana*, (1989-2003). Bologna: il Mulino.

Caruso, M., & Brown, J. (2021). L'italiano all'università tra aspirazioni di cittadinanza globale e magnetismo dell'Italia contemporanea. In Rubino, A., Tamponi, A. R., & Hajek, J. (Eds.), *L'italiano in Australia: lingua e cultura nell'attuale panorama dell'insegnamento dell'italiano. Italian in Australia. Perspectives and Trends in the Teaching of Language and Culture*, (pp. 115-132). Florence: Franco Cesati.

Castellani, A. (2000). *Grammatica storica della lingua italiana. I. Introduzione*. Bologna: Il Mulino.

Cella, R. (2015). *Storia dell'italiano*. Bologna: Il Mulino.

Ceravolo, M., & Finozzi, A. (Eds.), (2022). *Italian Studies across Disciplines. Interdisciplinarity, New Approaches, Future Directions*. Rome: Aracne.

Clivio, G., Danesi, M., & Maida-Nicol, S. (2011). *An introduction to Italian dialectology*. Muenchen: LINCOM Europa.

Clyne, M. (2008). The monolingual mindset as an impediment to the development of plurilingual potential in Australia. *Sociolinguistic Studies*, 2(3), 347–366.

Coletti, V. (1993). *Storia dell'italiano letterario*. Torino: Einaudi.

Cortelazzo, M., Marcato, C., De Blasi, N., & Clivio, G. P. (Eds.) (2002). *I dialetti italiani: storia, struttura, uso*. Torino: UTET.

De Mauro, T. (1963). *Storia linguistica dell'Italia unita*. Bari: Editori Laterza.
De Mauro, T. (2016). *Storia linguistica dell'Italia repubblicana dal 1946 ai nostri giorni*. Roma: Laterza.
Duberti, N., & Tosco, M. (2021). Teaching Piedmontese. A challenge? In Tamburelli, M., & Tosco, M. (Eds.). *Contested Languages. The Hidden Multilingualism of Europe*, (pp. 199–208). Amsterdam: John Benjamins.
Durante, M. (1981). *Dal latino all'italiano moderno: saggio di storia linguistica e culturale*. Bologna: Zanichelli.
Elcock, W. D. (1975). *The Romance languages*. London: Faber & Faber.
Formentin, V. (2010). Grammatica storica. In: *Enciclopedia dell'italiano* Available online at: https://www.treccani.it/enciclopedia/grammatica-storica_%28Enciclopedia-dell%27Italiano%29/.
Gensini, S. (1982). *Elementi di storia linguistica italiana*. Bergamo: Minerva Italica.
Glynn, R., Keen, C., & Pieri, G. (2020). Key Directions in Italian Studies. *Italian Studies*, 75(2), 121–124.
Grassi, C., Sobrero, A. A., & Telmon, T. (1997). *Fondamenti di dialettologia italiana*. Laterza: Roma-Bari.
Harris, M., & Vincent, N. (Eds.), (1988). *The Romance languages*. London: Croom Helm.
Joseph, B. D., Janda, R. D., & Vance, B. S. (Eds.), (2020). *The Handbook of Historical Linguistics. Volume II*. Malden, MA: Blackwell Publishers.
Kinder, J. J. (1996). The Role of Linguistics in Italian Departments. *Italica*, 73(4), 516–528.
Kinder, J. J., & Savini, V. M. (2004). *Using Italian: a guide to contemporary usage*. Cambridge: Cambridge University Press.
Kinder, J. J., & Scotellaro, G. (2020). *A Linguistic History of Italy*. Canberra: ANU ePress. Retrieved from https://press.anu.edu.au/publications/textbooks/linguistic-history-italy.
Lausberg, H. (1965-1969). *Romanische Sprachwissenschaft, I. Einleitung und Vokalismus. II. Morfologia*. Berlin: de Gruyter.
Lebsanft, F., & Tacke, F. (Eds.), (2020). *Manual of Standardization in the Romance Languages*. Berlin: De Gruyter.
Ledgeway, A. (2011). Il ruolo del dialetto nell'apprendimento dell'italiano L2: alcuni esempi napoletani. In Cennamo, M., & Lamarra, A. (Eds.), *Scuola di formazione di italiano lingua seconda/straniera: competenze d'uso e integrazione* (pp. 125–138). Naples: Edizioni Scientifiche Italiane.
Ledgeway, A., & Maiden, M. (Eds.), (2016). *The Oxford Guide to the Romance Languages*. Oxford: Oxford University Press.
Loporcaro, M. (2009). *Profilo linguistico dei dialetti italiani*. Bari: Laterza.
Lubello, S. (Ed.), (2016). *Manuale di linguistica italiana*. Berlin: De Gruyter.
Luraghi, S. (2016). *Introduzione alla linguistica storica*. Rome: Carocci.
Lyle, C. (1999). *Historical Linguistics: An Introduction*. Cambridge: Massachusetts: MIT Press.
Magni, E. (2014). *Linguistica storica*. Bologna: Patron.

Maiden, M. (1995). *A Linguistic History of Italian.* London & New York: Longman.

Maiden, M. (2004). A necessary discipline: historical Romance linguistics. *La Corónica,* 32, 215–221.

Maiden, M., & Parry, M. M. (Eds.), (1997). *The Dialects of Italy.* London: Routledge.

Maiden, M., Smiths J. C., & Ledgeway, A. (Eds.), (2011). *The Cambridge History of the Romance Languages. Volume 1: Structures.* Cambridge: Cambridge University Press.

Maiden, M., Smith, J. C., & Ledgeway, A. (Eds.), (2013). *The Cambridge History of the Romance Languages. Volume 2: Contexts.* Cambridge: Cambridge University Press.

Marazzini, C. (1994). *La lingua italiana: profilo storico.* Bologna: Il Mulino.

Migliorini, B. (1960). *Storia della lingua italiana.* Florence: Sansoni.

Morgana, S. (2003). *Capitoli di storia linguistica italiana.* Milano: LED.

Patota, G. (2007). *Nuovi lineamenti di grammatica storica dell'italiano.* Bologna: Il mulino.

Posner, R. (1996). *The Romance Languages.* Cambridge; New York: Cambridge University Press.

Repetti, L. (1996). Teaching about the Other Italian Languages: Dialectology in the Italian Curriculum. *Italica,* 73(4), 508–515.

Repetti, L. (2014). Where did all the dialects go? Aspects of the influence of Italian on dialects. *Forum Italicum,* 48(2), 219–226.

Robey, D. (2012). Italian Studies: The First Half. *Italian Studies,* 67, 287–299.

Rohlfs, G. (1966-1969). *Grammatica storica della lingua italiana e dei suoi dialetti. Vol. 3.* Torino: Einaudi.

Sabatini, F. (1990). Una lingua ritrovata: l'italiano parlato. In Lo Cascio, V. (Ed.). *Lingua e cultura italiana in Europa,* (pp. 260–276). Florence: Le Monnier.

Schlösser, R. (2005). *Le lingue romanze.* Bologna: il Mulino.

Serianni, L. (1998). *Lezioni di grammatica storica italiana.* Rome: Bulzoni.

Serianni, L. (2015). *Prima lezione di storia della lingua italiana.* Rome: Laterza.

Serianni, L., & Pizzoli, L. (2017). *Storia illustrata della lingua italiana.* Rome: Carocci.

Serianni, L., & Trifone, P. (Eds.). (1993). *Storia della lingua italiana. I. I luoghi della codificazione. II. Scritto e parlato. III. Le altre lingue,* 3 vols. Turin: G. Einaudi.

Sornicola, R. (2011). Romance linguistics and historical linguistics: reflections on synchrony and diachrony. In Maiden, M., Smith, J. C., & Ledgeway, A. (Eds.). *The Cambridge History of the Romance Languages,* (pp. 11–49). Cambridge: Cambridge University Press.

Tamburelli, M., & Brasca, L. (2018). Revisiting the classification of Gallo-Italic: a dialectometric approach. *Digital Scholarship in the Humanities,* 33(2), 442–455.

Tekavčić, P. (1980). *Grammatica storica dell'italiano. I Fonematica. II Morfosintassi. III Lessico.* Bologna: Il Mulino.

Telmon, T. (2018). Dialects of Italy. In Boberg, C., Nerbonne, J., & Watt, D. (Eds.). *The Handbook of Dialectology*, (pp. 486–497). New Jersey: Wiley.

Tesi, R. (2001). *Storia dell'italiano: la formazione della lingua comune dalle origini al Rinascimento*. Rome: Laterza.

Web references

Accademia della Crusca. Retrieved 25 April 2022 from https://accademiadellacrusca.it

Atlante Linguistico Italiano. Retrieved 24 April 2022 from www.atlantelinguistico.it

Atlante sonoro delle lingue e dei dialetti d'Italia. Retrieved 25 April 2022 from https://atlas.limsi.fr/?tab=it

CliMAlp: salvaguardia delle lingue minoritarie in Piemonte e Valle d'Aosta. Retrieved 24 April 2022 from www.archiwals.org

Corpus Epistolare Ottocentesco Digitale. Retrieved 25 April 2022 from http://ceod.unistrasi.it

Corpus OVI dell'Italiano antico. Retrieved 25 April 2022 from http://gattoweb.ovi.cnr.it

CRL: Clitics of Romance Languages. Retrieved 25 April 2022 from https://crl-database.herokuapp.com

Korpus im Text. Retrieved 24 April 2022 from www.kit.gwi.uni-muenchen.de/?p=12110

Lessico Etimologico Italiano. Retrieved 24 April 2022 from www.lei-digitale.org

LISA. Retrieved 24 April 2022 from www.lilec.it/lisa/category/strumenti-linguistici/corpora-online

MIDIA (Morfologia dell'Italiano in DIAcronia). Retrieved 24 April 2022 from www.corpusmidia.unito.it

OL, Orbis Latinus. Retrieved 24 April 2022 from www.orbilat.com/index.html

Oxford Online Database of Romance Verb Morphology. Retrieved 25 April 2022 from http://romverbmorph.clp.ox.ac.uk

Parole di Toscana. Retrieved 25 April 2022 from http://serverdbt.ilc.cnr.it/altweb

Romance Linguistics and Related Fields. Retrieved 24 April 2022 from www2.sal.tohoku.ac.jp/~gothit/ro

TLIO, Tesoro della Lingua Italiana delle Origini. Retrieved 25 April 2022 from http://tlio.ovi.cnr.it/TLIO

Chapter 3

Telecollaborating in Italian

Stefania Chiapello and Carmen González Royo
University of Alicante

Abstract: Exchanges between foreign and native language learners who establish a bilateral collaborative relationship have been adapting to everyday technologies throughout. Tandem philosophy naturally provides a new concept of linguistic immersion. Over the years, it has incorporated different technological tools to carry out oral exchanges pursuing communication. Telecollaboration allows participants to interact autonomously, provide reciprocal knowledge and come into contact with the authentic language, mainly through their native speakers. The goals vary, but mechanisms are activated to improve grammatical, pragmatic-communicative, and intercultural aspects and can focus their work on a wide variety of topics. Within the EHEA, this method has acquired great projection and continues to improve the design of telephones that are organized. This chapter intends to review some examples of telecollaboration aimed at learning Italian with another language. Although far from presenting an exhaustive scenario, we intend to approximate a sample of existing realities, leading to the diversity of both projects and objectives.

Keywords: Telecollaboration, Tandem, Technologies, Communication, Italian

***

1. Introduction

In this contribution, we will focus primarily on virtual collaboration for teaching/learning in Italian (IFL), in particular, when these experiences are framed in a university setting. Evidently, it is not an exhaustive catalogue but a sample that contributes to creating a diversified scenario of the current situation on this subject.

We will begin with a brief review of the literature framing the telecollaborative activity. In this regard, we observe that from a terminological point of view, the activity has acquired multiple definitions depending on the author who has adopted this methodology (Carreras, 2018; Aranha and Leone, 2017; O'Dowd, 2019). Warschauer (1996) and Belz (2001) started talking about telecollaboration. A few years later, Belz, together with Thorne (2006), argued about "internet-mediated intercultural foreign language education". Subsequently, it was the case of O'Rourke (2013), who began to define the activity as 'e-tandem', then Starke-Meyerring and Wilson (2008), who spoke of a "globally networked learning environments context", O'Dowd (2007: 2–3) together with Lewis (2016) of "online intercultural exchange", Leone and Telles (2010) and Chiapello, González Royo and Pascual Escagedo (2010) of "teletandem" to finish with Helm (2015), Rubin (2016), Schultheis, Moore and Simon (2015) that went on to define the activity as a "virtual exchange" (VE). In addition to an evolution in terms of nomenclature, over the last three decades, there has been an adaptation and improvement based on the multiple technological advances that have been offering increasingly sophisticated tools. This has made it possible to work on more skills (written, oral or kinesthetic) at the same time.

The compilation of the proposals has been carried out through published bibliographies and questionnaires completed by teachers who are responsible for this activity within their institutions. In the sections that develop the methodology followed by the different proposals, the common elements have been highlighted, but also the particularities that were found. Even so, it is evident that all of them obey the same fundamental principles: authenticity, due to the contribution of native speakers (N); reciprocity, because each one is N and non-native (NN) in alternate phases, and autonomy, due to the possibility of developing the activity without depending on the teacher (Holec, 1981); all through the implementation of a relatively simple activity (Brammerts, 2001; Munari, 1981). Consequently, the same principles ensure Internationalization at Home by guaranteeing accessibility, inclusivity, sustainability (less mobility) and democratization according to UNESCO goals (1990) for sustainable development, besides skill development in FL and ICT; educational innovation (Council of Europe, 2020: 191–241; Instituto Cervantes, 2018); institutionalization, integration or non-integration in the curricula; organization of European projects (ERASMUS +/ European Commission, Horizon 2020).

Procedures and objectives are also a matter of interest because they provide original perspectives to create a wide range of possibilities that take into account the theoretical approaches on didactics according to social constructivism (Vygotsky, 1978); autonomy in second language acquisition (SLA) (Little, 1991); global symmetry by reciprocity (Linell and Luckmann, 1991; Orletti, 2000); intrinsic motivation (Ryan and Deci, 2000; Schunk, 2014) and, finally, connectivism (Siemens, 2005.) The results, it will be taken into account, above all, the impact that teletandem has on the learning of the students in a sample of the various projects that have been selected. While general objectives have remained invariable, the specific ones have undergone modulation, in some respects, for attending to specific interests and allow the practice of macro-functions (descriptive, narrative, etc.), intercultural aspects (music, cinema, free time, studies, traditions, etc.) or others. In addition, institutional participation (Leone, 2018) has gone from being voluntary (i.e., non-integrated) to being evaluated and graded (integrated.)

2. Methodology

2.1. Contexts and Participants

The overview presented here focuses on projects taking place at the EHEA, mostly among university students of foreign languages and translation. However, on occasion, we have interacted with users from non-university centres, although the age range is in what we could call young adults (LiceoStabili-UA; UniCatt/USal/EOI; UnivSalento/Univ.SaoPaulo/GU). Generally, N/NN dyadic interactions are established, although there may be some phases of sharing activity and group-produced material, equally N/NN (UniTO-UMCS Polonia and LiceoStabili-UA.) In terms of language pairs with Italian, there is a great variety among the projects consulted: Arabic, English, French, German, Korean, Polish, Portuguese, and Spanish. In platforms that interconnect speakers, such as those facilitated by Language Centres (CLA, Centro Linguistico di Ateneo) like in UNIBO-Lyon2, UNIRoma3-GU, or UNILINGUA and other multilingual projects such as INTENT, EVOLVE or EVALUATE include a substantially larger number of languages as they do not usually include qualitative evaluation monitoring but only satisfaction monitoring. That said, we are not including those in our analysis.

In more specific telecollaborative projects, there is often a limit to the proficiency levels of the trainees due to the demands of the proposed practices, whereas in projects and platforms with less open conditions, the competence level does not limit the participation of the trainees (Council of Europe, 2020.)

Similarly, projects perform in terms of channel: platforms that leave the content of the activity to the decision of each participating pair do not limit between oral and written (UNILINGUA); however, more structured projects have more specific objectives and tend to define channel, production and delivery of the materials which have been produced (UniCatt-USal-EOI, UNISA-UNISOB-UA and the UniSalento projects.) On the other hand, all projects have a time limit for the completion of their stages and activities: the experiences are limited to a few months (UNISA-IES OC UNISA/Argentina), a six-week period (UniTO-UMCS) or a full course (UNIBO-Lyon2; UniSal/GU). The more concrete the proposal, the more the participants are required to respect the timeframe set out in the teaching plan.

2. 2. Tools

In line with what is promulgated by the connectivist theory (Siemens, 2005), technology is part of the everyday life of individuals; in this sense, it has been asserting itself as a tool in linguistics applied to language teaching-learning. In light of the information obtained from the telecollaboration proposals consulted, we note several recurring circumstances related to the use of ICT. Firstly, the technology used is generally limited to that which the participants in each experience have at their disposal at any given time and has therefore been modified over time in parallel and as these ICTs have evolved. Even if a project has started with certain tools, it has adapted them in favour of others with more up-to-date features. Secondly, students have been involved in using them to carry out tasks outside the classroom, choosing the most useful ones. For a few years, this accessible and everyday technology has given rise to Computer-Assisted Language Learning (CALL) methodologies and, more recently, Mobile-Assisted Language Learning (MALL), with devices that significantly increase portability, such as smartphones, tablets, e-books and other electronic readers.

We have drawn up a table (in Appendix) that attempts to summarise the digital tools that are necessary for accomplishing these tasks: making contact, written or oral interactions, with a recording, all wrapped up in a portfolio with a final survey or questionnaire that evaluates the participants' experience.

In the initial experiments carried out, contact was made exclusively via e-mail, and the written activity took place in Yahoo groups, for example, which were very close to the services provided by the distribution lists. In 2006 we pointed out LiceoStabili-UA and in 2016 UniCatt-USal-EOI, as an e-tandem experience. In the telecollaboration experiences initiated after 2009 (UNISA-UNISOB-UA, UNISA-IES OC), email is maintained for making contact. Applications such as Facebook start to be used as soon as users access this social network en masse; telecollaboration moves towards oral interaction, and Skype and Pamela for Skype/CAllburner are introduced for the recording of materials, which are maintained for a long time (UNIRoma3-GU, UNISA-UNISOB-UA). Later, Instagram (Telegram and Google Hangouts, in some cases) and Whatsapp were added, replacing the previous contact systems, taking advantage of their regular use and practicality. Due to the pandemic, from 2020 (UNISA-UNISOB-UA) platforms such as Google Meet, Zoom (UniSalento/GU; UniTO-UMCS) and Microsoft Teams burst onto the scene in full force, overtaking the previous applications, thanks to their ease of use and their everyday nature in interpersonal relations, as well as integrating the recording function, thus eliminating the need for complementary programmes as in previous years. In projects oriented to the practice of oral interaction, VoiP technology is undoubtedly used, with Skype at the undisputed lead as a reference in this type of virtual exchanges, due to the multimodality of its benefits. Other applications such as GoogleForms, Google Drive or shared walls such as Padlet and Google Classroom have contributed, to a greater extent, to the preparation of materials in the reflection and evaluation phases of the completed activity.

Parallel to the tools used in the above-mentioned telecollaboration projects, platforms are emerging that are hosted in the virtual contexts of certain universities. They create virtual meetings by managing and providing contacts to the students enrolled in the universities, leaving it up to the participants to decide on the digital tools to be used in their individual tandems. Examples would be the projects managed by the *CLA*, like in UNIBO-Lyon2, UNIRoma3-GU or the UNILINGUA proposals.

In some of the projects (LiceoStabili-UA, UniCatt-USal-EOI, #3# UNISA-UNISOB-UA), or at certain stages of them, unique and common tools were provided to complete the tasks. Among them is the participation of students in a Yahoo group, using e-mail, to establish contact with the group that will carry out a real exchange in their respective centres and accommodation in the student's homes. While the focus of the activity was on communicating through the written channel, students soon adopted other media to transmit audio or video information, as well as referring to websites or sending personal pictures by e-mail. The Yahoo group allowed all participants to access all posts submitted by any of its members, functioning as a mailing list (LiceoStabili-UA). The selection of the tools was decided by the teachers in order to facilitate the achievement of the pre-set objective: email, Skype and Pamela for Skype or Callburner covered the requirements for completing the three stages of the activity. Subsequently, Facebook, Hangouts, Instagram, etc., were introduced, gaining space and displacing the former applications with new ones that serve at least the same function or improve on it. In the last three years, students have been imposing their preferences, and we observe that Instagram is preferred over Facebook. In some projects, WhatsApp has become the favourite application for immediate contact between pairs as opposed to Facebook's Messenger (i.e., UNISA-UNISOB-UA). As mentioned, from 2020 onwards, communication via platforms such as Google Meet, Zoom or Microsoft Teams has become the most widely used communication tools to interact and record conversations. The same naturalness with which the first ICTs were introduced has manifested itself in today's pandemic times.

2. 3. Procedure

After having studied the telecollaboration proposals that combine various languages with Italian, three key phases are fundamentally observed in most of them: planning, implementation and evaluation (Nunan, 1993).

1) The planning phase consists of designing the activity according to the objectives, deciding on the participants and providing them with the instructions for action, the tools and the necessary contacts. All the telecollaboration proposals have drawn up an initial document specifying the guidelines to be respected to carry out the tasks, with the expression of the objectives, the suggested tools and the expected deadlines to complete each period of activity. We have found examples in which the proposal has defined the tasks quite completely depending on their level of proficiency (UNIRoma3-GU, UniCatt-USal-EOI, UniUrb-COLUMBIA) or the objectives to be achieved, for example, limiting itself to one channel (written channel LiceoStabili-UA or UniCatt-USal-EOI; audio channel UNISA-UNISOB-UA, video UniSalento, UNISA-IES OC, UniUrb-COLUMBIA.) Other projects limit participation to certain levels of competence, such as UniUrb-COLUMBIA, which distinguishes between advanced level participants and those enrolled in the master's degree in teaching, or as in UniTO-UMCS, in which the apprentices belong to an A1 level. Sometimes, pairs can be organized randomly (UNISA-UNISOB-UA) or, instead, questionnaires are used to obtain general information and identify similarities (UNISA-IES OC). It should be noted an original proposal at the University of Manchester that foresees a seminar to instruct participants in strategies to provide corrective feedback to their NN peers during tandem face-to-face meetings. The students "have to attend a workshop on giving effective corrective feedback... We (the teachers) were able to show that, with adequate preparation, students have the capacity to provide pertinent feedback of very high quality (Morley and Truscott, 2001)]" (Morley, 2018: 20). Other proposals offer greater or even total decision-making capacity to the participants about the activity, their offer functioning as a platform that provides contacts to carry out virtual exchanges between those enrolled in the participating universities. We cite the case of UNILINGUA, in which the number of languages and combinations is equally open, or UNIBO-Lyon2 and UNIRoma3-GU, in which the Language Centre provides general instructions for the operation of virtual exchanges and, at the same time, each person responsible for the languages can publish 'teaching aids' that lead the carrying out of the exchanges.

2) The implementation phase is developed within the established deadlines and depending on the design of each proposal. Several more or less differentiated stages can be distinguished. The participants, organized in pairs, prepare the activity according to the explicit guidelines received through a document, email or web page. In UniSalento/Sorbonne Abu Dhabi and UNIRoma3-GU, for example, it is a thematic list on which to direct the exchange, in UNISA-UNISOB-UA, UniUrb-COLUMBIA, with a free topic, the participants agree on how to carry out the exchange in pairs or separately prepare some elements that will allow them to interact. In other cases, there is prior preparation of materials, as in UniTO-UMCS in which other projects have been prepared on what to focus the telecollaboration. It is true that, even if the participants do not have guidelines, their level of proficiency and affinities between the interlocutors will find adequate arguments to start a conversation that will have the cooperation of the N and the learner, who will receive feedback and support in each situation (Morley, 2018: 23–26). Once the meeting is over, we move on to the phase of reflection on the experience (reflection on action), which, as we have observed, is based on different practices, depending on the performance of exercises of different types. In UNISA-UNISOB-UA and UNISA-IES OC, for example, the oral production is transcribed, with the consequent exhibition and reflection of the apprentice on his own work; the elaboration of specific exercises based on the stage of interaction in pairs, as in UniTO-UMCS. In more flexible proposals, the metalinguistic reflection is also left to the personal decision of the interlocutors (UNIRoma3-GU, and UNILINGUA.)

3) The evaluation phase, finally, reflects on both the development and the content of the practice. It has been noted that numerous projects have presented participants with evaluation surveys of the entire process, for example, UNISA-UNISOB-UA, UniSalento/Sorbonne Abu Dhabi, and UniUrb-COLUMBIA. In projects with less or no control over the virtual exchanges carried out, the surveys deal with user satisfaction with respect to the experience.

3. Results

On a regular basis, the immersion of the language learner in advanced courses in a country of the language of study has been used, with the consequent cost of these services; and an alternative immersion was to take advantage of specially designed job placements so that the apprentices themselves could help mitigate these often-high expenses. Before introducing the new technologies among the activities outside the classroom in the teaching-learning of FL, to facilitate contact with N at zero cost, it was established through other available means and at a distance. An example of this was a face-to-face conversation or mail exchange between students and N, the latter known as penfriends, in tandem. With technological advances, these relationships by mail or face-to-face have led to electronic correspondence or virtual meetings (Telles and Vassallo, 2006). In our research, we have found multiple examples of these practices with ICT between N and learners through the CALL and MALL methodologies.

We can label e-tandem LiceoStabili-UA (González Royo, 2006) and UniCatt-USal-EOI (Bailini, 2016) with written activities where Italian students of SFL and Spanish students of IFL establish an epistolary relationship. In LiceoStabili-UA (2003-04), students enrolled in the BA in Translation and Interpretation at the UA participate in an exchange programme promoted by an official agreement between UA and Liceo Classico F. Stabili together with Istituto Magistrale Trebbiani of Ascoli Piceno. One action entails the use of email to allow members of a Yahoo group to get in touch, initially virtually and in person later, being hosted by one student. Although the focus of the activity was to communicate through the written channel, soon the students chose other supports to transmit audio or video information as well, as they referred to web pages or sent personal photographs by email.

UniCatt-USal-EOI proposal is dual and parallel: similar participating entities, themes and procedures. The activity consists of emailing informal e-tandem letters on a free topic or proposed by the teacher, in which SFL trainees from the Catholic University of the Sacred Heart of Milan (Brescia Campus) and IFL trainees participate from the University of Salamanca and the Language School of Barcelona (Terrassa). This activity generated two parallel and longitudinal corpora (Bailini, 2018: 119) that were analysed in some monographs on teaching and SLA (IFL and SFL). From the activity carried out by these groups of apprentices, two corpora have been generated. The collection of texts in Spanish (CORpus del ESPañol de los Italianos - CORESPI) were recorded in 2013, with informants from levels A1 to B2; and in Italian (CORpus del ITaliano de los Españoles - CORITE) for 7 months (2008-2009) (Bailini, 2018: 115–118).

We have also observed inter-department or inter-university projects with specific structures and objectives. In 2009, UNISOB and UA started a Spanish-Italian bilingual teletandem activity, which incorporated, in 2010, UNISA, with students of BA in Modern Languages and Translation & Interpretation from SFL and IFL (Chiapello, González-Royo and Pascual Escagedo, 2010). This virtual exchange continues uninterruptedly to the present day, and numerous promotions of students from the three universities have participated in it. The participation of UA students started not being integrated to be soon converted into an integrated activity within the curriculum of the subjects involved. Regarding the substance of its methodological approaches, participation and general objectives have remained unchanged, focusing on the practice of descriptive and narrative macro functions in oral interaction and intercultural issues such as music, cinema, free time, studies, traditions, etc. Over the years, there has been a (visible evolution of technological instruments that has fluently incorporated new applications and new devices.) The recordings in SFL (A2 to C1) and IFL (A1 to B2) have been compiled to analyse the interlanguage of the learners in the CORINÉI (Corpus Oral de Interlengua Español-Italiano) (González-Royo and Martín Sánchez, 2019).

With the same Italian-Spanish linguistic combination as in Argentina, we documented a telecollaboration experience between SFL students from UNISA and students from the Olga Cossettini Institute of Higher Education in Rosario (UNISA-IES OC) in 2015. This project is part of a macro-project framework convened by the Secretary of State for Science, Technology and Innovation of the province of Santa Fe, which includes other research institutions in the country. It is a brief "pilot project" that focuses on interlingual, interdisciplinary telecollaborative practice on developing intercultural communicative skills, in particular, the connection maintained with the culture of origin of Italian immigrants in Argentina (Theiner, 2018: 93–114.) Italian-Argentinian informants hold conversations and debates with Italian-speaking Spanish students about intercultural issues that relate to them.

The Italian-Polish virtual exchange project (UniTO-UMCS), like other proposals already mentioned, is an initiative focused on a class activity: Polish as FL learners from the University of Turin and IFL of the University of Maria Curie-Skłodowska in Lublin, at a beginner level A1. It can be divided into two different stages: 1) syncronous or asyncronous preparatory tasks in groups with an exchange of materials (ej. pictures); 2) Zoom meetings of all groups at the same time. The objective is twofold: linguistic and intercultural. (Pieczka, 2021: 156–157).

Another example of virtual exchange is UniUrb-COLUMBIA, a project between advanced-level students of IFL of Columbia University and "pre-service teachers (PSTs) studying to become instructors of Italian as a second and foreign language in a Master's program at the University of Urbino, Italy" (Carloni and Franzè, 2021: 136) has obtained very favourable mentions and has been awarded by this American university. The objectives of both groups find a point of common interest in the practice of the use of a foreign language in a computer-assisted language learning (CALL) environment. In the case of the Urbino master's students, in addition to dealing with the issues that have been set in Grammar & Communication, they also get involved in the first person in the pedagogical activity offered by technology and, therefore, telecollaboration. It is a project in which the teachers provide the participants with documentation to prepare all the phases of the activity:

preparation, implementation and evaluation; it takes place via Skype video call and, as we read in the quote that follows: "As reflective practitioners, PSTs need to become aware of their belief systems by consistently analysing how their teaching practices, that is their theories-in-action, reflect their espoused theories, that is the theories they believe in." (Argyris and Schön, 1978 cited in Carloni and Franzè, 2021: 138).

At the University of Salento Apulia, there are several telecollaboration programmes with different universities and for different purposes. Initially, UniSalento joined Teletandem Brasil (UNESP/SJRP) in 2008 to organize Teletandem programmes and carrying out research on the matter. The exchanges are institutionalized, but they have been integrated into the curricula only from 2011 onward. In this respect, UniSalento promoted, later on, Tandem Oral Sessions (TOS) with Université Sorbonne-Abu Dhabi (IT - Arabic), being their Bachelor and Master students specialized in foreign languages (IT-Arabic-SP). The experience also explored inter-comprehension (IC), adding the Moroccan variant and English as a *lingua franca* in the same recorded video conferences to dig more into interculturality (Manta, 2015.) In UniSalento-GU, the Teletandem Exchange Program is established between Georgetown Italian learners with others from the University of Salento Apulia, Italy (https://italian.georgetown.edu/teletandem-exchange-program). It is proposed as an open virtual exchange by Zoom and foresees 8 hours in as many sessions, half for each language. It recognizes an academic credit to apprentices, but it is not necessarily integrated into the curriculum. It maintains a reflection phase so that students receive feedback on action and for action. Furthermore, the University of Salento also develops a telecollaboration programme with the University of Lyon 2, recognised by the acronym IOTT: Intercomprehension Orale et Teletandem (Garbarino and Leone, 2020). The programme, integrated/inserted in Miriadi's project (Leone, 2022), is defined on its website as a "Teletandem based Learning Scenario using VoIP technologies and is developed following the usual multilingual learning procedure of "computer-mediated synchronous communication across two different disciplines: an inter-comprehension program and a foreign language teaching methodology course." (see Appendix) The pairs are made up of learners with different mother tongues, and their level of proficiency in the target language is low or non-existent. A great deal of space is given to metalinguistic, communicative and interlinguistic reflection (Bonvino and Jamet, 2016: 8). Based on these tasks, Databank of Oral Teletandem Interactions (DOTI) has been created as a compilation of TOS (PT-EN, IT-EN) video recorded with the final purpose to transform it into a LETEC (Learning and Teaching Corpora) (Aranha and Leone, 2017).

Below, we group together several multilingual telecollaboration projects that show a different modality from those presented above. They share a unitary platform for all languages and a common organisation that gives these projects an official status within the faculty or university. This would be the case of the Language Centres of Italian universities (UNIBO-Lyon2, UNIRoma3-GU) and the UNILINGUA platform, launched in 2020. All of them offer the possibility to the user, registered in the partner universities, to carry out oral language practice and include Italian in their language catalogue. All these proposals tend to be more flexible in their regulations insofar as they are not tied to a subject curriculum.

In UNIBO-Lyon2, we highlight the Italian French partnership that has recently started its virtual exchanges depending on the Language Centre but with autonomy to manage and prepare materials if the trainees require it, according to the current head of the centre. In UNIRoma3-GU, there is an open website where the guidelines for the teletandem activity are published, which, it is underlined, is directed towards "authentic conversation", not didactic. The languages paired with Italian are not only English or French but also Spanish and German, and they provide online resources, thematic lists for UniRoma3 users to interact with their pairs and a diary of activities, "un formulario di feedback", to help them with metalinguistic reflection: the user is reminded to be motivated, but also to "*gestire [il Tandem] secondo criteri di reciprocità e autonomia.*" (see Appendix.)

We have found other multilingual projects of great magnitude and subsidized by official funds, such as INTENT, EVOLVE or EVALUATE, which are mainly focused on teachers or pre-service teachers (PST), but also, among others, V-PAL, Collaboration at Padua and The Trans-Atlantic Network (Guth, Helm and O'Dowd, 2012: 50) which focus on learners (Nunan, 1988). Nevertheless, we decided not to analyze them for lack of space, although we will make a reference to their rich existing bibliography.

4. Conclusions

This contribution has explored some of the proposals for virtual exchanges which are framed in EHEA and include Italian in their language offer. This language is present in a varied typology of projects and in different language combinations. As mentioned in the preceding pages, this is not an exhaustive but an exploratory study, and very representative examples of the offer covering these parameters have been taken into consideration. Some projects, such as INTENT, EVOLVE or EVALUATE, which are of great projection and interest, have not been included as they mainly focus on teacher preparation.

We will now review some of the types of teletandem discussed and to which the Italian participates fully in the project to which it belongs. E-tandem projects have been found to be oriented towards the practice of written communication. Others, the most numerous, focus on the practice of oral interaction, with more specific objectives such as intercultural information, authentic conversation or inter-comprehension. Some models have established telecollaboration agreements with language or translation departments or universities, while others adopt a multilingual format and, in general, leave a greater degree of autonomy to users in deciding their own virtual exchange modalities. Some even behave as a platform which, subject to conditions, offers all students enrolled in a school the possibility of contacting N with the aim of perfecting their chosen foreign language skills. In this way, in the projects more linked to a group activity or a subject, the participants respond to these parameters and follow a curricular programme. However, we have verified many more open offers that are extended to the participation of students of all levels in any of the partner universities. These projects fall under the label CALLT or even MALLT, since they are Teletandem Computer-Assisted Language Learning, but also increasingly Mobile Assisted Language Learning or work simultaneously according to the decision of the users. In addition, we highlight the extensive list of applications and digital tools that have been used, suggested by the teachers in the planning stage or determined by the choice of the participants. These tools cover all the stages of the methodological procedure and are selected based on their adaptability to the utilities of the project and of the moment.

A few years ago, email was systematically used to establish contact with the partner; as of 2015, social networks such as Facebook and, more recently, Instagram and Whatsapp are gaining ground by integrating these apps into daily communication. In the stage of carrying out the tasks, we have been able to verify the use of email, including Yahoo or Facebook groups that allow the sharing of notices, files and materials with all members. In projects oriented to the practice of oral interaction, VoIP technology is undoubtedly used, with Skype at the undisputed lead as a reference in this type of virtual exchanges, due to the multimodality of its benefits. Other applications such as Google Forms, Google Drive, or shared walls such as Padlet and Google Classroom have contributed, to a greater or lesser extent, to the preparation of materials in the reflection and evaluation phases of the completed activity.

Each project establishes a period of completion, the duration and the treatment of the linguistic product that adjusts to the specific objectives of the proposal: from a few weeks to an entire academic year, the most open projects. As for the duration and conditions of the tasks, they vary between 15' and 30' for each language involved, up to the platforms that do not limit these parameters. Furthermore, some projects have been integrated into the academic curriculum of the respective institutions varying from either a proposal or a mandatory task rewarded with academic credits to self-study practice that does not entail any teacher tutoring or monitoring. As for the realization phases, the classic ones are distinguished in planning, implementation and evaluation of the activity. Each project introduces, depending on its objectives and previous materials, accepts free-topic conversation or leads the theme towards grammatical, communicative or intercultural questions.

It should be noted that, despite the differences in the approaches, the respondents agree in underlining the very positive result of all the proposals. They are also capable of introducing suggestions and aspects for improvement, but although the degree of satisfaction is always high, the dedication that all activities require is not an obstacle. Therefore, this methodology is validated. In all projects, the common principles of telecollaboration are maintained: internationalization at home, accessibility, inclusiveness, sustainability, democratization, learning autonomy management (learner autonomy in managing their own learning), etc.

From the more specific proposals, we identified that the data obtained could innovate the curricula in line with action research. The teacher takes on the role of teacher-researcher and obtains real data on the interlanguage of the learners at their level of proficiency. Finally, we point out that interesting corpora have been compiled based on telecollaboration activities, and these are CORITE/CORESPI, CORINÉI and DOTI.

References

Aranha, S., & Leone, P. (2017). DOTI: Databank of Oral Teletandem. In Fišer, D. & Beißwenger, M. (eds.) *Investigating computer-mediated communication: Corpus-based Approaches to Language in the Digital World*, (pp.172–192). Ljubljana: University of Ljubljana.

Bailini, S. (2016). *La interlengua de lenguas afines. El español de los italianos, el italiano de los españoles*. Milan: Edizioni Universitarie di Lettere Economia Diritto.

Bailini, S. (2018). CORESPI y CORITE: criterios de construcción, características y potencialidades. In Chiapello, S., González Royo, C., Martín Sánchez, T. & Puigdevall Bafaluy, N. (Eds.), *Telecolaboración y corpus para el estudio de la lengua y la cultura*, (pp. 115–128). Alicante: Publicacions Universitat D'Alacant.

Bonvino, E., & Jamet, M. C. (2016). Storia, strategie e sfide di una disciplina in espansione. In Bonvino, E. & Jamet, M. C. (Eds.) *Intercomprensione: lingue, processi e percorsi* (pp. 7–26). Venice: Edizioni Ca' Foscari http://edizionicafoscari.unive.it/libri/978-88-6969-135-5/storia-strateg

Brammerts, H. (2001). Autonomes Sprachenlernen im Tandem: Entiwicklung eines Konzepts. In Brammerts, H. & Kleppin, K. (Eds.), *Selbstgesteuertes Sprachenlernen im Tandem: Ein handbuch,* (pp. 9-6). Tübingen: Stauffenburg-Verlag.

Carloni, G., & Franzè, F. (2021). A Telecollaborative International Exchange for Foreign Language Learning and Reflective Teaching. In Carloni, G., Fotheringham, C., Virga, A., & Zuccala, B., (Eds.), *Blended Learning and the Global South Virtual Exchanges in Higher Education* (pp. 131-158.). Venezia: Edizioni Ca' Foscari.

Carreras Goicoechea, M. (2018). La enseñanza colaborativa y sus aplicaciones a la didáctica de lenguas en Italia y España. In Chiapello, S., González Royo, C., Martín Sánchez, T. & Puigdevall Bafaluy, N. (Eds.) *Telecolaboración y corpus para el estudio de la lengua y la cultura,* (pp. 13-28). Alicante: Publicacions Universitat D'Alacant.

Chiapello, S., González-Royo, C., & Pascual Escagedo, C. (2010). Tareas colaborativas fuera del aula, a través de las TICs. Interacción nativo/no nativo en el aprendizaje de lenguas para la traducción. In Álvarez Teruel, D., Tortosa Ybáñez, M. T., & Pellín Buades, N. (Eds.), *VIII Jornadas de Redes de Investigación en Docencia Universitaria. Nuevas Titulaciones y cambio universitario,* (pp. 1554-1565). Universidad de Alicante. Retrieved from http://hdl.handle.net/10045/1988

Council of Europe (2020). (CEFRL) *Common European Framework of Reference for Languages: Learning, teaching, assessment – Companion volume.* Strasbourg: Council of Europe Publishing.

ERASMUS. EU programme for education, training, youth and sport. Retrieved 5th April 2023 from https://erasmus-plus.ec.europa.eu/projects.

Garbarino, S., & Leone, P. (2020). Innovation dans un projet de télécollaboration orale en intercompréhension: bilan et perspectives du projet IOTT. *Alsic,* 23(2). Retrieved online http://journals.openedition.org/alsic/4790

González-Royo, C. (2006). De la relación virtual a la real. In Oster, U., Ruiz Madrid, M. N., & Sanz Gil, M. (Eds.) *Towards the Integration of ICT in Language Learning and Teaching: Reflection and Experience* (pp. 48-59). Comunidad Valenciana: Servicio de Publicaciones de la Universitat Jaume I de Castellón.

González-Royo, C., Martín Sánchez, M. T. (2019). Corpus oral de interlengua español-italiano (CORINÉI). In Hidalgo, A. (Ed.) *Pragmática del español hablado. Hacia nuevos horizontes* (pp. 531-546). Comunidad Valenciana: Publicacions de la Universitat de València.

Guth, S., Helm, F., & O'Dowd, R. (2012). *University Language Classes Collaborating Online. A Report on the Integration of Telecollaborative Networks in European Universities with the INTENT project team.* Retrieved online www.unicollaboration.org/wp-content/uploads/2016/06/1.2-Telecol laboration_report_Final_Oct2012.pdf

Holec, H. (1981). *Autonomy in Foreign Language Learning.* Oxford: Pergamon.

European Commission (2020). *HORIZON 2020.* Retrieved from https://ec.europa.eu/info/research-and-innovation/funding/funding-opportunities/funding-programmes-and-open-calls/horizon-2020_en

Instituto Cervantes (IC) (2018). Las competencias clave del profesorado de lenguas segundas y extranjeras. Retrieved from https://cvc.cervantes.es/ENSENANZA/biblioteca_ele/competencias/default.htm

Leone, P. (2022). Teletandem and Intercomprehension. *The ESPecialist*, 43(1).

Leone, P. (2018). Co-costruzione di competenze linguistiche e culturali attraverso la riflessione e la discussione. *inTRAlinea*, 20, 1–8.

Leone, P. (2017). Migrazioni virtuali: teletandem per l'apprendimento di una L2. *Incontri. Rivista europea di studi italiani*, 31, 48–65.

Linell, P., & Luckmann, T. (1991) Asymmetries in dialogue: some conceptual preliminaries. In Markova, I., & Foppa, K. (Eds.), *Asymmetries in dialogue*, (pp 1-20). Hemel Hempstead: Harvester Wheatsheaf.

Little, D. (1991). *Learner Autonomy 1: Definitions, Issues and Problems*. Dublin: Authentik.

Manta, T. (2015). *La dimensione culturale nello scambio teletandem Università del Salento – Paris Sorbonne Abou Dhabi: studio di caso*. Tesi di laurea in didattica delle lingue moderne. Corso di Laurea Magistrale in Lingue Moderne, Letterature e Traduzione Letteraria. Università del Salento. Retrieved from www.dropbox.com/s/91tzdpmjj17597v/MANTA%20TESI%20MASTER%202015.pdf?dl=0

Morley, J. (2018). Tandem learning at the University of Manchester: Principles and challenges. In Martos Ramos, J. J., Tejedor Cabrera, J. M., & Trapassi, L. (Eds.), *Aplicaciones de la metodología Tándem en la formación universitaria*. Berlin: Peter Lang.

Munari, B. (1981). *Da cosa nasce cosa. Appunti per una metodologia progettuale*. Bari: Laterza.

Nunan, D. (1993). Task-based syllabus design: Selecting, grading and sequencing tasks. In Crookes, G., & Gass, S. (Eds.), *Tasks and language learning: Integrating theory and practice* (pp. 55–68). Clevedon: Multilingual Matters.

Nunan, D. (1988). *The Learner-Centred Curriculum: A Study in Second Language Teaching*. Cambridge: Cambridge University Press.

Orletti, F. (2000). *La conversazione diseguale*. Roma: Carocci.

O'Dowd, R. (2007). Intercultural communicative competence in telecollaborative partnerships. In R. O'Dowd (ed.), Online Intercultural Exchange: Policy, Pedagogy, Practice. Routledge.

O'Dowd, R. (2019). A transnational model of virtual exchange for global citizenship education. *Language Teaching Journal*, 53.

O'Rourke, B. (2013). Form-focused interaction in online tandem learning. *CALICO Journal*, 22(3), 433–466.

Pieczka, A. (2021). Virtual Exchanges as a Form of Learning which Affects the Development of Online Interaction Skills. *Neofilolog*, 57(1), 151–166. Retrieved from https://doi.org/10.14746/n.2021.57.1.10.

Ryan, R. M., & Deci, E. L. (2000). Intrinsic and Extrinsic Motivations: Classic Definitions and New Directions. *Contemporary Educational Psychology*, 25(1), 54–67.

Schunk, D. H. (2014). *Motivation in Education: Theory, Research, and Applications*. New York: Pearson Education, Inc.

Siemens, G. (2005). Connectivism: a learning theory for the digital age. *Int. J. Instruc. Technol. Dist. Learn*, 2(1). Retrieved from www.itdl.org/Journal/Jan_05/article01.htm

Starke-Meyerring, D., & Wilson, M. (eds.) (2008). *Designing Globally Networked Learning Environments: Visionary Partnerships, Policies, and Pedagogies*. Rotterdam: Sense Publishers.

Tejedor Cabrera, J. M., Martos Ramos, J. J., & Trapassi, L. (Eds.), (2018). *Aplicaciones dela metodología Tándem en la formación universitaria*. Series: Foreign Language Teaching in Europe. Berlin: Peter Lang.

Telles, J. A., & Vassallo, M. L. (2006). Foreign language learning in-tandem: Teletandem as an alternative proposal in CALLT. *ESPecialist*, 27(2), 189–21.

Theiner, I. M. (2018). Telecolaboración y desarrollo de la competencia comunicativa intercultural: un proyecto piloto. In Chiapello, S., González Royo, C., Martín Sánchez, T. & Puigdevall Bafaluy, N. (Eds.), *Telecolaboración y corpus para el estudio de la lengua y la cultura*, (pp. 93–114). Alicante: Publicacions Universitat D'Alacant.

UNESCO (1990). *World Declaration on Education for All and Framework for Action to Meet Basic Learning Needs. International Consultative Forum on Education for All*. UNESCO. Retrieved from https://unesdoc.unesco.org/ark:/48223/pf0000127583

Vygotsky, L. (1978). *Mind in Society. The Development of Higher Psychological Processes. Cambridge*. MA: Harvard University Press.

Warschauer, M. (1996). Computer-assisted language learning. An introduction. In Fotos, S. (Ed.), *Multimedia language teaching*, (3-20). Tokyo Logos International.

Web references

Centro Linguistico di Ateneo. Retrieved 27 April 2022 from www.cla.uniroma3.it/Tandem-IT.aspx

Miriadi. Retrieved 27 April 2022 from https://www.miriadi.net/4809-iott-2-intercomprensione-orale-e-teletandem-2018-19

Teletandem Brasil. Retrieved 27 April 2022 from www.teletandembrasil.org/partner-institutions.html

Teletándem – CORINÉI. Retrieved 27 April 2022 from https://dti.ua.es/es/teletandem-corinei/corinei/corinei.html

Teletandem Exchange Program. Retrieved 27 April 2022 from https://italian.georgetown.edu/teletandem-exchange-program/#

UniLingua: intercambio lingüístico interuniversitario Complutense. Retrieved 27 April 2022 from www.ucm.es/unilingua

Appendix

In the annexe, we intend to exhibit a general summary of the telecollaboration projects that we have explained in this contribution. Each table highlights a schema with the information related to the participating institutions; duration and range of time within which the projects reach completion; languages involved and level of language proficiency; tools and goal; methodology; and last, a link or bibliography related to the key information of each of the considered project.

LiceoStabili-UA	Liceo Stabili (Trebbiani), Ascoli Piceno / Universidad de Alicante
IT-SP	A1-B2
	Written; e-tándem
2003-2004 (Feb-May)	e-mail, Yahoo groups
	student-centred, from group communication to pair interaction
	González Royo, C. (2006: 48–59)

UniCatt-USal-EOI	Università Cattolica del Sacro Cuore (Brescia) Universidad de Salamanca / Escuela Oficial de Idiomas de Barcelona (Terrassa)
IT-SP	A1-B2
CORITE 2008-2009	Written; e-tándem; CORITE / CORESPI
	e-mail, questionnaires
CORESPI 2014	Methodology: guided task with given or free topics; no length limits and no time limits
	Bailini, (2018: 115–118)

UNISA-UNISOB-UA	Università Suor Orsola Benincasa di Napoli / Università degli Studi di Salerno / Universidad de Alicante
	Spanish: A2-C1; Italian: A1-B2
IT-SP	Oral diadic interaction; TELETÁNDEM > CORINÉI

2009-at present	Email, Facebook, Instagram, Whatsapp, Skype, Meet, Zoom, Teams, Jitsi, Pamela for Skype, device, digital questionnaires, Google Classroom, Google Forms, and Debates online or face-to-face.
	student-centred, audio-video recordings, transcriptions and auto-evaluation of the process
	https://dti.ua.es/es/teletandem-corinei/corinei/corinei.html

2008-at present	Università del Salento Apulia teletandem network www.teletandembrasil.org/partner-institutions.html
UNISalento-Sorbonne (Abu Dhabi) IT-ARABIC (Standard, Dial. Morroccan) -SP (EN Lingua Franca)	Università del Salento Apulia / Université Paris-Sorbonne Abu Dhabi
	Low intermediate - Advanced
	ICT management: video conferencing and recording CERFL and European Language Portfolio IC Intercomprensione
	email, Moodle, Skype and Evaer Google Image, Youtube, Wikipedia, dizionari online
	45 to 75 minutes (8 to 15 sessions); topics list. Autonomous work: preparation, video conferencing, journal of reflection on action (language and interculturality) / Discussion: characteristics of TOS, digital resources in a learning scenario, the role of a teacher as a mediator, and how mediation sessions are organized. Institutionalized but non-integrated
	Manta, T. (2015) Leone, P. (2016)
UNISalento-GU IT-EN	Università del Salento Apulia - Georgetown University
	The Teletandem Exchange Program (ITAL 408/ITAL 409) allows Georgetown students to partner with students from the University of Salento in Apulia, Italy.
	Oral interactions (TOS) - D.O.T.I. (Databank of Teletandem Interactions) - LETEC (Language and Teaching Corpura, Wigham and Chanier, 2013)
	Zoom
	student-centred
	https://italian.georgetown.edu/teletandem-exchange-program/#

UNISalento-UNIVLyon2	Università del Salento-UNIVLyon2
	Romance languages students must have limited knowledge or no knowledge of the foreign language used by the partner.
IT-FR - MULTILINGUAL	Oral Interaction, reflective journal on the communicative and comprehension strategies used, inter-comprehension; IOTT
	VoIP
2017-	Inter-comprehension programme and a foreign language teaching methodology course
	https://www.miriadi.net/4809-iott-2-intercomprensione-orale-e-teletandem-2018-19 Leone, P. (2022)

UniUrb-COLUMBIA	Università degli Studi di Urbino "Carlo Bo" / Columbia University
	Advanced Italian (LLs) at Columbia University, and Italian pre-service teachers (PSTs) enrolled in an MA in Teaching IFL at the University of Urbino, Italy
IT-EN	Oral Interaction, questionnaires
2014	Skype (Videoconferencing), CALLBURNER recording software, questionnaires
	student-centred with telecollaboration; for MA students and their reflection on methodology
	Carloni, G. and Franzè, F. (2020: 131–158)

UNISA-IES OC	Università degli Studi di Salerno / Instituto de Educación Superior Nº 28 "Olga Cossettini" de Rosario (IES OC) Argentina
IT-SP	Lengua Española III (UNISA, 43 participants);
	Oral Interaction, Intercultural exchange
2015 (October)	email, Skype (videoconferencing), Interviews with outside informants
	preparation to telecollaboration; interviews with outside informants and conversations transcription
	Theiner, I. M. (2018: 93–114)

UNIRoma3-GU IT-EN (March-May) 2016	Università ROMA TRE (CLA) / Georgetown University (TT Brasil)
	from A2 (UniRomaTre: Undergrad, Master, PhD, Erasmus, Marco Polo Project.)
	Oral Interaction, authentic conversation not included in the CV; Teletandem
	email, Skype (videoconferencing), informative meeting prior to starting (CLA), guidelines, agenda and monitoring by CLA (www.cla.uniroma3.it/Tandem-IT.aspx)
	ca. 10 meetings of 1 hour each
	www.cla.uniroma3.it/AvvisiRisultati%5CTeletandem_201602.pdf

UNIBO-Lyon2 IT-FR 2019 - present	Università degli Studi di Bologna (CLA) / Université de Lyon
	A2-C1
	Oral Interaction
	email, Facebook (groups), CLA platform, materials w/o questionnaires
	mín. 5 meetings (Sept-Dec and Feb. - May)

UniTO-UMCS IT-POL 2020-2021 (6 weeks)	Università degli Studi di Torino / Maria Curie-Sklodowska University of Lublin
	(Pre-A1) A1 and A2
	Oral Interaction, other Intercultural learning activities
	Facebook, Platforms, Padlet, Google Docs, Zoom
	Preparation for telecollaboration in groups of different types. Parallel use of both languages: Italian and Polish, mainly asynchronous. The teacher can access all the materials but does not intervene during the meetings except during the final oral presentation of the activity.
	Pieczka, A. (2021)

UNILINGUA	Universidad Complutense de Madrid, Université de Bourgogne, University of Cambridge, Chonbuk University, University of Edinburgh, Moscow State University, Universidad Libre de Berlín, Università di Palermo, Università degli Studi di Verona
IT-MULTILINGUAL	objectives/apps/method: any
2020- active	Universities just put learners in contact to practice the FL. Then they freely decide about the tools and channel to carry out exchanges (written, oral etc.)
	www.ucm.es/unilingua

Chapter 4

Teaching Italian (with) comics

Sara Dallavalle
University of Chicago

Abstract: In this chapter, I will explore ways in which comics can be integrated into Italian language courses at the university level, both in terms of teaching *comics* as standalone cultural products and teaching *with* comics, isolating specific elements as a means to discuss linguistic aspects. As reading comics involves the development of comics literacy, I will start with an overview of different comics formats and their features, and I will also offer a useful glossary of terms that are necessary to understand and describe comics sequences. I will then examine in detail the benefits of adopting comics, drawing from recent studies on multimodal literacy and its importance in contemporary communication. Finally, I will provide some suggestions on designing syllabi that focus on comics products, as well as some practical examples of activities and assessments that adopt comics as authentic sources of grammar, vocabulary, and contexts of use.

Keywords: Comics, Multimodal literacy, Communication, Italian, Teaching

***

1. Introduction

In recent years, foreign language teaching in higher education has advocated for an increasingly multimedia and interdisciplinary approach, enabling teachers to expand course materials and integrate various cultural products. In this regard, the medium of comics provides original pedagogical applications, both teaching *with* comics, isolating specific elements to discuss linguistic, narrative, or thematic aspects, and teaching comics, focusing on them as cultural objects. Integrating cartoons, comic strips, comic books, and graphic novels into lower- and upper-division curricula at the university allows for an expansion of the canon of Italian culture, enhancing students' curiosity toward non-common sources and fostering multimodal literacy, which is increasingly necessary to comprehend and navigate contemporary communication.

This chapter explores various ways to integrate comics into the teaching of Italian as a foreign language. The initial part examines the issue from a theoretical standpoint, starting with an overview of some primary issues pertaining to comics, such as sequentiality and simultaneity; it also includes a taxonomy of comics formats and a brief glossary of comics terminology. The following section reviews the literature on multiliteracies and multimodal literacy, particularly applying these frameworks to comics teaching in literature and FL courses. The second part of the chapter is devoted to practical pedagogical applications of comics in the context of Italian as a foreign language. At this point, the chapter draws a distinction between teaching *with* comics and teaching comics and provides instructional models that teachers can apply at all levels of the Italian language and culture. In order to facilitate the reproducibility of the proposed activities, the chapter does not dwell on specific examples from comics. Instead, it provides frameworks that can be adapted based on each teacher's available material.

2. Terms and definitions

The first question we need to address when we approach comics is clarifying what comics are. In reality, scholars have yet to agree on a univocal definition that encapsulates the complexities of this medium and art form. It can be established, however, what comics are not. They are not a genre, but instead, they have genres. Despite what the Anglo-Saxon term might suggest, they are not just funny or humorous. Not always do they have balloons, as the Italian word *fumetti* alludes to. They come in various formats, not just in strips, even though they are called *bandes dessinées* in French. They do not necessarily have a narrative, as the Hispanic terms *historietas* suggests. For scholar David Kunzle (1973: 2), for example, for a comic strip to be considered so, "there must be a sequence of separated images". In 1985 Will Eisner (2008: xi) stated that a comic – which he calls 'sequential art' – is an "arrangement of pictures or images and words to narrate a story or dramatize an idea". The most oft-quoted definition is Scott McCloud's (1993: 9), which reads: "juxtaposed pictorial and other images in *deliberate sequence,* intended to convey information and/or produce an aesthetic response in the viewer". One potential pitfall of all these definitions is the omission of a fundamental aspect of many comics: simultaneity or their unique ability to be perceived both sequentially and holistically. Already in 1976, Pierre Fresnault-Deruelle discussed the notions of 'linear' and 'tabular' (Fr. *linéaire* and *tabulaire*), whereby strips are read in a linear, chronological order, while pages are perceived in a tabular fashion as a global spatial composition. Similarly, in his seminal *Système de la bande dessinée*, Thierry Groensteen (1999: 21) introduced the concept of the 'iconic solidarity' (Fr. *solidarité iconique*): images are simultaneously separated and semantically over-determined on a comics page because they co-exist *in praesentia*. While sequential progression is still the most common mode employed, there are various instances of comics that take advantage of simultaneity to vary the reading rhythm and elicit a specific emotional response. In these cases, the action of 'looking at,' as Daniele Barbieri (2017: 55) would say, precedes (and sometimes prevails over) that of 'reading'.

This examination shows the complexity of the interplay between visual and verbal content in comics. Becoming aware of the hybridity of the medium is a necessary step for any teacher wishing to make comics part of their teaching materials. It also offers a valuable foundation to sort out the various formats in which comics can appear. In this regard, the most common are the following.

- **Cartoons** (It. *la vignetta*): single-panel comics, usually presenting words and images, often used to convey political or social commentary in a satirical or humorous tone (see Figure 4. 1.). Some examples of Italian cartoonists whose works can be found in newspapers and magazines and on social media are Altan, Sergio Staino, Vauro Senesi, Mauro Biani, Makkox, Silvia Ziche, Maicol and Mirco, Sio, Pat Carra.

- **Comic strips and comics pages** (It. *la striscia* and *la tavola*): a series of panels, usually arranged horizontally, that present a narrative or a chronological sequence (see Figure 4. 1.). A collection of comic strips can form a comics page; on social media, panels can be posted as a 'carousel': instead of all panels being next to each other, readers can swipe between them. Some famous Italian strips are Bonvi's *Sturmtruppen*, Silver's *Lupo Alberto* and *Cattivik*, Sio's *Scottecs*, Giacomo Bevilacqua's *A Panda Piace*, Labadessa's strips with his iconic man-bird protagonist, Leo Ortolani's and Fumettibrutti's strips on Instagram (Toninelli, n.d.).

- **Comic books** (It. *l'albo a fumetti*): a bound collection of comic strips or comics pages that typically present a single story with the same protagonists or a series of different stories of the same narrative genre (humour, action, horror, detective story, etc.). Generally, they are published weekly or monthly and sold on newsstands. Popular Italian comic book series are Panini Disney's (*Topolino, Paperinik*, etc.) and Sergio Bonelli

Editore's (*Tex, Martin Mystère, Dylan Dog, Julia, Orfani*, etc.), *Diabolik, Rat-Man*, among others.

- **Comics magazines** (It. *la rivista a fumetti*): a comic book featuring a portion of editorial content, such as articles, letters to the editor, and games (e.g., Panini Disney's *Topolino*). Some magazines publish a selection of comic stories of various authors, genres, and styles and interpolate them with editorial or literary contributions. A famous example is Baldini and Castoldi's *Linus*.

- **Graphic novels** (It. *il graphic novel*): a re-packaged collection of previously serialized comics or self-contained narratives, usually created by a recognizable authorial figure. Graphic novels are published as hardcover or paperback books and sold in bookstores. The offer of Italian graphic novels is constantly growing; among the most acclaimed authors, we can mention Paolo Bacilieri, Takoua Ben Mohamed, Lorena Canottiere, Marco Corona, Daniel Cuello, Gipi, Manuele Fior, Fumettibrutti, Francesca Ghermandi, Igort, Leila Marzocchi, Lorenzo Mattotti, Tuono Pettinato, Teresa Radice and Stefano Turconi, Alessandro Tota, Zerocalcare, Silvia Ziche.

- **Webcomics**: digital cartoons and comic strips created to be read online. Sometimes webcomics reproduce a printable format; other times, they take advantage of the 'infinite canvas,' that is, their ability to extend vertically and horizontally for an infinite distance (McCloud, 2000). Various comics artists keep personal blogs in which they post their webcomics, such as Zerocalcare, Leo Ortolani, and Sio.

In addition to knowing the various formats in which comics are published, teachers of Italian as FL should also get familiar with some fundamental terms used to describe comics features. Comics studies terminology is not formalized in the way other fields are and often borrows descriptors from art history, film studies, photography, narratology, publishing studies, etc. However, some standard terms are generally recognized as valid (see Figure 4. 2.).

- **Panel** (It. *la vignetta*): an area that contains a segment of action. Usually, a panel has a visible square or rectangular border; however, sometimes, it may be borderless. A row of panels is called 'tier' (It. *la striscia*), while a page containing a regular number of panels – such as two by three or three by three – is called 'grid' (It. *la griglia*). Some comics may present irregular layouts or have no recognizable panels; in this case, we just talk about a comics page (It. *la pagina* or *la tavola*).

- **Balloon** (It. *la nuvoletta o il balloon*): an area containing characters' spoken dialogues or inner monologue. It usually has a tail pointing to the character uttering or thinking the words. Depending on its shape, the balloon may convey paralanguage. A bubble-shaped balloon represents normal speech; a cloud-shaped balloon reproduces thoughts; a balloon with a jagged outline conveys screams (see Figure 4. 2, bottom tier).

- **Caption** (It. *la didascalia*): generally, a rectangular box placed near the top edge of a panel. It includes narrative or descriptive information, such as time and place. Captions can also express the narrator's commentary.

- **Gutter** (It. *lo spazio bianco*): the space that separates panels, and it is typically associated with the concept of 'closure' (see pp. 65).

- **Onomatopoeia** (It. *l'onomatopea*): words that phonetically imitate sounds, such as 'stunk' or 'mumble mumble' in Figure 4. 2.

- **Emanata** (It. *la metafora visualizzata*): graphic signs that convey information that goes beyond the visual and the aural, such as emotions (e.g., pain, surprise, anger, love, etc.) or physical properties (e.g., warmth, shine, smell, etc.). For example, in Figure 4. 2. (third panel), the character's spiral eyes and the star rotating over her head represent confusion and disorientation. These signs are conventional and might differ in various comics culture.

Figure 4. 1. On the left, an example of a cartoon or single-panel comics (It. vignetta). On the right, an example of comic strip (It. striscia)[1]

---

[1] Illustrated (for this chapter) by Gaia Fredella.

Figure 4. 2. This is a comics page with its main elements: gutter (It. lo spazio bianco), caption (It. la didascalia), balloon (It. la nuvoletta or il balloon), onomatopoeia (It. l'onomatopea), emanata (It. la metafora visualizzata), and panel (It. la vignetta). In the bottom tier, you see three types of balloons: a bubble-shaped balloon for normal speech a balloon with a jagged outline for screams; a cloud-shaped balloon for thoughts[2].

---

[2] Illustrated (for this chapter) by Gaia Fredella.

3. Pedagogical approach

The adoption of comics in FL teaching in higher education is not as widespread a practice as it is, for example, using audio-visual material. Nonetheless, the body of scholarship that discusses the pedagogical benefits of comics has been growing in the past two decades. Two related concepts that are often mentioned in this regard are "multiliteracies" and "multimodal literacy." In 1996 the New London Group came together to discuss the future of literacy pedagogy. They discussed literacy as the ability 1) "to read the ordinary texts of modern society – newspapers, information books, novels"; 2) "to write using correct spelling and grammar"; and 3) "to appreciate high-cultural values through exposure to a taste of the literary canon" (Cope and Kalantzis, 2015: 1). According to these scholars, "the conventional understandings of literacy were becoming anachronistic" (Ibid., 1), and they proposed a "pedagogy of multiliteracies." Multiliteracies addressed the changing patterns of meaning-making in contemporary society, which is multilingual – "communication and representation of meaning today increasingly requires that learners become able to negotiate differences in patterns of meaning from one context to another" (Ibid., 3) and multimodal – "written-linguistic modes of meaning interface with oral, visual, audio, gestural, tactile, and spatial patterns of meaning" (Ibid., 3). The multiliteracies framework (New London Group, 1996; Cope and Kalantzis, 2009; Cope and Kalantzis, 2015) has been advocated as a pedagogical model to carry out integrated, text-based curricula that can bridge the divide in FL teaching between language-focused lower divisions and content-focused upper divisions (Allen and Paesani, 2010; Allen, Paesani and Dupuy, 2016). "Multimodality," in particular, has been studied extensively in the context of pedagogy (Kress and Van Leeuwen, 2001; Kress, 2003; Jewitt and Kress, 2003; Jewitt, 2008): "Key to multimodal perspectives on literacy is the basic assumption that meanings are made (as well as distributed, interpreted, and remade) through many representational and communicational resources, of which language is but one" (Jewitt, 2008: 246). According to Jewitt (2008), a tenet of this approach is "the promotion of a pluralized notion of literacy and forms of representation and communication to help students negotiate a broader range of text types and modes of persuasion" (Ibid., 255). "Multimodal literacy" has been applied to teaching visual texts (Chan and Chia, 2014; Lim-Fei et al., 2015; Lim-Fei and Tan, 2017; Chia and Chan, 2017) and has also been invoked by scholars interested in the pedagogical applications of comics in composition as well as FL courses. According to Daniela Elsner (2013),

> Twenty-first-century learners of foreign languages need to be able to decode and comprehend mono- and multimodal, linear and non-

linear, mono- and multilingual, audio- or visual, traditional or digital text forms; they moreover need to be able to analyse and understand the interplay of pictures, sound, texts and symbols. Learners must learn how to interpret and critically evaluate the same in terms of their content-relevance, their validity and authorship. (2013: 57).

At the same time, "teachers need to offer a wide variety of text and media combinations – just as learners find those in real-world contexts accordingly" (Elsner and Viebrock, 2013: 28). While Elsner acknowledges the difficulty in "fostering all dimensions of multiliteracies at the same time" (Elsner and Viebrock, 2013: 27), she also recognizes the potential of graphic novels to promote a multiliteracies approach. An even stronger advocate of comics in the university is Dale Jacobs. Refuting the notion that comics are "a debased or simplified word-based literacy" (2007: 19), Jacobs acknowledges the benefits that this medium can bring to students. He argues, "we can help students engage critically with ways of making meaning that exist all around them since multimodal texts include much of the content on the Internet, interactive multimedia, newspapers, television, film, instructional textbooks, and many other texts in our contemporary society" (Ibid., 19). While the tendency is to foreground the linguistic mode of comics, found in captions and speech balloons, words are but one element and not nearly enough to manifest comics' complex meaning-making environment. As a word/image medium, the other equally important mode is the visual, a sort of 'macro-mode' that allows materializing the audio, gestural, and spatial modes.

Unlike non-illustrated prose, sounds can be visualized in comics in various ways, primarily through balloons (voices) and onomatopoeias (sounds). To a certain extent, variations in balloon shapes and in the lettering style of both onomatopoeias and spoken words even convey paralanguage, such as volume, emphasis, and vocal quality. For example, while round or square balloons generally represent normal speech, a jagged outline conventionally manifests a louder sound or tone of voice, while a dashed outline reproduces whispers. By varying the size, thickness, and shape of words, artists can convey a particular emotional tenor – and this is especially true when the lettering is hand-drawn by the author itself, as is the case of Zerocalcare's comics.

The gestural mode has to do with facial expression and body posture. Whether the style is naturalistic and representational, or symbolical and 'cartoony' – in this case, emanata are often present to convey physiological or emotional states (e.g., sweat beads, light bulbs, heart eyes, etc.) – "the practitioner has to distill a hundred intermediate movements of which the gesture is comprised into one posture. This selected posture must convey nuances, support the dialogue, carry out the thrust of the story and deliver the message" (Eisner, 2008: 104).

The spatial mode involves the position and physical arrangement of objects in space. As Jacobs explains, it "can be conceived as the layout page and the relation between these panels through the use of gutter space" (2007: 22). The spatial mode also acts within each panel in how each scene is framed (i.e., depth of field, perspective, angle of framing, etc.). This mode is possibly the most peculiar and complex one because spatial forms systematically translate time (Baetens and Pylyser, 2017: 303). This is what McCloud calls 'closure': when reading a comics sequence, readers move spatially from one panel to the other, and in doing so, they also progress temporally, "connecting these moments and mentally constructing a continuous, unified reality" (1993: 67). At the same time, the images represented within single panels often depict time and movement: regardless of their posture, when characters say their lines, time is passing; in some cases, actions are depicted with the aid of motion lines and motion blur (often seen in manga); in other cases, a single panel may depict various, subsequent instants (e.g., Gianni De Luca's Shakespearean trilogy).

Finally, from a purely visual point of view, comic artists rely on lines, white spaces, shading, colours, and other pictorial or photographic techniques to make meaning. All these modes co-exist on the page; therefore, reading comics is neither immediate nor reducible solely to the linguistic element. In reading comics, we actively engage with the 'grammar' or the rule and conventions of the medium. Those who know these conventions have an advantage in terms of ways of reading and understanding texts. Vice versa, those who are not familiar with comics grammars need guidance. Eventually, "by teaching students to become conscious and critical of how they make meaning from multimodal texts such as comics, we can also teach students to become more literate with a wide range of multimodal texts" (Jacobs, 2007: 24).

Despite the complexity of the comics medium, a less subtle argument is often made when discussing the benefits of teaching comics in FL classes. Lovisa Källvant (2015) argues that "comics have a lot of potential within the second or foreign language classroom as they provide students with authentic language, but with a reduced amount of texts, that can nevertheless be quite advanced. Images also assist students and help them understand texts" (Ibid., 18). While this argument raises some doubts in its tendency to conceive comics as a monomodal, or better, a two-modal medium, comics can indeed be approached from various angles, depending on the pedagogical focus teachers have set for their classes.

4. Pedagogical applications

Teaching (with) comics refers to two ways of using comics in the FL classroom. As a variation to the definitions provided by the Kennedy Center (n.d.), this chapter understands teaching *with* comics in terms of an "arts-enhanced curriculum, when arts (=comics) are used as a device or strategy to support other curriculum areas," such as the Italian language curriculum. Parkes and Ryan (2015) note that the arts-enhanced curriculum is widely adopted in FL teaching at the university. However, it does not commonly "introduce the specific vocabulary, physical tools, modalities of creation, or culture of critique as part of formal learning goals for assessments" (Ibid., 2). Moreover, teachers do not need special training or expertise in the art form.

On the other hand, teaching comics go in the direction of an "arts-integrated curriculum," where "students meet dual learning objectives when they engage in the creative process to explore connections between an art form and another subject area to gain greater understanding in both" (Kennedy Center, n.d.). Parkes and Ryan advocate for the latter approach, in which art is employed as content and the foreign language as "one primary means or modality for understanding, interpreting, and experiencing it" (2015: 2). Arts-integrated courses in FL do not all look the same. The Kennedy Center, for example, posits students' engagement in the creative process as a fundamental step (n.d.). Other scholars reflect on the context of the art, its creator's intentions, and its relationship with cultural insiders and outsiders (Barnes-Karol and Broner, 2010); or, in general, they speak of 'object-based learning,' where the object is used "to generate a creative exchange of ideas and reflections" (Parra and Di Fabio, 2015: 15).

The following sections focus on a comics-enhanced approach first, or teaching *with* comics, and on a comics-integrated approach after, where Italian comics are investigated holistically in their textual and contextual features.

A) Teaching with comics

This section gathers instructional models and examples of activities that teachers can adapt to various language levels and classroom settings. Activities are grouped into three conceptual categories: activities with a 1) focus on language, 2) focus on narration, and 3) focus on theme. These categories are by no means fixed, and some activities could have more than one focus, depending on teachers' learning goals.

A1) Activities with a focus on language

One way of approaching comics is from a linguistic standpoint. This approach does not require much experience with reading comics, as activities generally focus on the verbal content included in balloons and captions. In contrast, the visual content most often just provides support. Teachers can select cartoons, comic strips, or comic pages based on the grammar structures and vocabulary they are interested in and create mechanical or meaningful activities. It should be noted that the language used in comics is exceptionally variegated. The early comic strips feature poetic language and rhymed couplets in place of dialogues. Serial comic books mix standard Italian, colloquialism, dialect expressions, idiomatic expressions, and set phrases. Graphic novels can range from standard Italian to poetic language or regionalisms (Morgana, 2020). Disney comic books, such as *Topolino*, employ a particularly creative language, including slang, 'pseudo-jargon,' 'Anglicism,' and even the language of television (Pietrini, 2020). Not to mention the number of comic adaptations of Italian and international classics, which interpolate direct quotations from original sources (e.g., Dino Battaglia's and Sergio Toppi's) and even re-work them in comical terms (e.g., Disney's parodies).

A1. 1. Cloze & fill-in-the-blanks activities

In cloze exercises, a selected text presents blanks students fill with meaningful words, which can be provided with word banks or multiple choices. In some cases, students must conjugate verbs that are given in the infinite form. Instructors can remove words from balloons and captions by editing PDF copies or manipulating printed copies by erasing or covering words and successively scanning the edited pages.

A1. 2. Sentence transformation

In this kind of activity, students work on transforming sentences that present specific grammar structures. One-panel cartoons are particularly indicated in this case, as they often reproduce dialogues about routine tasks and use a variety of verb constructions. Students can be asked to re-write speech balloons transforming all verbs from the *indicativo presente* to the *passato prossimo*, or from the *congiuntivo presente* to the *congiuntivo imperfetto*, etcetera. The new sentence should still make sense in the context of the cartoon.

A1. 3. Sentence creation

In order to have students work communicatively with grammar structure and vocabulary, teachers can adopt single-panel cartoons or strips with little or no dialogue as prompts for sentence creation. Teachers might ask students to create individual sentences or a story focusing on a particular grammar structure (e.g., a major time frame), a function of speech (e.g., description, narration, expressing opinions), or vocabulary. Working with images can promote students' imaginative processes and creative responses. At the same time, these images are culturally relevant; even with the simple act of looking at them, students engage in cultural exploration and can start to recognize particular gestures, facial expressions, locations, and a variety of other products and practices of the target culture. Students' linguistic experience is thus enriched with an authentic cultural context.

A1. 4. Translation

Translation activities can take many forms and varying degrees of involvement with the visual content of the comics. At a basic level, students can work on translating captions and balloons from L2 to L1 or L1 to L2 (in this case, instructors should provide Italian comics in translation), focusing on pragmatics. Students can practice various functions depending on the selected text, such as narrating and describing (captions) or written conversations (balloons). While the latter are often found in cartoons and comic strips, narrative and descriptive passages are more common in graphic novels or comic books. At advanced levels, students can also practice translating texts into L1 with different linguistic styles, from the colloquial to the neutral to the literary. Teachers can select literary and poetic excerpts in comic adaptations of classics or in comic parodies. Moreover, as mentioned, early comics often had rhymed couplets in place of balloons (e.g., Attilio Mussino's, Antonio Rubino's, and Sergio Tofano's comics); this way, students could practice creative translations.

A1. 5. Table-read

Pronunciation and fluency are essential aspects of foreign language classes. Frequently, final projects require students to deliver a presentation or perform a dialogue. Students must have enough class practice to work on their delivery skills in these cases. Instructors can include table-reads activities and ask students to read out captions and dialogues. Unlike film scripts, comics allow students to see characters' facial expressions and body postures and the paralanguage conveyed by lettering and balloon shapes. This way, students can practice their pronunciation and gain awareness of some pragmatic aspects of the language (intonation, emphasis, body language, etc.).

A2) Activities with a focus on narration

When class activities focus on storytelling, teachers can take advantage of the complex relationship between words and images, engaging students in verbal but also in visual analysis. The activities focused on narration promote various abilities, mainly writing, reading, creative thinking, and problem-solving skills.

A2. 1. Jigsaw puzzle

Many Italian comics have a grid layout, with panels arranged in three or four tiers per page; pages read from left to right, top to bottom. For this reason, strips or even whole pages can be disassembled into individual panels, like pieces of a puzzle. To reorder the panels, students must work on both the textual and the visual aspects of the comic, understanding the communicative context and engaging with the gutters and the already-mentioned notion of 'closure' (McCloud, 1993). They have the active task of interconnecting the images in each panel to create a coherent story. As noticed by Elsner, "they, therefore, need to bring in their personal knowledge of the world and their experiences, as a big part of the story occurs in the invisible spaces between the panels and thus in the mind of the readers themselves" (2013: 66). For this reason, a jigsaw puzzle activity activates students' linguistic, social, and cultural knowledge and experience, which the New London Group calls 'Available Design' (1996) and involves linguistic, as well as schematic, visual, audio, gestural, or spatial resources (Paesani, Allen, and Dupuy, 2016: 28–29). In some cases, re-assembling a comic sequence requires such a degree of interpretation and sequencing that students will have to negotiate their decisions and think critically to justify their choices to their classmates.

A2. 2. Inventing missing panels

If, in jigsaw puzzles, students have all panels at their disposal, and need to reorder them, in this activity, they are presented with a sequence missing one or more panels, be it at the beginning, in the middle, or at the end. Once again, students must first understand the comic's context, the characters involved and their actions, and the communicative functions involved in the dialogues. When they ideate the missing panel – either in a verbal form or pictorially – they engage in sequencing and prediction skills and creative thinking. After they have ideated the missing panels, teachers may present students with the original panel and ask them to compare it with their rendition.

A2. 3. Inventing missing dialogues

The activity of filling missing dialogues can be adapted with various goals, be they linguistic or narrative. Teachers can remove words from captions and balloons in a whole strip or even on a whole page and ask students to create a story through dialogues. While creativity and coherence are the primary learning goals, students must also pay attention to the visual content of the comic, making sense of the setting, characters' facial expressions, body posture, and the relationship between characters.

A2. 4. Retelling

Verbal retelling is a form of adaptation. According to Linda Hutcheon, adaptations are a product or a "transcoding ... that can involve a shift of medium (a poem to a film), or genre (an epic to a novel), or a change of frame and therefore context" (2006: 8). Adaptation is also a process of creation that "always involves both (re-)interpretation and then (re-) creation" (2006: 8). When students retell a comic, they are moving "across modes of engagement and thus across media" (Hutcheon, 2006: 35) and are manipulating and refocusing the content of a comic. Students can be involved in retelling activities in which they transpose the setting of a comic and the captions into a descriptive text and the sequence of actions and dialogues into a narrative text. In order to carry out this assignment, students must interpret the comic before progressing to the retelling. They need to combine the visual content with the verbal, selecting essential information and leaving out secondary details. They also need to balance description, narration and reported speech. In a retelling activity, the selection of comics cannot be random: depending on how detailed a sequence is, it may take students fifty or five hundred words to describe it. More naturalist rendering styles tend to be full of background and foreground details. At the same time, numerous comic strips are minimal. This difference is immediately visible when confronting, for example, a page from any Bacilieri's graphic novels with a strip by Sio. A significant number of comics presents a good balance in terms of the number of details; Disney comics, for example, combine a simple, cartoony style with explicit cultural references in the depiction of objects and places.

A3) Activities with a focus on theme

Comic books and graphic novels deal with a vast array of themes, which they explore with a serious as well as a humorous tone. In light of this, teachers can adopt comics productions as a springboard to explore thematic paths. However, unlike films, which require a short time to be watched and understood in their entirety, reading comics is a slower activity that can take students days to complete. For this reason, while the thematic analysis of a whole work is certainly more comprehensive, time constraints might prompt to select portions of longer texts, short stories, or works featuring little verbal content.

A3. 1. Word clouds

Word cloud activities are an effective way to engage students in class discussions. When focusing on thematic aspects, word clouds can be used at various stages of the reading process – as a pre-, during, and post-reading activity. Teachers can survey their students, asking them to predict what the text is about (pre-reading) or to identify the fundamental topics explored in the comic (during and post-reading). This type of polling – particularly when interactive, as allowed by Mentimeter™ and Poll Everywhere™ – can help teachers quickly collect students' answers, visually highlighting and presenting them to the class in real time. To engage students in critical thinking, teachers can ask them to discuss why specific themes appear more frequently and others less so, justifying their answers with examples from the comic itself.

A3. 2. Characters biographies

Italian comics feature many well-rounded characters that appear in comic book series and graphic novels. Corto Maltese, Valentina, Tex Willer, Diabolik, Martin Mystère, Dylan Dog, and the five young protagonists of *W.I.T.C.H.* are examples of characters with a well-known biography and many adventures. Students can familiarize themselves with these characters by reading short passages and then researching more information online. Once they have collected details about these characters, students can perform creative, communicative activities, such as ideating imaginary interviews, performing conversations among different comics characters, and writing the subject of a movie or a television show adaptation of the comic(s) in question. Since most serial comics belong to specific genres (adventure, western, mystery, fantasy, horror, etc.) and are set in various historical periods and places of the world, activities focused on characters encourage students to reflect on contextualization and allow them to practice a more extensive vocabulary than they would otherwise do.

B) Teaching comics

Teaching comics may refer to the applied approach of comics production or have the critical, cultural, historical, and aesthetic focus of comics studies. In the first case, students learn how to make comics; in the second case, they learn how to perform a close reading and analyse comics contextually. While comics-making is beyond the scope of this chapter, some form of comics production can be present in comics-integrated courses. Some language professors, such as Kathy Korcheck at Central College (Iowa), challenge students to draw and write their own comic panels: "there's a part of me that feels strongly about the idea that you can't truly understand the comics and graphic novels you're studying unless you try to feel what it means to draw something and put your ideas into images" (Korcheck, 2022). This choice is entirely personal and requires teachers to be comfortable with assessing students' creation skills; otherwise, students could use comics creation software, such as Pixton™, StoryboardThat™, and Canva™, to invent digital stories. While adopting these tools can be fruitful from a linguistic and narrative point of view, they generally take away control of visual information, colours, emphasis, and even page layout.

In the following pages, the chapter presents pedagogical reflections and paths that teachers can follow, with a predominant 1) focus on the text, 2) focus on the material object, and 3) focus on the context. Activities in this section do not have clear boundaries and should be combined to enable students to have a more holistic and nuanced understanding of comics. Indeed, teaching comics implies a more advanced knowledge of the specificities of the medium and a deeper reflection on the relationship between visual and verbal content.

Before or while engaging in these activities, students might need to consult some reference works in English or Italian. Manuals to consider are *Understanding Comics, The Power of Comics* (McCloud, 1993), *Il linguaggio del fumetto* (Barbieri, 1991), and *Fumetto! 150 anni di storie italiane* (Bono and Stefanelli, 2016). Simone Castaldi's chapter *A Brief History of Comics in Italy and Spain* in *The Routledge Companion to Comics* is essential for a brief yet comprehensive historical contextualization of Italian comics. The blog posts' Show vs Tell' and 'List of Terms for Comics Studies by Andrei Molotiu' are helpful for students to understand terms and notions. However, since they are written in English, teachers might want to share a detailed glossary of terms in Italian. In addition, since comics studies borrow terms from other fields (art history, film studies, photography, narratology, publishing, etc.), teachers should create their lists of agreed-upon words to help students navigate the complex interdisciplinary nature of comics.

B1) Path with a focus on the text

Focusing on the text means adopting an overall approach to the analysis of comics, one that equally considers the pictures and the words. Traditionally, the visual content has been considered subservient to the verbal; in reality, the interaction between these two aspects varies from comic to comic. Notably, McCloud (1993) proposes seven main word/picture combinations: 1) in 'word-specific' combinations, pictures illustrate words; 2) in 'picture-specific' combinations, words add the soundtrack to a visual sequence; 3) in 'duo-specific' combinations, words and pictures convey the same message; 4) in 'additive' combinations, words amplify the images or vice versa; 5) in 'parallel combinations' words and pictures seem to follow non-intersecting narrative paths; 6) in 'montage' combinations words are part of the picture; 7) in 'interdependent' combinations, words and pictures are both necessary to convey an idea. An eighth category could be added too, the 'ironic combinations,' in which words and pictures contradict each other (Molotiu, 2013). Moreover, while some comics develop sequentially and present a regular panel grid, others experiment with more complex layouts where a traditional Western reading strategy is not enough to convey the meaning of the sequences. In this case, reading is propelled by a different progression, such as by the size (bigger-smaller), position (centre-periphery), or definition of the images (more detailed-less detailed).

Students should receive guidance in approaching comics as text, as they might not have yet developed the necessary 'grammar' to understand and explain comics. Depending on time constraints, amount of material, and learning goals, teachers can use a deductive approach, presenting explanations followed by examples, or an inductive approach, providing students with information and asking them to figure out the medium's conventions. To practice their skills, students can then engage in visual analyses. Of course, visual analyses can be enriched by activities focusing on language, such as table-reads, narration, such as retelling, or theme, such as word clouds.

B1. 1. Visual analysis

Visual analysis activities are fundamental to training students' visual literacy and developing their comics literacy. To build a successful visual analysis assignment, teachers should offer students a selection of comics pages. If the page is electronic, it should have high resolution and retain all properties it had originally. Students should disregard artist, date information, and historical context and focus only on what they can learn by looking at the comics page. The goal here is to reflect on what the combination of images and words tells us and what effect they produce.

To avoid overwhelming students, teachers should provide them with guiding questions about page layout, art style, framing, and effect on viewers. The following are some questions that students may find helpful in approaching a visual analysis.

- Layout della pagina
    o Com'è organizzata la pagina?
    o Che ordine hanno le vignette? Come capisci qual è l'ordine delle vignette?

- Le vignette e i bordi delle vignette hanno la stessa forma e dimensione o variano?
- Quale effetto provoca uno schema vignettistico regolare vs. uno non regolare?

- Stile artistico
  - È un fumetto in bianco e nero o a colori? Se è a colori, qual è la palette (monocromo, bicromo, tricromo, ecc.)?
  - Lo stile è astratto, caricaturale, cartoonistico, realistico, iperrealistico (=simile a una foto)?
  - Lo sfondo è ricco di dettagli o semplice? Qual è l'effetto?
  - I contorni sono sottili, spessi, o tratteggiati?
  - Le linee sono omogenee/spezzate, verticali/orizzontali, dritte/curve, sottili/spesse, pulite/sporche, ecc.?

- Inquadrature
  - Tutte le vignette hanno la stessa inquadratura? Se no, come cambia l'angolo?
  - Qual è l'effetto provocato dal cambio o dalla mancanza di cambio di inquadratura?

- Rapporto immagini/testo
  - Come sono i testi (didascalie, balloon, onomatopee)?
  - Che rapporto c'è tra i testi e le immagini?
    - Il testo è più importante. Le immagini illustrano il testo ma non aggiungono significato.
    - L'immagine è più importante. Il testo è una sorta di colonna sonora.
    - Testo e immagini sono ugualmente importanti, illustrano la stessa scena.
    - Le immagini aggiungono qualcosa al testo o il testo aggiunge qualcosa alle immagini.
    - Il testo e le immagini seguono due linee indipendenti.
    - Il testo è parte dell'immagine stessa.

- Il testo e l'immagine si contraddicono a vicenda.

- Contenuto e genere
  - Che genere di fumetto è? Come lo capiamo?
  - Che cosa succede nella pagina/sequenza?
  - Chi sono i personaggi principali? Che rapporto c'è tra i vari personaggi?

- Domande generali
  - Qual è il rapporto tra lo spazio (la sequenza disegnata) e il tempo evocato?
  - Qual è il rapporto tra le scelte formali (layout, inquadrature e stile) e il contenuto?
  - Quali sensazioni pensi che il fumetto trasmetta? In che modo le trasmette?

B2) *Path with a focus on the material object*

The materiality of comics is a rarely discussed issue but an essential one. While adopting films, songs, commercials, or works of literature in an FL class does not necessarily prompt reflections about medium and physical object, this question in relation to comics is conducive to understanding the relationship between the content and the audience.

Integrating comics in class means deciding what format of primary sources is better using. Teachers have the choice of adopting digital reproductions or paper copies and should weigh the pros and cons of each solution in light of their learning goals. On the one hand, digital copies are reproducible, generally accessible, often free, or cheaper than paper copies. These characteristics allow for the integration of a greater variety of source materials. Scanned comics and e-books, in particular, allow students to enjoy the authentic reading experience of an entire work (or even series) in a portable fashion. The cons, however, are multiple. If we talk about JPEG images, they are usually lower quality and fragments of more extensive works whose features are impossible to grasp. Scanned comics and e-books, on the contrary, might be uncomfortable to read; frequently, readers need to zoom in and scroll the page, losing that overall perception of the page that is essential to the medium. In addition, some e-books are not available offline, which certainly limits accessibility.

On the other hand, paper copies are hard to find outside Italy, are more expensive, and in some cases, fragile too. Usually, teachers who want to use hard copies rely on the material they own or what is made available by libraries. Despite these challenges, pedagogically, the pros of using paper copies are incomparable. For students, leafing through a comic book or a graphic novel means getting a tactile interaction with the object; this close encounter is often a unique experience for most. Students gain immediate awareness of comics as objects and understand how materiality has to do with context – cultural positioning (highbrow vs lowbrow), role in society, and audience.

B2. 1. Object analysis

To perform object analysis, teachers should present students with various formats of comics – possibly a comic book, a graphic novel, a magazine, and a collection of comic strips. Students could be asked to approach comics without any guidance to train their reasoning ability and give them the agency to make informed speculations. Otherwise, students' analysis could focus on editorial information (title, author, date), format information (format itself, hardcover or paperback, b&w or colours), cover (art style, layout, price), and tactile and visual sensations. Some guiding questions could be:

- Qual è il titolo del fumetto? Chi è l'autore? Quando è stato pubblicato?

- Che tipo di fumetto è (graphic novel, albo a fumetti, rivista, raccolta di strisce)? È in cartonato o in brossura? È un oggetto da collezione o usa e getta? È a colori o in bianco e nero?

- Com'è la copertina? Quali informazioni contiene? Qual è lo stile? Qual è il prezzo?

- Che sensazioni si provano nel toccare e vedere questo fumetto?

- A chi è indirizzato questo fumetto? Come lo capisci?

The last question allows connecting object and aim, encouraging students to think about readership. In a related activity, teachers could create some readers' profiles and ask students to suggest a comic to each of these readers, justifying their suggestions with references to the object's properties. This activity could also be integrated after performing an edition comparison (see below).

B2. 2. Edition Comparison

Comparing editions tells how interconnected aesthetic values and the media industry are. It allows students to focus on the changes that might have undergone between an early and a later edition of a graphic novel (especially if its/the author became particularly famous meanwhile), previously serialized strips that have been collected in an anthology, instalments of stories that are bound in a graphic novel format; comic books that are reprinted in colour and hard-paper copies; and so on. A comparison of this kind can prompt reflections about the cultural role of a particular comic or offer more information on the kind of audience that it might have reached in being repurposed.

When exploring early comics, with comics magazines being the only format, students could be asked to analyse the same story as published in the original American newspapers and in Italy. For example, in comparing episodes of Richard F. Outcault's *Buster Brown* or Winsor McCay's *Little Nemo* and their Italian adaptations, *Mimmo* and *Bubi*, students may notice how the Italian version turned balloons into captions and eliminated some panels. The reason was related to space constraints but also pedagogical concerns – while the target of American comics was adult readers, comic strips were addressed only to children in Italy. Another activity could revolve around the censorship that some publishers (such as Bonelli) self-imposed in the 1950s on their previously printed comic books to eliminate any sexual reference (e.g., skirts that were too short) or less than proper speech. Indeed, teachers should also equip students with historical, social, and factual knowledge to draw such conclusions.

B3) Path with a focus on the context

A comics-integrated course must assess the historical and social context in which comics were published. Some issues to consider in this regard are genres, authors, social commentary, repurposing of comics in other media, and readership. Teachers who prefer a thematical approach to Italian comics classes may want to assign students secondary sources to supplement contextual information, such as the already mentioned chapter by Castaldi to address Italian comics history or selections from *Fumetti!* to address authors and movements.

B3. 1. Genre comparison

Exploring genres is rather pivotal, as they "provide us with a shorthand for discussing trends and motifs that characterize given narratives" (Duncan, Smith and Levitz, 2015: 164). Analysing the degree of standardization (i.e., matching the conventions of the genre) or differentiation (i.e., bringing innovation to the genre) helps position a specific comic within its bigger historical and social context and reflect on its role in the cultural industry. In

Italy, genre comics are generally fruitful in serial comics, while graphic novels tend to be independent. Some popular genres in Italian comics are detective and police fiction (e.g., *Julia, Il commissiario Ricciardi*), adventure (e.g., *Martin Mystère*), horror (e.g., *Dylan Dog*), crime (e.g., *Diabolik*), sci-fi (e.g., *Nathan Never, Orfani*), western (e.g., *Tex*), fantasy (*Dragonero, W.I.T.C.H*), autobiography (e.g., Zerocalcare's, Gipi's, Fumettibrutti's graphic novels), satire (e.g., Sio's, Ziche's, Ortolani's strips and graphic novels), and comedy (e.g., *Topolino*).

To compare genres, students need to focus on common characteristics: character types, settings, narrative patterns, themes, and visual conventions (Duncan, Smith and Levitz, 2015). In order for students to assess these characteristics, they need to employ their comics literacy holistically, practising their linguistic, narrative, thematic, and visual skills. To come up with the features of character types, for example, students analyse their visual properties – such as clothes and accessories, but also facial expressions and body gestures. Moreover, they need to consider the characters' language to recognize typical expressions or a particular way of speaking. Alternatively, asking an American student to discuss the representation of the Far West in the late 1800s *Tex* or a British student the depiction of a 1990s London in *Dylan Dog* could prompt more profound reflections on the influence of foreign culture on Italian popular culture imagination.

Finally, students could also compare genres typical of Anglo-Saxon and Italian comics. Reflecting on the lack of superhero comics in Italy, for example, leads to discussing the different perspectives that Italian people have regarding notions such as individualism, self-reliance, the sense of community, the role of the res publica, and so on.

B3. 2. Authors survey

Surveying authors and their work is another possible way to access comics both diachronically and synchronically. Students can investigate authors from a variety of perspectives, within genres (such as satirical or autobiographical) or groups (the Cannibale group, the Valvoline group, the Disney group), for their particular art style (i.e., Toppi, Pazienza, Bacilieri, Gipi), for their connections with other media (i.e., Zerocalcare on Netflix). Since women authors are usually less represented, courses could also focus on their contribution and role in attracting female readers to comics.

B3. 3. Society and History

When integrated into courses on on 20th- and 21st-century Italian history and society, comics allow students to have a first-hand experience with the cultural production of the time, relating to the cultural objects that people used to consume. The birth of comics in Italy dates back to 1908, and changes in comics formats mark pivotal historical moments:

- Giolittian Era: early comics addressed to children to develop their literacy, such as those published in *Il Corriere dei Piccoli*.

- Fascism Era: censorship of international comics and fascist propaganda in comics; development of an Italian school of Disney comics.

- Post-WWII: the fascination with American culture and development of Western comics.

- Economic boom: more money and wealth, the desire for amusement, and the birth of adult crime comics (It. *fumetti neri*) that reflect the dark side of this exponential development.

- Counterculture: youth protests and counterculture manifest strongly in underground comics and the work of the Cannibale group, but also in auteur comics magazines that help make comics a recognized art form.

- The Eighties, the disengagement, and the television: while forms of civic engagement and protest start to disappear, comics series show post-modern traits (such as *Dylan Dog*).

- The Berlusconi Era: Italian culture is flooded with foreign cultural content, and similarly, Italian readers replace Italian comics with American superhero comic book series and manga.

- The Internet Era: in the last twenty years, comics had to adapt to survive the explosion of digital content. Graphic novels now discuss every possible theme and are increasingly involved with representing minorities (e.g., second-generation Italians and the LGBTQ+ community); webcomics are everywhere, and comics authors take full advantage of social media to share their work. Satirical comics are published in real-time and represent one of the most popular forms of political commentary.

These are just some parallelisms that might help consolidate students' understanding of Italian history, society, and culture, but many more can be drawn. In a course like this, students might have "an almost complete outlook into what was going on in society at the time," recognize that a culture can be represented through the works of the time, understand "how the economy changed and what the people of Italy were feeling," and relate more easily "with the timeline of Italy" (Dallavalle, 2019).

5. Further readings

For the history and development of Italian comics, see Barbieri (2009), Brancato (2000), Bono and Stefanelli (2016), and Tosti (2016). For an overview of the most famous Italian comics characters, see Raffaelli (2009); Zanatta et al. (2009) focuses mainly on female characters. Useful magazines of comics criticism are *Lo Spazio Bianco* (online), *Fumettologica* (online), and *Fumo di China* (in print). In addition, the website *Slumberland* includes details on the history and format of many international and Italian comics, while *ComiXtime* is a database that gathers thousands of authors, stories, series, genres, etc., and provides valuable metadata.

References

Allen, H. W., & Paesani, K. (2010). Exploring the Feasibility of a Pedagogy of Multiliteracies in Introductory Foreign Language Courses. *L2 Journal*, 2, 119–142.

Baetens, J., & Pylyser, C. (2017). Comics and Time. In Bramlett, F., Cook, R.T., & Meskin, A. (Eds.), *The Routledge Companion to Comics*, (pp. 303–311). New York: Routledge.

Barbieri, D. (1991). *I linguaggi del fumetto*. Milano: Bompiani.

Barbieri, D. (2009). *Breve storia della letteratura a fumetti*. Roma: Carocci.

Barbieri, D. (2017). *Semiotica del fumetto*. Roma: Carocci.

Barnes-Karol, G., & Broner, M. (2010) Using Images as Springboards to Teach Cultural Perspectives in Light of the Ideals of the MLA Report. *Foreign Language Annals*, 422–445.

Bono, G., & Stefanelli, M. (2016). *Fumetto!: 150 anni di storie italiane*. Milano: Rizzoli.

Brancato, S. (2000). *Fumetti: guida ai comics nel sistema dei media*. Roma: Datanews.

Castaldi, S. (2016). A brief history of comics in Italy and Spain. In Bramlett, F., Cook, R. T., & Meskin, A. (Eds.), *The Routledge Companion to Comics*, (pp. 79–87). New York: Routledge.

Chan, C., & Chia, A. (2014). *Reading in the 21st Century: Understanding Multimodal Texts and Developing Multiliteracy Skills*. Singapore: McGraw-Hill.

Chia, A., & Chan, C. (2017). Re-defining "Reading" in the 21st Century: Accessing Multimodal Texts. *Beyond Words*, 5(2), 98–105.

ComiXtime. (n.d.). Retrieved 15 April, 2022, from: https://comixtime.it/home.php.

Cope, B., & Kalantzis, M. (2009). "Multiliteracies": New Literacies, New Learning. *Pedagogies*, 4(3), 164–195.

Cope, B., & Kalantzis, M. (2015). The Things You Do to Know: An Introduction to the Pedagogy of Multiliteracies. In Cope, B., & Kalantzis, M. (Eds.), *A Pedagogy of Multiliteracies*, (pp. 1–36). London: Palgrave Macmillan.

Dallavalle, S. (2019). Questionnaire Individual Report for FRIT M301 4338 Italian Reading & Expression.

Duncan, R., Smith, M. J., & Levitz, P. (2017). *The Power of Comics*. London: Bloomsbury.

Eisner, W. (2008). *Comics and Sequential Art*. New York and London: W. W. Norton.

Elsner, D. (2013). Graphic Novels in the Limelight of a Multiliteracies Approach to Teaching English. In Elsner, D., Helff, S., & Viebrock, B. (Eds.) *Films, Graphic Novels & Visuals. Developing Multiliteracies in Foreign Language Education - An Interdisciplinary Approach* (pp. 55–71). Berlin: LIT Verlag.

Elsner, D., & Viebrock, B. (2013). Developing Multiliteracies in the 21st Century: Motives for New Approaches of Teaching and Learning Foreign Languages. In Elsner, D., Helff, S., & Viebrock, B. (Eds.), *Films, Graphic Novels & Visuals. Developing Multiliteracies in Foreign Language Education - An Interdisciplinary Approach*, (pp. 17–32). Berlin: LIT Verlag.

Fresnault-Deruelle, P. (1976). Du linéaire au tabulaire. *Communications*, 24, 7–23.

Fumettologica (no date). Retrieved 13 April. 2022, from: https://fumettologica.it.

Groensteen, T. (1999). *Système de la bande dessinée*. Paris: Presses Universitaires de France. https://gupea.ub.gu.se/bitstream/handle/2077/41223/gupea_2077_41223_1.pdf;jsessionid=CC359ABBD578FD34AC414FA731B8DBC0?sequence=1

Hutcheon, L., & O'Flynn, S. (2006). *A Theory of Adaptation*. (2nd Edition). New York: Routledge.

Jacobs, D. (2007). More than Words: Comics as a Means of Teaching Multiple Literacies. *The English Journal*, 96(3), 19–25.

Jewitt, C. (2008). Multimodality and Literacy in School Classrooms. *Review of Research in Education*, 32, 241–267.

Jewitt, C., & Kress, G. (Eds.), (2003). *Multimodal Literacy*. New York: Peter Lang.

Källvant, L. (2015). *Reading comics in the language classroom. A literature review*. Retrieved 15 April, 2022, from https://gupea.ub.gu.se/bitstream/handle/2077/41223/gupea_2077_41223_1.pdf;jsessionid=CC359ABBD578FD34AC414FA731B8DBC0?sequence=1

Kennedy Center, The (n.d.). *What is Arts Integration? Explore the Kennedy Center's comprehensive definition*. Retrieved 20 April, 2022, from https://www.kennedy-center.org/education/resources-for-educators/classroom-resources/articles-and-how-tos/articles/collections/arts-integration-resources/what-is-arts-integration/

Korcheck, K. (2022). 'KAPOWerful'. Retrieved 20 April, 2022, from https://civitas.central.edu/2022/04/kapowerful/

Kress, G., & Van Leeuwen, T. (2001). *Multimodal discourse: The modes and media of contemporary communication*. London: Arnold.

Kress, G. (2003). *Literacy in the new media age*. London: Routledge.

Kunzle, D. (1973). *The History of tlie Comic Strip. Vol 1: The Early Comic Strip: Narrative Strips and Picture Stories in the European Broadsheet from c. 1450 to 1825*. Berkeley, CA: University of California Press.

Lim-Fei, V., & Tan, K. Y. S. (2017). Multimodal Translational Research: Teaching Visual Texts. In Seizov, O., & Wildfeuer, J. (Eds.), *New studies in multimodality: conceptual and methodological elaborations*, (pp. 175–200). London: Bloomsbury Academic.

Lim-Fei, V., O'Halloran, K. L., & Tan, S. et al. (2015). Teaching Visual Texts with Multimodal Analysis Software. *Educational Technology Research and Development*, 63(6), 915–935.

Lo Spazio Bianco - Nel cuore del fumetto (n.d.). Retrieved 15 April, 2022, from: www.lospaziobianco.it

McCloud, S. (1993). *Understanding comics. The invisible art*. New York: Harper Collins.

McCloud, S. (2000). *Reinventing Comics: How Imagination and Technology are Revolutionizing an Art Form*. New York: Harper Collins.

Molotiu, A. (2013). List of Terms for Comics Studies by Andrei Molotiu', *Comics Forum*. Retrieved 14 April, 2022, from https://comicsforum.org/2013/07/26/list-of-terms-for-comics-studies-by-andrei-molotiu/

Morgana, S. (2020). Avventure dell'italiano a fumetti. In Ciociola, C., & D'Achille, P. (Eds.), *L'italiano tra parola e immagine: graffiti, illustrazioni, fumetti*, (pp. 167–206). Firenze: GoWare.

New London Group (1996). A Pedagogy of Multiliteracies: Designing Social Futures. *Harvard Educational Review*, 66, 60–92.

Paesani, K., Allen, H. W., & Dupuy, B. (2016). *A Multiliteracies Framework for Collegiate Foreign Language Teaching*. Boston: Pearson.

Parkes, L., & Ryan, C. (2015). Introduction. In Parkes, L. & Ryan, C. (Eds.), *Integrating the Arts: Creative Thinking about FL Curricula and Language Program Direction*, (pp. 1–10). Boston: Cengage.

Parra, M. L., & Di Fabio, E. (2015). Languages in Partnership with the Visual Arts: Implications for Curriculum Design and Training. In Parkes, L., & Ryan, C. (Eds.), *Integrating the Arts: Creative Thinking about FL Curricula and Language Program Direction*, (pp. 11–36). Boston: Cengage.

Pietrini, D. (2020). Verso l'italiano contemporaneo in compagnia di Topolino. In Ciociola, C. & D'Achille, P. (Eds.), *L'italiano tra parola e immagine: graffiti, illustrazioni, fumetti*, (pp. 207–218). Firenze: GoWare.

Raffaelli, L. (2009). *Tratti & ritratti: i grandi personaggi del fumetto da Alan Ford a Zagor*. Roma: Minimum Fax.

Show vs. Tell (n.d.). Understanding Comics. Retrieved 14 April, 2022, from https://understandingcomics177.wordpress.com/about/1-2/

Slumberland - L'Enciclopedia del Fumetto (n.d.). Retrieved 13 April, 2022, from www.slumberland.it

Toninelli, M. (n.d.). Strisce italiane: ieri e oggi. *Giornale Pop*. Retrieved 22 March, 2022, from www.giornalepop.it/strisce-italiane

Tosti, A. (2016). *Graphic novel: storia e teoria del romanzo a fumetti e del rapporto fra parola e immagine*. Latina: Tunué.

Zanatta, S., Zanghini, S., & Guzzetta, E. (2009). *Le donne del fumetto. L'altra metà dei comics italiani: temi, autrici, personaggi al femminile*. Latina: Tunué.

Chapter 5

Teaching and understanding Italian through the language of the press

Marta Kaliska
Nicolaus Copernicus University in Toruń

Abstract: The press constitutes a large source of knowledge of contemporary languages; thus, it may be employed to develop diverse learners' competencies regarding linguistic forms, intercultural communication, languages for specific purposes, and specialised translation. These objectives seem particularly important for the higher education context, where students are expected to acquire professional knowledge and skills, and language proficiency is not an end in itself.

In the first theoretical part, journalistic language will be defined with particular regard to its main text genres. Then, I will analyse one of the most important European documents (such as the CEFR and its Companion Volume of 2018) in terms of descriptors referring to the mass media and especially to the press. In the second part, the focus will shift to Italian language teaching in higher education, specifically possible subject areas and teaching methodologies aimed at enhancing learners' communicative, professional, and intercultural competencies.

Keywords: Italian, Press, Journalism, Mass media, Teaching

***

1. Introduction

The press constitutes a substantial source of varied and interesting information on contemporary language use and the socio-cultural reality of a given language area. It offers a broad range of text genres and other communication formats, such as graphs, images, and videos, that can be used in different educational contexts as useful teaching material (Grundy, 1993). Such resources may also increase learners' motivation, which in turn increases the effort they devote to learning (Cohen and Dörnyei, 2002). Due to technological development in the media market, different journalistic means of conveying information have become more and more interrelated with each other. Both teachers and learners can take advantage of these press materials to keep up-to-date with current affairs and observe novel language use while remaining in their country of origin or outside the target language area.

In my opinion, press resources can be effective in (young) adults' education, particularly in the higher education setting, where students of various degree courses often learn foreign languages not only for the language itself but often to increase their potential in a job market that, nowadays, has acquired an international dimension. Therefore, including press texts in the teaching process can contribute to enhancing their language proficiency, as well as intercultural competence (Byram, Gribkova, Starkey, 2002; Council of Europe, 2018). Additionally, the availability and abundance of such resources on the Internet facilitate their selection and adaptation to learners' needs. By using innovative pedagogical approaches and new technologies, textual press samples can be developed into effective and stimulating teaching materials accompanied by original teaching activities focused on language form, cultural content, or communication modes. This has gained new importance with the pandemic and the accompanying forced remote learning (Jelińska, Paradowski, 2021), when traditional paper handouts are less and less convenient, being superseded by other ways of presenting content, e.g. screen sharing, scans of teaching materials, and "classroom" websites (Rocha, Baldissera, Rosa Filho, 2021).

The Italian press consists of many newspaper and magazine titles targeted at a variety of audiences. Amidst the nationally-distributed publications with the highest circulation, it is possible to identify such newspapers as *Corriere della Sera*, *La Stampa*, *La Repubblica*, and *Il Sole 24 Ore*. As for the most popular magazines, the list is much wider and more thematically diverse; therefore, Italian language teachers may select those which better address learners' needs in a given educational context. According to sales data, at the top of the ranking, we find *Di Più, TV Sorrisi e Canzoni, Telesette, L'Espresso, D - la Repubblica delle donne,* and *Io Donna*[1]. Obviously, the number of magazine titles is much higher; however, the list of those with a circulation of over 100,000 runs to approximately 20. All the titles possess their own websites, which are available free of charge or lie behind a paywall.

The main objective of this chapter is to examine possible subject courses and methodological teaching proposals that make use of Italian press

---

[1] https://bubinoblog.altervista.org/i-settimanali-piu-venduti-in-italia-dipiu-supera-tv-sorrisi-e-canzoni-chi-al-14-posto/ (Accessed 19.04.2022).

resources in the higher education context. I will first focus on the specifics of journalistic language in terms of discourse and press genres and their adaptability to various learners' proficiency levels according to the CEFR documents (2001, 2018). Secondly, I will shift our focus to possible subject courses organised by faculties specialising in applied linguistics or Italian studies. Thirdly, our attention will move on to teaching methodology, i.e. which approaches seem to be best suited for developing teaching materials and organising lesson structure to enhance given learners' competencies.

2. Theoretical assumptions

2. 1. Defining the language of journalism and press text genres

The contemporary version of the journalistic language used by the press oscillates between a paper-based tradition and a screen-based dimension (Bonomi, 2002; Kress, 2003). It is often defined in terms of discourse and genre analysis, according to which text genres constitute models or prototypes (Ficek, 2013) or 'routine' texts (Maingueneau, 2010) used within a given communicative context. However, the conceptualization of journalistic language seems more complex, depending both on a theoretical perspective of language and discourse as well as the concept of journalism itself. In brief, following Richardson, journalism "exists to enable citizens to better understand their lives and their position(s) in the world. Journalism's success or failure [...] rests on the extent to which it achieves this fiduciary role" (Richardson, 2007: 7). Thus, journalistic discourse undoubtedly represents a social phenomenon that can be defined as a set of language units that are interrelated at formal, organisational, and semantic levels (Cameron, 2001; van Dijk, 2008). It involves processes of producing, conveying and consuming messages that, in turn, display a certain form and content (Richardson, 2007). The form is represented by various styles of (news) writing within the communicative framework of the text genres specific to thematic press categories, while the content concerns various topics. According to Maingueneau, press genres fall within "instituted" genres which include both genres "imposed by the authors, sometimes by an editor with paratextual indications" and an author's subjective opinion, as well as "routine" genres based on "a pre-established framework" embracing certain repetitive components (2010: 28).

Journalistic discourse is formulated by the press in both printed media and electronic media. The first category includes periodic newspapers and various magazines, while the latter covers radio, television, and the Internet (Pisarek, 2008: 126). In this chapter, I will combine these two categories by focusing on different textual forms typical for Italian newspapers, magazines, and their online editions. I will then examine possible ways of fitting such language materials into the teaching process. Undoubtedly, the selected sources offer a plethora of text genres that can be perceived as "communicative events" occurring in a particular "speech community" of "given language users" (Hymes, 1972; Maingueneau, 2010). The press audience, on the basis of their own sociocultural knowledge, is able to recognise these events by identifying components typical of given text genres. Among traditional written journalistic genres, it is possible to identify such ones as news reports, press releases, articles, reportage, interviews, reviews, (opinion) essays, photo-stories, columns, letters, agony aunt columns, sports commentary, advertisements, celebrity news and even images accompanying texts (Bauer, 2008; Pisarek, 2008; Gualdo, 2014; Jastrzębski, 2017; Lewandowska 2021). These genres reveal various linguistic and stylistic features: advertisements and sports and celebrity news are often briefer, more concise, or simpler compared to opinion essays, articles on economics, and political issues, which in turn include more specialised terminology and complex syntactical structures (Kula, 2010). Nonetheless, all these various textual characteristics collocate within the press framework imposed by the nature of the medium of communication, and they demonstrate certain typical mediatic forms of textuality.

The advent of the digital era and the press's move online have contributed to transforming printed press genres into Web genres or hyper genres (Herring et al., 2005). This notion is not merely restricted to the Internet communication context because, historically, it refers to a broader category of a genre that comprises a range of texts with co-occurring components but without clearly defined boundaries (Maingueneau, 2010). Therefore, a hyper-genre category seems particularly useful for analysing novel textual forms used on press websites, where traditional text genres have become more and more blurred, being subject to such factors as technical requirements, the necessity of continual and rapid updating of news, as well as the audience's needs. Initially, with the development of digital journalism, new textual and paratextual forms of conveying content appeared, however, over time, these new forms have become more and more uniform, acquiring certain specific characteristics related to the nature of the medium itself. Among those, it is possible to identify conciseness, linguistic and structural simplifications, as well as a tendency to accompany textual forms with images, infographics, and videos (Bonomi, 2002).

Another important characteristic of the Internet press is hypertextuality, which means that users can create their own individual path of reading and research, not in a linear, sequential way, but cross-textually by clicking on the links contained in a text. Even single words can constitute links that enable users to pass from one text to many other texts according to their interests and needs. This process of web questing has a beginning, but it may not have an end unless the reader decides to stop.

To sum up, the press has developed in parallel with sociocultural evolution, always reflecting changes occurring in modern and postmodern societies, and today it has entered the digital space to avoid exclusion from the mass, and social media, market. Traditional journalistic language has adapted to the requirements of new models of screen-mediated communication (Kress, 2003), in which visual and spatial aspects dominate (Weninger, 2020), and language has increasingly made way for the image. However, it should be emphasised that some of its linguistic features still display points of convergence with the paper-based formats (Bonomi, 2002).

Especially worth noticing is the commercial and political aspect of journalistic language which characterises texts published in certain newspapers and magazines. These publications must sell to a particular audience; therefore, on the one hand, advertising revenue plays an important role, while on the other political bias seems necessary and obvious (Reah, 1998). A press language analysis, both from a linguistic and didactic perspective, requires the ideological context of an examined press title to be taken into account. In this chapter, I will use the notions of press or journalistic language interchangeably as synonymous usages referring to a broad range of press or journalistic text-based genres published in newspapers, magazines and journals that disseminate meaningful information.

The typological diversity of traditional or virtual press texts offers multiple teaching possibilities at different competency levels. Specific texts may address given learners' needs, e.g. linguistically simplified text genres appear to be suitable for beginners in the general language teaching context; brief news reports may constitute language sources for intermediates, whilst more difficult, composite and specialised texts are ideal for advanced learners or students of linguistic fields whose aim is to gain a deeper knowledge of the language, often at a professional level.

2. 2. Press resources in foreign language teaching

As stated in the previous section, press resources provide learners and teachers with samples of authentic and thematically varied texts typical of the mass media dimension, which may illustrate both linguistic-communicative structures and cultural content inherent to a particular aspect of life in the target language. Obviously, there are certain limits concerning the implementation of press texts in the teaching process. These mostly concern the press language's textual character resulting from its nature as a means of communication itself and the fact that journalistic styles lack communicative naturality, sociolinguistic varieties and particular communicative functions.

Press texts are undoubtedly subject to the technical medium's requirements; they must keep to a specific word count, fit under the headings, or present a given graphic form (Bonomi, 2002; Pisarek, 2008). The latter factor refers to the objectives the press pursues, which mainly include conveying news (the informative function) and presenting opinions or commentary (the impressive function) (Pisarek, 2008). Importantly, the press must sell; thus, to attract an audience, it makes use of colourful and eye-catching headlines, images, as well as expressive or emotive texts. All these press features, both paper-based ones and digital ones, should be taken into account while planning and organising the teaching process. Press genres reveal different journalistic styles, expressive forms, as well as sociocultural aspects of life in the target language. To a certain extent, they constitute formidable authentic teaching materials that can easily be adapted to specific learners' needs.

As for the concept of authenticity itself, it relates to all types of materials used in the language teaching and learning processes which have not been specially developed for teaching purposes but to address communicative objectives for a given language community (Spinelli, 2000; Janowska, 2011). This means that texts belonging to this category represent samples of real-life language usage and are carriers of sociocultural values and beliefs found in a given language area which, in turn, serve to enhance learners' intercultural competence. The richness and variety of such texts should surely be considered to be of pedagogical benefit; however, at lower proficiency levels, they are usually tailored to the learners' abilities by simplifying the structures and vocabulary contained in them in order to align them with relevant teaching objectives, which to a certain extent can be detrimental to their authentic communication value (Guariento, Morley, 2001).

2. 3. CEFR and journalistic language

Undoubtedly, the *Common European Framework of Reference for Languages* constitutes one of the most important documents in foreign language education, providing teachers, examiners, textbook writers, and other language education professionals, as well as indeed language learners, with special guidelines on teaching methodology, learners' competency descriptors and assessment criteria (CEFR, 2001: 4). It has enabled the uniformisation of European language educational systems by introducing coherent proficiency scales with common reference levels and a clear definition of learners' communicative-language competences.

In 2018, an updated and extended version of the document was published entitled *Companion Volume with New Descriptors*. Its main goals are to better promote inclusive education and quality in second/foreign language teaching and learning, as well as enhance plurilingual and intercultural language pedagogy by emphasising certain key concepts, such as plurilingual competence, interaction, and mediation. Compared to the CEFR document of 2001, the last notion has been specifically delineated and divided into two main categories: mediation activities and mediation strategies. The former relates to three language use domains – texts, concepts, and communication – while the latter covers such strategies as explaining new concepts and simplifying texts. Pluricultural/intercultural communication phenomena are described within the subcategory of communication, in which the activity of the pluricultural facilitator and the intermediary is clearly underlined.

As for journalistic language and respective text genres, both the CEFR document (2001) and *Companion Volume* (2018) primarily perceive the manipulation of these texts as a component of learners' skills classified progressively in line with the scale of common reference levels. Texts are defined as a broad category that refers to "any piece of language, whether a spoken utterance or a piece of writing, which users/learners receive, produce or exchange" (2001: 93). The properties of given texts are determined by the nature of the particular medium they are conveyed via. Newspaper and magazine texts are classified as written text types that provide learners with specific information and enhance their language proficiency - according to the CEFR, mostly in relation to reading, writing, and mediating skills. The most frequent texts listed in different sections of the document are articles, essays, editorials, and news reports.

The press constitutes one of the many thematic subcategories found within the broader thematic area of "free time and entertainment, " alongside "leisure", "hobbies and interests", various mass media and so on (p. 52). Interestingly, press texts are also related to the ludic use of language, such as verbal joking (p. 56) or expressing folk wisdom (p. 120), e.g. in advertisements and newspaper headlines. The CEFR generally recommends learners experience direct exposure to authentic, pedagogically untreated language materials, amongst which newspaper and magazine texts are often listed (p. 143, 146).

Referring to the common reference levels, the first mention of press texts appears in the self-assessment grid as early as at the A2 level relating to the ability to read, where advertisements are listed. As for writing skills, the CEFR specifies level descriptors starting from A1, where learners are expected to write simple, isolated sentences, and concluding with C2, which envisages clear and smooth writing of complex texts in an appropriate style. Furthermore, among general writing activities, "writing articles for magazines and newspapers" is introduced (p. 61), which represents a rather difficult skill for a language learner and requires a high proficiency level.

With regard to reading skills, the ability to identify the content of news items and articles appears at the B2 level as part of "reading for orientation", whereas descriptors of the second subcategory, "reading for information and argument", appear at the A2 and B1 levels, where they point out that the learner is firstly able to identify specific information in short textual forms and secondly to recognise "significant points in straightforward newspaper articles on familiar subjects" (p. 70). Text-based press genres also appear in mediating activities and strategies in the area of written mediation, where learners are expected to summarise the content of newspaper and magazine articles between L1 and L2. It seems obvious that samples of press texts, i.e. samples of written language use, are perfectly suitable for developing learners' skills in reading with comprehension, searching for information, and mediating the meaning of a text.

As for the *Companion Volume* of 2018, reading authentic texts drawn from newspapers, magazines, as well as literature, among other places, falls under leisure-time activities. For example, the learner can read short newspaper/magazine accounts and reviews on films, concerts, and books, understanding their main points (p. 65).

Additionally, press texts appear at the C1 common reference level in the general written reception category, according to which the learner "can understand a wide variety of texts including literary writings, newspaper or magazine articles, and specialised academic or professional publications" (p. 60). At the less advanced B1 and B2 levels, these texts are listed in the subcategory "reading for orientation", where the learner is firstly expected to assess their connection to the required topic and then, to identify the content and the key concepts presented in the news items and articles (p. 62). As for the "reading for information and argument", the respective references emerge at the C2, B1 and A2 levels. In the first one of these, it is established that the learner should understand the implications of the content; at the B1 level, the learner's skills limit them to merely recognising significant points in rather straightforward articles on familiar topics, whereas at the least advanced level, the learner is expected to identify certain pieces of information in simple and short articles (p. 63).

Another relevant reference to newspaper/magazine texts can be found in the mediation section. Learners are supposed to relay specific information from articles and reports: starting at the A1 level, they should focus only on simple information, graduating to more specific details in straightforward texts at the B1 and B2 levels. With regard to processing text in speech, they should be able to summarise the main information contained in straightforward magazine articles on familiar topics. However, the ability to summarise such content in writing is only expected at the C1 level (p. 112).

What is new in the *Companion Volume* is the inclusion of "strategies to explain a new concept": at the B1 level, the learner can paraphrase relevant points presented in short magazine articles, facilitating the comprehension of the text by others.

To sum up, it should be noted that various newspaper and magazine text genres, mostly articles, editorials, essays, and news reports, are classified in the two QCER documents as authentic materials which guarantee a learner the appropriate exposure to real use of L2 language, i.e. to texts not created for teaching purposes. Additionally, reading them may be a useful way of spending leisure time so that it leads to an improvement in one's L2 competence.

As for the common reference levels, press texts are mainly listed in the sections dedicated to reading, writing and mediating skills. However, in the case of mediation, their inclusion in the teaching/learning process may also enhance learners' oral production by means of activities such as relaying specific information, explaining data, summarising, or paraphrasing a text or a concept in speech. Undoubtedly, many press texts constitute useful and significant language materials, even if they are not subject to pedagogical manipulation.

2. 4. Language education in higher education

With the signing of the Bologna Declaration in 1999 by 29 European ministers, a long reform process towards the unification of higher education systems began. The Bologna Process was aimed at implementing common structural and administrative arrangements in Europe. In this regard, the European Higher Education Area (EHEA) was later established, and it is now responsible for monitoring, as well as evaluating, the adaption of universities to the Bologna reforms (Kushnir, 2016). The primary objectives of these measures were, firstly, to increase the competitiveness of European universities, secondly, to boost the technological and economic potential of the old continent, and finally, to create a knowledge-based modern society (Buchner-Jeziorska, 2010).

As far as language education is concerned, European policy has mostly focused on promoting plurilingualism and pluriculturalism to both raise awareness of Europeans' own diversity and to build a new European community not limited by national constraints (Gâz, 2011). For the last 30 years, both the European Commission and the Council of Europe have published a considerable number of documents and recommendations concerning language education in Europe, according to which higher education institutions have become particularly significant in encouraging students to know more than one foreign language. One of the most important documents for language education in a higher education context is a Berlin Communiqué published in 2003[2]. Its authors emphasise the importance of foreign language teaching, and learning, as part of European integration at a political level. Furthermore, certain specific objectives were established for European universities, such as (1) the promotion of mobility and international collaboration, (2) the establishment of a common system of credits, and (3) the introduction of comparable degrees.

Other documents that have contributed to unifying language education are the CEFR, published in 2001, the *Guide for the Development of Language Policies in Europe* from 2007 (Beacco, Byram 2007), and *Universities and their Policy in Europe: Reference Document* (2001). The first one of these has become a reference point for introducing a common language proficiency scale, level descriptors, types of assessment, as well clear definitions of certain key concepts, e.g. communicative-language competence. The second concentrated on promoting plurilingualism, but importantly, it served to explain many notions used in various European documents on language policies. Universities have been assigned the role of raising students' awareness of the importance of foreign language competency in their private and professional lives. It has also been emphasised that language education should be continuous, which is in line with the European policy promoting lifelong learning (Cybulska, 2009).

The main objective of the third document, produced by the European Language Council (2001), is to support university authorities in implementing European language policy at structural and administrative levels. The authors recommend that students learn at least two foreign languages and have an opportunity to develop intercultural communicative competence by participating in various mobility programmes (Semplici and Tronconi, 2015).

Language teaching and learning in higher education display a dual character. On the one hand, university language centres and schools organise general language courses dedicated to all the students who may choose and attend a course in a language they intend to learn outside their core curriculum. On the other, language courses constitute a substantial part of the curriculum of those fields of study which train future language teachers and translators, such as applied linguistics or specific foreign language studies (Piasecka, 2007). In the latter case, the number of teaching hours and ECTS credits per language is significantly higher, which allows students to achieve a level of language proficiency at a professional level.

---

[2] Conference of Ministers responsible for Higher Education (2003). Realising the European Higher Education. Retrieved 10 April, 2022, from www.ehea.info/media.ehea.info/file/2003_Berlin/28/4/2003_Berlin_Communique_English_577284.pdf

Furthermore, within different fields of study, subject courses in foreign languages are offered to provide students with both content knowledge in line with a degree profile and linguistic knowledge and skills. This combination is aimed at enhancing their career opportunities in an increasingly complex and demanding job market. The language that prevails as a teaching tool is English, the *lingua franca* of today's professional communication, though, to promote plurilingualism effectively, it is necessary to develop such courses in a wide variety of European languages. Not only would this allow students to gain linguistic competence in more than one language, but it would contribute to the better implementation of European policy objectives.

3. Italian language teaching: methodological proposals

In this section, I focus our attention on methodological proposals concerning Italian language teaching by using press text genres. Since I ended the previous section with considerations on content-based language learning (CBLL), I will begin our review of possible teaching solutions from this point, and then I will move on to two other issues: general Italian courses and languages for specific purposes.

At an academic level, combining language and content seems a highly effective teaching method because, within one course, two types of knowledge are conveyed, which is beneficial for students and young adults preparing to enter the job market. The CBLL involves immersing oneself in a foreign language, and this constitutes both a means of communication and a teaching objective in itself (Coyle, 2007; Gajo and Serra, 2002). Subjects related to the press or journalistic language make up the content and having considered their complexity and variety, a range of courses can be created. On the one hand, they may be included within a broader theme of mass media phenomena and communication, as well as politics, while on the other, specific courses related to press text genres and journalistic writing may be offered to students of different majors. As for the latter category, journalistic writing in Italian seems especially appropriate for students of linguistic fields aimed at training translators, interpreters, and language teachers, who will need to use the language in their future professional life. In their case, knowledge of journalistic means of expression, article structures, and styles seems particularly significant in translation and teaching activity. Newspaper and magazine text genres may also be introduced with Content and Language Integrated Learning (CLIL), which represents a further version of language teaching through content. The method involves combining language with subject materials: language represents both tools facilitating the learning process and teaching objectives, while the content falls within teaching objectives. However, the CLIL method is primarily implemented in primary and secondary schools (Ruiz De Zarobe, 2009).

Apart from content-based language learning, press text genres to constitute authentic teaching materials implemented in general Italian language courses at different proficiency levels. They are examples of real language use specific for journalistic discourse, where particular forms, styles, and ways of creating meaning are in use. Due to the application of these resources, students can observe socio-linguistic differentiation, as well as cultural differences between their own and the target language. As stated in the previous chapter, press genres vary at a linguistic level, and they can also be included not only at intermediate or advanced levels but also at A1 or A2 levels. On these terms, simpler texts, such as advertisements, commercials, article titles, or slogans, may be introduced in order to demonstrate single words, expressions, or cultural phenomena. The difficulty level of texts should be appropriately adapted to learners' language levels: shorter articles, news reports, interviews, photo stories, letters, celebrity news, relationship advice, sports commentary, and graphs all seem suitable for B1 and B2 learners, while structurally and thematically more complex texts, such as columns, newspaper articles, reports, and reviews are ideal both for intermediate and advanced learners. When introducing Italian press texts into the teaching process, it is a good idea to characterise the main press titles from a political and commercial perspective to allow students to gain additional knowledge of the Italian journalistic landscape. As for task development, the press, mostly its digital version, represents a formidable source of linguistic, factual, and cultural information teachers can choose by themselves, or else one can ask students to search for given data on selected press websites. Tasks that seem particularly useful to stimulate learners' autonomy and active engagement are WebQuests or other forms of discovery learning, such as problem-solving, answering problematic questions, and discussing controversies (Dodge, 2001; March, 2008; Tuan, 2011). WebQuests represent "a scaffold learning structure that uses links to essential resources on the World Wide Web and an authentic task to motivate students' investigation of a central, open-ended question" (Tuan, 2011: 666). They are suitable both in the classroom and remote education contexts, allowing learners to build up their own knowledge and expertise. Students may be encouraged to prepare a presentation on a topic defined by the teacher, who in turn indicates appropriate websites to be used, deadlines, and the main points of the task. He/she is also responsible for assigning specific sub-tasks to the learners. Due to the implementation of such innovative methodology, students can observe deeper relationships between socio-cultural phenomena, discern the rationale behind particular opinions, as well as better comprehend life in a foreign language area.

The third approach to introducing the Italian language as part of academic language courses relates to teaching languages for specific purposes (LSP), something incredibly important in professional communication. Considering the importance of the Italian economy in Europe and the widespread popularity of Italian design, promoting Italian LSP should constitute a major part of most university curricula, not only those of a linguistic profile.

LSPs, defined in Italian as 'lingue speciali' o 'sottocodici', constitute situational varieties which depend "dall'argomento del discorso e dall'ambito esperienziale di riferimento" (Berruto, 1993: 70). Their internal diversification occurs vertically according to the criterion of specialisation, and horizontally according to the specifics of the discipline. Therefore, some of them demonstrate a high level of specialization and terminological density, while for others, these features are less saturated (Sobrero, 1993; Balboni, 2000). The nature of LSP remains strictly correlated with a given professional domain of language use and the respective professional group of language users. Newspapers and magazines often constitute a means of communication between professionals and laypersons, offering columns on topics such as economics, trade, politics, technology and innovation, science, the environment, healthcare, motoring, fashion, and art (columns drawn from popular *Corriere della Sera*). All these sections can provide language learners with samples of terminology and specific linguistic structures used at the popular-science level. The respective texts seem useful for the development of various teaching activities and tasks, including translation ones devoted to students of different fields of studies and being suitable both for the training of professional translators as well as for specialists in various disciplines. Their appropriateness results from the fact that, on the one hand, such press texts contain specialised terminology used in professional communication, and on the other, the density level of such terminology and the structure are simplified in relation to highly specialised texts used exclusively in communication between professionals. Thus, these types of newspaper and magazine articles can be introduced as an initial part of LSP courses to make students acquainted with a popular science discourse which is more approachable to non-specialists. According to the CEFR (2001), learners who begin LSP courses should at least be at the B1 proficiency level, which means that, especially at the beginning, simplified texts should be used to gradually develop learners' linguistic and communicative competence within LSP domains.

As we have seen, the Italian journalistic language can be introduced in various forms of academic language teaching, from general courses to content-based teaching and courses in specialised languages. This type of text constitutes useful authentic material that, on the one hand, is often used in its original version without any pedagogical adaption and, on the other, may be tailored to learners' needs by simplifying lexical and structural dimensions and by adding supplementary exercises or tasks. Another benefit of using press texts is their availability on the Internet, which allows a broad range of press materials to be accessed and tasks to be developed based on discovery learning, e.g. WebQuests, searching for given topics, projects, and so on.

4. Conclusion

Teaching the Italian language using newspaper and magazine texts in the higher education context is useful and advantageous because the press constitutes an efficient source of linguistic and socio-cultural, continuously updated information on the Italian language and the community of its users. Nowadays, due to the Internet, it is also one of the most accessible authentic materials, providing language teachers and learners with samples of language that have not been pedagogically adapted and serving as an actual means of communication. Another benefit results from the vast range of available text genres that can be introduced at different proficiency levels, e.g. short texts, such as advertisements, suit beginners, while longer texts (news reports, celebrity or sports commentary, and short articles on familiar topics) are ideal for intermediates, and finally, complex articles on political and economic issues, essays, and specialised columns are appropriate for advanced, independent learners.

The Italian press constitutes useful teaching material in a higher education setting, where not only do students need to learn a language, but they must also immerse themselves in its culture, as well as observe particular sociolinguistic phenomena. This group of learners, i.e. young adults who are about to set out on their professional careers, must develop intercultural competence, critical thinking, and mediation abilities, and press content not aimed at pedagogical objectives perfectly fulfils these requirements.

References

Balboni, P. (2000). *Le microlingue scientifico-professionali. Natura e insegnamento.* Torino: Petrini.

Bauer, Z. (2008). Gatunki dziennikarskie. In Bauer, Z. and Chudziński, E. (Eds.), *Dziennikarstwo i świat mediów* (pp. 255–329). Kraków: Universitas.

Beacco, J. C., & Byram, M. (2007). *From linguistic diversity to plurilingual education: Guide for the development of language education Policies in Europe. Main Version.* Strasbourg: Council of Europe.

Berruto, G. (1993). Le varietà del repertorio. In Sobrero, A. A. (Ed.), *Introduzione all'italiano contemporaneo. La variazione e gli usi*, (pp. 3–36). Roma/ Bari: Laterza.

Bonomi, I. (2002). *L'italiano giornalistico. Dall'inizio del 900 ai quotidiani online.* Firenze: Franco Cesati Editore.

Buchner-Jeziorska, A. (2010). Polska wobec wyzwań strategii lizbońskiej. In Buchner-Jeziorska, A., & Dziedziczak-Foltyn, A. (eds.), *Proces Boloński: ideologia i praktyka edukacyjna*, (pp. 11–32). Łódź: Wydawnictwo Uniwersytetu Łódzkiego.

Byram, M., Gribkova, B., & Starkey, H. (2002). *Developing the Intercultural Dimension in Language Teaching: A Practical Introduction for Teachers*. Strasbourg: Council of Europe.

Cameron, L. (2001). *Teaching Languages to Young Learners*. Cambridge: Cambridge University Press.

Cohen, A. D., & Dörnyei, Z. (2002). Focus on the Language Learner: Motivation, Styles and Strategies. In Schmitt, N. (Ed.), *An Introduction to Applied Linguistics*, (pp. 170–190). London: Arnold.

Council of Europe (2001). *Common European Framework of Reference for Languages: Learning, Teaching, Assessment.* Cambridge: Cambridge University Press.

Council of Europe (2018). *Common European Framework of Reference for Languages: Learning, Teaching, Assessment. Companion Volume with New Descriptors.* Retrieved 10 April 2022 from https://rm.coe.int/common-european-framework-of-reference-for-languages-learning-teaching/16809ea0d4.

Coyle, D. (2007). Content and language integrated learning: towards a connected research agenda for CLIL pedagogies. *Working Papers on Bilingualism*, 19, 121–129.

Cybulska, K. (2009). Różnojęzyczność a kształcenie językowe w szkolnictwie wyższym. In Komorowska, H. (Ed.), *Kształcenie językowe w szkolnictwie wyższy*, (pp. 97–114). Warszawa: Wydawnictwo SWPS Academica.

Dodge, B. (2001). Focus: Five rules for writing a great WebQuest. *Learning & Leading with Technology*, 28(8), 6–9.

European Language Council, (2001). *Multilingualism and New Learning Environments. Workshop 1: Universities and language policy in Europe. Reference Document.* Berlin: Freie Universität Berlin.

Ficek, E. (2013). *Poradnik. Model gatunkowy i jego tekstowe aktualizacje.* Katowice: Wydawnictwo Uniwersytetu Śląskiego.

Gajo, L., & Serra, C. (2002). Bilingual teaching: Connecting language and concepts in mathematics. In So, D., & Jones, G. (Eds.), *Education and Society in Plurilingual Contexts*, (pp. 75–95). Brussels: VUB Brussels University Press.

Gâz, R. M. (2011). Language policies in European higher education area. Babeș-Bolyai University – a case study. *Romanian Review of International Studies*, III, 1, 51–70.

Grundy, P. (2013). Humanistic language teaching. In Byram, M., & Hu, A. (Eds.), *Routledge Encyclopedia of Language Teaching and Learning*, (pp. 322–5). Abingdon: Routledge.

Gualdo, R. (2014). *L'italiano dei giornali*. Roma: Carocci Editore.

Guariento, W., & Morley, J. (2001). Text and authenticity in the EFL classroom. *ELT Journal*, 4, 347–353.

Herring, S., Scheidt, L. A., Bonus, S., & Wright, E. (2005). Weblogs as a bridging genre. *Information, Technology and People*, 18 (2), 142–171.

Hymes, D. (1972). On Communicative Competence. In Pride, J. B., & Holmes, J. (Eds.), *Sociolinguistics*, (pp. 269–293). Harmondsworth: Penguin Books.

Janowska, I. (2011). *Podejście zadaniowe do nauczania i uczenia się języków obcych*. Kraków: Universitas.

Jastrzębski, J. (2017). Prasowe gatunki dziennikarskie we Włoszech. In Wolny-Zmorzyński, K., Morawieski, J., & Urbaniak, P. (Eds.), *Gatunki dziennikarskie w Europie. Wstęp do genologii porównawczej*, (pp. 127–141). Wrocław: Wydawnictwo Uniwersytetu Wrocławskiego.

Jelińska, M., & Paradowski, M. (2021). Teachers' Perception of Student Coping With Emergency Remote Instruction During the COVID-19 Pandemic: The Relative Impact of Educator Demographics and Professional Adaptation and Adjustment. *Frontiers in Psychology*, 12. Retrieved 8 April 2022 from www.frontiersin.org/articles/10.3389/fpsyg.2021.648443/full

Kress, G. (2003). *Literacy in the new media age*. Abingdon, UK: Routledge.

Kula, A. (2010). *Cechy stylowe publicystyki ekonomicznej na materiale „Polityki" z lat 1957–2004*. Poznań: Wydawnictwo Poznańskie.

Kushnir, I. (2016). The Role of the Bologna Process in Defining Europe. *European Educational Research Journal*, 15(6), 664–675.

Lewandowska, M. J. (2021). *Grazia. Consigli che hanno formato le italiane. Un'analisi del discorso*. Warszawa: Wydawnictwa Uniwersytetu Warszawskiego.

Maingueneau, D. (2010). Analyse du discours et champ disciplinaire. *Questions de Communication*, 2(18), 185–196.

Piasecka, M. (2007). Jakość kształcenia w szkole wyższej w Polsce i w innych krajach europejskich. In Komorowska, H. (Ed.), *Nauczanie język w obcych. Polska a Europa*. (pp. 181–190). Warszawa: Academica SWPS.

Pisarek, W. (2008). *Wstęp do nauki o komunikowaniu*. Warszawa: Wydawnictwo WAiP.

Reah, D. (1998). *The Language of Newspapers*. London: Routledge.

Richardson, J. E. (2007). *Analysing Newspapers. An approach from Critical Discourse Analysis*. New York: Palgrave Macmillan.

Rocha, V., Baldissera, L. G., & Rosa Filho, J. A. (2021). Digital Resources to Teaching and Learning English as a Foreign Language in Remote Classes. *Revista X*, 16 (3), 687–702.

Ruiz De Zarobe, Y., & Jiménez Catalán, R. M. (Eds.), (2009). *Content and language integrated learning: evidence from research in Europe*. Bristol: Multilingual Matters.

Semplici, S., & Tronconi, E. (2015). Insegnare l'italiano a studenti universitari. In Diadori, P., (Ed.), *Insegnare italiano a stranieri* (pp. 240–253). Milano: Le Monnier.

Sobrero, A. A. (1993). Lingue speciali. In Sobrero, A. A., (Ed.), *Introduzione all'italiano contemporaneo. La variazione e gli usi* (pp. 237–278). Roma/Bari: Laterza.

Spinelli, B. (2000). L'utilizzo dei materiali autentici nell'insegnamento dell'italiano come LS. In Dolci, R. & Celentin, P. (Eds.), *La formazione di base del docente di italiano a stranieri* (pp. 133–147). Roma: Bonacci Editore.

Tuan, L. T. (2011). Teaching Reading through WebQuest. *Journal of Language Teaching and Research*, 2 (3), 664–673.

Van Dijk, T. (2010). *Discourse and Power*. New York: Palgrave Macmillan.

Weninger, C. (2020). Multimodality in critical language textbook analysis. *Language, Culture and Curriculum*, 34(3), 1–14.

Web references

Conference of Ministers Responsible for Higher Education (2003). Realising the European Higher Education. Retrieved 10 April, 2022, from www.ehea.info/media.ehea.info/file/2003_Berlin/28/4/2003_Berlin_Communique_English_577284.pdf

Chapter 6

Teaching and learning Italian word-formation patterns

Irene Lami
Lund University

Abstract: A knowledge of word-formation patterns can have considerable benefits on competence in a second language. A dynamic view of the lexicon can reveal recurring patterns in the vocabulary of a language, representing a useful tool to improve receptive fluency. Unfortunately, reflections on word-formation are not often considered an essential part of second language teaching, and grammar books often tend to take morphological processes for granted. However, while native speakers can make use of word-formation rules to construct new words out of the already existing ones, the same cannot be said of foreign learners, who lack native intuitions on productive mechanisms. This chapter aims to give an overview of the main word-formation patterns in Italian, organizing them in relation to the different parts of speech. Importance is given to their productivity, semantic regularities, and specialisations, allowing learners to familiarize themselves with a regular system rather than considering words as isolated linguistic objects.

Keywords: Word-formation, Morphological processes, Semantic, Pattern, Italian

***

1. Introduction

Teaching and acquiring languages have fluency as their main goal. Fluency is an evanescent concept, often described from the point of view of the listener (i.e., based on the perception that the listener has of a speaker's language) and very often according to functional principles (i.e., based on what we can practically communicate with the level of language we have acquired so far). Hence, 'fluency' implies both subjective perceptions and objective criteria, and rather than constituting a fixed point, it represents a construct defined by several different viewpoints.

Particularly, vocabulary plays a fundamental role in language acquisition, and proficiency in vocabulary use is considered one of the most important elements that concur to obtain language fluency. However, vocabulary tends to be studied in terms of semantics rather than in terms of a productive process. Even more dangerously, vocabulary is often described as if words were static objects, which need to be memorized and appropriately used in different contexts and communicative situations. This static and functional view of vocabulary fails to provide truthful insights into the nature of the lexicon and, more generally, language structures; above all, it runs the risk of hindering exactly the goal that we are aiming for, i.e., fluency.

Word-formation patterns are very rarely included in didactic material directed to second-language students, hence very few are books include exercises specifically thought to allow learners (or teachers) to practice this important aspect of language. Moreover, studying a language at an academic level implies a different type of knowledge that not only focuses on the active practice of linguistic structures, but that also involves familiarity with theoretical concepts. For these reasons, in the following chapter, we aim to provide teachers and learners with instruments that can allow metalinguistic reflections on Italian vocabulary. We will see how a dynamic approach to Italian word-formation processes can help to improve the acquisition of Italian vocabulary. We will see some regularities and irregularities, and more importantly, we will try to understand how to act when facing them. Having an overview of the main word-formation patterns can give learners a clearer idea of how fluid the creation of new words is, and delimiting this creative force by grasping its underlying mechanisms will be a valid help in increasing language fluency.

The chapter will give a summary of the field of word-formation. After that, an illustration of the main formation mechanisms will be given, stressing the importance of distinguishing between new words and word forms. Then the main mechanisms of Italian word-formation will be analysed, related to the different parts of speech. Reflections on how to infer the meaning of unknown words will be made, and exercises will be suggested to help students feel familiar, even in non-familiar words. This will not only be useful in language perception but also in production.

2. Morphology and word-formation theory

The study of word-formation theory investigates the processes whereby new words are created in a language. It is an important branch of morphology, the study of the internal structure of words and their relations with the other components of language architecture.

Even though this might seem strange, the very concept of 'word' is far from being established once and for all in morphological theory. Scholars have tried to isolate the notion of 'wordhood', often relating it to other linguistic domains (e.g. phonology, syntax, semantics, etc.), but a theoretical definition that unequivocally represents what a word truly is, universally shared among different linguistic systems, has not been formulated yet.

If 'word' is still a debated concept, no wonder that on word-formation mechanisms, linguistic research is also debating: is the lexicon 'stored' somewhere in the brain, and are words listed individually no matter how complex they are? Or, on the contrary, are there bases on which word-formation patterns are idiosyncratically applied during language processing? And if so, how are these mechanisms applied? Is there an order? Is there a scale from the most minimal element to the most complex one? And if so, is this scale made of discrete units or is it rather a continuum?

These and many other issues were at the basis of morphological research until the very first Sanskrit grammarians started to reflect upon language structures. On some of these complex issues, we have a better understanding nowadays, but on many others, clear answers are still far from being given.

Despite all these debates, on which language science is constantly researching and going forward (also thanks to new technologies that allow us to study, for instance, neurolinguistic processes), the fact that words are formed by patterns is evident to anyone who reflects even slightly metalinguistically. Words are formed through mechanisms. This does not mean that there are strict rules at the foundation of word creation, or that native speakers consciously apply some norms when they need to express concepts with new words. It is more precise to think of this creation as rule-governed creativity (Bauer, 1983).

Rather than rules, we can talk about tendencies. These tendencies can be described as relations between regular forms associated with regular meanings. E.g. in Italian, *ammira-***zione** 'admiration', *corre-***zione** 'correction', *intui-***zione** 'intuition', all are actions derived from verbs, respectively *ammirare* 'to admire', *correggere* 'to correct', *intuire* 'to realize'. So, we can say that when in Italian, a new word is created that represents the nominalization of an action conveyed by an existent verb, a possibility is that of adding the suffix *-zione* to the verb base (we will explain this and other possibilities further in the chapter).

Deepening the knowledge of these tendencies is useful to expand not only our vocabulary but also our understanding of it. Our capacity to infer meaning when facing unfamiliar words might translate into an improvement in our receptive fluency.

3. Derivation and compounding (but not inflection)

In the previous section, we have seen an example of nominalization employing affixation, i.e., the attachment of a morpheme to a word-base to create a new noun. The affix *-zione* bears indeed a meaning ('the act of': *ammirazione* is 'the act of admiring'), but this string of letters possesses this meaning only when attached to a base that specifies which kind of action we are talking about. *-Zione* does not exist as a free form but only as a suffix, i.e., a bound form. This process, where a word is created by adding bound forms to a root word, is called **derivation**.

It is important to underline that not every time we have affixes, we are in front of a case of derivation. Let's take two sentences such as:

1) a. I usually go to the movies.
   b. Mary usually go*es* to the movies.

(1b) shows the use of the affix -es indeed; however, this affix does not create a new word but rather another form of the same word (in this case, the same verb but with a 3rd person). In the case of derivation, instead, the new word represents a new concept: the process of derivation can create a new word changing the meaning of the original word from which it derives, and it can even change the part of speech (as we have seen, a noun can be created from a verb). Even when the mechanism is simpler, and the meaning can easily be inferred from the original word, the new word created is not another word-form, but it represents a new concept (e.g. *happy → un-happy*). For this reason, the use of affixes should not be misleading: we could say that the term 'affix' represents a formal category, while the terms 'derivation' or 'inflection' represent functional categories (Booij, 2008).

Since inflection creates new forms and not new words, it is not considered a word-formation process. Hence, this chapter will not address inflection.

Words can also be created by joining two autonomous words: e.g. *fine* 'end' + *settimana* 'week', *fine settimana* 'weekend'. The case where a new word is created by joining two free forms is called **compounding**.

4. Word-formation in Italian

Making a complete overview of all the known word formation patterns in Italian is not only impossible in the space limits of this chapter, but it would risk becoming a tedious list of word fragments, thus representing a poor tool for students who want to expand their fluency in Italian. Hence, rather than seeking exhaustiveness, we will try to give a context to the most productive mechanisms, showing how word-formation is related to many different dimensions of language and trying to find some order in apparent chaos.

4.1. Italian derivation

So far, derivation has been referred to in terms of addition, where affixes are added to roots. This might be inaccurate in absolute terms since derivation also includes processes of subtraction such as that of back-formation, i.e., the creation of a new word by removing affixes from an already-existent word. Back-formation is quite common in English; however, Italian allows back-formations to a much lesser extent than English. Derivational processes in Italian, in fact, tend to show a quite regular directionality (Iacobini, 1996), and usually, words with a simpler structure expand to a more complex structure, i.e., a process of addition. Hence, the addition of **suffixes** (affixes added at the end of the root), **prefixes** (affixes added before the root), and the process known as **parasynthesis** (the simultaneous addition of a prefix and a suffix, which is particularly productive in some particular cases), are primarily investigated. Suffixes will be here much more investigated compared to prefixes since they bear the grammatical information of the word: for students of Italian as a foreign language, it might be more useful to establish a relation between the verb *approvare* 'to approve' with the noun *approvazione* 'approval', rather than with the prefixed verb *dis-approvare* 'to disapprove', since this is a merely semantic relation, while the other example implies a change in part of speech, thus representing a less intuitive process.

We are already starting to see that word-formation patterns are intertwined with other linguistic factors: etymology, phonology, and many other domains that we will see in the next sections.

4.1.1. Nominalization

Nominalization is the process by which a noun is created from another linguistic element. In Italian, nouns are generally created by adding a suffix to a word base.

A very productive kind of nominalization in Italian is the creation of **deverbal nouns**, i.e., nouns that derive from a verb, exactly as we have seen in the example *ammira-zione* 'admiration' from the verb *ammirare* 'to admire'.

4.1.1.1. Action suffixes

We have seen that it is possible to use the suffix *-zione* to indicate 'the action of X', being X as the base verb. However, *-zione* is not the only suffix that we can attach to a verb to form a noun. If we look at any written text, we will see that deverbal nouns can be created by means of different patterns. Table 6. 1. shows a list of the most common suffixes used to express nominalizations of verbs indicating actions, processes, or states.

-Ø	*ritorno; arrivo; verifica*
-zione	*ammira-zione; corre-zione; intui-zione*
-mento	*allena-mento; cambia-mento; anda-mento*
-tura	*abbronza-tura; rasa-tura; bolli-tura*
-aggio	*atterr-aggio; lav-aggio; monitor-aggio*
-ío	*formicol-io; cigol-io; brontol-io*
-ata / -uta / -ita	*mangi-ata; bev-uta; dorm-ita*
-anza / -enza	*conosc-enza; part-enza; toller-anza*
-gione	*impicca-gione; guari-gione; pianta-gione*

Table 6. 1. Deverbal suffixes

The first example in table 1 is not a suffix, strictly speaking, at least not in the sense we used the word 'suffix' so far. In this case, in fact, we have words created without adding explicit affixes, in a process called **conversion** or **zero-derivation**. It is a very productive process in English, while in Italian, it is less frequent (Grossman and Reiner, 2013). However, we can find many words created by zero derivation among deverbal nouns.

Consider now the following suffixes in table 6. 1.: *-zione* and *-mento*. These two suffixes are very productive in Italian and are normally used in competition to indicate actions, processes, or states. They have normally been introduced already at level A1 thanks to their wide presence in the Italian language and to their regularity regarding gender: while nouns ending with *-zione* are, in fact, always feminine, the ones ending in *-mento* are always masculine. It might be useful to notice that verbs that end with *-izzare* or *-ificare* are normally nominalized with the suffix *-zione* (e.g. *alfabetizzare* 'to literate' → *alfabetizzazione* 'literacy'; *purificare* 'to purify' → *purificazione* 'purification'), while *-mento* is used with verbs ending with *-eggiare* (e.g. *patteggiare* 'to negotiate a plea bargain' → *patteggiamento* 'plea bargain'). Moreover, *-mento* is the only suffix that can be used with nominalizations of parasynthetic verbs, i.e., verbs that are formed simultaneously with a prefix and a suffix (we will see them better in section 4.1.2).

However, the differences in the use of suffixes are not only dependent on the formal structure of the verb. Sometimes a semantic difference guides which suffix is more correct in a given utterance. For instance, consider the nouns *congelamento - congelazione*: this is a pair of two perfectly acceptable nouns with the meaning 'freezing'. However, there is a difference in terms of process vs. result of the process (Thornton, 1990). Consider these sentences:

2) a. Non   è   consigliato   il   congelamento   del   prodotto.

   not   is   recommended   the   freezing   of.the   product

   'The product is not suitable for freezing.'

   b. Alcuni prodotti si   rovinano dopo   la   congelazione.

   some   products themselves   waste   after   the   freezing

   'Some products get ruined after freezing'

Congelamento can, in fact, be translated as "the act of freezing", while *congelazione* means "the state of being frozen".

These are subtle differences: sometimes, they can be difficult to grasp even by native speakers' metalinguistic reflections. However, it is important to see that there is an underlying order, or better, there are different principles and limitations, and all of them concur in the creation of new words.

For instance, the feminine suffix *-tura*, is found preferably in certain contexts, thus, is introduced to learners probably at later stages, being largely used to indicate technical or professional activities (e.g. *saldatura* 'welding', *muratura* 'brickwork'). The same is true for the masculine suffix *-aggio*, which is, however, much less productive (e.g. *imballaggio* 'packaging', *montaggio* 'assembly').

Another semantic preference is expressed by the masculine suffix *-io*, which is normally used to express prolonged and repetitive actions, often descriving sounds (e.g. *cigolio* 'squeaking', *brontolio* 'grumble').

The opposite is true in the case of suffixes *-ata / -uta /-ita*, i.e., verb participle forms, which indicate single occurrences of the action indicated by the verb, and it can never refer to the action in general. These suffixes can be introduced quite early in the study of language, normally at level A1+ or A2, when students are taught present perfect. Due to their occasional value, many of the nouns ending with these suffixes have established in the lexicon as entities having a concrete value (e.g. *ferire* 'to hurt' → *ferita* 'wound'; *salire* 'to climb up' → *salita* 'rise'). As it has been said, word formation patterns are tightly intertwined with all the other aspects of language, so also with linguistic factors: suffixes *-ata* / *-uta* /*-ita*, for instance, are very productive in Italian often belonging to colloquial language or youth jargon, even together with calques from other languages (e.g. from English *spoilerare* 'to spoil a movie or a book' → *spoilerata* 'the act of spoiling a movie or a book'). They often create periphrastic structures with the verbs *dare* 'to give' and *fare* 'to do, to make' adding a nuance of concision to the simple verb form: e.g. *dare una pulita* 'to clean up briefly', lit. 'give a cleaning' vs *pulire* 'to clean continuously or thoroughly[1]. Students can practice these nouns with exercises similar to those used for the present perfect, underlining the verbal nature of these nouns, e.g. filling the gaps: *una mangi__* (from the verb *mangiare*).

The use of the suffixes *-anza* / *-enza* is largely determined by chronological factors. These suffixes were imported in Italian from Occitan during the fourteenth century but have largely fallen into disuse, been substituted in time mainly by a zero derivation (e.g. *perdonanza* → *perdono* 'forgiveness') or by the suffix *-zione* (e.g. *consolanza* → *consolazione* 'solace'). The same thing happened to the suffix *-gione* (Gallo-Romance variant of the suffix *-zione*), which has remained in a few words.

4. 1. 1. 2. Agentive, instrumental, locative suffixes

Nominalizations can be formed not only to refer to actions but also to agents of actions. Nowadays, the most productive agentive suffix appears to be *-ista*, which is not only used to identify professionals (e.g. *gommista* 'tire dealer') and specialists (e.g. *dietista* 'dietitian') but also people expressing a sense of belonging to social group (e.g. *animalista* 'animal-rights activist'). This suffix is present in several languages, and the nouns ending with this suffix can be both masculine and feminine, depending on the article (e.g. *un regista*, a film director, is masculine, while *una regista* is feminine).

It normally expresses the characteristics of nouns ending with the concept suffix *-ismo* (see next subsection) even as an adjective form (e.g. *partito comunista* 'communist party', see section 4.1.3), but this is not always true: the extension of the suffix *-ista* reached nouns with different bases, even loan words (e.g. *rugbista* 'rugby player'), and made this suffix extremely productive in contemporary Italian.

Other very productive suffixes indicating agents are masculine *-tore* and the feminine *-trice* (e.g. *lavorare* 'to work' → *lavoratore* - *lavoratrice* 'worker'). These

---

[1] The suffix -ata is also largely used in nominalizations based on other nouns, e.g. *spaghettata* 'spaghetti dinner'. In these cases, only the -ata is used and not the other participial forms probably due to the productivity of verbs in -are in Italian, and hence, on the basis on the most frequent participial form.

suffixes are normally introduced at level A1 when students learn how to form masculine and feminine nouns. Exercises can focus on the differences in gender, e.g. filling the gaps: *un lavora___; una lavora___*.

As often across different languages, the concept of agent is linked to that of instrument, and this is reflected by the use of suffixes as well (Gaeta, 2002): many of the suffixes used to indicate agents are often used to indicate instruments as well (e.g. *frullare* 'to blend' → *frullatore* 'blender'; *lavare* 'to wash' → *lavatrice* 'washing machine'). The structure of these nouns is quite transparent, so even if the speaker never heard of the word *affettatrice* 'slicer', it can easily identify the instrument if he or she knows the base verb (i.e., *affettare* 'to slice'). An exercise that aims to further the knowledge of this structure might underline the verbal nature of the nouns ending with these suffixes together with gender agreement with the article, e.g. *Uno strumento che frulla (dal verbo* frullare*) è un ___* 'An instrument that blends (from the verb *to blend*) is a ___'.

The parallelism between agent/instrument suffix is also evident in the suffix *-nte*, both masculine and feminine, which comes from present participle. Some nouns ending with this suffix are introduced already at the first levels of language learning; however, the formation of present participle is normally presented at B1-B2 levels. To identify agents, this suffix is particularly productive in designating professions and conditions (e.g. *cantare* 'to sing' → *cantante* 'singer'; *abitare* 'to inhabit' → *abitante* 'inhabitant'). With an instrumental reading, this suffix is particularly productive in identifying pharmaceuticals or cosmetic products or, in general, substances that are supposed to cause a reaction of some sort (e.g. *abbronzante* 'tanning', *dimagrante* 'slimming')[2]. Exercises can underline the verbal nature of the nouns ending with these suffixes, e.g. *Una persona che per lavoro canta (dal verbo* cantare*) è un o una ___* 'A person that sings (from the verb *to sing*) professionally is a ___'.

Other recurrent suffixes for agents and instruments, although much less productive, are *-ino* (masculine) and *-ina* (feminine) (e.g. *spazzare* 'to sweep' → *spazzino/a* 'street cleaner'; *macinare* 'to grind' → *macinino* 'grinder'). The suffixes *-one* and *-ona* are also used with agentive nouns to indicate someone doing something frequently or excessively, often with a pejorative nuance (e.g. *mangione* 'glutton'). Both *-ino/a* and *-one/a* originally belonged to the class of modifying suffixes, i.e., suffixes that assign a value to the base noun adding a particular shade of meaning (e.g. *casa* 'house' → *cas-ina* 'small house', *cas-ona*

---

[2] The past participle is also used, but it more often represents a passive voice (e.g. *divorziato* 'divorced') or identifies the noun as belonging to a class of individuals (e.g. *immigrato* 'immigrant').

'big house', *cas-etta* 'nice house', etc.). Modifying suffixes can be difficult for learners, due to the absence of fixed rules (Grandi, 2009), hence exercises presenting at least the most frequent nouns are suggested. These suffixes are largely used with denominal nouns (i.e., nouns that are created from other nouns) to create concrete nouns, where the evaluative interpretation has been lost with time (e.g. *forca* 'hayfork', which originated *forcina* 'hairpin', *forcella* 'wishbone', *forchetta* 'fork', *forcone* 'pitchfork', *forchettone* 'carving fork', etc.).

Not only agents and instruments are related concepts, but also the places where a given action occurs. The suffixes *-iere* and *-iera* are, for instance, quite productive for all the three instances (e.g. *romanziere* 'novelist'; *tagliere* 'chopping board'; *cappelliera* 'luggage rack', or cases where distinguishing between instrumental and locative value is not simple, such as *braciere* 'brazier'). The same can be said for the suffixes *-aio* and *-aia* (e.g. *benzinaio* 'gas station attendant', *rotaia* 'rail', *bagagliaio* 'trunk'). Exercises in relation to professions can be made focusing on the memorization of the different suffixes, e.g. *Il romanz___ scrive romanza* 'The novelist writes novels'; *Il calzol___ aggiusta le scarpe* 'The cobbler fixes shoes'.

Table 6. 2. shows agentive, instrumental, and locative suffixes.

Suffix	Agent	Instrument	Place
-ista	gomm-ista		
-tore / -trice	lavora-tore	lava-trice	
-nte	canta-nte	abbronza-nte	
-ino	spazz-ino	macin-ino	
-iere / -iera	romanz-iere	tagl-iere	cappell-iera
-aio / -aia	benzin-aio	rot-aia	bagagli-aio

Table 6. 2. Agentive, instrumental, locative suffixes

4. 1. 1. 3. Abstract concept suffixes

Giving a definition of an 'abstract' concept is not as easy as it might seem at first glance. The concept of abstractness is not clearly definable from a semantic point of view, and sometimes the idea of 'abstract noun' overlaps with that of 'collective noun' or 'quality noun'. In this section, "abstract concept suffixes" will be defined as suffixes indicating concepts and qualities that are not akin to actions consciously performed by a subject.

Syntactically, nominalizations to express conceptualizations can be created by means of conversion from other parts of speech simply by placing the definite article in front of the part of speech that we want to change. We can conceptualize infinite verbs (e.g. *il soffrire* 'woe'), adjectives (e.g. *il bello* 'beauty'), and even adverbs (e.g. *il male* "wickedness'). Particularly infinite verb nominalizations can be difficult to acquire for students since this structure requires quite advanced syntactic competencies and hence are usually presented at the most advanced levels (C1).

More frequently, Italian makes use of concept suffixes to create nouns that represent various concepts with different semantic values. I have said in the previous section how the agentive suffix *-ista* has a strong relation with the concept suffix *-ismo*. Even though the productivity of the agentive suffix *-ista* has led it to develop an independent existence, one thing that is shared with its cognate *-ismo* is great productivity. *-Ismo* is, in fact, one of the most productive abstract concept suffixes in Italian, and it creates nouns referring to scientific, ideological, artistic, and literary movements (e.g. *futurismo* 'Futurism'), social phenomena (e.g. *femminismo* 'feminism'), individual attitudes (e.g. *altruismo* 'selflessness'), athletic activities (e.g. *ciclismo* 'cycling'), medical conditions (e.g. *daltonismo* 'colour-blindness'), or other specialist terms (e.g. linguistics, *gallicismo* 'Gallicism'). *-Ismo* is etymologically related to the other concept suffix *-esimo*, which has, however only remained for religious beliefs (e.g. *cattolicesimo* 'Catholicism') and few other occurrences belonging to the earlier stages of the language.

An etymologically related suffix is the feminine concept suffix *-istica*, widely used for academic disciplines (e.g. *linguistica* 'linguistics') but also for other nouns to add a general interpretation (e.g. *componentistica* 'component industry'), something which has led this suffix to adopt the meaning of a collective whole made up of single entities (e.g. *oggettistica* 'group of items and accessories of various nature').

So far, we have seen mainly denominal nouns; however, many conceptual nouns are deadjectival, i.e., they derive from adjectives. The suffixes that we can add to adjectives to create concept nouns are many, but only a few of them are productively used to create new words.

-Ità or *-ietà* are the most productive, and their differentiation depends exclusively on phonological principles: the suffix *-ietà* is only used with adjectives ending with *i* + vowel, e.g. *precario* 'uncertain' → *precarietà* 'uncertainty'). It is important to remind learners of the importance of the grave accent: in Italian, in fact, any word finishing with accented *à* has a grave accent and is invariable in plural form (e.g. *la precarietà* 'the uncertainty'; *le precarietà* 'the uncertainties'. Phonological reasons are at the basis of the differentiation between *-ità* / *-ietà* and *-ezza*: while the first suffixes are

preferably used with adjectives having more than two syllables, *-ezza* tends to be rather used with bysyllabic bases (e.g. *alto* 'tall' → *altezza* 'height') and lexicalized past participles (e.g. *raffinato* 'refined' → *raffinatezza* 'refinement').

-ía is also well established in Italian to create concept nouns from bases that are not derived adjectives (e.g. *allegro* 'cheerful' → *allegría* 'cheerfulness'). However, nowadays, its productivity relies on adjectives ending with formative elements of Greek origins (e.g. *autonomo* 'independent' → *autonomía* 'independence'). In order to learn how to pronounce these words correctly, students might be presented with phonetic exercises stressing the position of the accent.

A suffix that is generally considered non-productive is *-itudine*, normally linked to abstract Latin nouns (e.g. *grato* 'thankful' → *gratitudine* 'thankfulness'). However, recent research appears to suggest that this suffix has found a new way: ethnic adjectives make use of this suffix to suggest a sense of identity (e.g. *sardo* Sardinian' → *sarditudine* 'the quality of being Sardinian') and, by extension, adjectives that evoke life habits, ways of life or inclinations, even with loan words (e.g. *single singletudine* 'singleness') (Frenguelli, 2008).

Two more interesting concept suffixes are *-aggine* and *-ería*. They are used with adjective basis expressing a negative quality associated with human behaviour. *-Aggine* is generally used from adjectives ending in *-ato* and *-oso* (e.g. *sbadato* 'careless' → *sbadataggine* 'carelessness'; *scontroso* 'surly' → *scontrosaggine* 'surliness'). *-Ería* prefers adjective bases ending with *-one*, instead (e.g. *cialtrone* 'sloppy' → *cialtroneria* 'sloppiness').

A summary of abstract concept suffixes is presented in Table 6. 3.

- Ø	*il male*
-ismo	*femmin-ismo*
-esimo	*cattolic-esimo*
-istica	*lingu-istica*
-ità / -ietà	*sever-ità*
-ezza	*gentil-ezza*
-ía	*allegr-ia*
-itudine	*grat-itudine*
-aggine	*sbadat-aggine*
-ería	*cialtron-eria*

Table 6. 3. Abstract concept suffixes

4.1.2. Verbalization

In languages with little inflectional morphology, such as English, forming verbs can be made by means of conversion. Consider an English word like *water*: it can indicate the liquid, but it can also be a verb depending on the context (e.g. *I have to water the plants*). In the Italian language, which possesses a rich verbal morphology, this way to create verbs cannot be applied; hence verb formation in Italian needs to make use of suffixation.

As known, in Italian, there are three verbal conjugations, *-are* (e.g. *cant-are* 'to sing'), *-ere* (e.g. *scriv-ere* 'to write'), *-ire* (e.g. *dorm-ire* 'to sleep'). However, the only productive conjugation is the first one; hence new verbs are formed almost exclusively with the suffix *-are*. This suffix is attached to both noun bases and adjective bases, and verbs formed by means of this process are mainly used in bureaucratic language (e.g. *scadenza* 'deadline' → *scadenz-are* 'to set a deadline') or are based on loan words (especially from English, e.g. *blog* → *blogg-are* 'to create and manage a blog'). It is interesting to notice that the high sectoriality of verbs created this way can give the impression that these formations are odd or, anyway, belong to a peculiar language variation ('bureaucratese' in the first case, or youth jargon with English loan words, for instance).

Even though new verbs are almost exclusively formed with *-are* conjugation, many are the verbs using the other conjugations that are still present in the language. An obstacle for early learners of Italian is represented by the differentiation present in *-ire* conjugation between 'infixed' verbs and 'pure' verbs[3]. The majority of verbs in *-ire*, in fact, shows the infix *-isc-* in first-second- and third-person singular and third-person plural of present indicative and subjunctive (e.g. *pulire* 'to clean' *io pul-isc-o* 'I clean' vs *dormire* 'to sleep' *io dorm-o* 'I sleep"). It is very common that learners might overgeneralize the pattern even with pure verbs. Exercises presenting the most frequent verbs might help students to memorize these occurrences.

Very common suffixes are *-eggiare*, *-izzare* and *-ificare*. They all can create both denominal verbs and deajectival verbs and the main differences among them are related to their productivity and their context of usage.

-Eggiare, for instance, belongs to previous stages of the language, and nowadays is not as productive as before. Verbs with ending *-eggiare* are usually intransitive and express actions, behaviors or qualities implied by the nominal/adjectival base, sometimes with a nuance of repetitive action (e.g.

---

[3] The infixed verbs are sometimes improperly defined as inchoative verbs, based on Latin. However, the infix is in Italian semantically inert, hence we preferred the formal definition 'infixed verb'.

ondeggiare 'to sway'). It is often used with color adjectives (e.g. *rosseggiare* 'to become red').

Despite *-eggiare* is the popular variant of the etymologically related *-izzare*, the latter is nowadays much more productive in all registers, and verbs formed with this suffix, contrarily to the ones formed with *-eggiare*, are mainly transitive and indicate a process (e.g. *stabilizzare* 'to stabilize'). A difference in *-eggiare* and *-izzare* can be found in the aspect of the verb. Consider the pair *latineggiare / latinizzare*: it is easy to identify that the basis has something to do with Latin, so it should not be difficult to paraphrase these two verbs as 'to act as Latins'. However, while the first has the focus on the action, i.e., 'to behave in a Latin fashion', the verb with *-izzare* implies an ending point (in what is known as 'telicity'), i.e., 'to make something or someone Latin'.

-Ificare is less common and not much productive; however, it is semantically more specialized. It is used mainly in formal registers and in scientific domains, and it indicates 'the process of making something X' where X represents the nominal/adjectival base, therefore, it mostly has a transitive reading (e.g. *acidificare* 'to acidify').

A very productive process in verb formation not only in Italian, but across Romance languages in general, is the one known as parasynthesis, i.e. the simultaneous combination of a prefix and a suffix, both with nouns (e.g. *bottone* 'button' → *abbottonare* = *a-* + *bottone* + *-are* 'to button up') and with adjectives (e.g. *vecchio* 'old' → *invecchiare* = *in-* + *vecchio* + *-are* 'to get old'), where the word exists only when both affixes are present, and it is not possible to only have either prefix or suffix (e.g. **abbottone* or **bottonare* are not possible). A limited number of parasynthetic verbs is formed by adverbs (e.g. *vicino* 'near' → *avvicinare* = *a-* + *vicino* + *-are* 'to place near'); however, this process is not productive anymore. Moreover, while, as I have said, the only productive verbal conjugation is *-are*, in the case of parasynthetic verbs, we can also find *-ire*, however much less common than *-are* (e.g. *morbido* 'soft' → *ammorbidire* = *a-* + *morbido* + *-ire* 'to soften'). Exercises might focus on the formal structure of these verbs, for instance, asking the student to compose a verb based on the constituents (e.g. forming the verb with a + bottone + are). The difficulty of this type of exercise might be easily increased for students at higher levels asking to pick the right preposition among several of them. Another exercise might focus on the semantics of these constructions, asking to infer the meaning of a parasynthetic verb based on the main constituent.

Table 6. 4. illustrates verb formation patterns both based on adjectives and on nouns.

Affix(es)	Deadjectival verb	Denominal verb
-are	*calm-are*	*blogg-are*
-eggiare	*ross-eggiare*	*ond-eggiare*
-izzare	*stabil-izzare*	*ospedal-izzare*
-ificare	*acid-ificare*	*spon-ificare*
prep + X + -are	*in-vecchi-are*	*ab-botton-are*
prep + X + -ire	*am-morbid-ire*	*in-cener-ire*

Table 6. 4. Verb suffixes

4. 1. 3. Adjectivation

Not only do adjectives express qualities, but also relations with nouns. Consider the use of the adjective *nervoso* 'nervous':

3) a. Gianni è un bambino nervoso.
   Gianni is a child nervous
   'Gianni is a nervous child'

   b. Il sistema nervoso si trova nel cervello
   the system nervous itself finds in.the brain
   'The nervous system resides in the brain.'

Exactly as in English, while *nervoso* in (3a) expresses a noun's quality and hence is a qualifying adjective, the same adjective in (3b) expresses a relation with a noun and hence is a relational adjective. This is only an example to show that there can be many semantic nuances that occur between a noun and its adjective, sometimes regularly identified with the form of a suffix. Due to space limits, only a limited number of suffixes will be analyzed, exemplifying the relations that they can have with the nouns. Due to the extreme variety of adjectival suffixes, in fact, a choice has been made in their selection based on specific semantic reasons or peculiarities that may help the acquisition of these patterns.

We have seen in example (3) the suffix *-oso*. This suffix is mainly attached to nouns, but it can also create deverbal adjectives (e.g. *scivolare* 'to slip' → *scivoloso* 'slippery'). It has quite a wide range of meanings:

- Presence and/or abundance of the quality implied by the base, e.g. *fangoso* 'muddy, full of mud';
- Inclination towards the quality implied by the base, e.g. *avventuroso* 'adventurous, that has a propensity for adventure';
- That provokes the quality implied by the base, e.g. *disgustoso* 'disgusting, that provokes disgust';
- Affinity to the quality/qualities implied by the base, e.g. *farinoso* 'powdery, that resembles flour'.

The suffix *-ale* is very productive in its relational meaning, e.g. *settiman-ale* 'weekly, of the week'. It is mainly used in specialized language, especially from nouns ending with *-zione* (e.g. *gravitazione* 'gravitation' → *gravitazionale* 'gravitational') and *-mento* (e.g. *strumento* 'instrument' → *strumentale* 'instrumental'), and it becomes *-iale* with some nouns ending with *-ore* (e.g. *genitore* 'parent' → *genitoriale* 'parental'), *-nza* (e.g. *essenza* 'essence' → *essenziale* 'essential'). It is not applicable to nouns ending with *-ità*, for which the suffix *-ario* needs to be used (e.g. *autorità* 'autority' → *autoritario* 'authoritative'. *-Ale*'s variant *-are* is also quite productive, and it must be used when an /l/ or the trigraph /gli/ is present in the last syllable (e.g. *sole* 'sun' → *solare* 'solar'; *famiglia* 'family' → *familiare* 'familial/familiar').

Largely used for relational adjectives is also the suffix *-istico*, formed by *-ista* + *-ico* (e.g. *specialista* 'specialist' → *specialistico* 'specialized'). We have seen *-ista* in section 4.1.1. The differences between adjectival forms in *-ista* and adjectives in *-istico* are subtle; however, the latter might possess a slightly pejorative nuance that nevertheless largely depends on the context (e.g. *femminista* 'feminist' vs *femministico* 'acting in a feminist way'). It is largely used from nominal bases in *-ale* and *-ione*, and relational adjectives ending with this suffix usually refer to ideologies, artistic movements, and sports.

It is important to mention that with relational adjectives, often the adjective does not resemble the base form at all (e.g. *guerra* 'war' → *bellico* 'related to war', as in *ordigno bellico* 'wartime bomb'). This might be confusing to international students. It is a morphological process known as suppletion, or the lexical polymorph, i.e., the use of phonologically distinct allomorphs, where one form has been supplied by another paradigm due to etymological reasons. In the case of relational adjectives, given that they often belong to specific semantic fields, such as technical or scientific terminology, Italian prefers an erudite etymology (usually Latin or Greek) next to a more popular form that has been subject to modification in oral language: in the example shown, *guerra* has Germanic origin and *bellico* a Latin one, but sometimes we see only a phonological transformation of the noun form (e.g. *oro* 'gold' → *aureo* 'golden', as in *periodo aureo* 'golden time') due to its evolution in the spoken language, a transformation that the adjective did not have due to its erudite use. These suppletive forms are especially used in medical terminology (e.g. *cuore* 'heart' → *cardiaco* 'cardiac'), in legal language (e.g. *denaro* 'money' → *pecuniario* 'monetary') and sometimes for ethnic nouns (e.g. *Napoli* 'Naples' → *partenopeo* 'from Naples').

A typically qualifying suffix, instead, is *-uto*, which is mostly denominal and often used to indicate the human body. Denominal adjectives ending in *-uto* tend to express the considerable presence of something indicated by the nominal base (e.g. *naso* 'nose' → *nasuto* 'big-nosed'), often with pejorative sense.

The suffix *-iano* deserves a special mention, both for qualifying and relational adjectives, for its tight relation with its base. *-Iano* in fact, is extremely productive in creating onomastic adjectives, i.e., derived from proper nouns. It can be used to simply refer to the person without any connotation (e.g. *cinema felliniano* 'Fellini's cinematography'), but also to indicate someone's supporters, also without adapting the proper noun to Italian phonology (e.g. *i trumpiani* 'Trump supporters' pronounced /trampiani/ and not /trumpiani/). To indicate somebody supporting somebody else, the suffix *-ista* is also very productive (e.g. *macronista* 'Macron supporter').

The suffix *-ese* is also highly specialized to indicate geographical origin both for cities (e.g. *milanese* 'from Milan, Milanese') and nations (e.g. *francese* 'from France, French'). Its conversion into a noun is used to indicate foreign languages (e.g. *il giapponese* 'Japanese language').

Adjectives can also be deverbal. An interesting deverbal suffix is *-bile*. In fact, while deverbal adjectives include several semantic meanings, the formation through *-bile* appears to be very regular and is also the most productive deverbal adjective suffix and one of the most productive processes of Italian derivation. Its meaning is incredibily regular, and it can be translated as 'that can be X', where X represents the verbal base (e.g. *lavare* 'to wash' → *lavabile* 'that can be washed, washable'). It can virtually be applied to any transitive verb that can be expressed with a passive voice.

Etymologically related to *-bile*, we find *-evole*, also deverbal, much less productive but still largely present in the Italian vocabulary. It can have an intransitive (e.g. *girevole* 'that revolves, revolving') or transitive reading (e.g.

incantevole 'enchanting'). Nouns deriving from adjectives with *-evole* only select suffix *-ezza* (e.g. *piacevole* 'pleasant' *piacevolezza* 'pleasantness').

We have seen the participial suffix *-nte* in section 4.1.1.2. This suffix has a wide range of applications, and its deverbal feature can be available to both an agentive/instrumental nominal reading and an adjectival meaning (Rainer, 1989) (e.g. *pesare* 'to weigh' → *pesante* 'heavy', i.e., 'that weigh much'). It is common to have a primary adjectival function with nominal use (e.g. *abbronzante* 'tanning' as in *(lozione) abbronzante* 'tanning (lotion)') or viceversa (e.g. the noun *partecipante* 'participant' as *soggetto partecipante* 'participant individual').

Finally, another quite productive suffix is *-ivo*, mainly deverbal (e.g. *difendere* 'to defend' → *difensivo* 'defensive') but denominal in some cases (*sportivo* 'related to sports'), largely used for qualifying adjectives, even though a relational reading is not uncommon.

4.1.4. Adverbialization

The way to form adverbs in Italian is almost exclusively by adding the suffix *-mente* (Grossmann and Rainer, 2013). This suffix is a typical example of the process known as grammaticalization, i.e., the process by which a lexical word becomes a grammatical marker. *-Mente*, in fact, meant 'mind' in Latin (as the Italian *mente*) in the ablative case, hence 'with an X mind', where the meaning of X was determined by the qualificative adjective preposed to *mente*, e.g. *forte mente* 'with a strong mind, with a strong temperament'. This meaning has been grammaticalized and started to be intended as 'in an X way', so *fortemente* 'in a strong way, strongly'. This is why, even though it is not visible with adjectives ending with *-e*, such as *forte*, the adjective before *-mente* is always feminine in Italian, being *mente* 'mind' feminine (e.g. *chiara* 'clear' feminine form + *mente*, i.e., *chiaramente* 'clearly').

However, in Italian, suffixation is not the only way to create an adverb. Especially in colloquial registers, adverbs can be created through conversion, and adjectives can be used with ad adverbial function:

4) Il   tempo   scorre   lento
   The   time   goes.by   slowly
   'Time goes by slowly.'

In 4), the use of *lentamente* would be more correct, however, this form is largely used to the point that some adverbs formed by conversion of adjectives are now commonly established in the lexicon (e.g. *vicino* 'close' but also 'nearby').

4. 2. Italian compounding

Whilst Italian makes use mainly of derivation to expand its vocabulary, research shows that compounding has increased in the most recent phases of the language.

In section 3 we have seen that while in derivation bound forms are attached to the word-base, in compounding, free forms combine with each other, and so an example like *fine settimana* 'weekend' shows two words (*fine* 'end' and *settimana* 'week') existing as free forms and that do not necessarily need to be joined together to get to be used in a sentence[4].

Since 'word' is not a clearly established concept, the distinction between compounds and derivatives is not always clear. However, space limits do not consent us to address theoretical considerations in this chapter, and here information will be given on the internal structure of compounds, in order to help international students to have a more structured view.

In order to give tools to be able to interpret a compound, the concept of **head** needs to be introduced. The head of a compound is the element that gives us syntactic and semantic information, e.g. *pescespada* 'swordfish' is a specific type of *pesce* 'fish', not a type of *spada* 'sword' and this is even more visible if we consider syntactic information such as gender agreement:

5) Il grosso pescespada nero
the:M big:M fish:M.sword:F black:M
'The big black swordfish'

In 5) gender is transmitted to the article and the adjectives by the masculine noun *pesce* and not by the feminine noun *spada*. This structure made of two nouns, where the second one represents an entity evoking a property of the first noun, is extremely productive in Italian (Radimský 2015). Common are also cases where the right noun is a complement of the head (e.g. *caposquadra* 'team leader', lit. 'leader.team'). Normally, being the left noun the

---

[4] It is important to mention that there is a high variety in the orthography of compounds: sometimes even the same compound can be written as a joined word (e.g., *finesettimana*), the elements can be separated by a hyphen (e.g., *fine-settimana*), or they can be written as two separate words (e.g. *fine settimana*).

syntactic head, the plural inflection is identified in the first noun, and hence *pescispada* 'swordfishes', lit. 'fishes.sword' or *capisquadra* 'teamleaders', lit. 'leaders. team'.

If we consider English, we might be tempted to see a reverse pattern: while in English, the head is the rightmost element (and so, a *houseboat* is a type of boat, while a *boathouse* is a type of house), in a language where adjectives normally follow the noun, such as Italian, the head should be the leftmost element. And indeed, this structure, where the head is at the left of the compound, has been considered to be archetypal Italian (Scalise, 1990). However, Italian shows examples like:

6) a. scuolabus

   school.bus

   'schoolbus'

   b. musicoterapia

   music.therapy

   'music therapy'

   c. alcoldipendenza

   alcohol.addiction

   'alcoholism'

In (6a), we see a word directly borrowed from English, while in (6b), we see a structure derived from Greek. With the expression 'derived from Greek', we do not imply that the word *musicoterapia* did exist in Ancient Greek, but that the words *mousikē* '(art) of the Muses' and *therapeia* 'healing' existed, and they were combined at a later stage. These compounds are called neoclassical compounds and are widely used in Italian, especially in technical and scientific language, but also for common words (e.g. *termometro* 'thermometer', from Greek *thermos* 'hot' and *meter* 'measure') (Dardano, 2009). On the other hand, case (6c) is original of the Italian language instead: these formations are increasing in the language, probably subject to the pressure of the English language, and it is more and more common to find them in neologisms. We see that these types of compounds show their head in the rightmost position: in order to know how to identify the head to extrapolate syntactic information, it is always useful to apply the *IS A* rule (e.g. *alcoldipendenza* 'alcoholism' is a *dipendenza* 'addiction', not an *alcol* 'alcohol', hence modifiers will be feminine as the word *dipendenza* is). It is interesting to mention that while left-headed compounds can often be written separately, right-headed compounds tend to strongly prefer to be joined in a single word (Radimský, 2013).

We have seen now compounds that can have the head either on the left or on the right. These compounds are called endocentric compounds, i.e., the head is inside the compound. However, there are also compounds whose head lies outside the compound itself, i.e., exocentric compounds. Consider:

7) a. pettirosso

   chest.red

   'robin'

   b. senzatetto

   without.roof

   'homeless person'

   c. apriscatole

   open.cans

   'can opener'

   d. bagnasciuga

   wet.dry

   'foreshore'

If we try to apply the *IS A* rule, we see that it does not work: in 7a), a robin is not a 'chest' and is not a 'red'; in 7b), a homeless person is not a 'without' and is not a 'roof'; in (7c) a can-opener is not an 'open' and is not a 'can'[5]; in 7d) a foreshore is not a 'wet' and is not a 'dry'.

In 7a), contrarily to what happens with the word *pescespada* 'swordfish', where a fish is identified and qualified by an object that resembles it, the word *pettirosso* does not give us any element to understand we are referring to a bird: the meaning of the compound refers to something outside of it, where

---

[5] It is indeed an 'opener' in English, but in Italian an *apritore* 'opener' is not mentioned, rather only the verbal stem *apri* 'open' is present. Hence, while in English can-opener is endocentric, the Italian *apriscatole* is exocentric.

the first element is of the quality indicated by the second element. This structure, where we find a noun plus an adjective that modifies that noun without, however, referring to an explicit head, is very productive.

Likewise, in 7b), we see that a word such as *senzatetto* 'homeless' (lit. 'without.roof') indicates somebody or something whose state is described by the joining of a preposition with a noun. These compounds are quite productive, and the preposition is always before the noun. In 7c), one of the most productive ways to create compounds in Italian languages (and in general across Romance languages) is shown. Compounds like *apriscatole* 'can-opener' show a verbal stem (which is always presented as second person imperative) plus the argument of the verb, nearly always the direct object of the verb. These compounds are normally used to refer to instruments, and when the second element is in plural form, the compound is invariable, e.g. *un apriscatole* 'one can opener' *due apriscatole*, 'two can openers'.

In 7d), being the word a noun, it is clear that this compound must be exocentric, since it is made by coordination between two verbs: *bagnasciuga* 'foreshore', lit. 'wet [and] dry'. These structures are not productive in the language; however, an interesting case is that of reduplications of the same verb to indicate nouns characterized by repetitive event performed by multiple agents, e.g. *un fuggi fuggi* 'a stampede', lit. 'a run away, run away'.

5. Conclusion

This chapter has underlined the importance of an approach that puts emphasis on word-formation in teaching and learning Italian as a second language.

When first approaching a foreign language, the great variety of morphological possibilities can appear confusing and intimidating, and therefore creating some order is crucial in language acquisition. Understanding how words are created, in fact, represents an important tool to be able to acquire new vocabulary and a morphological awareness that might aid the learning process.

Here, we have seen the most productive processes that Italian word-formation shows nowadays. Due to space limits, it has not been possible to analyse all the known patterns or other processes such as loanwords, portmanteau words, multi-word expressions, acronyms, etc. This chapter has tried to give a systematic view of the most common and productive mechanisms to help learners to organize their knowledge of the lexicon.

Teachers might find great help in reflecting on word-formation patterns and focusing their didactic in order to increase students' morphological awareness. When presenting new texts to students, teachers might work on a word level, underlining word-formation considerations, especially when new vocabulary is presented. The teachers can create exercises focused on the mechanism of formation of those words (e.g. ask the students to write words that have the same structure as the word presented; ask to change the part of speech of the words; create sentences that the students have to finish using a derivative word created based on a word suggested by the teacher, etc.).

Activities would be, of course, varied depending on the level of the students, but even at beginner levels, creative exercises focusing on word-formation reflections might offer a new perspective on the study of language (e.g. let students make hypotheses about how some compounds have been created on the basis of the two elements presenting their translations; show different words with the same suffix and their translation and ask students to think about their similarities; matching suffixes to word class and ask students to organize them in a table; try to show comparatively the same mechanisms in other languages students are familiar with; ask students to break down morphologically complex words, etc.).

The students, in fact, would greatly benefit if vocabulary were presented as a net of morphological building blocks rather than a chaotic list of strings of letters that need to be memorized. Not only, in fact, might word-formation awareness expand learners' understanding, but also production, autonomy and creativity.

References

Booij, G. (2008). Inflection and derivation. In Booij G., Lehmann, C., Mugdan, J., Kesselheim, W., & Skopeteas, S. (Eds.), *1. Halbband: Ein internationales Handbuch zur Flexion und Wortbildung* (pp. 360–369). Berlin, New York: De Gruyter Mouton.

Dardano, M. (2009). *Costruire parole. La morfologia derivativa dell'italiano.* Bologna: Il Mulino.

Frenguelli, G. (2008). Che cosa c'è di nuovo nella formazione delle parole. In Dardano M., & Frenguelli, G. (Eds.), *L'italiano di oggi: Fenomeni, problemi, prospettive.* (pp. 137–148). Roma: Aracne.

Gaeta, L. (2002). *Quando i verbi compaiono come nomi. Un saggio di morfologia naturale.* Milano, Franco Angeli.

Grandi, N. (2009). Restrictions on Italian verbal evaluative suffixes: the role of aspect and actionality. *York Papers in Linguistics,* 2(10), 46–66.

Grossmann, M., & Rainer, F. (2013). *La formazione delle parole in italiano.* Berlin, Boston: Max Niemeyer Verlag.

Iacobini, C. (1996). Il principio di direzionalità nella morfologia derivazionale. *Lingua e stile* 31(2), 215–237.

Radimský, J. (2013). Position of the head in Italian N-N Compounds: the case of mirror compounds. *Linguistica Pragensia* 23(1), 41–52.

Radimský, J. (2015). *Noun+Noun Compounds in Italian. A corpus-based study.* České Budějovice: Jihočeská univerzita, edice Epistémé.

Rainer, F. (1989). *I nomi di qualità nell'italiano contemporaneo.* Wien: Braumüller.
Scalise, S. (1990). *Morfologia e lessico.* Bologna: Il Mulino.
Thornton, A. M. (1990). Sui deverbali italiani in -mento e -zione. *Archivio glottologico italiano* (75), 169–207.

Chapter 7

Teaching Italian Dialectology

Adam Ledgeway
University of Cambridge

Abstract: The chapter exemplifies and explores some of the apparent problems that the formal study of the dialects of Italy can raise for both the teacher and the student, as well as investigating some methodological and practical solutions to the same, including an outline of the topics and material to be covered and an overview of some of the most useful pedagogical resources. Among other things, it highlights the necessity and advantages of studying (and teaching) Italian dialectology, how it can enrich both literary and linguistic modules and, in particular, how it can also enhance the teaching of standard Italian as well as throw considerable light on the peculiarities of spoken Italian, the *italiani regionali* which in large part represent the outcome of language contact between standard Italian and dialect (Berruto 1987; Telmon 1990; Cardinaletti and Munaro 2009).

Keywords: Dialectology, Dialects, italiani regionali, Standard Italian, Italian

***

1. Introduction

As Dante reminds us in the *De vulgari eloquentia* in (1), Italy has since at least medieval times been a deeply multilingual country (cf. also Vincent, 2006) in which there has been widespread diglossia between the *dialetti*, the regional vernacular languages which developed from spoken Latin largely without any interference from education and learning, and Latin, the official language of writing and learning which was to be replaced in the course of time by Tuscan-Italian in this role.

1) Quapropter, si primas et secundarias et subsecundarias vulgaris Ytalie variationes calcolare velimus, et in hoc minimo mundi angulo non solum ad millenam loquele variationem venire contigerit, sed etiam ad magis ultra. (Dante, *De vulgari eloquentia* I, x.9)

'For this reason, if we wished to calculate the number of primary, and secondary, and still further subordinate varieties of the Italian vernacular, we would find that, even in this tiny corner of the world, the count would take us not only to a thousand different types of speech, but well beyond that figure.'

From a linguistic perspective, Italy's regions are today still spectacularly fragmented after barely a century and a half of political unity such that mutual linguistic intelligibility between different Romance dialects, although closely related, remains just as great as that between, say, Romanian and Catalan. And even with the ever-growing expansion of Italian across the peninsula and the islands, in no small part assisted by major advances in technology, education, literacy, mass communication and social mobility, the dialects are still spoken by just over half the population (Jones, Parry and Williams 2016: 615), with even higher rates of usage in such regions as the Friuli-Venezia-Giulia, Basilicata, Calabria and Sicily where dialect is typically spoken by over 70% of the local populations (Istat, Statistiche Report, 2017: 5f.).

Given the undeniable importance and prominence of dialects in Italy, both in the past and present, in what follows, I exemplify and consider some of the apparent problems that the formal study of the Romance dialects of Italy can raise for both the teacher and the student, whilst exploring some methodological and practical solutions to the same, including an outline of the topics and material to be covered and an overview of some of the most useful pedagogical resources (cf. Appendices A and B). Among other things, I highlight the advantages and indeed the necessity of studying and teaching Italian dialectology, demonstrating how it can enrich both literary and linguistic modules and, in particular, how it can also enhance the teaching of standard Italian, as well as throw considerable light on the peculiarities of spoken Italian, the *italiani regionali* which in large part represent the outcome of language contact between standard Italian and dialect.

2. Why teach Italian dialectology?

In a book like the present one focused on *Italian as a Foreign Language*, an article on Italian dialectology might, at first sight, seem somewhat surprising, not to say out of place. Yet, the dialects have played, and continue to play, an important role in the internal and external linguistic history of Italy. Indeed, it hardly needs repeating that Italian itself has its roots in the dialect of Florence and was, for centuries, as Maiden (2002: 323) accurately puts it, 'a mere face in the crowd' among a myriad of dialects. Exemplary in this respect is the first Italian document, the *Placito capuano* dating from March 960, written not in (Tuscan) Italian but, rather, a Campanian variety (cf. Bartoli, 1944-45; Michel, 1996; Ledgeway, 2011a; 2012a).

2) Sao   ko   kelle   terre,   per   kelle   fini   que ki   contene,   trenta
   know.1SG   that   those   lands   for   those   limits that here contain.3SG thirty

   anni   le   possette   parte   sancti   Benedicti. (OCmp.)
   years   them=   possess. PST.PFV.3SG part   saint.OBL Benedict.OBL

'I know that, those lands, within those borders which are contained here [in the document/map before me], have belonged for thirty years to the part [= monastery] of St. Benedict [of Montecassino].'

And even when a Tuscan literary vernacular began to emerge a little over two centuries later, as embodied most notably in the literary works of the *Tre Corone*, it represented just one of several competing literary vernacular traditions that had sprung up in different parts of medieval Italy (Migliorini and Griffith, 1984:ch. 4), including the Sicilian school of poetry (e.g. Giacomino Pugliese, Stefano Protonotaro), Umbrian religious poetry (e.g. S. Francesco, Iacopone da Todi), northern Italian didactic poetry (e.g. Patecchio, Barsegapé, Bonvesin da la Riva, Uguccione da Lodi), and the Bolognese school of vernacular grammatical and rhetorical studies (e.g. Guido Fava).

Although by the end of the fifteenth century, a form of Tuscan dialect (notably Florentine) was beginning to emerge as a national literary language, the *questione della lingua* was far from settled as long as the numerous other regional literary traditions of the peninsula and islands continued to flourish. Indeed, these regional vernaculars, now relegated to dialects proper, came to represent in many cases important vehicles of literary expression, affording Italy an alternative, rich and valuable body of authors, including, to name just a few, for Piedmont, Alione, Tana, Isler, Calvo, Pietracqua, Pacotto; for Liguria, Foglietta, Cavalli, De Franchi, Piaggio, Firpo; for Lombardy, dagli Orzi, Maggi, Balestrieri, Porta, Grossi, Tessa, Loi; for the Veneto, Ruzante, Calmo, Venier, Goldoni, Baffo, Giotti; for Emilia-Romagna, Pincetti, Croce, Masdoni, Bancheri, Manfredi, Guerrini, Spallicci; for Umbria, Ceccoli, Nuccoli, Bartocci, Torelli, Dell'Uomo, Leonardi; for Lazio, Berneri, Belli, Pascarella, Zanazzo, Trilussa; for Abruzzo/Molise, Parente, De Titta, Clemente, Giannangeli; for Campania, Cortese, Basile, Sarnelli, Scarpetta, Di Giacomo, De Filippo; for Apulia, D'Amelio, Abbrescia, Consiglio, De Dominicis, Gatti; for Basilicata/Calabria, Piro, Ammirà, Pane, Butera, De Marco, Curcio; and for Sicily, Veneziano, Maura, Gambino, Meli, Tempio, Martoglio.

Significantly, this body of early and modern dialect literature, far from being demoted to a peripheral position within the literary canon, is widely read and studied by scholars of Italian and is even given varying degrees of coverage in both undergraduate and postgraduate university courses. Yet, the non-trivial practical and pedagogical linguistic issues associated with teaching, reading, and studying dialect literature are typically overlooked by scholars and students alike, who, apart from some rather superficial inferences about the structure of the linguistic system in which their texts are written, progressively accrued during the course of their readings, generally approach such texts without any formal study or knowledge of the relevant linguistic variety. Undoubtedly, the potential difficulties for comprehension are enormous, as they are for anyone expected to read a text in a 'foreign' language, a point convincingly made by Vincent (2005) in relation to old Italian. Here too, he argues, scholars and students of Italian all too frequently fail to appreciate the many, often subtle, linguistic differences, especially those of a morphosyntactic nature, that distinguish old Italian from modern Italian. In short, knowledge of the latter, however expert, is simply not sufficient to invariably guarantee a correct reading of the former. By way of illustration, consider the representative late thirteenth-century Tuscan example in (3a).

3) a. Vedi, donna: l' uscio mi lascerai aperto
   see.IMP.2SG lady the door me= leave.FUT.2SG open

   istanotte però ch' io mi sono costumato di
   tonight but that I me= be.1SG accustomed of

   levare a provedere le stelle. (OTsc., *Il Novellino* XXXVIII)
   raise.INF to watch.INF the stars

   'Look, woman, leave the house door open tonight, for I am accustomed to get up and study the stars.'

b. e tu mi prometterai che tu mi dara' mille
   and you.SG me= promise.FUT.2SG that you.SG me= give.FUT.2SG thousand

   livre al primo piato che tue vincerai. (OTsc., *Il Novellino* LVI)
   pounds at.the first lawsuit that you.SG win.FUT.2SG

   'and you will promise me that you will give me a thousand pounds when you win your first lawsuit.'

If read from the perspective of modern Italian, the uninitiated reader can easily misinterpret a number of features of the syntax of this sentence. First, the fronted complement *l'uscio* exemplifies the Verb Second (V2) syntax of early Tuscan and early Romance in general,[1] which in main clauses requires a constituent, and not necessarily the subject, to be fronted to a position before the finite verb where it receives a pragmatically salient interpretation. Whereas in modern Italian constituent fronting typically requires a resumptive clitic in the case of topicalisation, e.g. *La porta me **la** lascerai aperta* 'As for the door, you'll leave it open for me', or is otherwise interpreted as a case of contrastive or corrective focalisation, e.g. *La porta mi lascerai aperta (, e non la finestra)* 'You'll leave the door open for me (, and not the window)', in old Tuscan such fronted constituents can be interpreted either as topics or, as in (3a), as an instance of pure informational focus conveying new information which in modern Italian would be placed after the verb, namely *Mi lascerai la porta aperta*. Equally deceiving is the presence of the overt subject pronoun *io* 'I' in the following embedded clause in (3a). Modern Italian is a classic example of a null subject language in which subject pronouns are by default null in the unmarked case, only occurring in overt form when needed to mark contrast (e.g. **Io** *me ne vado ma* **tu** *rimani* 'I'm going but you are staying') or switch reference (e.g. *Eva$_i$ dice che* **pro**$_i$/ **lei**$_j$ *ha già pagato* 'Eva$_i$ says that she$_{i/j}$ has already paid'). However, neither of these pragmatic requirements are met in (3a), such that in modern Italian, the subject would be null, namely *...perché sono abituato...*. Rather, the occurrence of *io* in the embedded clause simply represents another reflex of the language's V2 syntax which imposes an asymmetric setting of the null subject parameter, whereby in embedded clauses pronouns are always phonologically realised, irrespective of their pragmatic interpretation. This is shown more spectacularly in examples such as (3b), where the second-person singular pronoun *tu(e)* first introduced in the main clause is repeated in the following two embedded clauses giving rise to a structure which, from a modern perspective, would be interpreted as pleonastic and typical of non-null subject languages such as English. We thus see that naively reading a sentence such as (3a), as well as (3b), according to the grammatical principles of modern Italian, will lead to a number of misunderstandings: the fronted object *l'uscio* is not a case of contrastive focus, and the presence of the subject pronoun *io* does not mark a contrastive reading or switch reference.

---

[1] See, among others, Vanelli, Renzi & Benincà (1985), Vanelli (1986; 1999), Benincà (1995; 2006; 2013), Salvi (2004; 2012; 2016:1005-1009), Ledgeway (2007a; 2008a; 2021), Wolfe (2015a,b,c; 2018).

Similar arguments apply to the dialects, whether in their earlier or modern attestations, which, although related to (Tuscan) Italian, frequently differ in subtle yet radical ways that the unwitting reader will quite simply fail to appreciate (cf. Vincent, 2006; Ledgeway, 2008b; 2011b). Illustrative in this respect are examples such as (4, a-c):

4) a. J   eu   vist   la   jer. (Mondovì, CE)
       SCL.1SG   have.1SG   seen   =her   yesterday
       'I saw her yesterday.'

   b. si   'viʃto   a   'fra:timo (Colonna, Rome)
       be.2SG   seen   DOM   brother=me
       'Have you seen my brother?'

   c. Vorzi   mi   vaci   m'   u   faci. (Reggio Calabria)
       want. PST.PFV.3SG that.IRR   go.3SG   that.IRR it=   do.3SG
       'He wanted/has wanted to go and do it.'

In (4a), for instance, all lexemes are shared with standard Italian, but nonetheless, knowledge of modern Italian – or indeed any modern Romance variety – is not of much help in understanding the sentence, inasmuch as in many contexts, local phonological process have disrupted or destroyed superficial cognacy (cf. EGO > *j* : *io*, (H)A(B)EO > *eu* : *ho*, HERI > *jer* : *ieri*). Furthermore, morphosyntactic patterns may also diverge considerably. First, as a northern Italian dialect, the finite verb requires an overt subject clitic *j*, a feature which aligns this dialect more readily with modern French (cf. **(j')ai*) than modern Italian (cf. *(io) ho*), which lacks the category of subject clitics. Second, the object clitic pronoun *la* follows the typical Piedmontese rule of attaching to the participle rather than to the auxiliary (cf. Parry, 1994; Tortora, 2014), giving rise to a clitic placement whose nearest equivalent is found in modern Romanian, e.g. *am văzut-o ieri* lit. 'have.1sg seen=her yesterday' (cf. Ledgeway, 2018). Third, as part of a process of aoristic drift (Schaden, 2012; Bertinetto and Squartini 2016: 944f.), the dialect generalises the analytic perfect to situations such as (4a) whose interpretation lacks any present relevance, although standard Italian, at least traditionally, marks a distinction between a synthetic perfect (e.g. *La vidi ieri*), without present relevance, and an analytic perfect with present relevance (e.g. *L'ho appena vista* 'I've just seen her'). Nonetheless, in this case, we know that this is one area where the influence and prestige of northern dialects has led to the generalization of the analytic perfect in northern regional Italian and, at the same time, has also set the scene for its increasing expansion in neo-standard Italian (Berretta, 1993: 212).

Equally opaque are the examples in (4b-c). In the former, ˌsi and ˈvːiʃto might individually be sufficiently transparent to speakers of modern Italian (viz. *sei, visto*), but when combined in the central dialect of Colonna they do not license the passive reading of Italian *sei visto* 'you are seen', but, rather, give rise to an active interpretation (Loporcaro, 2007; Ledgeway, 2019) and one characterized by present relevance which excludes the aoristic readings of northern Italy. While the nominal root of ˈfːraːtimo too might prove relatively transparent, it represents a potential area of misunderstanding given its conservative meaning 'brother' (cf. Lat. FRATER) in contrast to Italian *frate* with the more specialised meaning of 'religious brother, monk'. Again, other features find no parallel in Italian such as the use of enclitic first-person singular possessive *-mo* 'my' typical of dialects of central and upper southern Italy (Lombardi, 2007; Ledgeway, 2009:ch.7; 2016a:258; Loporcaro and Paciaroni, 2016: 243f.; Ledgeway, Schifano and Silvestri, 2020), as well as spoken Romanian (cf. Ro. *frate-meu* 'brother=my'; Maiden, 2016: 117), and the differential marking of typically animate and specific direct objects with the preposition *a* 'to' in line with a pattern characteristic, for example, of Spanish, e.g. *¿Has visto **a** mi hermano?* (Ledgeway, 2023 a). Similar degrees of opacity surround (4c) where, despite considerable lexical transparency (e.g. (*volsi* >) *vorzi*: *volle, vaci*: *va, faci*: *fa*), the syntax of Reggino, and in particular the general replacement of the infinitive with finite clauses introduced by *mi* 'that' (< (QUO)MODO 'how') on a par with complementation patterns closely paralleled only in Romanian within Romance, e.g. *a vrut să meargă să-l facă* lit. 'have.3SG wanted that.IRR go.SBJV.3 that.IRR=it do.SBJV.3' (Joseph, 1983; Ledgeway, 2023 b) is such that the sentence proves largely impenetrable to speakers of Italian and other Romance languages. Also notable is the use of the synthetic perfect *vorzi*, which represents the mirror image of the northern analytic paradigm in that its aspectual range includes situations marked by present relevance as well as those without.

Consequently, we conclude that at least a working knowledge of Italian dialectology should form part of the basic competence of all Italianists, ultimately constituting a compulsory element of all degree programmes and graduate training. At present, Italian dialectology, if taught at all, tends to form part of those specialist linguistic courses referred to under the generic title of *Storia della lingua*, although, as we have seen, a knowledge of the dialects, including early (Tuscan) Italian, is essential for all students and scholars who wish to access a whole body of 'Italian' literature, including cinema which increasingly forms a core ingredient in many degree programmes, as well as to engage and participate in the linguistic and cultural reality of over half of the Italian population whose first language is one of the many dialects.

2. 1. Regional Italian

One of the major linguistic developments within Italy since at least the latter half of the previous century has been the rise of regional varieties of Italian, which have their origins in so-called *italiano popolare* (Cortelazzo, 1972). In particular, there has been a gradual shift from original diglossia between (written) Italian and the dialects to a situation of dilalia (Berruto, 1987) in which written standard Italian has come to coexist, not only alongside the traditional local spoken dialects but increasingly also alongside spoken Italian, albeit characterised by some quite marked regional features (Istat, Statistiche Report, 2017: 1-5). In particular, the latter represents the outcome of language contact between Italian and the dialect adstrate and/or substrate, giving rise to new dialects of Italian which betray regional provenance at all levels of analysis (for a selection of representative sources for the study of regional Italian, see Appendix B). By way of example, consider the regional Italian equivalents of the dialect sentences in (4, a-c) illustrated in (5, a-c).

5) a. L'   ho   vista   ieri. (northern Italy)
      =her   have.1SG   seen   yesterday

   b. Hai   visto   a   mio   fratello? (central Italy)
      have.2SG   seen   DOM   my   brother

   c. Lo   volle   andare   a   fare. (extreme southern Italy)
      it=   want. PST.PFV.3SG   go.INF   to   do.INF

Although unquestionably examples of Italian in which the most marked dialect features of (4a-c), such as enclisis of the object clitic on the participle, the selection of perfective auxiliary BE, and the replacement of the infinitive with a finite complement have all disappeared, the regional provenance of the speaker is still clearly betrayed in all three cases by, for example, the aoristic extension of the analytic perfect in (5a), the use of the differential object marker *a* in (5b), and the generalization of the synthetic perfect and obligatory climbing of *lo* in (5c). At the phonological level, too, there are further clues. For instance, in accordance with the phonological tendency of northern Italian dialects to shorten long consonants, in (5a), the perfect auxiliary *ho*, a trigger of *rafforzamento fonosintattico* in the standard, fails to produce lengthening of the initial consonant of the following participle in the north (viz. NIt. [ɔ 'vista] vs Tsc.-It. [ɔ v'vista]). This contrasts with the regional varieties of central and southern Italy in (5b-c), where the preposition *a* regularly produces *rafforzamento*, yielding [a m'mio] and [a f'farɛ]. These and many further details and examples which, for reasons of space we cannot explore here, highlight the reality and rich complexities of everyday spoken Italian, which cannot be overlooked, either by teachers or students. While it is perfectly natural in the first instance to set out to encourage students to acquire a written and spoken mastery of the standard language, the fact remains that authentic spoken Italian is always regionally marked (cf. the title of Crocco's 2017 article 'Everyone has an accent'), albeit to different degrees in accordance with various sociolinguistic variables, such that any student who aspires to both speak and understand Italian with a (near) native competence must reckon with this linguistic reality. The obvious route to achieving this is through the study of the dialects which continue to surface to varying degrees, even in the speech of non-dialect speakers, in the often unconscious phonological, morphosyntactic and lexical structures of the *italiani regionali*.

3. Teaching Italian dialectology

Having established in section 2 that a knowledge of Italian dialectology offers numerous advantages to scholars and students, not to say it represents a *sine qua non* for any serious, all-round scholar of Italian Studies who want to access a rich and diverse body of literary, cultural and sociohistorical material, we may now ask how Italian dialectology should be formally taught. In the same way that first-year students standardly study medieval Italian literature through the works of the *Tre Corone*, Italian dialectology should, ideally, also be taught from the very beginning of any degree programme as an independent course or, at the very least, as a substantial part of a general course in Italian linguistics in which, given the particular Italian linguistic situation, the dialects cannot but figure heavily in the curriculum. There exists a growing range of teaching and research sources for the study of the dialects (for some selective examples, see Appendix A), which can be further supplemented, with notable literary and cultural advantages, by authentic materials from Italian cinema (cf. Italian neorealism), drama (e.g. Goldoni, De Filippo), and popular music (cf. *la canzone napoletana*). In addition to detailed information about the external linguistic history of Italy and, in particular, the *questione della lingua* (Vitale, [1960] 1978; Marazzini, [1999] 2009; Scarpa, 2012), any such course must also provide students with detailed information about the internal history, structures and classification of the dialects. Indeed, for didactic purposes, it is best to divide the teaching of

Italian dialects into a least two, if not three, separate submodules in accordance with standard classifications of the dialects.

Starting with Dante's Apenninic west-east divide into 14 *vulgaria* (*De vulgari eloquentia* 1.x.6-9; cf. Coletti, 1995), there is a long tradition in Italian dialectology to classify the dialects by geographical criteria. Putting aside many of the details (see Pellegrini, 1975; Bruni, 1987: 290f.; Cortelazzo, 1988; Maiden, 1995: 233-248; Loporcaro, 2009), today the dialects are conventionally, though not uncontroversially, classified according to a north-south axis which, although excluding Sardinian (Bossong, 2016: 65; Mensching and Remberger, 2016: 270), recognises the three broad linguistic areas of the north (cf. Benincà, Parry and Pescarini, 2016), centre (cf. Loporcaro and Paciaroni, 2016) and south (cf. Ledgeway, 2016a), characterised, in turn, by a series of internal subdivisions (e.g. Gallo-Italic vs Venetan northern dialects; Tuscan vs non-Tuscan central dialects; upper vs extreme southern dialects). Variously coinciding with early administrative, political and cultural divisions and, in part, with the distribution of the ancient peoples of the peninsula and their substrate languages (Ascoli, 1882; Merlo, 1933; 1937), these three macro-areas constitute a geographic continuum with the linguistic distance increasing proportionately with geographic distance, allowing us to recognise two principal isoglosses (see Rohlfs, [1972]1977a; Savoia, 1997): the La Spezia–Rimini Line – more accurately a bundle of phonetic and lexical isoglosses running from Carrara to Fano – traditionally delineates northern dialects from those of the centre-south which, in turn, are only more loosely differentiated from each other through the bundles of phonetic, lexical and some morphological isoglosses traditionally grouped together under the Rome–Ancona Line. Given the frequent time and space constraints of the curriculum, it is therefore often most practical to organise the teaching of Italian dialectology in terms of the broad division between northern and central-southern dialects focusing, in turn, on the most salient local features of phonology, morphosyntax and lexis. By way of illustration and putting aside many finer details of local variation, below we review some representative examples from each of phonology, morphosyntax and lexis, which, it will be shown, can also help to reinforce the distinctiveness of Italian and throw light on its own structures.

3. 1. Phonology

Within the realm of phonology, one of the most distinctive features among the dialects is the behaviour of unstressed vowels. With the exception of word-final unstressed -[a], in the north, unstressed vowels tend to fall (cf. Bol. [gaːt] vs It. *gatto/-i* 'cat/s', [ˈfjɔwr] vs It. *fiore* 'flower', but [ˈbokɐ] 'mouth'), often giving rise word-finally to consonantal devoicing (e.g. Bol. [ˈɔv(u)] > [ɔf] 'egg') and word-internally producing consonantal clusters which are otherwise unattested elsewhere in the peninsula (e.g. Bol. [zbdal] vs It. *ospedale* 'hospital'). In the centre and south, by contrast, unstressed vowels are either retained, as happens in the centre on a par with the standard (cf. Mac. [ˈboːnu/-i], [ˈbɔːna/-e] and It. *buono/-i/-a/-e* 'good.MSG/MPL/FSG/FPL') or are neutralised with the concomitant loss of many morphosyntactic distinctions, as happens in the south. In the latter case, there are two patterns: in dialects of the upper south, unstressed vowels tend towards the indistinct central vowel schwa [ə] (cf. Nap. [ˈfiʎʎə] 'son(s), daughter(s)'), whereas in the extreme south, they merge into one of the three vowels [i (> ɪ), a, u (> ʊ)] (cf. Sic. [ˈfiɟɟʊ/-a] 'son/daughter', [ˈfiɟɟɪ] 'sons/daughters'). It is precisely these same dialectal differences which explain the differential integration of learnèd and foreign loans across different varieties of regional Italian illustrated in Table 7. 1.

Standard	North	Centre	Upper South	Extreme South
atmosfera 'atmosphere'	admosˈfɛra	ammosˈfɛra	atəmosˈfɛrə	atɪmosˈfɛra
taxi	takˈsi	tasˈsi	ˈtakəsi	ˈtakɪsɪ
club	klɛp	ˈklɛbbe	ˈklɛbbə	ˈklɛbbɪ
smog	zmɔk	ˈzmɔgge	ˈzmɔggə	ˈzmɔggɪ

Table 7. 1. Integration of learnèd and foreign loans in Italian

Non-native word-internal consonantal clusters and word-final consonants like those in rows 2-3 and 4-5, respectively, are simply tolerated, albeit with assimilatory voicing (e.g. /tm/ > [dm]) or devoicing (e.g. /b/ > [p]), in the north where we have seen that the phonotactics of the underlying dialects regularly produce consonantal clusters and voiceless word-final consonants. However, in the centre and south, they are 'repaired' either by complete assimilation, as in the centre in the case of word-internal consonantal clusters (e.g. /tm/ > [mm]), or by epenthesis or paragoge of the unmarked unstressed vowel [e] (centre), [ə] (upper south) and [ɪ] (extreme south).

In the same way, when teaching and studying a modern standard foreign language, these new concepts and discoveries can and should be reinforced and further underpinned by gap-filling and translation exercises in both directions in class and through homework like those exemplified in Tables 7.2-4 (solutions are provided in brackets). Not only do such exercises serve to support further and embed the relevant dialect structures in the learning process, but they also force the student to assess and compare them in relation to Italian, strengthening and reinforcing in the process the student's knowledge of, and active competence in, standard Italian as well as enriching their lexis in a number of cases.

Pdm.	pjat (piatto/-i)		gal (gallo)		tlɛ (telaio/-ai)		fnuj (finocchio)
Bol.	sɲa (segnare/-to)		vdut (veduto/-i/-e)		s'tmana (settimana)		vdes (vedessi/-e)
Rml.	fɔrpʃ (forbice/-i)		drɔ (dirò)		d'mɛnga (domenica)		stil (sottile/-i)
Eml.	'pɛgra (pecora)		stɔŋk (stomaco/-ci)		mstir (mestiere/-i)		'frasne (frassino)

Table 7. 2. Translate the following forms into Italian (note that a single dialect form might correspond to several forms in Italian)

Italian	Neapolitan	Italian	Neapolitan	Italian	Neapolitan	Italian	Neapolitan
vestito	(vəs'titə)	fumate	(fum'matə)	belli	(b'bɛllə)	belle	(b'bɛllə)
cenate	(ʃə'natə)	correte	(kur'ritə)	bella	(b'bɛllə)	pane	('panə)
venire	(və'ni)	portate	(pur'tatə)	belli	(b'bɛllə)	mare	('marə)

Table 7. 3. Translate the following Italian forms into Neapolitan (the only relevant differences of interest are unstressed vowels)

favuri (favore/-i)	*cunfissuri* (confessore/-i)	*cunigghiu* (coniglio)	*culuri* (colore/-i)
diri (dire)	*ùtili* (utile/-i)	*vuliri* (volere)	*vìnniri* (vendere)
dici (dice/-i)	*paisi* (paese/-i)	*misi* (mese/-i)	*pinzeri* (pensieri)
pilusu (peloso)	*vintitrì* (ventitrè)	*vulpi* (volpe/-i)	*midicari* (medicare)
distinari (destinare)	*picchì* (perché)	*udiari* (odiare)	*viali* (viale/-i)
paci (pace/-i)	*milli* (mille)	*cani* (cane/-i)	*cunfini* (confine/-i)
mmitari (invitare)	*putiri* (potere/-i)	*giùvini* (giovane/-i)	*luci* (luce/-i)

Table 7. 4. Translate the following Sicilian forms into Italian (note that a single dialect form might correspond to several forms in Italian)

3. 2. Morphosyntax

In the area of morphosyntax, the differences among the dialects are numerous and show a remarkable degree of microvariation. One example of particular note concerns the behaviour of sentential negation (cf. Zanuttini, 1997; Parry, 1997; 2013; Manzini and Savoia 2005, III: 127-155; Poletto, 2008; 2016; 2017; Garzonio and Poletto, 2018). Now, on a par with standard Italian (6a), in the dialects of central and southern Italy (6b), sentential negation is marked by a simple reflex of Latin preverbal NON 'not', so-called Stage I of Jespersen's Cycle. In most dialects of northern Italy, by contrast, negation is either at Stage II, where negation is expressed discontinuously by both a preverbal and postverbal negator (6c-d) or at Stage III, as in many north-western dialects in which negation is expressed by a single postverbal negator (6, e-f).

6) a. **Non** fumavo. (It.)

    NEG   smoke.PST.IPFV.1SG

    'I wasn't smoking.'

b. **Un** duarmu. (Cos.)

    NEG   sleep.1SG

    'I don't sleep.'

c. u   n   ɛ   **pɑ/nɛŋ**   vny (Pdm.)

    SCL   NEG   be.3SG   NEG   come

    'He didn't come.'

d. **nu** drom ˈ**mia** (Soglio, Pdm.)

    NEG   sleep.1SG   NEG

    'I don't sleep.'

e. el ˈtʃamʊ ˈ**miyɛ** (Premana, Lmb.)

    him=   call.1SG   NEG

f. mi lu ˈtʃamu ˈ**nɛŋ** (Cuneo)

    I   him=   call.1SG   NEG

    'I won't call him.'

Besides the relevance of these Italo-Romance dialectal data for our understanding and reconstruction of Jespersen's Cycle and, in particular, the cross-linguistically widespread historical development of negation from Stages I to III, the data in (6) also help us to explain a number of developments in modern Italian. First, structures such as those in (6c-f) in conjunction with *mica* are increasingly frequent today in Italian and, not by chance, exclusively in the speech of northern speakers where non-standard examples such as (7a-b) perfectly replicate the underlying Stage II and Stage III structures found in the dialects of northern Italy (Molinelli, 1984; 1987; Molinelli, Bernini and Ramat, 1987; Bernini and Ramat, 1996; Penello and Pescarini, 2008).

7) a. Giovanni **non** mangia **mica** pasta. (Ven.)

   Giovanni NEG eat.3SG NEG pasta

   'Giovanni doesn't eat pasta.'

   b. Insomma va **mica** male. (Cremona)

   after.all eat.3SG NEG bad

   'Things aren't so bad after all.'

Second, structures such as (6c-d) and (7a) invite us as teachers, speakers and learners of Italian to ask what is the status of standard Italian structures containing the negator *mica* (cf. 8a-b), cognate with northern Italian dialect forms such as *mi(n)ga* and *mia* (< MICA 'crumb'), and whether Italian too can be considered to have reached Stage II of Jespersen's Cycle.

8) a. **Non** piove **mica.** (It.)

   NEG rain.3SG NEG

   'It's not raining.'

   b. **Non** fumo **mica.** (It.)

   NEG smoke.1SG NEG

   'I don't smoke.'

Standard grammars are generally of little or no help in this respect, limiting themselves to the traditional and essentially incorrect observation that *mica* has a reinforcing function equivalent to English 'not at all'. However, a close examination of examples such as (8a-b) reveals that utterances of this kind only prove appropriate in specific, pragmatic contexts, such that the use of *mica* in standard Italian cannot be considered an example of unmarked Stage II negation on a par with northern structures such as (6d, 7a). Rather, as demonstrated by Cinque (1976), *mica* in standard Italian functions as a presuppositional negator, serving to deny an explicit or implicit presupposition or assumption that a certain situation holds true. For instance, (8a) would be pragmatically appropriate as a response to a previous assertion such as *Prendi l'ombrello!* 'Don't forget your umbrella!', but not as a simple unsolicited observation whilst casually looking out of the window. In a similar vein, (8b) would be an appropriate response for a non-smoker if offered a cigarette by another who incorrectly assumed that they too are a smoker but would not be appropriate in a context in which the sentence continues ...*perché non ho più soldi*, namely with the intended meaning 'I'm not smoking as I've run out of money'. In short, English translations of (8a-b) with 'not at all' fall seriously short of the mark and fail to highlight the marked pragmatic value of standard Italian *mica*. Indeed, northern dialects today at Stage II can be shown through historical documentation to have passed through an identical intermediate phase between Stages I and II, in which the value of postverbal negators such as *mica* was precisely that of a presuppositional negator which progressively underwent pragmatic weakening over time to become the unmarked negator observed today. From this comparative historical perspective, we can indeed conclude that standard Italian negation is still at Stage I.

3. 3. Lexis

As with phonology and morphosyntax, variation in the realm of lexis across dialects is truly spectacular and is often more readily, and probably unwittingly in many cases, transferred into Italian, where regional variations in both form (geosynonyms) and meaning (geohomonyms) are legendary (Varvaro, 1997). In what follows, we limit our observations to a representative selection of the most general lexical tendencies and recurrent lexicalized patterns for the expression of temporal deixis according to a largely onomasiological approach (cf. Rohlfs, 1969: 264-279; Ledgeway, 2015).

The principal temporal adverbs indicating past ('then'), present ('now'), and future ('after, then') show considerable variation across the dialects. Regarding the first, northern dialects continue a form of ILLA HORA 'at that hour' (e.g. OPdm. *antlor*, Gen. *allantoa*, OLmb. *enlora/inlora*, Bormiese *ilora*, Sondriese *igliura*), whereas central and southern varieties display an analogical formation on QUANDO 'when' (cf. QUANTO/TANTO), namely SCal./Sal. *tando/-u*, Cmp./Bas./NCal./Sic. *tanno/-u*, Laz./Abr. *(a)ndanno*, Abr. *allundannə*. For 'now' there are three principal forms and distributions: north AD IPSUM 'at this (moment)' (Pdm./Lmb./Rml. *adès*, Eml. *adèsa*, Ven. *desso*), centre (and southern Calabria, Sicily) HORA > *ora* 'at (the present) hour' (cf. also HAC HORA 'at this hour' > Lig./SWPdm. *áu(ra)/aú(ra), aó(v)a, aú*), and south (and also parts of Lombardy) MODO 'presently' > *mo*. For 'after, then', there are three principal forms. While most dialects continue a form of POS(T) 'after', e.g. Lig./Pdm. *pöi*, Eml. *pò*, Rml. *pu*, Cmp. *pò*, Cal. *pu(e)*, Sal. *puei*, we also find reinforced forms DE-POST in Lombardy and the Veneto (*dop(o), despò*), Lazio (*da(p)pó*) and large parts of the south (*doppu/-ə, dipoi*), not to mention Sic. *appò(i), appuói* (AD POST). The third form concerns a reflex of AD-PRESSUM 'pressed closely together', principally found in Campania (*appriesso*) and Calabria (*appriessu*).

Table 7. 5. provides a selection of the cross-dialectal variation found in relation to the basic day-based divisions gleaned from a variety of sources and individual dialects within each region:

	DAY BEFORE YESTERDAY	YESTERDAY	TODAY	TOMORROW	DAY AFTER TOMORROW
Pdm.	*l'autrèr, r'atra saira*	*jer, sèira*	*ancöi*	*dumaŋ*	*pasadumaŋ*
Lig.	*avantèi, ra'tra saira*	*saira, sèira, sèja, aieri, véi* (Gen.)	*ancö*	*dumaŋ*	*pödmáŋ*
Lmb.	*l'alrér, puſiér*	*ieri*	*incö*	*dumaŋ*	*pasadomá, puſdumá*
Eml.-Rml.	*ier d'là, jirlètər*	*ieri, (a)jìr*	*incö, incuo, incú*	*ədmáŋ, dmân*	*pasdmèn*
Ven.	*gerialtro, gerla'tro, ierlaltro*	*gèri, ièri, ngèr*	*ancúo, anc(u)ò, ancòi, incò(i), oncuò, unquò*	*domáŋ, dimáŋ*	*dopodomáŋ, domanlaltro, domanealtro, passà doman*
Umb.	*l'altro ieri*	*jere*	*ogge*	*d(i)man(e), domene/-a*	*doppodomane, domane llà, dimane llà*

	DAY BEFORE YESTERDAY	YESTERDAY	TODAY	TOMORROW	DAY AFTER TOMORROW
Laz.	l'artro jjère, vantièri	jjère	ògge	domane, dimane, dumane	dopodomani, domà ll'altro
Abr., Mol.	l'atraddejére	ieri, iere	ogge, uojje	crajə, dumane, addimane	doppedumane
Cmp.	iterza, jesterza	ajerə	oggə	crajə/rimanə	pəʃcrai
Nap.		ajíerə	oggə	rimanə	
Bas.	avandjerə, rətɛrze, diterza	(a)jerə	ɔjə, òscə	crai(ə), rimànə	pòirimanə, ròppərimànə, pəscrai
Pgl.	nustèrza/-ə, nəsterzə	ajirə, jire	jòje, joscə, osci	crà, crè(i)	pescrà, pəscrè, piscrèi
Sal.	nustierzu	jeri	òsci	crai	puscrai, bbuscrai
NCal.	nustierzu, 'stèrzə, diterza, 'itèrzə	ìeri, ajèra, jírə	òja, oji, gójə	crai, crèjə, dumani/-u	doppudumani/-u, puscrai/piscrai, puscrèjə
SCal.	avantèri, pusèri		òje, oji	crai/domani	podomani
Sic.	avantèri, passannajèri, pusèri	ajèri	òji	dumani	passannu dumani

Table 7. 5. Basic day-based divisions

As a general tendency, Table 7. 5. highlights how the dialects of the north, and to a lesser degree of the centre, show a larger number of lexical innovations than those of the south. For instance, whereas central-southern dialects straightforwardly continue Latin HODIE 'today', northern dialects display a reflex of the reinforced form HINC-HODIE lit. 'this today'. Similarly, many (especially rural) southern varieties continue Latin CRAS 'tomorrow', whereas central and northern varieties all opt for the innovative formation DE MANE 'of morning'. The term for 'yesterday', by contrast, is uniform across all areas (viz. < (AD)HERI), with the exception of some Ligurian and Piedmontese (Monferrino) dialects which have extended reflexes of SERAM 'evening' from an initial innovative shift 'yesterday evening' to the more general meaning 'yesterday' (Rohlfs, 1969: 266; cf. DE MANE 'of morning' > 'tomorrow morning' > 'tomorrow'). This initial semantic extension of SERAM (> 'yesterday evening') is attested beyond Liguria and Piedmont and is also found throughout the south (Rohlfs, 1969: 266; Gioscio, 1985: 88): Laz./Cmp. *sera*, Abr. *sairə*, Bas. *serə*, Cal. *sira*. This observation highlights how greater lexical conservatism in the south does not necessarily imply semantic conservatism. For instance, although HODIE is continued throughout the south, in many varieties, it has also come to mean 'this afternoon' (Rohlfs, 1969: 264): Pgl. *joscə*, SCal./Sic. *òji* (Cal. *ndi vidimu òji* 'we'll meet up this **afternoon**'), exceptionally giving rise to a lexical differentiation in Procidano (Parascandola, 1976: 135f.; Ledgeway, 2009: 734) between *jojə* 'this afternoon' and *oggə* 'today'.

The two core terms 'yesterday' (HERI) and 'tomorrow' (CRAS, DE-MANE) are also involved in many dialects in neologisms to indicate the day before and the day after, respectively. In the former case, the principal formations are HERI ALTERUM/ALTERUM HERI '(other) yesterday (other)' (north, centre), AB-ANTE-HERI 'before-yesterday' and POST-HERI 'after-yesterday' (north, southern Calabria, Sicily) and, in the south (excluding southern Calabria and Sicily) NUSTERTIUS (< NUDIUS TERTIUS 'day before yesterday') and/or DIES TERTIA 'third day'. In addition to the latter, some of these same dialects – but not all of them, cf. isolated Nap. *jesterza* (Ledgeway, 2009: 734), Mormannese *diterza*, Tarantino *nusterza* 'day before yesterday' – also present another related term to indicate 'the day preceding the day before yesterday' which is usually distinguished from the former by the presence of a sibilant (Rohlfs, 1969: 266f.; cf. also SCal. *appressavanteri* lit. 'after-before-yesterday', Sic. *avantirazzu* < *avantèri* 'day-before-yesterday' + augmentative). See Table 7. 6.:

	2 DAYS AGO	3 DAYS AGO
Veroli (Rohlfs 1969: 267)	*itèrza*	*ištèrza*
Campania (Rohlfs 1969: 266)	*itèrza*	*istèrza*
Calvello (Gioscio 1985: 88)	*rətɛrze*	*rəsterzə*
Castrovillari (Battipede 1987: 240)	*ditèrza*	*distèrza*
Saracena (Viola 2006: 122)	*'itèrzə*	*'stèrzə*
San Giorgio (Rohlfs 1969: 266)	*nustèrza*	*diatèrza*
Parabita (Romano 2009: 51, 113)	*nustierzu*	*nustierzignu*

Table 7. 6. Lexicalizations of '2 / 3 days ago'

As for the 'day after tomorrow', three broad areal patterns can be identified. In the north (and southern Calabria and Sicily), formations based on *pasa*+DE-

MANE 'pass-tomorrow' and POS(T)+DE-MANE 'after-tomorrow' are preferred,[2] in the centre DE-POS(T)+DE-MANE, and in the south POS(T)-CRAS. Once again, southern varieties traditionally present a rich array of innovative lexicalized variation in this area (cf. Table 7. 7.) through the use of diminutive (typically in -*i*-) and augmentative (typically in -*(u)o*-) suffixation to forge corresponding terms to indicate in three and four days time, respectively (Rohlfs, 1969: 265). In rarer cases, we even find a further augmentative form to indicate 'in five days' time'.

	IN 2 DAYS	IN 3 DAYS	IN 4 DAYS	IN 5 DAYS
Amaseno	pəscrai	pəscrigna	pəscròcca	
Mol.	pəskra(jə)	pəskrílle, pəskrəllucca	pəskrəllacca, pəskrónə, pəskrwóttə, pəskrwózzə	
ONap.	pescraie	pescrigno	pescru(o)zzo	
Nap.	pescraje	pescrigno	pescrotte	pescruozzo
Procida (NA)	piscreje	piscrigno	piscrogna	
Pisticci (MT)	pəscrai	piscriḍḍə	piscròttu	
Calvello (PZ)	pəskrayə	pəskridde	pəskrwofələ	marwofələ
Trecchina (PZ)	pescraje	pescriddro	pescroddro	pescruddro
Aieta (CS)	piscrai	piscriḍḍu	pəscronə	
Saracena (CS)	puscrèjə	puscriḍḍə		
Castrovillari (CS)	piscraj	piscriddu	piscrotti	
Mormanno (CS)	piscrai, puscrai	piscriddru		
Vico (FG)	pəscrai	pəcriddə	pəšcrògna	
S. Nicandro (FG)	pescrà	pescridde	pescròzze	
Otranto (LE)	pusscrai	piscriḍḍi	piscruófələ	
Nardò (LE)	puscrai	puscriḍḍi	puscriḍḍazzu	piscriḍḍòne

Table 7. 7. Lexicalizations of 'in 2 / 3 / 4 / 5 days time'

---

[2] The frequent linguistic similarity between northern Italy and southern Calabria and Sicily is a consequence of the neoromanization of this part of southern Italy following the Norman conquest of southern Italy (cf. Rohlfs, 1997a,b [1972]).

The basic terms '(day before) yesterday' and '(the day after) tomorrow' can also be productively combined in all dialects with the individual divisions of the day: (i) 'yesterday morning': Viterbese *jjerammattina*, Trecchinese *jerematina*, Nap. *aierammatina*, Cos. *aieri matina*; (ii) 'yesterday evening': Pdm. *jersèira*, Viterbese *jjeresséra*, Abr. *jeresére*, Nap. *aierassera*, Trecchinese *jeresera*, Sannicandrese *jierséra*, SCal. *arzira*, Sic. *arsira*, though we saw above that many dialects (also) employ here simple *saira/sèira* (Lig.), *sera* (Laz., Cmp.), *sére* (Abr.); (iii) 'yesterday (/last) night': Viterbese *jjerannòtte*, Abr. *jennòtte*, Teramano *jinottə*, Casacalendese *jenòtte*, Trecchinese *jerannotte*, Nap. *aierannotte*, Cos. *aieri notte*; (iv) 'tomorrow morning': Viterbese *domattina*, Nap. *dimanassera*, Castrovillarese *cramatina*, Pgl. *cremmènə*, Sannicandrese *crammatina*, Parabitano *crammatina* (cf. also Mosorrofa *matinu* 'tomorrow morning'); (v) 'tomorrow afternoon': Viterbese *domane doppopranzo*, Nap. *rimane ô iuorno*; (vi) 'tomorrow evening': Viterbese *diman'a sséra*, Mol. *krajesséra, pəskrajjesssérə*, Nap. *dimanassera*, Castrovillarese *craj a sira*, Parabitano *crassira*; (vii) 'tomorrow night': Nap. *dimanannotte*, Cos. *dumani notte*.

4. Linguistic theory

One of the major advantages of teaching and studying Italian dialectology is the numerous possibilities that it offers for the scientific study of language more generally. In particular, it is known that languages vary through time and space, raising profound questions about how such variation is related to differences between: (i) standard vs non-standard languages; (ii) synchrony vs diachrony; (iii) direct attestation vs inferred reconstruction; and (iv) language-internal vs language-external motivations. These questions are best studied within a single 'family' of languages where differences between otherwise highly homogeneous linguistic systems of the family are often minimal, allowing us to pinpoint what precisely may vary and the linguistic mechanisms underpinning such variation. The richly-documented diachronic and synchronic variation exhibited by Italo-Romance dialects offers privileged access to a range of variation through time and space unparalleled for other Western languages. Indeed, Italo-Romance dialects have proven to be an inexhaustible testing ground with a central role to play in challenging established beliefs in linguistics and forming new ideas and perspectives about language structure, change, and variation. In this context, the lessons learnt from Italo-Romance, with a long-recorded history and vast dialectal variation, are extremely valuable far beyond the Romance languages: they enable us to understand the role and relevance of reconstruction and internal and external causes of change in establishing the histories of languages in many parts of the world where such documentation is not available. At the same time, a firm grasp of existing linguistic theories is indispensable for understanding the structures and typological patterns of Italo-Romance. This is especially true with varieties we only know imperfectly through the texts of earlier periods: without native speakers to provide the missing empirical pieces of the puzzle, the traditional tension between attested and reconstructed forms has to be resolved by invoking established principles of endogenous and exogenous linguistic change. Italian dialects, therefore, offer us an experimental testbed to investigate with tried-and-tested techniques ways in which current theories claim that it is possible for the structures of languages to vary. More specifically, detailed, expert knowledge of the full extent of the Italo-Romance evidence can both test and challenge our theories of language and expand the empirical linguistic data on which they are based, as well as reveal how earlier stages may have diverged from what the written record of Latin tells us. Alas, non-standard varieties such as the dialects of Italy are too often overlooked in this respect, even though they offer fertile, frequently uncharted territory in which to study microvariation, frequently revealing significant differences of real theoretical significance. Such differences would not be visible by simply comparing the grammars of standard languages, as is so often done. Moreover, such microvariation can be read both 'horizontally' as synchronic variation across varieties through space and 'vertically' as different stages of variation through time, thereby helping to bridge the often unhelpful and unnecessary division between synchronic and diachronic approaches. In sum, these perspectives enable us to identify which phenomena are correlated with particular 'parametric' options, by which we mean a finite set of binary choices which determine the possible limits of linguistic variation and what kind of syntactic structures are associated with them.

To give a concrete example, consider the distribution of agreement of the active past participle across Italo-Romance (cf. Loporcaro, 1998; Ledgeway, 2012b: 317f.; 2016b), a representative sample of which is given in (9, a-g):

9) a. Li   piatti   ll'   eri   lavatu? (Bova Marina, RC)
       the.MPL plates.M them.MPL= be.PST.IPFV.2SG washed.MSG

   'The dishes, have you washed them?'

   b. Nu   seme   magnite   lu   biscotte   / Ji   so
      we   be.1PL eaten.MPL   the.MSG biscuit.MSG / I   be.1SG

      magnite   li   biscutte. (Arielli, CH)
      eaten.MPL the.MPL biscuits.MPL

   'We ate the biscuit / I ate the biscuits.'

c. [ɔ   kæ'maðæ   'kala   'fomlæ] (Bagolino, BS)
    have.1SG   called.FSG   that.F   woman.F
    'I called that woman.'

d. euna   feille   que   dz'   ayò   vuya (Valdostano)
    a.F   girl.F   that I   have.1SG   seen.FSG
    'a girl that I have seen'

e. Li   /   Ni   a   visti. (Cos.)
    them.M=   /   us=   have.2SG   seen.MPL

f. Los   /   Nos   as   vistos/vistu. (Lula, Sardinian)
    them.M=   /   us=   have.2SG   seen.MPL/MSG
    'You saw them/us.'

Assuming active participle agreement to be the surface reflex of an underlying agreement relation for gender/number features between the participle and a given nominal, we can recognise at least six different parametric specifications across Italo-Romance. Their distribution is modelled by the hierarchically-organized parametric choices exemplified in (9a-f), where the gradual cascading effect not only mirrors the gradual diachronic contraction of Italo-Romance participle agreement, but also highlights how synchronic variation in relation to the ability of the participle to spell out the agreement features of specific nominals is not uniform, but, rather, licenses differing degrees of surface variation in accordance with the growing markedness conditions that accompany the available parametric options as one moves down the hierarchy of examples in (9).

The simplest and least constrained system is exemplified by Bovese (9a), where the participle quite simply never displays any agreement with any nominal. Its mirror image is the pattern of participial agreement found in eastern Abruzzese (9b), where the participle simply agrees with any plural argument, be it the subject or the object (cf. non-meta phonetic singular form of the participle *magnate* 'eaten.SG'). In this respect, Bovese and Ariellese represent rather simple and relatively unmarked options in that the participle in these varieties either indiscriminately fails to agree or, on the contrary, systematically agrees with all (plural) arguments. Slightly more constrained, though still liberal by general Romance standards, is the conservative pattern found in Bagolinese (9c), where the participle only agrees with a subset of nominal arguments, namely those marked accusative, whereas in Valdostano (9d), a variety of Francoprovençal spoken in the Aosta Valley, there is the further proviso that the accusative nominal undergo overt fronting under relativization or *wh*-fronting. In all four cases, however, we are dealing with a case of 'mesoparametric' variation, in that the four options can be subsumed within a naturally definable class: they exclusively make reference to a single nominal category, in turn further specified for the feature [+acc] in Bagolinese and Valdostano and also for the relevant fronting feature in the latter. We observe, however, a shift from meso- to microparametric variation as we move to Cosentino (9e), which proves even more restrictive insofar as the relevant class of triggers for participial agreement is no longer represented *tout court* by a naturally definable class of nominals, but now makes reference to a small and lexically definable subclass of nominals, namely the pronominal clitics *mi* 'me', *ti* 'you.sg', *u/a* 'him/her', *si* 'him-/herself/themselves', *ni* 'us; thereof', *vi* 'you.PL', *i* 'them'. Incidentally, this behaviour also characterises modern Italian, which today no longer shows the more liberal types of agreement found in (9c-d), witness the Manzonian *le ciarle che avrebbe fatte e sentite* (*I promessi sposi* ch. III) lit. 'the.FPL gossips.F that have.COND.3SG done.FPL and heard.FPL', but restricts agreement to pronominal objects. Finally, in the case of Sardinian, this lexically definable subclass is broken down further: the participle is now restricted to agreeing with the ever more marked pronominal categories of the third person (9f), again a tendency found in many varieties of spoken Italian, including modern spoken Tuscan (Pieraccioni, 1951: 26). We see then that, while an examination of earlier and modern Italian would only yield a partial picture, the integration of various dialects (9a-f) provides missing pieces of the puzzle which reveal parametric choices and diachronic steps which cannot otherwise be readily inferred.

The dialects also have much to contribute to our understanding in the area of so-called 'universal principles' of language, a system of rules forming part of the genetic endowment known as Universal Grammar. An illustration of the valuable role that Italian dialects can play in testing linguistic universals concerns the licensing of nominative subjects. Within the current theory, it is assumed that Infl(ection), the locus of verbal inflexion, may be specified as [±tense], featural specifications, in turn, argued to correlate with the verb's ability to license a nominative subject. This distinction is supported by the evidence of many of the world's languages, including Italian, where tensed verbs license nominative subjects (10a), but untensed verbs such as infinitives only allow null (caseless) subjects (10b):

10) a. **Lei** torna a casa. (It.)
       she return.3SG to home
       'She returns home.'

   b. Prima di Ø$_i$ / *lei$_j$ tornare, Gianni$_i$ telefona. (It.)
      before of Ø / she return.INF Gianni telephone.3SG
      'Before his/her returning home, Gianni rings through.'

Yet, the evidence of the dialects of Italy reveals that the supposed universal correlation between the specification of Infl and the availability of nominative is spurious (Ledgeway, 1998; 2000: ch. 4; Mensching, 2000). Dialects from the length and breadth of the peninsula and the islands demonstrate an abundant use of overt nominative subjects in conjunction with infinitival verbs; witness the examples in (11, a-c):

11) a. L'   üsu   l'   è   d'   acatâ   tütu **u**   **padrùn**. (Lig.)
       the usage SCL be.3SG of   buy.INF all   the   boss
       'It is customary for the boss to buy everything.'

   b. E'   di   prima   à   mettasi   **idda** in   vinochju, altari ùn
      and of   before to   put.INF=self   she   in   knee   altar   NEG
      si   ni   fighjulaia   più. (Crs.)
      self= of.it=   look.PST.IPFV.3SG   more
      'Until she knelt down, you couldn't look at the altar.'

   c. Me   patri   morsi   prima   di   arrivari   **la** **figghia**. (Sic.)
      my   father die.PST.PFV.3SG before of   arrive.INF the   daughter
      'My father died before his daughter arrived.'

Data like these also illustrate how investigations of the dialects frequently reveal that the extent of typological variation within Italo-Romance, and indeed even within and beyond Indo-European, can prove to be considerably greater than traditionally assumed and often of a typologically 'exotic' nature. In this respect, one only has to think of such examples as the inflected infinitives, gerunds, past and present participles of old Neapolitan illustrated in (12a-d), which, as intermediate hybrid categories, clearly throw into turmoil traditionally narrow interpretations of finiteness in terms of a binary finite vs non-finite dichotomy (cf. Loporcaro, 1986; Vincent, 1996; 1998; Ledgeway, 1998: 41-46; 2000: 109-114; 2007b; 2009: 585-590).

12) a. oramay èy   hora   de   nne   **levaremo**   da   lo   liecto (ONap.,)

   now   be.3SG   time   of   us=   raise.INF.1PL   from   the   bed

   'now it is time for us to get up.'

b. **Tirandono**   certi   piscatori   la   reta

   pull. GER.3PL   certain   fishermen   the   net

   dal   mare,   senterono   essere pisante [...]

   from.the   sea   feel.PST.PFV.3PL be.INF heavy

   credendonose   haverno   incappati   multi   pesci
                                                                (ONap., VFE 133.23–5)

   believe. GER.3PL =selves   have.INF3PL caught   many   fish

   'Some fishermen drawing in the net, felt it to be heavy [...] believing themselves to have caught many fish.'

c. E   **datonosse**   insembla   salute   como   convenne, (ONap.)

   and   given.3PL=selves together   greeting   as   be.necessary.PST.PFV.3SG

   'And after having greeted one another as was customary'

d. in   questa /   città   di   Napoli   erano

   in   this   city   of   Naples   be.PST.IPFV.3PL

   duo   mariti   e   mugliere **timentino**   Dio (ONap.)

   two   husbands   and   wives   fear.PTCP.3PL   god

   'in this city of Naples there were two husbands and wives in fear of God'

Lexically, the verbal forms in bold (12a-d) prove unproblematic. Formally, however, they are certain to disorientate and mislead the unwitting reader, for they instantiate typologically marked verbal categories which find no direct parallel in Italian (and within Romance are only found in Portuguese, Galician, old Leonese and in Sardinian) whose meanings cannot be simply or transparently guessed at. For instance, in (12a), the first-person plural inflected infinitival form *levaremo* is more likely to be interpreted as a first-person plural future form. Equally puzzling is the first instance of the third-person plural inflected gerund in (12b), which *prima facie* might be erroneously analysed as a third-person plural present tense form (albeit with an odd postnasal dental in the verbal stem, viz. *tirand-ono), not to mention the complex sequence of a third-person plural inflected gerund followed by a third-person plural inflected infinitival complement *credendonose haverno*. No reader could be blamed for being unable to process such a bewildering and unfamiliar sequence. Similarly difficult to segment and parse for the uninitiated reader are the third-person plural participial forms in *dato**no*** and *timenti**no*** in (12c-d), inasmuch as cross-linguistically explicit agreement with such non-finite verb forms represents an extremely rare option, yet Neapolitan highlights how models of language need to accommodate it.

In conclusion, the examples reviewed in this section show that the Italo-Romance data — when they take into account not just the standard language but also the extraordinarily rich but often neglected stock of diachronic and synchronic dialectal variation — are crucial for our understanding of parametric variation, linguistic universals, and typological variation and what these can tell us about the cross-linguistic mechanisms underpinning language variation through time and space.

5. Conclusion

This chapter has explored some of the methodological and practical problems that the formal study of the dialects of Italy can raise for both the teacher and the student. Among other things, it has highlighted not only the advantages but has also made a case for the necessity of integrating the teaching of Italian dialectology into (under)graduate degree programmes in Italian Studies: a knowledge of Italy's *ricco patrimonio dialettale*, which, by European standards, stands unparalleled for the wealth of linguistic variation concentrated into such a compact area, can greatly enrich both literary and linguistic modules whilst at the same time enhancing the teaching of standard Italian, including a greater awareness and understanding of the nature of the peculiarities of spoken Italian, the *italiani regionali*. Finally, we have also observed how the vast typological variation found throughout the peninsula and the islands can be profitably exploited by dialectologists to throw light on issues in general linguistic theory, demonstrating how the dialects present the linguist with relatively unexplored experimental territory in which to investigate new ideas about language structure, language change and language variation. In the face of such variation, which frequently even baffles the most experienced of dialectologists, one cannot legitimately expect those with little or no formal training in dialectology to recognise or fully understand the often complex structural subtleties masked by an unfamiliar grammar without some formal instruction in Italian dialectology.

References

Ascoli, G. I. (1882). L'Italia dialettale. *Archivio glottologico italiano*, 1, 98–128.
Avolio, F. (2009). *Tra Abruzzo e Sabina. Contatti e reazioni linguistiche sui 'confini' dialettali nel contado aquilano*. Alessandria: Edizioni dell'Orso.
Bartoli, M. (1944-45). Sao ko kelle terre. *Lingua nostra* 6, 1–6.
Battipede, B. (1987). *Studio linguistico tra Calabria e Lucania. Il dialetto di Castrovillari*. Castrovillari: il Coscile.
Benincà, P. (1995). Complement clitics in medieval Romance: the Tobler-Mussafia Law. In Battye, A., & Roberts, I. (Eds), *Clause Structure and Language Change*, (pp. 325–344.). Oxford: Oxford University Press.
Benincà, P. (1996). *Piccola storia ragionata della dialettologia italiana*. Padua: Unipress.
Benincà, P. (2006). A detailed map of the left periphery of medieval Romance. In Zanuttini, R., Campos, H., Herberger, E., & Portner P. (Eds.), *Crosslinguistic Research in Syntax and Semantics. Negation, Tense and Clausal Architecture*, (pp. 53–86). Washington: Georgetown University Press.
Benincà, P. (2013). Caratteristiche del V2 romanzo. Lingue romanze antiche, ladino dolomitico e portoghese. In Cognola, F., & Bidese, E. (Eds), *Introduzione alla linguistica del* mòcheno, (pp. 65–84). Turin: Rosenberg & Sellier.
Benincà, P., Parry, M., & Pescarini, D. (2016). The dialects of northern Italy. In Ledgeway A., & Maiden M. (Eds), *The Oxford Guide to the Romance Languages*, (pp. 185–205). Oxford: Oxford University Press.
Bernini, G., & Ramat, P. (1996). *Negative Sentences in the Languages of Europe. A Typological Approach*. Berlin: de Gruyter.
Berretta, M. (1993). Morfologia. In Sobrero A. (Ed.), *Introduzione all'italiano contemporano. Le strutture*, (pp. 197–222.). Bari: Laterza.
Berruto, G. (1987). Lingua, dialetto, diglossia, dilalìa. In Holtus, G., & Kramer, J. (Eds), *Romania et Slavia adriatica. Festschrift für Zarko Muljačić*, (pp. 57–81.). Hamburg: Buske.
Bertinetto, P. M., & Squartini, M. (2016). Tense and aspect. In Ledgeway, A., & Maiden, M. (Eds), *The Oxford Guide to the Romance Languages*, (pp. 937–953). Oxford: Oxford University Press.
Bossong, G. (2016). Classifications. In Ledgeway, A., & Maiden, M. (Eds), *The Oxford Guide to the Romance Languages*, (pp. 63–72). Oxford: Oxford University Press.
Bruni, F. (1987). *L'italiano. Elementi di storia della lingua e della cultura*. Turin: UTET.
Cinque, G. (1976). Mica. *Annali della facoltà di lettere e filosofia dell'Università di Padova*, (pp. 101–112).
Coletti, V. (Ed.) (1995). D. Alighieri, *De vulgari eloquentia*. Milan: Garzanti.

Cortelazzo, M. (1972). *Avviamento allo studio della dialettologia italiana. III. Lineamenti dell'italiano popolare.* Pisa: Pacini.

Cortelazzo, M. (1988). Ripartizione dialettale. In Holtus, G., Metzeltin, M., & Schmidt, C. (Eds), *Lexikon der Romanistischen Linguistik. Band 4. Italienisch, Korsisch, Sardisch,* (pp. 445–453.). Tübingen: Max Niemeyer.

Crocco, C. (2017). Everyone has an accent. Standard Italian and regional pronunciation. In Cerruti, M., Crocco, C., & Marzo, S. (Eds), *Towards a New Standard: Theoretical and Empirical Studies on the Restandardization of Italian,* (pp. 89–117). Berlin/Boston: de Gruyter.

De Blasi, N. (2006) *Profilo linguistico della Campania.* Bari: Laterza.

Garzonio, J., & Poletto, C. (2018). Sintassi formale e micro-tipologia della negazione dei dialetti italiani. In Brincat, J., & Caruana, S. (Eds), *Tipologia e 'dintorni': Il metodo tipologico alla intersezione di piani,* (pp. 83–102.). Rome: Bulzoni,

Gioscio, J. (1985). *Il dialetto di Calvello.* Stuttgart: Steiner.

Istat (2017). Statistiche Report. *Istat 27 dicembre 2017.* Retrieved from https://www.istat.it/it/files//2017/12/Report_Uso-italiano_dialetti_altrelingue_2015.pdf

Jones, M., Parry, M. & Williams, L. (2016). Sociolinguistic variation. In Ledgeway, A., & Maiden, M. (Eds), *The Oxford Guide to the Romance Languages,* (pp. 611–623) Oxford: Oxford University Press.

Joseph, B. (1983). *The Synchrony and Diachrony of the Balkan Infinitive.* Cambridge: CUP.

Ledgeway, A. (1998). Variation in the Romance infinitive: the case of the southern Calabrian inflected infinitive. *Transactions of the Philological Society,* 96, 1–61.

Ledgeway, A. (2000). *A Comparative Syntax of the Dialects of Southern Italy: a Minimalist Approach.* Oxford: Wiley-Blackwell.

Ledgeway, A. (2007a). Old Neapolitan word order: some initial observations. In Lepschy, A. L. & Tosi, A. (Eds), *Histories and Dictionaries of the Languages of Italy,* (pp. 121-149). Ravenna: Longo.

Ledgeway, A. (2007b) Diachrony and finiteness: subordination in the dialects of southern Italy. In Nikolaeva, I. (Ed.), *Finiteness: Theoretical and Empirical Foundations,* (pp. 335–365). Oxford: Oxford University Press.

Ledgeway, A. (2008a). Satisfying V2: *sì* clauses in old Neapolitan. *Journal of Linguistics,* 44, 437–40.

Ledgeway, A. (2008b). Understanding dialect: some Neapolitan examples. In Ledgeway A., & Lepschy, A. L. (Eds), *Didattica della lingua italiana: testo e contesto,* (pp. 99–111). Perugia: Guerra.

Ledgeway, A. (2009). *Grammatica diacronica del napoletano.* Tübingen: Max Niemeyer Verlag.

Ledgeway, A. (2011a). When data meet theory: the case of the *Placiti cassinesi.* In Adamson, S., & Bennett, W. (Eds), *Linguistics and Philology in the Twenty-first Century.* Oxford: Blackwell. Special Issue of the *Transactions of the Philological Society* 109, 213–219.

Ledgeway, A. (2011b). Il ruolo del dialetto nell'apprendimento dell'italiano L2: alcuni esempi napoletani. In Cennamo M., & Lamarra, A. (Eds), *Scuola di formazione di italiano lingua seconda/straniera: competenze d'uso e integrazione*, (pp. 125-138.). Naples: Edizioni Scientifiche Italiane.

Ledgeway, A. (2012a). I *Placiti cassinesi*: punti di incontro tra teoria e dati. *La lingua italiana. Storia, strutture, testi* 8, 9-21.

Ledgeway, A. (2012b). *From Latin to Romance. Morphosyntactic Typology and Change*. Oxford: Oxford University Press.

Ledgeway, A. (2015). Varieties in Italy. In Jungbluth, K. & Da Milano, F. (Eds), *Manuals of Romance Linguistics. Volume 6. Manual of Deixis in Romance Languages*, (pp. 75-113). Berlin: de Gruyter.

Ledgeway, A. (2016a). The dialects of southern Italy. In Ledgeway, A. & Maiden, M. (Eds), *The Oxford Guide to the Romance Languages*, (246-269). Oxford: Oxford University Press.

Ledgeway, A. (2016b). Grammatiche diacroniche e teoria linguistica. In Benedetti, M., Bruno, C., & Tronci, L. (Eds), *Grammatiche e Grammatici. Teorie, Testi e Contesti. Atti del XXXIX Convegno Annuale della Società Italiana di Glottologia*, (pp. 39-51). Rome: Il Calamo.

Ledgeway, A. (2018). Romanian clitic placement: parallels in clausal and nominal structures. In Pană Dindelegan, G., Dragomirescu, A., Nicula, I. & Nicolae, A. (Eds), *Comparative and Diachronic Perspectives on Romance Syntax*, (pp. 23-52). Newcastle: Cambridge Scholars Publishing.

Ledgeway, A. (2019). Parameters in the development of Romance perfective auxiliary selection. In Cennamo, M., & Fabrizio, C. (Eds), *Historical Linguistics 2015. Selected Papers from the 22nd International Conference on Historical Linguistics, Naples, 27-31 July 2015*, (pp. 343-384). Amsterdam / Philadelphia: Benjamins.

Ledgeway, A. (2021). V2 beyond borders: the *Histoire Ancienne jusqu'a César*. In Meklenborg, C. & Wolfe, S. (Eds), *Secrets of Success*, special issue of *Journal of Historical Syntax* 5(29), 1-65.

Ledgeway, A. (2023 a). Parametric variation in differential object marking in the dialects of Italy. In Irimia M., & Mardale, A. (Eds), *Differential Object Marking in Romance*. Amsterdam: Benjamins.

Ledgeway, A. (2023 b). The final stronghold of the infinitive: (silent) modals in Romanian and southern Italy. In Alboiu, G., & Mardale, A. (Eds), special issue of *Revue roumaine de linguistique* 68, 25-39.

Ledgeway, A., Schifano, N. & Silvestri, G. (2020). I possessivi in italo-greco e italo-romanzo: paralleli strutturali in un'area di contatto. *Archivio glottologico italiano* CV, 85-114.

Lombardi, A. (2007). Definiteness and possessive constructions in medieval Italo-Romance. In Lepschy, A. L. & Tosi, A. (Eds), *Histories and Dictionaries of the Languages of Italy*, (pp. 99-118). Ravenna: Longo.

Loporcaro, M. (1986). L'infinito coniugato nell'Italia centro-meridionale: ipotesi genetica e ricostruzione storica. *Italia dialettale* 49, 173-40.

Lopocaro, M. (1998). *Sintassi comparata dell'accordo participiale romanzo*. Turin: Rosenberg & Sellier.

Loporcaro, M. (2007b). On triple auxiliation. *Linguistics* 45, 173-222.

Loporcaro, M. (2009). *Profilo linguistico dei dialetti italiani*. Rome-Bari: Laterza.

Loporcaro, M. & Paciaroni, T. (2016). The dialects of central Italy. In Ledgeway, A., & Maiden, M. (Eds), *The Oxford Guide to the Romance Languages*, (pp. 228–245). Oxford: Oxford University Press.

Maiden, M. (1995). *A Linguistic History of Italian*. London: Longman.

Maiden, M. (2002). The definition of multilingualism in historical perspective. In Lepschy, A. L., & Tosi, A. (Eds), *Multilingualism in Italy: Past and Present*, (pp. 31–46). Oxford: Legenda.

Maiden, M. (2016). Romanian, Istro-Romanian, Megleno-Romanian, and Aromanian. In Ledgeway, A., & M. Maiden, M. (Eds), *The Oxford Guide to the Romance Languages*, (pp. 91–125). Oxford: Oxford University Press.

Manzini, R. & Savoia, L. (2005). *I dialetti italiani e romanci. Morfosintassi generativa. (3 vols)*. Alessandria: Edizioni dell'Orso.

Marazzini, C. ([1999] 2009). *Da Dante alla lingua selvaggia. Sette secoli di dibattiti sull'italiano*. Rome: Carocci.

Mensching, G. (2000). *Infinitive Constructions with Specified Subjects. A Syntactic Analysis of the Romance Languages*. Oxford: Oxford University Press.

Mensching, G. & Remberger, E. M. (2016). Sardinian. In Ledgeway, A., & and Maiden, M. (Eds.), *The Oxford Guide to the Romance Languages*, (pp. 270–291). Oxford: Oxford University Press.

Merlo, C. (1933). Il sostrato etnico e i dialetti italiani. *Revue de linguistique romane* 9, 176–194.

Merlo, C. (1937). Lingua e dialetti d'Italia. In Merlo, C. (Ed.), *Terra e nazioni: Italia*, (pp. 257–280). Milan: Vallardi.

Michel, A. (1996). Für eine Textlinguistiche Interpretation der *Placiti campani* aufgezeigt am Beispiel des *Placito capuano* (960). In Gil, G. & Schmitt, C. (Eds), *Kohäsion, Kohärenz, Modalität in Texten romanischer Sprachen. Akten der Sektion „Grundlagen für eine Textgrammatik der Romanischen Sprachen" des XXIV. Deutschen Romanistentages, Münster (25.-28.9.1995)*, (pp. 271–309). Bonn: Romanistischer Verlag.

Migliorini, B. & Griffith, T. G. (1984). *The Italian Language*. London: Faber.

Molinelli, P. (1984). Dialetto e italiano: fenomeni di riduzione della negazione. *Rivista Italiana di Dialettologia* 8, 73–90.

Molinelli, P. (1987). The current situation as regards discontinuous negation in the Romance languages. In Ramat, R. (Ed.), *Linguistic Typology*, (pp. 165–172). Berlin: Mouton de Gruyter.

Molinelli, P., Bernini, G. and Ramat, P. (1987). Sentence negation in Germanic and Romance languages. In Ramat, P. (Ed.), *Linguistic Typology*, (pp. 165–188). Berlin/New York: de Gruyter.

Parascandola, V. (1976). *Vèfio. Folk-glossario del dialetto procidano*. Naples: Alfredo Guida Editore.

Parry, M. (1994). Posizione dei clitici complemento nelle costruzioni verbali perifrastiche del piemontese. In Clivio, G. P. & Pich, C. (Eds), *At dël VIII Rëscontr antërnassional dë studi an sla lenga e la literatura piemontèisa*, (pp. 247–259). Alba: Famija Albèisa.

Parry, M. (1997). Variazione sintattica nelle strutture interrogative piemontesi. Strutture interrogative dell'Italia settentrionale. In Benincà, P. & Poletto, C.

(Eds.), *Quaderni di lavoro dell'ASIS*, (pp. 91–103). University of Padua: Consiglio Nazionale delle Ricerche.

Parry, M. (2013). Negation in the history of Italo-Romance, In Willis, D., Lucas, C. & Breitbarth, A. (Eds.), *The History of Negation in the Languages of Europe and the Mediterranean*, (pp. 77–118). Oxford: Oxford University Press.

Pellegrini, G. (1975). Tra lingua e dialetto in Italia. In Pellegrini, G. (Ed.), *Saggi di linguistica italiana*, (pp.11–54). Turin: Boringhieri.

Penello, N. & Pescarini, D. (2008). Osservazioni su *mica* in italiano e in alcuni dialetti veneti. *Quaderni di Lavoro ASIt* 8, 43–56.

Pescarini, D. (Ed.) (2009). *Studi sui dialetti della Calabria* (Quaderni di lavoro ASIt n. 9). Padua: Unipress.

Pieraccioni, D. (1951). Intorno all'accordo del participio passato. *Lingua Nostra* 12, 26.

Poletto, C. (2008). On negative doubling. In Cognola, F., & Pescarini, D. (Eds.), *La negazione: variazione dialettale ed evoluzione diacronica* (Quaderni di lavoro dell'ASIt n.8), (pp. 57–84). Padua, Unipress.

Poletto, C. (2016). Negation. In Ledgeway, A., & Maiden, M. (Eds), *The Oxford Guide to the Romance Languages*, (pp. 833–846). Oxford: Oxford University Press.

Poletto, C. (2017). Negative doubling: in favor of a "Big NegP" analysis. In Cruschina, S., Hartmann, K., & Remberger, E. M. (Eds), *Studies on Negation: Syntax, semantics, and variation*, (pp. 81–104). Göttingen: Vienna University Press.

Rohlfs, G. ([1972] 1997). L'Italia dialettale (Dal Piemonte in Sicilia). In Rohlfs, G. (Ed.), *Studi e ricerche su lingua e dialetti d'Italia*, (pp. 26–31). Turin: Sansoni.

Rohlfs, G. ([1972] 1997b). Le due Calabrie (Calabria greca e Calabria latina), in: Gerhard Rohlfs (Ed.), *Studie e ricerche su lingua e dialetti d'Italia*, (pp. 246–259). Florence: Sansoni.

Rohlfs, G. ([1972] 1997c). Latinità ed ellenismo nella Sicilia d'oggi (aspetti di geografia linguistica). In Rohlfs, G. (Ed.), *Studi e ricerche su lingua e dialetti d'Italia*, (pp. 273–293). Florence: Sansoni.

Rohlfs, G. (1977) *Nuovo dizionario dialettale della Calabria*. Ravenna: Longo Editore.

Romano, A. (2009). *Vocabolario del dialetto di Parabita*. Lecce: Grifo.

Salvi, G. (2004). *La formazione della struttura di frase romanza. Ordine delle parole e clitici dal latino alle lingue romanze antiche*. Tübingen: Niemeyer.

Salvi, G. (2012). On the nature of the V2 system of medieval Romance. In Brugè, L., Cardinaletti, C., Giusti, G., Munaro, N., & Poletto, C. (Eds.), *Functional Heads. The Cartography of Syntactic Structures, Volume 7*, (pp. 103–111). New York: Oxford University Press.

Salvi, G. (2016). Word order. In Ledgeway, A., & Maiden, M. (Eds.), *The Oxford Guide to the Romance Languages*, (pp. 997–1012). Oxford: Oxford University Press.

Savoia, L. (1997). The geographical distribution of the dialects. In Maiden, M., & Parry, M. (Eds.), *The Dialects of Italy*, (pp. 225–234). London: Routledge.

Scarpa, R. (2012). *La questione della lingua: antologia di testi da Dante a oggi*. Rome: Carocci.

Schaden, G. (2012). Modelling the "aoristic drift of the present perfect" as inflation. An essay in historical pragmatics. *International Review of Pragmatics*, 4, 261–292.

Telmon, T. (1990). *Guida allo studio degli italiani regionali*. Alessandria: Edizioni dell'Orso.

Tortora, C. (2014). *A Comparative Grammar of Borgomanerese*. New York: Oxford University Press.

Vanelli, L. (1986). Strutture tematiche in italiano antico. In Stammerjohann, H. (Ed.), *Tema-Rema in Italiano*, (pp. 248–273). Tübingen: Narr.

Vanelli, L. (1999). Ordine delle parole e articolazione pragmatica nell'italiano antico: la "prominenza" pragmatica della prima posizione nella frase. *Medioevo Romanzo*, 23, 229–246.

Vanelli, L., Renzi, L. & Benincà, P. (1985). Typologie des pronoms sujets dans les langues romanes. In *Actes du XVIIe Congrès International de Linguistique et Philologie Romanes, III*, (pp. 163–176). Aix-en-Provence: Université de Provence.

Varvaro, A. (1997). Lexical and semantic variation. In Maiden, M. & Parry, M. (Eds), *The Dialects of Italy*, (pp. 214–221). London: Routledge.

Vincent, N. (1996). L'infinito flesso in un testo napoletano del Trecento. In Benincà, P., Cinque, G., De Mauro, T., & Vincent, N. (Eds), *Italiano e dialetto nel tempo: saggi di grammatica per Giulio C. Lepschy*, (pp. 389–409). Rome: Bulzoni.

Vincent, N. (1998) On the grammar of inflected non-finite forms (with special reference to old Neapolitan). *Copenhagen Studies in Language* 22, 135–58.

Vincent, N. (2005). Come insegnare l'italiano antico. In Lepschy, A. L. & Tamponi, A. R. (Eds), *Prospettive sull'italiano come lingua straniera*, (pp. 33–40). Perugia: Guerra.

Vincent, N. (2006). Languages in contact in medieval Italy. In Lepschy, A. L., & Tosi, A. (Eds), *Rethinking Languages in Contact: the Case of Italian*, (pp. 12–27). Oxford: Legenda.

Viola, L. (2006). *Idiomi del Pollino. Grammatica del dialetto Saracenaro*. Castrovillari: il Coscile.

Vitale, M. ([1960] 1978). *La questione della lingua*. Palermo: Palumbo.

Wolfe, S. (2015a). *Microvariation in Medieval Romance Syntax: a Comparative Study*. University of Cambridge: doctoral thesis.

Wolfe, S. (2015b). Microvariation in old Italo-Romance syntax: the view form old Sardinian and old Sicilian. *Archivio glottologico italiano*, 100, 3–36.

Wolfe, S. (2015c). The nature of old Spanish verb second reconsidered. *Lingua*, 164, 132–155.

Wolfe, S. (2018). *Verb Second in Medieval Romance*. Oxford: Oxford University Press.

Zanuttini, R. (1997). *Negation and Clausal Structure. A Comparative Study of Romance Languages*. Oxford: Oxford Univerisity Press.

Appendix A: selective sources for the study of the dialects

Argiolas, M., & Serra, R. (Eds) (2001). *Limba lingua language: lingue locali, standardizzazione e identità in Segna nell'era della globalizzazione*. Cagliari: CUEC.

Avolio, F. (2009). *Lingue e dialetti d'Italia*. Rome: Carocci.

Battisti, G. B. (1998) *Salento. Monografia regionale della Carta dei Dialetti italiani*. Lecce: Grifo.

Benincà, P., Ledgeway, A., & Vincent, N. (2014). *Diachrony and Dialects. Grammatical Change in the Dialects of Italy*. Oxford: Oxford University Press.

Benincà, P., Parry, M., & Pescarini, D. (2016). The dialects of northern Italy. In Ledgeway, A., & Maiden, M. (Eds), *The Oxford Guide to the Romance Languages*, (pp. 185-205). Oxford: Oxford University Press.

Bentley, D., & Ledgeway, A. (2007) *Sui dialetti italoromanzi. Saggi in onore di Nigel B. Vincent (the Italianist* 27, Special supplement 1). Norfolk: Biddles.

Brunale, A. (2003). *Grammatica e sintassi descrittive del dialetto di Campobasso*. Campobasso: Enne.

Bruni, F. (1984). *L'italiano. Elementi di storia della lingua e della cultura*. Turin: UTET.

Canobbio, S., & Telmon, T. (Eds) (2003). *Atlante linguistico ed etnografico del Piemonte occidentale, ALEPO*. Ivrea: Priuli & Verlucca.

Coco, F. (1982). *Introduzione allo studio della dialettologia italiana*. Bologna: Pàtron.

Cruschina, C., Ledgeway, A. & Remberger, E-M. (2019). *Italian Dialectology at the Interfaces (Linguistik Aktuell / Linguistics Today)*. Amsterdam: John Benjamins.

D'Alessandro, R., Ledgeway, A. & Roberts, I. (2009). *Syntactic Variation: the Dialects of Italy*. Cambridge: Cambridge University Press.

D'Alessandro, R., Di Felice, C., Franco, I. & Ledgeway, A. (2014). *Approcci diversi alla dialettologia italiana contemporanea*. Special issue of *L'Italia dialettale*, 75.

D'Alessandro, R. & Pescarini, D. (Eds), (2018). *Advances in Italian Dialectology*. Leiden, Brill.

De Angelis, A. (2022). 'Central-southern Italo-Romance', in M. Loporcaro and F. Gardani (eds), *The Oxford Encyclopedia of Romance Linguistics*. Oxford: Oxford University Press. Advance online publication. doi: https://doi.org/10.1093/acrefore/9780199384655.013.738.

De Mauro, T., & Lodi, M. (1993) *Lingua e dialetti*. Rome: Riuniti.

Devoto, G., & Giacomelli, G. (1994). *I dialetti delle regioni d'Italia*. Milan: Bompiani.

Frattolillo Di Zinno, R. (2003). *Lingua e dialetto a Montagano nel Sannio tra passato e presente*. Ferrazzano: Enne.

Grassi, C. (1996). Italiano e dialetti. In Sobrero, A. (Ed.), *Introduzione all'italiano contemporaneo. La variazione e gli usi*, (pp. 276-307). Bari: Laterza.

Grassi, C., Sobrero, A. & Telmon, T. (1997). *Fondamenti di dialettologia italiana*. Bari: Laterza.

Grassi, C., Sobrero, A. & Telmon, T. (2003). *Introduzione alla dialettologia italiana*. Bari: Laterza.

Jones, M. (1993). *Sardinian Syntax*. London: Routledge.

Ledgeway, A. (2000). *A Comparative Syntax of the Dialects of Southern Italy: a Minimalist Approach*. Oxford: Blackwells.

Ledgeway, A. (2009). *Grammatica diacronica del napoletano*. Tübingen: Max Niemeyer Verlag.

Ledgeway, A. (2016a). Italian, Tuscan, and Corsican. In Ledgeway, A., & Maiden, M. (Eds), *The Oxford Guide to the Romance Languages*, (pp. 206–227). Oxford: Oxford University Press.

Ledgeway, A. (2016b). The dialects of southern Italy. In Ledgeway, A., & Maiden, M. (Eds), *The Oxford Guide to the Romance Languages*, (pp. 246–269). Oxford: Oxford University Press.

Loporcaro, M. (2009). *Profilo linguistico dei dialetti italiani*. Rome / Bari: Laterza.

Loporcaro, M., & Paciaroni, T. (2016). The dialects of central Italy. In Ledgeway, A., & Maiden, M. (Eds), *The Oxford Guide to the Romance Languages*, (pp. 228–245). Oxford: Oxford University Press.

Maiden, M., & Parry, M. (1997). *The Dialects of Italy*. London: Routledge.

Manzini, R., & Savoia, L. (2005). *I dialetti italiani e romanci. Morfosintassi generativa*. (3 vols), Alessandria: Edizioni dell'Orso.

Marcato, C. (2002). *Dialetto, dialetti e italiano*. Bologna: il Mulino.

Marcato, G. (2004). *Parlar veneto: istruzioni per l'uso*. Padua: Unipress.

Parry, M. (2005). *Parluma 'd Còiri. Sociolinguistica e grammatica del dialetto di Cairo Montenotte*. Savona: Società Savonese di Storia Patria and Editrice Liguria.

Poletto, C. (2000). *The Higher Functional Field. Evidence from Northern Italian Dialects*. Oxford: Oxford University Press.

Rohlfs, G. (1966) *Grammatica storica della lingua italiana e dei suoi dialetti. I. Fonetica*, Turin: Einaudi.

Rohlfs, G. (1968). *Grammatica storica della lingua italiana e dei suoi dialetti. Morfologia*. Turin: Einaudi.

Rohlfs, G. (1969). *Grammatica storica della lingua italiana e dei suoi dialetti. Sintassi e formazione delle parole*. Turin, Einaudi.

Rohlfs, G. (1997). *Studi e ricerche su lingua e dialetti d'Italia*. Florence: Sansoni.

Tekavčić, P. (1980). *Grammatica storica dell'italiano (3 vols)*. Bologna: Pàtron.

Telmon, T. (2001) *Piemonte e Valle d'Aosta*. Rome: Laterza.

Vanelli, L. (1998). *I dialetti italiani settentrionali nel panorama romanzo*. Rome: Bulzoni.

Appendix B: selective sources for the study of regional Italian

Amenta, L. (2017). Contact between Italian and dialect in Sicily: the case of phrasal verb constructions. In Cerruti, M., Crocco, C., & Marzo, S., *Towards a New Standard: Theoretical and Empirical Studies on the Restandardization of Italian*, (pp. 242–266). Berlin/Boston: de Gruyter.

Bentley, D. (1997). Language and dialect in modern Sicily. *The Italianist*, 17, 204–230.

Bentley, D. (2001). Standard e dialetto nella Sicilia odierna. In Lamberti, M. & Bizzoni, F. (Eds), *La Italia del siglo XX. Jornadas internacionales de estudios italianos*, (pp. 347–363). Mexico City: Cátedra Extraordinaria Italo Calvino, Universidad Nacional Autónoma de México.

Bentley, D. (2008). L'italiano regionale e l'insegnamento dell'italiano oggi. In Ledgeway, A. & Lepschy, A. L. (Eds), *Didattica della lingua italiana: testo e contesto*, (pp. 85–97). Perugia: Guerra Edizioni.

Berretta, M. (1988). Linguistica delle varietà. In Holtus, H. Meltzeltin, M. & Schmitt, C. (Eds), *Lexikon der Romanistischen Linguistik. Band IV. Italienisch, Korsisch, Sardisch*, (pp. 762–774). Tübingen: Max Niemeyer.

Berrutto, G. (1987). *Sociolinguistica dell'italiano contemporaneo*. Rome: La Nuova Italia Scientifica.

Cardinaletti, A., & Munaro, N. (2009). *Italiano, italiani regionali e dialetti*. Milan: FrancoAngeli.

Cerruti, M. (2011). Regional varieties of Italian in the linguistic repertoire. *International Journal of the Sociology of Language* 210, 2–28.

Cerruti, M., Crocco, C., & Marzo, S. (2017). On the development of a new standard norm in Italian. In *Towards a New Standard: Theoretical and Empirical Studies on the Restandardization of Italian*, (pp. 3–28). Berlin/Boston: de Gruyter.

Cortelazzo, M. (1972). *Avviamento allo studio della dialettologia italiana. III. Lineamenti dell'italiano popolare*. Pisa: Pacini.

Crocco, C. (2017). Everyone has an accent. Standard Italian and regional pronunciation. In Cerruti, M., Crocco, C. & Marzo, S. (Eds), *Towards a New Standard: Theoretical and Empirical Studies on the Restandardization of Italian*, (pp., 89–117). Berlin/Boston: de Gruyter.

De Pascale, S., Marzo, S., & Speelman, D. (2017). Evaluating regional variation in Italian: towards a change in standard language ideology? In Cerruti, M., Crocco, C. & Marzo, S. (Eds), *Towards a New Standard: Theoretical and Empirical Studies on the Restandardization of Italian*. (pp. 118–142). Berlin/Boston: de Gruyter.

De Mauro, T. (1976). *Storia linguistica dell'Italia unita*. Bari: Laterza.

Ledgeway, A. (2010). Lingua italiana in bocca calabra: Italian in Calabria. In De Gasparin, V. (Ed.), *Ciò che potea la lingua nostra. Lectures and Essays in Memory of Clara Florio Cooper*, (*The Italianist* 30, Special supplement 1), (pp. 95–120). Norfolk: Biddles.

Maiden, M. (1995). *A Linguistic History of Italian*. London: Longman.

Regis. R. (2017). How standard regional Italians set in: the case of standard Piedmontese Italian. In Cerruti, M., Crocco, C. & Marzo, S. (Eds), *Towards a*

New Standard: Theoretical and Empirical Studies on the Restandardization of Italian, (pp.145–175). Berlin/Boston: de Gruyter.

Sobrero, A. (1988). Italiano regionale. In Holtus, G., Meltzeltin, M. & Schmitt, C. (Eds), *Lexikon der Romanistischen Linguistik. Band IV. Italienisch, Korsisch, Sardisch*, (pp. 732–748). Tübingen: Max Niemeyer.

Telmon, T. (1993). Varietà regionali. In Sobrero A. (Ed.) *Introduzione all'italiano contemporaneo. La variazione e gli usi*, (pp. 93–149). Bari: Laterza.

Telmon, T. (2016). Gli italiani regionali. In Lubello, S. (Ed.), *Manuale di linguistica italiana*, (pp. 301–327). Berlin / Boston: de Gruyter.

Chapter 8

Teaching and learning Italian indecent language

Alberto Regagliolo
UKSW University

Abstract: The Italian language is rich in vulgar expressions, figurative senses and incorrect expressions used in colloquial language, in the media, in magazines, but also in the cinematographic language. Knowing how to juggle within the linguistic richness is not a simple task because words are like stones, and their use can sometimes hurt, can lead to discrimination, but can also, for example, be criminally punished. This chapter will primarily focus on making a brief reflection on the role of the vulgar and colourful language in Italian, then offer some methodological teaching ideas, useful exercises for the linguistic reflection, as well as the revision of some useful materials to be used in the classroom. This chapter explores the role of the indecent and colourful Italian language at the university level to ensure that students of philology, future translators, and linguists, as well as teachers, can have new tools to deepen and understand even the less studied aspects of the language.

Keywords: Indecent language, Vulgarity, Colourful language, Italian, Teaching, Learning

***

1. Introduction

In 2012, the film *Viva l'Italia*, which was directed by Massimiliano Bruno, was released at cinemas. It is the story of Michele, a politician from the *Viva l'Italia* party, who, while having fun with his lover, suffers a stroke that causes damage to part of his brain, leaving him without inhibitions. In practice, he says everything he thinks without filtering his words in the relevant situations, even using offensive language with his loved ones. After the accident, he is admitted to the hospital, and his relatives visit to check on how he is doing and to speak to his doctor:

Michele: Andatevene tutti a **fanculo**!

Susanna (figlia): E dai, papà, bazta!

Michele: Zitta tu con 'sta *s* che non te se po senti'!

Dottore: Signora, al momento suo marito, purtroppo, è totalmente privo di freni inibitori, perciò, dice e fa tutto quello che gli passa per la testa, comprese le parolacce.

Giovanna (moglie): Una specie di sindrome di Tourette?

Dottore: Purtroppo è molto peggio.

Michele: Giovano', ma quanto magni? Sembri **un cinghiale**.

Antonio (Infermiere): Ma come te permetti?

Michele: A **fagocero**!

Antonio (Infermiere): A **rinojoni'**!

Michele: A **stonzo**!

Antonio (Infermiere): A **merda**!

Dottore: Antonio, ma che sei impazzito, veramente, su!

Michele: A **panzoni**, sembrate du' lottatori de sumo!

Dottore: Come potete vedere (ai famigliari) non può fare a meno di dire tutta la verità! Tutta la verità!

Michele: Scusi, dottore, ma lei continua a parlare con quel **coglione** di mio figlio!

Susanna (figlia): Eh, la verità!

Michele: Uno che si è sposato quel **troione** alle sue spalle! Prego, notate!

Elena (moglie di Valerio): Ma Valerio, lo senti tuo padre?

Valerio (figlio): È molto malato...

Michele: **Merde**!

Figli: Grazie![1]

From *Viva l'Italia* (2012)[2]

---

[1] IIF - Italian International Film (2015 February 9). Viva l'Italia, Scena divertente – Clip ufficiale. [YouTube video]. Retrieved January 15, 2022, from www.youtube.com/watch?v=roab3pmHgZo

The hilarious scene described above is just one example from the film where Michele, in addition to offending people he knows, such as his children and daughter-in-law, also offends the nurse who, being rather robust, is insulted with the term *boar, warthog, asshole* and *fatso*. The scene is symbolic because of the disproportionate and out-of-context use of vulgarity.

Although the scene is based on a serious accident, the use of indecent language is certainly not new to the public and readers. In fact, the Italian language is full of vulgar expressions, figurative senses and politically incorrect phrases used in colloquial language, in magazines and also in film.

Vulgarity was also around in the ancient era. Quite explicitly. Antonio Varrone, in the book *Erotica Pompeiana: Love Inscriptions on the Walls of Pompeii* tries to understand the reason for vulgarity in an objective way. According to him, "in a society that knew neither the sense of guilt nor the prudishness or the hypocrisy of much modern literature, love became man's worldly domain; the obscene did not exist, or was transformed" (Varrone, 2002: 16). Although morality in ancient Rome was different from that of today, edicts were issued against offences to safeguard the honour of people (Lenel, 1907: §§ 191–197) like the *De Cunuicio*, the edict *Ne quid infamandi causa fiat* the *De iniuriis quae servis fiunt*, among others. For example, the *Lex de adtemptata pudicitia* was a law that defended the honour of women and young people who still wore *toga praetexta*. The walls of Pompeii knew this well, as one of the engravings still tells us: *admiror paries te non cecidesse ruinis, qui tot scriptorum taedia sustineas* (wall, that you do not collapse under the weight of so much nonsense) (Zangemeister and Schöne, 1871: 122). Words such *as Indecens* (repugnant), *barbarus* (boor), *stercus* (shit), *mentula* (male member), *meretrix* (prostitute), verbs such as *periat* (to die) or *futuere* (to fuck) have weighed down several walls, and today, if an ancient Roman was catapulted in the twenty-first century to hear an Italian speak or to see an Italian comedy with the excessive use of profanity, s/he probably wouldn't be surprised! Quite the opposite, s/he'd probably recognise a few words!

Knowing how to handle linguistic richness is not an easy task because words can hurt, they can cause discrimination, and words are punishable under civil law if they are deemed as offensive. This chapter will focus *primarily* on setting out a brief reflection on the role of vulgar speech and colourful language in the Italian language. The second half puts forward some methodological ideas, useful exercises for linguistic reflection, as well as a review of some useful classroom materials. Here, I want to explore the role of

---

[2] Directed by Massimiliano Bruno, written by Massimiliano Bruno Edoardo and Maria Falcone and Produced by Fulvio e Federica Lucisano. It was not been possible to retrieve the original screenplay, so, the dialogues have been transcribed by the author.

the indecent Italian language so that philology students, future translators and linguists, as well as teachers, will have new tools to deepen and understand the least studied aspects of the language.

2. Part one: theoretical foundation

2. 1. What is indecent language, and why do we use it?

Society has evolved, but the human being remains essentially the same as always, a being who – as in the past – has feelings and emotions, such as anger, sadness, love, pain, disgust... and this is expressed through verbal and non-verbal language. Words are used in verbal language, whereas gestures are used on a non-linguistic level.

Indecent language is not normally used in certain situations because it is considered inappropriate and offensive and sometimes even obscene and outrageous. Inside it, one can find a language rich with expletives and swearing, such as **parolacce**, that is, those dirty and vulgar words (*vaffanculo, stronzo*); the **blasfemia**, irreverent words against someone who has religious beliefs and against sacred things (*dannazione, Cristo*, and all the words that include the word *Dio*) – in short, a type of profane language. Within the world of indecent language, there are then words or expressions **tabù** and those **oscene**, words that are considered indecent and not fit for saying in public (*farsi una sega, fare un pompino*). In fact, they can shock others or trigger significant awkwardness. There are also expressions that have a **scatological meaning**, which means they refer to excrement (*Sei una merda!*). It is also easy to find in Italian a colourful language (**linguaggio colorito**)– a set of lively and expressive words and expressions – not necessarily offensive, which can also be jokey (*Sei come il prezzemolo! È una zucca vuota!*).

It is not possible to fully understand human language without factoring in emotions. Without them, communication would not be accurate. Cursing is closely linked to emotions, and the two components cannot be separated. In linguistics, and specifically in language teaching, however, vulgar speech is not normally taken into account, neither in the study nor in actual teaching. The reality, however, is that it is precisely in the oral part of the language that cursing finds its place, intensifying and giving life and voice to emotions. Emotions that are translated into vulgar speech and that could not be expressed through any other word. And this is precisely because they are strong words, full of meaning that do not have other fitting correspondents. Without vulgar language, it would be impossible to understand the language *in its entirety* and, therefore, to understand the effective communications of human beings. Because without emotion, all linguistic studies would be in vain.

If it is true that the world is beautiful due to variation, the same could be said of language. The use of cursing is varied, and every adult fluent in a language implicitly acquires the knowledge and meaning of swear words. Vulgar language is part of all languages (Foote and Woodward, 1973) and is closely related to emotions, as already mentioned. In fact, language plays a fundamental role in their perception (Lindquist, MacCormack, and Shablack, 2015), given that profanity is actually a means for expressing language (Dewaele, 2006). Indecent language is linked to three main spheres: *neurological control, psychological restraints,* and *sociocultural restrictions* (Jay, 2000: 19). All three are found on the grounds of profanity and obscenities. Because it can change culture, it can change language, and even the actual profanities change over time.

It is thought that, from an early age, one is exposed to vulgar language. Then, depending on the social context, the type of education that one receives, and the type of relationship that parents have with cursing, a child will have a greater or lesser sensitivity to indecent language and its use and control. Undoubtedly, then, cursing is also used for getting attention, communicating honesty, hyperbolising and aiding social bonding (Stoker, 2013: 2).

According to Pinker (2007: 350), people would use vulgar language in five different ways: descriptively (Scopiamo!), idiomatically (È fottuto!), abusively (Fottiti!), empathically (È fottutamente pazzesco!), and cathartically (Cazzo!). On the other hand, cursing is not always controlled. Imagine, for example, spontaneous exclamations such as 'cazzo!' (Response cry), when, for example, one makes a mistake or hurts oneself. They are immediate verbal responses to a negative event and are usually not directed at others. Other types of profanity, on the other hand, are pronounced in other situations. Think of jokes, offences, assaults, for example. In this case, we are talking about controlled language, and it is up to the speaker to regulate its use.

It is estimated that two-thirds of swear words concern situations of anger and frustration (Jay, 2000) and also, in old age, for example, patients with Alzheimer's or dementia, although they forget facts and names, can still refer to swear words that sometimes recall a lexicon used when the person was back in their childhood.

Cursing expresses something that otherwise could not be expressed in a less vulgar way. Cursing has a main emotional and dysphemistic connotation (*lui scopa a casa*), and according to Jay (cited in McGuinness, 2013), "no other language is this efficient or effective at conveying emotional information as swear language". It can be used out of disappointment, wonder, sarcasm, humour, etc. Emotions are, therefore, the main trigger for more offensive and insulting language.

Think of the pragmatic situation of a tourist who, after paying EUR 120 for the train, arrives late and misses it. Expressions such as 'mannaggia', 'che rabbia', 'per dindirindina', 'mamma mia' or 'accidenti' to an Italian would sound out of context to be pronounced in this specific situation because they do not express an excessively strong degree of anger. A much more common response would be 'cazzo!', 'porca puttana!', 'ma vaffanculo!'. A stronger response or word, charged with meaning that reflects a state of significant anger.

Although language has an emotional force and may be hostile to the speaker, there is also a cultural element linked to the rules of the relevant country that gives extra weight to language. Indeed, cursing is less common in more religious communities (Janschewitz, 2008), as confirmed by a recent study where bilingual Polish students translating swear words from English to Polish, and vice versa, using a weaker lexical meaning in Polish translations, rather than stronger words (Gawinkowska, Paradowski and Bilewicz, 2013).

Many people, indeed, may be disturbed by saying, hearing, or using indecent and obscene language. This phenomenon, interdiction, is often replaced with a euphemism (Jay, 2005), a rhetorical figure where words or phrases are replaced for reasons of social convenience, fear of a religious, moral or political nature with others with a more attenuated meaning and less crude or violent meaning. Dysphemism, on the contrary, replaces a term and gives it a derogatory and offensive connotation. Sometimes, however, a mocking and joking tone is also hidden via dysphemism.

Set out below are some examples of these two rhetorical figures:

Euphemism	Dysphemism
Quel tuo amico **non mi sta per niente simpatico**.	Quel tuo amico **mi sta proprio sul cazzo**.
Loro due **cercano di ingraziarsi** il direttore.	Loro due **leccano il culo** al direttore.
Al vicino, visto quello che era successo, gli ho detto **in malo modo di tenersi lontano**.	Al vicino, visto quello che era successo, gli ho detto **di andare a farsi fottere**.
Mi ha detto che **è andato a letto** con qualcuno.	Mi ha detto che **ha scopato** con qualcuno.

The choice to use a euphemism or dysphemism is not, however, accidental. The pragmatic context, the register and the linguistic function are major players in this case. Understanding cursing, therefore, is a way to understand the emotions of the people that surround us and why vulgar words are part of our identity (Jay, 2000: 82).

2. 2. The linguistic function

Language is used to communicate with others and to communicate a message. Depending on the objective, the functions of communication vary. Roman Jakobson (1960: 354) proposes six linguistic functions: emotional, referential, poetic, phatic, metalinguistic and conative (table. 8. 1.).

Classification	Function
Referential	Describe, inform, warn
Emotive	Expresses feelings, emotions, moods
Conative	Persuade, Influence, Encourage Change
Phatic	Establishes contact between interlocutors, establishes and continues the conversation
Metalinguistic	Language analysis, reflection and language functioning
Poetic	Produces literary texts, choice of words

Table 8. 1. The linguistic function

Swearing can occur within various linguistic functions. For example, to draw attention to oneself (phatic). Between a teacher and a student, the latter could say: *Professore, Mi scusi, potrebbe ripetere?* While a man who walks along a sidewalk and is blocked from passing by idiots could say: *Ah stronzi, lasciate passare!* Therefore, even in other functions, such as poetics, the production of a text will not only be aulic, but we could find: *Fottiamci, anima mia, fottiamci presto perché tutti per fotter nati siamo* (Aretino, *Sonetti Lussuriosi*). Moreover, to express their emotions, we could find Carlo, a theatre actor, who can say to his friend: *Sono davvero troppo emozionato!*; whilst Joseph, before an audition, could say to his colleague: *Mi sto cagando addosso!* The linguistic function, therefore, must also be viewed from the perspective of the relevant register.

2. 3. Register

It is true that language changes in time and space. It changes according to the situation and the interlocutor with whom we interact. In fact, the same message can be conveyed differently if expressed through different registers. In Italian, thanks to the Berruto scheme, we can divide registers in a specific way: *formale aulico, tecnico-scientifico, italiano burocratico, standard letterario, neo-standard, italiano colloquiale, italiano regionale popolare, italiano gergale e trascurato.*

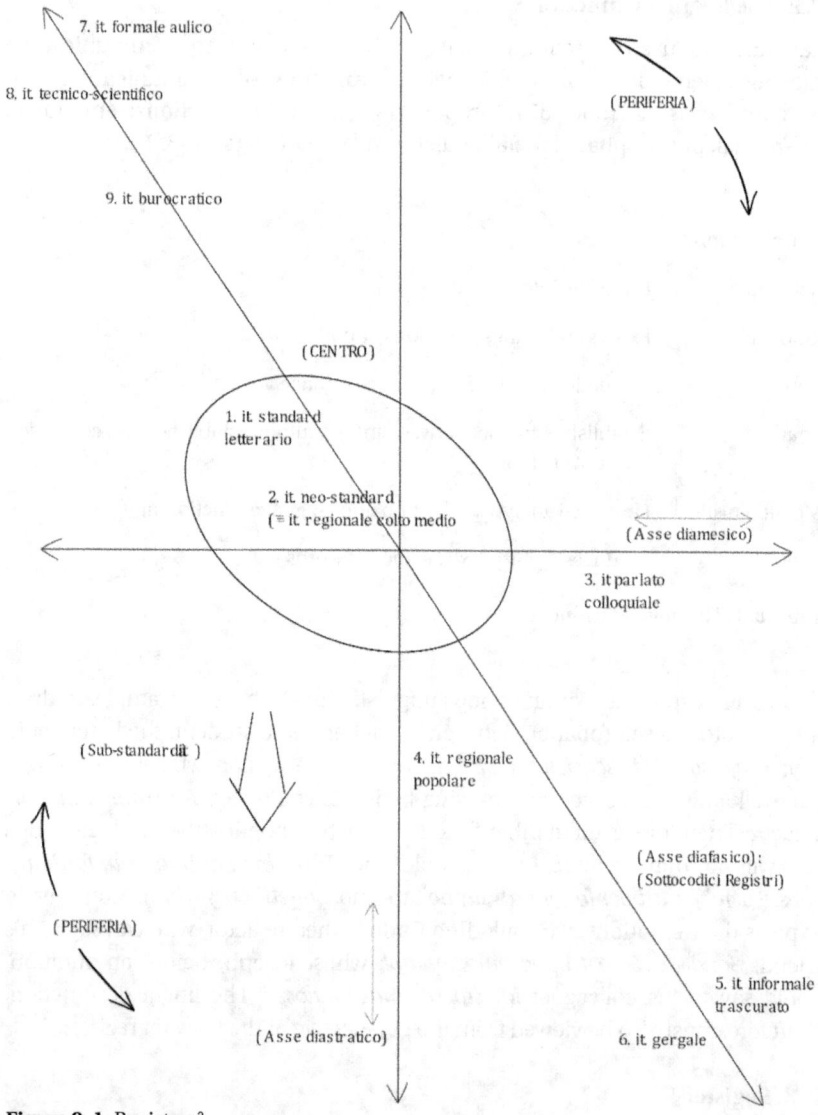

Figure 8.1. Registers[3]

---

[3] The scheme has been recreated.

Registers are based on variations: diatopic (geographic situation), diastratic (social position), diaphasic (communicative situation), diamesic (medium used) and diachronic (based on time). Depending on the situation and these variables, speech may vary drastically.

Note here Berruto's scheme (fig. 8. 1.) with the various registers that are distributed within the diamesic and diastratic axis, in which in the highest part there is the *formale aulico* register, while in the lowest part, the Italian *gergale*, register where there is dysphemism.

Berruto highlights how the same sentence can change according to the register. To make the change more evident, from the most refined to the most vulgar language, he uses as an example the phrase: *dire a qualcuno che non si può andare da lui* (1993: 13). We may note the change:

(2) Mi pregio informarla che la nostra venuta non rientra nell'ambito del fattibile (7, italiano formale aulico)

(3) Trasmettiamo a Lei destinatario l'informazione che la venuta di chi sta parlando non avrà luogo (8, italiano tecnico-scientifico)

(4) Vogliate prendere atto dell'impossibilità della venuta dei sottoscritti (9, italiano burocratico)

(5) La informo che non potremo venire (1, italiano standard letterario)

(6) Le dico che non possiamo venire (2, italiano neo-standard)

(7) sa, non possiamo venire (3, italiano parlato colloquiale)

(8) ci dico che non potiamo venire (4, italiano popolare)

(9) mica possiam venire, eh (5, italiano informale trascurato)

(10) ehi, apri 'ste orecchie, col cavolo che ci si trasborda (6, italiano gergale)

As we can see, the same sentence changes completely. Berruto points out, however, that such examples are not normally presented with all varieties because "obviously a certain type of message finds its normal formulation only in some variety, and above all each variety is linked to certain areas or preferential conditions of use"[4] (1993: 12). From a didactic point of view, however, it is interesting and key for students to be able to work mainly with Italian *gergale*, *colloquiale* and *standard letterario* in order to understand the

---

[4] Translated by the author.

changes and perceive that the vocabulary, the syntax and the linguistic structures in turn change according to the register.

2. 4. Denotative and connotative meaning

Terms may have a *denotative* and *connotative* meanings. The former corresponds to the objective meaning of a lexical unit that is disconnected from any applicable subjective and affective meaning. On the contrary, connotative language has an additional meaning in addition to denotative language. It is more metaphorical, figurative and emotional. The two levels coexist and are not distinctly separated. Cursing exists on a connotative level, which is essentially indecent Italian. The context, the situation itself, sometimes helps to separate the two levels and to perceive the true meaning. Think of the terms *pisello* and *patata*. Both are edible foods. The first a legume, the second a tuber. On a denotative level, therefore, they represent the two foods. On a connotative level, however, they are part of that taboo lexicon. The first represents the penis (*pisello, pisellino...*), and the second term can mean vagina or problem if it is associated with the adjective 'bollente'.

Another example is the term *pizza*, a word known internationally because it is associated with Neapolitan pizza, a distinctive dish of Italian cuisine par excellence. *Pizza* also has another meaning. In the example *Che pizza questo film!* Pizza refers to something that is boring. Therefore, it is obvious to the Italian speaker that in this precise context, *pizza* does not refer to the meaning of food. And again, *palla* is a noun that refers to a spherical object, for example, a ball game (football, volleyball, basketball, etc.). The term *palla*, however, in vulgar and jargon, has a totally different meaning. See examples (1, a-d and 2, a-d):

1) a. Che *palle* la lezione di fisica!

   b. C'ha due *palle* così quello, per esser andato in mezzo ai coccodrilli!

   c. Mia suocera è una *palla* al piede!

   d. Senti, bello, non raccontare *palle*!

The 'hidden' meaning is this:

2) a. Che *noia* la lezione di fisica!

   b. C'ha *un coraggio* così quello, per esser andato in mezzo ai coccodrilli!

c. Mia suocera è una *peso* al piede!

d. Senti, bello, non raccontare *bugie*.

The vulgarity, therefore, is also hidden in a second meaning that comes to life in a certain context and that also provides for cultural knowledge. For example, *essere una palla al piede* is an expression that refers to the way in which prisoners were tied with a ball strapped to their feet so they could not escape. The use of the connotative level is linked to the sphere of cursing, and it is essential to understand its meaning in order to understand its content.

2. 5. Metaphor

In addition to the denotative and connotative levels, it is important to underline the role of the rhetorical figure, in particular, the metaphor. The term derives from the ancient Greek: μεταφορά, from *metaphéro* which means 'to carry a meaning'. A meaning that will be richer and sometimes replaced. It can identify a character trait if it is associated with one person or something of the characteristics of another. The phrase *È un coniglio*, in fact, can mean a) herbivorous animal or b) a scared, frightened person. The metaphor can be used to express one's emotions, to charge even vulgarly with meaning and offend someone. Note the examples (3, a-b):

3) a. Sei una zucca vuota!

b. Sei una sanguisuga!

Comparing a person to one *sanguisuga* means transferring leech properties to someone specific. The leech is a common name for the species of annelids that sucks blood from other living beings. Transferring these characteristics to a person causes the description to be that of an avid person who exploits others. This is obviously a derogatory or joking definition at times.

There are many animals used in metaphors. Below are some examples (4):

4) Essere un coniglio, essere un mulo, essere un gufo, essere un manzo, essere una balena, essere una topaia, essere un topo, essere un uccel di bosco, essere una gallina, essere un porco, essere un maiale, essere una formica, essere un galletto, essere una vacca, essere un purosangue, essere uno stallone, essere una lumaca, essere una vipera, essere un farfallone...

They are sometimes used in a playful way; other times, they are more offensive. If a female is uttered the phrase *Sei una gallina!*, she will most likely be offended. If you said to a man *Sei un porco!* it would almost certainly not be taken as a compliment; in fact, it can mean a) person who eats like pigs; b) be fat; c) a slimy person, dirty.

In addition to animals, however, there are also other terms that are used to offend, such as: *merda* (*Sei una merda!*), *tappo* (*Sei un tappo!*) to underline that the person is not tall, *mozzarella* (*Sei una mozzarella!*) in which the features underlined are the clear complexion of the skin. These are just to name a few.

Using metaphor, in addition to being a very recurring rhetorical figure in literature, especially in poetry, is also a way to express emotions, such as the anger we lash out at others, loading our message with derogatory and offensive epithets.

2. 6. Cursing *grammar*

Just like with the Italian, even the indecent language has very precise rules that have to be respected. To a native Italian, the phrase *Sei un padre di puttana!* It would sound strange. Precisely because the vulgar expression fossilised and known is *Sei un figlio di puttana!* Sometimes, therefore, elements cannot be freely changed according to context or phrase. Here, too, it is important to respect grammatical rules.

Other times, however, variations are feasible. Take the expression *porca x* as an example. It can change, sometimes addressing a different term (example 5), such as:

5) *Porca vacca!*   *Porca puttana!*   *Porca troia!*   *Porza zozza!*

The adjective *porca* remains in its fixed position, but the second term can change. On the contrary, it is not possible to change position: **puttana porca! *zozza porca!*

At other times, the verb can change without affecting the vulgar meaning of the phrase (example 6, a-b):

6) a. *Prendere* per il culo   *Pigliare* per il culo

    b. *Essere* nella merda   *Stare* nella merda   *Rimanere* nella merda

As with transitive verbs, the same property is to be followed also with vulgar verbs that require the direct object; otherwise, they would be ungrammatical or could have a different meaning (example 7, a-c).

7) a. Non mi ha cagato!

b. Quello spande merda!

c. La prossima volta lo sputtano!

A noun can also have different meanings depending on the context. The masculine noun vulgar *cazzo* can have a different meaning depending on the elements accompanying it and, therefore, the context is fundamental to understanding the significance (example 8, a-d):

8) Examples — Meaning

a. Che *cazzo* vuoi? — Cosa

b. Ha parcheggiato alla *cazzo*! — Malamente

c. Non ho capito un *cazzo*! — Niente

d. Fatti i *cazzi* tuoi! — Affari

The meaning of *cazzo* in the first example cannot be substituted with others. It would be, in some cases, ungrammatical, or it would make no sense or change the meaning: **Che malamente vuoi / *Che niente vuoi / ¿Che affari vuoi?*

As an example, we can make reference to a sketch by Luciana Littizzetto as part of the programme *Che tempo che fa* dated 18/02/2018, where she begins by saying: *Altra cosa, volevo parlare del problema scopare*, leaving the conductor Fabio Fazio speechless, and clarifying immediately afterwards *Allora il problema scopare, ma non come pensi tu, Fabio!*, continuing later *Allora, il problema è il seguente: facciamo l'esperimento, dunque, facciamo che io devo scopare* (taking a broom) and showing the public that every time the dirt is collected with the broom, a little remains always on the floor (scopare, in fact, means 'to fuck' but also 'to sweep').

From a morphological point of view, even the vulgar can have affixes, such as prefixes (they are added before the word), infix (they are inserted inside the words) and suffixes (they are attached at the end). Various words / verbs/ expressions derive from the noun *cazzo*. Look at the examples (9, a-g):

9) Examples — Meaning

a. Ho fatto una *cazzata*! — Stupidata

b. *Cazzeggia* sempre tutto il giorno! — Ozia

c. Quello è un *cazzone*! — Sciocco

d. Che *cazzotto* che ho preso! — Pugno

e. Filipe è sempre *incazzoso* — Irascibile

f. È ancora *scazzato*. — Annoiato, giù di morale

g. Mo' gli faccio una *cazziata*! — Rimprovero

The same goes for other nouns. Take the noun *porco* (porcile, porcheria, porcone...); *palla* (palloso, pallone gonfiato); *culo* (culone) o *figa* (sfiga, figata) etc., as an example.

Below, the rules of word formation as diminutive or augmentative also work with some nouns (example 10, a-b):

10) a. *Cazziata   Cazziatone*

b. *Cazzata   Cazzatina*

However, *cazzone* refers to a) a person who does nothing or b) a person with a large penis.

Then look at the suffix -*ere* that is used in *puttaniere* (womaniser), a man who habitually frequents prostitutes. -*Ere* is a suffix derived from job names such as: *panettiere, infermiere, cameriere.*

To be noted then, the words composed as *leccaculo, paraculato, inculata, vaffanculo*, among others, have their own identity and autonomy.

There are also specific rules on the use of the plural (example 11, a-c):

11) a. È un *leccaculo*

b. Sono dei *leccaculo*

c. Quelle ragazze sono delle *leccaculo*

Leccaculo is an invariable masculine and feminine noun. It changes the article, the demonstrative or the articulated preposition, but the noun remains singular even in the plural. The same happens with the noun *rompipalle* or *cacasotto* whose plural is invariable (example 12, a-d):

12) a. Il mio amico è un *cacasotto*.

    b. Loro sono dei *cacasotto*.

    c. Quelle ragazze sono delle *cacasotto*.

    d. Sono dei *rompipalle*.

The noun *paraculato* (recommended) is different, which has a regular plural *paraculati/e*.

Even disparaging and offensive verbs work in the same way as regular verbs (example 13, a-d):

13) a. L'altro ieri *mi hanno infinocchiato* (infinocchiare)

    b. Ma perché *stai cazzeggiando* (cazzeggiare)

    c. Mentre guidavo *mi hanno inculato* (inculare)

    d. Li sentivo che *scopavano* nell'altra camera (scopare)

In addition, other rules must also be respected in vulgar expressions, such as the presence of certain prepositions in an expression (example 14, a-b):

14) a. *Il mio vicino di casa ha parcheggiato alla cazzo!*
    Not being able to say **in cazzo / *per cazzo*

    b. *Sono andati in culo al mondo*
    It would not be correct to say **in culo del mondo*.

Questions and exclamations must also be respected: *Che cazzo fa?* (although sometimes this may be omitted), *Che palle!*

Here are just a few examples to understand that indecent Italian, vulgar, obscene language, etc., always respond to rules that must be respected. The fact that, even behind vulgar speech, there is specific grammar regulating cursing becomes a point of study and reflection also for university students who study the Italian language, studying the various peculiarities.

2. 7. Teaching and learning the indecent language. Why?

For reasons that may seem obvious, vulgar language has been dismissed in teaching, but De Klerk adds that "how revealing use of such taboos can be of the social variables by which speakers are affected" (De Klerk, 1991: 164). One wonders why the teaching of cursing should be included in the classroom. There are, in fact, words that can block the interlocutor, that can make them feel uncomfortable. And this is normal because each of us comes from a different cultural background and uses a different language. In fact, there are five types of categories that would fall into the type of taboo words that could create embarrassment. These are expressions: *1. Supernatural, to evoke awe and fear often connected with religion 2. Bodily effluvia and organs to evoke disgust 3. Disease, death, and infirmity to evoke a sense of dread 4. Sexuality, to evoke revulsion and depravity 5. Disfavored people and groups, to evoke hatred and contempt* (Finn, 2017: 18).

Although it is evident from studies that, in general, indecent language is not present in foreign language courses and is especially not incorporated as part of the curriculum (Dewaele, 2004), various authors are interested in proposing the incorporation of indecent language in foreign language lessons (Mercury, 1995; Horan, 2013, Finn, 2017). In other courses of study, such as Law, it is normal, however, to find within the course of *Diritto Penale* the study of various articles and examples, such as the crime of insult (art. 594 of the Criminal Code, no longer a criminal offence since 2016 but a civil offence), the crime of defamation (art. 595 of the Criminal Code) or the crime of slander (art. 368 of the Criminal Code). In fact, these, although often confused, are three different types of offence and in the course mentioned above, one can study various examples to understand – through the expressions used as offences – the language and how the law works.

On the other hand, with reference to languages, the *Common European Framework of Reference for Language,* updated to 2020, clearly states that at the lexical level, an advanced level student "has a good command of a very broad lexical repertoire including idiomatic expressions and colloquialisms; shows awareness of connotative levels of meaning" (Council of Europe, 2020: 131). And indeed, vulgar language is part of the spoken language, has a dysphemistic connotation and is also part of the various idiomatic expressions also used publicly.

Certainly, international students who study Italian when they reach an advanced level know the rules well, know when to use verbal times, formulate clear and correct messages and use a rich and refined vocabulary. The deepening of the Italian language through the study of profanity is, I believe, a unique possibility that allows; therefore, the student to continue to increase their linguistic knowledge without limits or prejudices. The translator translates, the teacher teaches, and the writer writes. And going through the Italian language, it is inevitable to 'get your hands dirty' with swear words, albeit directly or indirectly. Those who work in the field of film translation, and subtitling, for example, work continuously with a rich and varied linguistic scenario and the professionalism of a translator also lies in always knowing how to operate on each project.

Mugford's direct opinion on why *Teaching impoliteness in the second-language classroom* is very useful. He argues that:

> impoliteness is part of everyday language use and L2 users need to be prepared to interact in impolite situations. Furthermore, I argue that students have the communicative right to be rude if they want to, as long as they are aware of the consequences of their actions. Teachers need to take the lead by preparing learners to communicate in pleasant, not so pleasant, and even abusive interactional and transactional situations. Preparation involves helping learners identify potentially impolite practices and offering ways of dealing with impoliteness. The alternative is to continue to ignore such issues and promote a Pollyanna EFL world (Mugford, 2008: 375).

Including a course on cursing in Italian is also useful to know which words in one language have a neutral meaning whilst in the other have a dysphemistic connotation. Think of the word *curva* (bend, curve) in Italian and the term *kurwa* in Polish, which means *shit, fuck*. Or the vulgar term *figa* to indicate the female genital organ and *figa* in Polish (nominative, singular) with the meaning of *fig*. Just pay attention to the menu of an Italian restaurant in Warsaw (*Semolino*) that offers a cocktail called *Viva la figa* (with wild turkey, Frangelico, sweet vanilla and fig): in short, the double meaning is obvious and perhaps done on purpose.

In addition to this, a course on Italian swear words is useful to understand the most varied pragmatic situations and the emotions of people; it is essential, therefore, to be able to understand that, in certain situations, they can contain unkind elements and it is important to know how to recognise them (Mugford, 2008: 382). Not to mention the sexist or offensive language that must be recognised and condemned.

Knowing a language 360º allows the student to have all the tools to be able to respond fully. These tools are also useful to gauge whether some expressions can also be used in public and, not least, to know their meaning to know if someone is being offensive. As language is a means to convey emotions, deciphering its real meaning is essential to understand the message of the speaker fully.

2. 8. Teaching materials

To learn Italian as a foreign language and a second language, there are numerous manuals and books available. Some books integrate more skills, others focus on writing or conversation, and others focus on speech or phraseology. In short, although the materials in Italian cannot be compared in quantity to those in English, Spanish or French, there is certainly a good range of choices. Unfortunately, however, there are not many teaching materials in terms of swear words, at least as far as the Italian market is concerned.

From a **theoretical** point of view, one may certainly include some books in other languages; however, in Italian, with reference to the historical aspect, one can consider: *Storia dell'insolenza. Offese, insulti e turpiloquio nella politica italiana da Cavour a Grillo* (Capurso, 2014), as well as *Elogio del turpiloquio. Letteratura, politica e parolacce* (Capuano, 2006) that refers to swearing in Italian literature, *Le parolacce di Dante Alighieri* (Sanguineti, 2021) or *Comunque anche Leopardi diceva le parolacce. L'italiano come non ve l'hanno mai raccontato* (Antonelli, 2014). The book *Insulti e pregiudizi. Discriminazione etnica e turpiloquio in film, canzoni e giornali* (Azzaro, Cohen and Malavolti, 2007) focuses on media and songs, while on sociology we recommend *Turpia. Sociologia del turpiloquio e della bestemmia* (Capuano, 2007) as well as *Parliamo di parolacce senza dire parolacce* (Cottarelli, 2018). I cannot fail to mention the bestseller *Parolacce. Parolacce. Perché le diciamo, che cosa significano, quali effetti hanno* (Tartamella, 2006), in addition to its web page, always rich in materials (www.parolacce.org). Furthermore, a book with the common sayings, *Acqua in bocca* (Bortoluzzi, 2016), can also be useful in teaching.

From a **practical** point of view, materials are scarce. There is *L'italiano indecente e colorito per studenti stranieri* (Regagliolo, 2022), which presents 10 chapters each one with a different topic: *Che cazzo fai? / Va' a cagare! / Che palle! / Che culo! / Sei un porco! / È una puttanata! / Sei una lumaca! / Siamo nella merda! / Al diavolo! / È una zucca vuota!* Each topic includes several expressions related to the title of the chapter: *Che cazzo fai*, for example, presents different expressions using the noun 'cazzo' (non c'è un cazzo, cazzata, alla cazzo, cazzatina, cazzi tuoi, 'sti cazzi, scazzato, cazzeggiare, incazzato...); while the chapter *Sei una lumaca* includes colorful expressions connected to animals (sei un farfallone, una vipera, uno stallone, una sanguisuga, mandare in vacca, essere un galletto, un uccel di bosco, among others). Each chapter also includes some linguistic exercises, readings related to the topic and a section called 'Modera il linguaggio' in which the student has to change from vulgar to standard language (thus *oggi non ho fatto un cazzo* will become *oggi non ho fatto niente / nulla*), or the student has to substitute some indecent expressions with others. The book always presents authentic materials and readings. For instance, at p. 204 we find 'La mafia è una montagna di merda'. In each chapter, there is also a section dedicated to the vulgar in the literature, in the actuality, in the cinema or in the songs. Examples in the literature are extracted from Dante, Boccaccio, and Pirandello, among others, while examples in the cinema are short screenplay elements where the vulgar language is contextualized.

It is also possible to rely on some blogs and web pages. In the latter, however, there is usually an explanation of some vulgar expressions such as, for example, learnamo.com/parolacce. The exercises are, however, few and far between, as on www.adgblog.it where you are asked to match the vulgar expressions with their definitions or to insert swearing within the sentences.

Some hints can be found in some Italian-language manuals. For example, in *Nuovo Espresso 5* di Alma Edizioni (Massei and Rosella, 2017). On page 26 of the second chapter, there is a reflection on bad language, presenting three words: *cazzo*, *fottiti* e *vaffanculo*. The three words are taken from a text by Fabio Volo, *La strada verso casa*. The student is required to find the synonyms for the three swear words.

In *Magari* (De Giuli, Gustalla, and Naddeo, 2012: 174-184), Chapter *Lingua non solo parolacce* presents some texts related to the indecent language: *Dare del 'rompic.' si può/non si può* (175), *Dire 'stro...' è non è offensivo* (176) *Il cinema e la parolac*cia (178), *Piccolo viaggio intorno alla parolaccia* (182-183), and *La direttrice le dà della 'rompipalle' e lei la denuncia* (184).

The online page lira.unistrapg.it offers a chapter titled *Quando le cose si mettono male* in which one may find the theme *Offendere, insultare e dire parolacce*. Here some activities are proposed, such as finding and recognising the offensive word in the various texts proposed or watching some videos with the transcription to reflect on the use of offensive language.

Generally, however, despite some shy approaches, vulgar language is excluded from teaching materials (Pugliese and Zanoni, 2015).

Not to be held less important, however, some collateral materials can always be used, such as linguistics manuals to understand the role of the metaphor, the meaning of denotation and connotation, but also a manual of the history of the Italian language and an etymological dictionary to respond to any doubts that may arise.

2. 9. Guidelines

To teach indecent language, Wedlock (2020: 41) proposes seven guidelines based on his personal experience. Here is a summary:

1. It is advisable to not only make the class itself an elective class but also to make each individual section/topic of the class elective.
2. I suggest allowing the students the opportunity to choose whether they wish to be instructed by a female or male teacher.
3. Introduce some historical background and interesting facts about SOTL.
4. Use prominent examples of SOTL from literature, movies, and celebrities.
5. It is advisable to explain how different lexical items have different degrees of "power" or "impact."
6. It is important to explain how certain rules that can be found within SOTL may not exist in "standard" English.
7. Using newspaper headlines and certain jokes incited the students to think more deeply about the intended meaning of the text or utterance.

Through the **L'italiano indecente** course, an optional course to its third edition that takes place at the Cardinal Stefan Wyszyński University in Warsaw and addressed to the students of the master's degree in Italian philology, other fundamental points have proved useful, including:

1. A reflection and familiarity with specific terminology.
2. Significant readings on the subject (literature, press, scripts...).
3. Reading and analysis of the content of magazines or books.
4. Watching and analysis of the content of movies, shows or video clips.
5. Examples of cursing in Italian music.
6. Exercises to check whether there was censorship of some verses of the songs, to understand how these verses were changed and why.

7. Direct and inverse translation exercises of some lines extrapolated from the original screenplay of a film.
8. Translation verification exercises from foreign language to Italian, and vice versa, to understand how the expressions were translated in the films.
9. Exercises with pragmatic situations to understand expressions in a given context.
10. Reflecting on the language through specific readings.
11. Exercises for creating various lines within a given script.
12. Linguistic register change exercises, offering three registers: Italian *gergale*, *colloquiale* and *standard letterario*.
13. Exercises on metaphor and connotation and denotation.
14. Swearing and the Italian law presenting examples of sentences through the *Corte di Cassazione* to understand which expressions have been condemned and which have not.

The aim of this course is to allow students enrolled in the specialisation in teaching and translation to be able to master the Italian language. The level required to access this course is C1 (advanced), and, speaking of an advanced level, it is necessary to be able to provide students with a linguistic range that goes beyond the Italian manual for foreigners, and that can be a starting point and metalinguistic reflection.

3. Part two: educational proposals

In this second part, various teaching activities are proposed to be put into practice in a course or in the various lessons on the teaching of indecent Italian. The proposals are varied and can be adapted and improved each time according to the working group.

3. 1. Introduction

A student studying a target language, as Husna points out, "is not immune to those swear or taboo words in the target language" (2019: 30). Therefore, it is assumed that a student who is studying Italian at an advanced level has already encountered numerous expressions and vulgar words on their own, especially through films, readings and songs. Also, it is quite unlikely to find real vulgarisms in the language manuals.

Attending a course in which the central theme is indecent language in the Italian language responds to specific needs.

A recent survey of students on the Master's Degree in Italian Philology at UKSW shows that students are interested in the course on indecent Italian for a variety of reasons.

Below is an excerpt of some student responses:

> For me studying indecent Italian is very useful for a philology student, translator or Italianist. In different thematic areas you can find various colloquial terms, swearing, but very common in everyday language. They often appear on key topics such as in media, magazines or movies. Undoubtedly, the knowledge of this variety allows us to broaden our horizons, better understand Italian culture, daily communication and prepare for the various unforeseen events that can happen to us during our stay in Italy. This knowledge can also be very important in the profession of a translator. Students of Italian philology should be specialists in the Italian language; therefore, not being familiar with an area such as vulgar Italian would be a major disadvantage.
>
> Student A, IV Year, Italian Philology

> In my opinion, it is not enough to study a foreign language only through grammar, phonetics, vocabulary, etc. We must add something more, something of culture and speech. Elements based on the use of everyday language (and not only in official writings) are an important part of the language, although often censored. Knowing the vulgar language is, in my opinion, of great value not only because it is interesting but because it shows the part of the language that we can observe by talking to mother-tongue speakers or watching a movie. Thus, we can notice swear words, derogatory words and react when necessary. Language also makes us more aware of the power of words themselves.
>
> Student B, IV Year, Italian Philology

> First of all, cursing is an integral part of the language, and to really know the language, in my opinion, you have to learn it all. This knowledge is very useful in practice. Vulgar expressions often appear in cinema and literature and, above all, in speech. How can we know, without knowing these words, if our Italian interlocutor is not insulting

us? Moreover, the degree of "indecency" of words and the situations in which they are used are very different and easy to misunderstand. It is therefore important to have the opportunity to acquire knowledge in this field in order to avoid communication problems as well.

Student C, IV Year, Italian Philology

Motivation is defined as the "enjoyment of school learning characterized by a mastery orientation; curiosity; persistence; task-endogeny; and the learning of challenging, difficult, and novel tasks" (Gottfried, 1990: 525 cited in Lai, 2011: 5) is relevant in following a course on the subject. It is counterproductive to force someone to do so, also because each of us has a sensitivity and an openness to a certain different language. It is, therefore, essential that the course is optional and requires, moreover, a minimum language level. In this regard, an advanced level is proposed for a complete course. Despite this, even at the elementary and intermediate levels, it is possible to work with original and/or adapted material.

3. 2. Terminology

Using correct terminology is essential for those who have an advanced level of a foreign language, especially at the university level. The world of vulgar language proposes, yes, even offensive and colourful expressions, but *first of all*, it is useful to understand the difference between the various groups within the indecent language, such as, for example, to understand the difference between blasphemy and sexist expressions. It is a specific lexicon that includes, in part, legal vocabulary because there are specific verbs present in criminal law, such as: defame, denigrate, violate, or other nouns such as vilification, harassment, obscenity, among others. Proposing a basic vocabulary – as guidelines – is useful and also enriches the student's vocabulary. Here is an example (15):

15)

Tipologia	**Significato**	**Esempio**
Oscenità		
Bestemmia		
Scatologico		
Sessista		
Parolaccia		
Colorito		

3. 3. Historical-Lliterary Part

In addition to an introduction, the initial part, as also underlined by Wedlock (2020), can be represented by a more historical part that makes students aware of the relevance that cursing has also had in the past. To think, in fact, that we are the only or the first to use swear words is quite wrong; it certainly remains interesting for students to start from ancient Greece and Rome. The Romans, according to what the inscriptions also attest, seemed to be true masters of obscenity and slander. Just think of Catullo and Martial, among others.

An introduction to the vulgar writings found in Pompeii could be an example (16, a-b):

16) a. **Fetida d'una puttana**, *restituisci i versetti, restituiscili tutti.*
Liber, *Carmen Proibiti*, Gaio Valerio Catullo

b. *Condanni l'immoralità tu, proprio tu, che degli efebi di Socrate sei il buco più noto?*
(Giovenale, *Satire*, Libro I)

Profanity is not new to Italian literature. In fact, it could be said that is a teacher of life. Indeed, great writers and poets of the past have given life to illustrious works even with the use of less aulic, less appropriate expressions. If we are not surprised by the great Latin authors, we will not be surprised by the Italians from the Middle Ages. Dante is an example, but with him, the queue is long (17).

17) Dante:

E mentre ch'io là giù con l'occhio cerco,
Vidi un col capo sì di **merda** lordo,
Che non parea s'era laico o cherco.

(Dante, Inferno, Canto XVIII. Verso 115-117)

18) But also, for example, Boccaccio:

Col malanno possa egli essere oggimai, se tu dei stare al fracidume delle parole di un mercantuzzo di feccia d'asino, che venutici di contado e usciti delle troiate, vestiti di romagnuolo, con le calze a campanile e con la **penna in culo**, come egli hanno tre soldi, vogliono le figliuole de' gentili uomini e delle buone donne per moglie»

(Decameron, Settima giornata).

Various Italian authors have used indecent language in their works. Think of Pietro Aretino, Giorgio Baffo, etc. A choice of some verses is a good start to justify the relevance of cursing also in the literature, as well as in the spoken language. Reading and understanding some literary texts can certainly be beneficial because, in addition to the linguistic part, students broaden their literary and cultural knowledge. One may, therefore, propose targeted research on certain Italian authors, even contemporary ones, and read some passages in class.

3. 4. The Topicality

The press is another example in which one can come across indecent language with a thousand nuances. Using texts extracted from newspapers and magazines, one can present examples and observe how cursing is presented and in what particular context. Many times, they are expressions reported by famous people and politicians. The various newspapers, in fact, also report facts and words uttered by others, both in the text of the article and in the title itself.

They can bring back the euphoric words of a singer after winning the Golden Globe, like Laura Pausini, who let slip a *porca vacca*:

> Più spontanea l'esultanza della cantante in una story postata poco dopo l'annuncio della vittoria: «Sìììììì! Aaaaah! **Porca vacca**! "Thank you"! Grazie mille, Italia», urla a squarciagola la 46enne circondata dai suoi collaboratori.
>
> Tuttich, Dario Ornaghi, 1/3/2021

In other cases, and this is very common, the words of politicians are reported. Interesting, in this regard, is the book by Antonelli *Volgare Eloquenza. Come le parole hanno paralizzato la politica* (2019), which is also reflected in the language of politicians that can also include profanity.

Sometimes the press also includes reflections on indecent language, and these can be used in class to encourage critical reflection:

> Pane al pane e vino al vino? O piuttosto uno scivolamento inesorabile, un bradisismo, qualcosa che non tiene e viene giù nelle abitudini linguistiche e di bon ton della comunicazione politica? Incominciò Sgarbi con la preside stronza e si proseguì con i giudici assassini, gli elettori coglioni, i consulenti rompicoglioni, i partner europei culattoni, i monsignori puttanieri e adesso il premier magnaccia. Vaffanculo qua e

vaffanculo là: una voluttà di turpiloquio e insulto che, come età mentale, pertiene ai neo-teenager, i maschi alle scuole medie inferiori.

> La Repubblica, Bartezzaghi Stefano 1/07/2008

These can be some of the extracts that one may propose. They are useful texts for the reader and encourage discussion and reflection on the topic, as well as being a *link* to study the Italian press and the language used in it.

Many times, however, articles report serious acts of verbal violence, hatred and vilification, including the exact words suffered by the victims. This topic is extremely sensitive because, in these episodes, the words used amplify hatred, homophobia, racism, and sexism, among others. In these cases, articles regarding people who have suffered violence – for obvious reasons –usually protect their anonymity and – in addition to the fact – make us reflect on the very violence that words can inflict, as well as physical violence. Someone said that words are stones because they hurt. Words, however, not only hurt but kill and nullify a person. They are a powerful weapon: a bullet that hits and knocks people out.

There are also many articles that are translated into other languages to ensure that they are also read by a wider audience. Think, for example, of the weekly magazine *Internazionale* (www.internazionale.it), which also contains articles translated and presented in other foreign magazines. The translation of headlines (but also of articles) is, however, a challenge. This task is much more difficult because – as Swan admits (2005: 211-212) – many times, the language used follows specific rules of that language, with syntactic structures, metaphors and a vocabulary that is, at times, difficult to translate. For example, a more unusual lexicon shorter for space issues and to attract attention and increase the dramatic impact for readers.

Sometimes, moreover, headings are modified according to the censorship policies of each newspaper. As underlined in newsassociates.co.uk:

> When it comes to newspapers publishing profanity, the supposed 'posh' papers have no qualms about exposing their readership to swear words. But their more rumbustious red top and mid-market cousins take a more conservative view.

Swear words in Italy are present "in newspapers inspired by a marked and extreme political line, even if of opposite sign, as for example the *Fatto Quotidiano* or *Libero*, which use a strongly expressive and obscure language, particularly in the lexicon" (Bonomi-Maraschio, 2017: 37).

Presenting different newspapers and comparing the various headlines and the presence of vulgarisms in some and not in others is also useful to understand the type of language adopted by the newspaper and to verify any censorship adopted.

Secondly, an example of indecent and colourful language can be found in today's **books**. A point of reflection certainly goes to the use of vulgar in the titles of books. It is known, in fact, that the heading of an article in a magazine or also the name of a book, as well as images, immediately attracts attention.

See here for some examples (19).

Author	Title	Year	Publishing house
Antonio De Francesco	*La palla al piede. Una storia del pregiudizio antimeridionale*	2012	Feltrinelli
Beppe Tosco	*Perché le donne credono nel colpo di fulmine, gli uomini **nel colpo di culo***	2012	Mondadori
Carlo Capotorto	*La strabiliante capacità di **mandare tutto a puttane***	2019	Youcanprint
Raffaella Crescenzi e Stefano Cervigni	*Chimica Organica e Biochimica.* **Cheppalle***!: Chi l'ha detto che studiare la chimica deve essere per forza **palloso**??*	2016	Autopubblicazione
Di Leccese Andrea ed Eric Cò	*La Costituzione italiana è **una cagata** pazzesca*	2013	Sovera Edizioni
Elisa Origi	*Partorire, **porca miseria**!*	2019	Hygeia Press
Emanuele Cavallaro	***In culo** alla mafia. Ignazio Cutrò, un testimone che ha cambiato le cose*	2019	Caracò
Gianfranco Zavalloni	*La pedagogia della **lumaca**. Per una scuola lenta e non violenta*	2015	Emi Editore
Gianluca Morozzi	*L'era del **porco***	2018	TEA
Giorgio Vallortigara	*Cervello di **gallina**. Visite (guidate) tra etologia e neuroscienze*	2005	Bollati Boringhieri Editore
Maria Bellonci	*Tu **vipera** gentile*	1972	Mondadori
Paolo Villaggio	*Vita, morte e miracoli di un **pezzo di merda***	2002	Mondadori

Bernardo Stamateas e Claudia Marseguerra	È facile liberarsi dei **rompipalle**	2014	TEA
Vincenzo Costantino	Chi è senza peccato non ha **un cazzo** da raccontare	2010	Marcos y Marcos

In addition to this, of course, is the reading of some steps within the book previously selected. The exercise stimulates reading and expands and gives the student the opportunity to discover new Italian authors.

With regard to articles and books, there are some activities that can be put into practice. Here are some exercises:

1. Give a colourful and impactful heading to articles so that the text is effective for the reader and can be intriguing.
2. Propose ambiguous headings in which a given word can have other meanings. Reflection on the proposed headings.
3. Analyse how censorship is treated in newspapers. For example, has the same vulgar element enunciated by a politician been taken from all the newspapers or has someone omitted it and perhaps used a euphemism?
4. Translate headlines and newspaper articles from other languages. It can also be translated using both swear words, if one tries to keep the same register, and with euphemisms.
5. Searching for books that contain a heading that incorporates profanity.

3. 5. Films and shows

Films, especially Italian comedies, are a very rich source of materials that can be proposed in the classroom, both as a real and pragmatic example, but also for the various exercises and this, and for the presence of the range of indecent expressions always contextualised, and for the various registers. In addition, films, short films and videos are very valuable tools for getting to know the various dialects, especially the Roman one, which is very present in Italian comedy. Take, for example, the comedy *Borotalco* by Carlo Verdone:

> Prete: Che state a fa'? Qua c'è gente che dorme! Questo è un convitto, non siamo al varietà! Mo ve lo dico per l'ultima volta: piantatela!

Altrimenti ve caccio via tutti e due! Quella poi la dovete leva' (riferito ad un poster con una donna). E quattro, va bene?

Marcello: Ma famme un piace'!

Sergio: **Che palle** questo!

Prete: **Che palle** lo dici a tu' padre! Intendo?

Verdone, Borotalco, 1986

The presence of swear words is very frequent and represents the speech of a specific register, even if it is not known whether certain linguistic uses were generated through the creativity of the media or if they are the result of the spontaneous speech of society (Messina, 2016: 114–115).

Theatre, however, can also offer inspiration for linguistic analysis and reflection. Especially comedy shows. Comedians such as Roberto Benigni, Checco Zelone, Ficarra and Picone, Teresa Mannino, and Anna Maria Barbera, among others, are loved by Italians, and their sketches and comedy monologues delight and make the public laugh (and reflect).

Teresa Mannino, in her latest theatrical monologues, *Terrybilmente divagante* (2010-2012), *Sono nata il ventitré* (2014-2017), and *Sento la Terra girare* (2018-2020), incorporates swear words in a fitting way in her convincing narrative, made up of anecdotes, environmental reflections and false dialogues between people[5].

From an educational point of view, there are several activities that can be carried out:

1. Looking at some scenes from a film (even if not the whole film) to understand the use of swear words within a specific context.//
2. Present various scenes from different films with the same vulgar expression and compare the various pragmatic situations, emotions and all the elements that can lead the actor to vulgarity.

It is, therefore, not only interesting but appropriate to provide various video documents that can be used to contextualise indecent Italian.

---

[5] Teleambiente (2021 December 16). Zelig, Teresa Mannino: Quando a Natale scarti i regali ti ritrovi alle spalle un'isola di plastica. Retrieved January 15, 2022, from www.youtube.com/watch?v=xAQOJTkGO_s

3. 6. Songs

Songs also play an important role in linguistic acquisition for both L1 and L2 because, as consolidated by relevant literature (Jalongo and Bromley, 1984; McCarthy, 1985, Caon, 2008; Costamagna, 2010), songs lower stress levels in students, they motivate, entertain and are easy to memorise. In addition, songs have lyrics that offer – as well as a more poetic language – also a spoken language used today (Shen, 2009), and this includes swear words. It's hard to quantify how many people use swear words in songs, but nowadays, it's pretty common.

The vulgar and obscene Aretino behind the *Sonetti Lussoriosi* of Italian music could be represented by Fabri Fibra, who already gives a *preview* of the content from the names of some of his songs: *Succhiateci ancora il cazzo, Vaffanculo scemo, Mi stai sul cazzo, Non fare la puttana, Che cazzata, Solo una botta*, to name a few. Other artists insert swear words inside their stanzas without overusing vulgar speech. Just think of the last musical festival, the Festival of Sanremo 2022, in which, on stage, several singers sang some verses that incorporated profanities: Emma sang *siamo sante o puttane*, while Mahmood and Blanco *scusa se poi mando tutto a puttane* or Dargen D'Amico *fottitene e balla, per restare a galla*. And this uncensored, considering Sanremo usually airs from 9: 00 to 1: 30. Without censorship, however, is also the programme called *Amici* that draws in 4.27% of the public between the ages of 8 and 14 and 9% between the ages of 15 and 24[6]. Tommaso's song *Solo per paura* (2021/2022 edition) is sung before the watershed and states: *E poter chiedere scusa. Se mando a puttane tutto a volte* (fuck it up). It would seem a justified vulgarism and also allowed for young people.

For the lesson, in addition to listening to and reading the song, it is important to be able to do research to understand how, when and if verses were censored, especially in a live concert and actually see how they were changed.

Lucio Dalla presents the song *Gesùbambino* (Sanremo 1971) whose title and a verse were changed:

Original	Live performance
Titolo: Gesùbambino	Titolo: 4 – 03 – 1943
e ancora adesso che **bestemmio** e bevo vino / **per i ladri e le puttane** mi chiamo Gesù Bambino	e ancora adesso che **gioco a carte** e bevo vino / **per la gente del porto** mi chiamo Gesù Bambino

---

[6] www.tvblog.it/post/35947/focus-ascolti-amici-vince-perche-e-invecchiato-il-suo-pubblico

In 1981, Luca Barbarossa sang a song at Sanremo that contained profanity, yes, but the name was changed:

Original	Live performance
Roma **puttana**	Roma **spogliata**

The vulgarity in the lyrics of Barbarossa's song, however, remains the same:

Original	Live performance
Roma **puttana**, quattro dischi, un gatto, una serata strana	Roma **puttana**, quattro dischi, un gatto, una serata strana[7]

Loredana Bertè in Sanremo (1997) sings *Luna*. Here, too, there is a linguistic change.

Original	Live performance
Vaffanculo, Luna	**Occhiali neri**, Luna

The 2006 Sanremo Festival featured Dolcenera presenting the song *Come è straordinaria la vita*. The live performance was slightly modified:

Original	Live performance
ti viene da prendere un treno, andare **affanculo**	ti viene da prendere un treno, andare **lontano**

Another change was seen with Zanicchi's song in 2022 which, together with the artistic direction, changed a verse of her lyrics because the lyrics were considered too daring:

---

[7] I magnetici anni (2018 February 20). 1981 Rai Rete 1 Sanremo 81 Luca Barbarossa (7 febbraio). Retrieved January 12, 2022, from www.youtube.com/watch?v=dSYDuJ5t6aI

Original	Live performance
*Voglio amarti, nelle braccia, **nel sudore, nella carne***	*Voglio amarti, nelle braccia, **nel calore della pelle.***

Not even the popular Måneskin have escaped censorship, having to change two verses of their song at the Eurovision Song contest of 2021:

Original	Live performance
*Vi conviene toccarvi i **coglioni***	*Vi conviene **non fare più errori***

Original	Live performance
*La gente non sa di che **cazzo** parla*	*La gente non sa di che **cosa** parla*

In addition, a further exercise is to reflect on censorship that concerns taboo issues, such as sex and drugs, among others. Here are some examples of censored verses in Sanremo.

Francesco Magni, *Voglio l'erba voglio* (1980):

Original	Live performance
Chi **si tira una pera solamente** il dì di festa	Chi **fa il gallo solamente** il dì di festa

Vasco Rossi, *Vado al Massimo* (1982):

Original	Live performance
Vado in Messico, voglio andare a vedere se come dice il droghiere, laggiù **masticano tutti foglie intere**	Vado in Messico, voglio andare a vedere se come dice il droghiere, laggiù **vanno tutti a gonfie vele**

Federico Salvatore, *Sulla porta* (1996):

Original	Live performance
Sono un diverso, mamma, un **omosessuale**	Sono un diverso, mamma, **e questo ti fa male**

In addition, it is appropriate to dwell on the moment in which the artist uses profanities. It could be a relevant point to understand if it is a 'more poetic', 'more daring' choice, or just simply reflects the use of the language at that particular time with a specific register.

3. 7. Movie translation

Regarding translation, the student must understand that translating from one language to another of a film responds to the need to find a valid semantic correspondent to the vulgarism used in the source language. Take, for example, the word *motherfucker*, which does not have an equal equivalent in Italian. In the absence of an equivalent, the student can translate using the expression *figlio di puttana*. Secondly, as the literature points out (Pavesi and Malinverno, 2000: 80), the technical aspect also is relevant. The English expression could be longer or shorter, and in dubbing, one tends to choose an alternative suitable for that particular lip movement. The choice, therefore, in the translation phase must respond to different needs[8].

Taking into account the translatological aspect, for the practical part, it is possible to propose some lines taken from a screenplay of a film in a language known to students (it can be the L1 or an, L2 or L3) and work on the translation of vulgar expressions. It will, therefore, be important to understand whether there is a valid consideration both from the point of view of meaning but also useful from a technical point of view. The translation of swear words, however, would seem more free and expressive, and sometimes the text would not require to be fully adherent to the original (Koolstra, Peeters and Spinhof, 2022), also because sometimes the use of speech in a language does not have the same value, the same sound, the same strength or meaning as in the original language.

Here is an example of a screenplay taken from *The Godfather* (1972) by Mario Puzo and Francis Ford Coppola. The student's task is to translate the lines paying attention to the vulgar part. In this precise example, the student will have to understand how to *translate smooth-talking son of-a-bitch* and *dago, guinea, wop greaseball goombahs*. The exercise can be done individually or in pairs / small groups.

---

[8] See Pavesi M., and Malinversno A. L. (2000). Uses of profanity in film translation in: Taylor C. (Ed.), "Translating Cinema." Atti Covegno (Trieste, 29-30 November 1996), Trieste, pp. 75-90.

Inglese	Italiano
WOLTZ Now listen to me, you **smooth-talking son of-a-bitch**! Let me lay it on the line for you and your boss, whoever he is. Johnny Fontane will never get that movie! I don't care how many **dago, guinea, wop greaseball goombahs** come outta the woodwork.	

The practical part can also include a reverse translation exercise: proposing lines from a film in Italian and translating them into one's own L1. This activity turns out to be more feasible, as it requires very advanced L1 skills. The following scene is taken from the film *Tre uomini e una gamba* (1997) by Aldo, Giovanni and Giacomo and Massimo Venier.

Italiano	L1
[Giacomo al telefono con Giovanni] Giovanni: Senti, le commissioni le hai fatte? Giacomo: Le ho fatte tutte, sì. Giovanni: Il vestito l'hai ritirato? Giacomo: Eh, secondo te mi sposo nudo? Giovanni: Eh... gli anelli? Giacomo: Ma **che palle che sei**! Certo che li ho ritirati gli anelli! Giovanni: Anche le scarpe? Giacomo: Le scarpe le ho ri... **Porca puttana**, le scarpe! Giovanni: Hai visto? Se non ti telefonavo io ti sposavi in ciabatte!	

The translation can be done individually or in small groups. Then, once the activity is finished, the various translations can be compared, and the proposed solutions can be discussed, including the vulgar and gergal parts.

As with songs, even in translation or subtitling, there can be censorship (Drozde and Vogule, 2008) or swear words that are left out, not so much because of technical issues or space, but precisely because they are omitted for different and other reasons.

An exercise to be carried out in class is also the analysis of the translation of the same script from the original language to Italian or from Italian to another language.

3. 8. Pragmatic situations

Context is fundamental in understanding specific vocabulary and expression and, therefore, in understanding cursing. In addition to the pragmatic context offered by the video, in which extra-linguistic elements (e.g. gestures) facilitate comprehension, in addition to the "social and psychological world in which the language user operates at any given time," (Oehs, 1979: 1- 2) also written texts can be an example of real communication. Including various pragmatic dialogues in which there is an expression that is useful for reflection and study. The teacher can offer more materials in the absence of authentic materials that are sometimes not available or available (Italian scripts, for example, are not easily found).

Note the example (20, a-c):

Example a	Example b	Example c
La **vacca** bruca l'erba.	(Le modelle) camminano così, secche che io in confronto sembro una **vacca**!	- Guarda, in questi giorni, dopo le mangiate di Natale, sembro una **vacca**!
	Mannino, *Sento la Terra girare*.	

In the above example, we find the literal meaning, which is the term *vacca* (cow) that grazes grass. In the other two, the meaning is figurative. The characteristics of the cow are associated with a person of big stature. *Cow*, however, is also a woman "*dai costumi immorali e licenziosi, in particolare, che si prostituisce (con valore fortemente spregiativo, e come ingiuria triviale)*" (Mature, 2008: 91). The context, in all cases, is fundamental. From the dialogue, *Guarda, in questi giorni, dopo le mangiate di Natale, sembro una vacca!*, one could add options (such as the exercises proposed in the manual by Zamora et al. (2006) to leave the student with the reflection on the meaning (example 21):

21) Guarda, in questi giorni, dopo le mangiate di Natale, sembro una **vacca**!

In questo contesto, *vacca* significa persona:
a. vegetariana
b. in forma
c. grassa

In addition to this, pragmatic scenes can be offered to observe how each individual student would react. Receiving an insult, being mocked, being offended as well as sometimes being punished by the law requires knowing how to deal with the situation. A useful exercise is to propose various dialogues and leave the student with a free choice on how to respond. One may also ask students not to use vulgar language but to try to react while still acting correctly.

3. 9. Language Reflection Exercises

An important note is a reflection through specific readings and scientific articles. Another issue to be addressed, for example, is certainly sexist language, whose discrimination is present both in "the use of the language and in the internal system of the language" (Biemmi, 2017). Terms like *zoccolo, squillo, uno che batte* have a precise meanings for the male: country footwear, cell phone ringtone, tennis player who serves; the female, however, changes its meaning: *una zoccola* (a prostitute), *una squillo* (a prostitute), *una che batte* (a prostitute).

As Sabatini (1987: 13) points out:

> "l'impostazione «androcentrica» della lingua [...] riflettendo una situazione sociale storicamente situabile, induce fatalmente giudizi che sminuiscono, ridimensionano e, in definitiva, penalizzano, le posizioni che la donna è venuta oggi ad occupare."

Examples are different and also include *cortigiano, un uomo con un passato, un uomo di mondo, un uomo con un protettore, gatto morto*, among others. They are taken from *Non si può più* (Bartezzaghi, 2010) and also made known by Paola Cortellesi's monologue at David di Donatello 2018[9].

---

[9] Rai (2018 March 26). Il monologo di Paola Cortellesi - David di Donatello 2018. Retrieved January 15, 2022, from www.youtube.com/watch?v=4WjhLSkXqTk

Although sexist language is not explored here, it will be important to propose one or more reflections on it.

In a course on vulgarism, one may include essays, readings and interviews on the use of offensive language that can be a source of reflection and linguistic understanding.

Some examples are as follows:

> La mafia è una montagna di merda: il ricordo di Peppino Impastato
> 9/5/2017 di Carlo Rombolà tratto da www.liberopensiero.eu
>
> Siamo coraggiose e le palle non c'entrano
> 31/10/2015 di Dana tratto da www.viaggiodasolaperche.com
>
> La provocazione. Ci siamo fatti prendere per il culo: l'Eliseo è il film di un regista cieco, il finale lo conosciamo già.
> 3/12/2015 di Maria Fioretti tratto da www.orticalab.it
>
> I maiali di Pasolini: "Porcile" tra apologo e autoritratto.
> 2008 di Marco Sabbatini tratto da Rivista svizzera delle letterature romanze.
>
> Ok, i trentenni italiani sono nella merda. Ma ora possiamo smettere di piangerci addosso?
> 4/12/2015 di Virginia W. Ricci tratto da www.vice.com

3. 10. Screenplay

An original production work that entails having proper knowledge of the indecent language is creative writing, in particular, when it comes to script writing for a film or for theatre. In addition to deciding the plot, and the title, one has to choose the different scenes and lines that the actors will say. A script is very long to write, but focusing on a specific and limited situation can be a stimulus to put swearing into practice as if one were, in effect, a screenwriter. In this case, the student must keep in mind the situations that will lead the actor to use profanities. Is there an escalation? Did an accident happen? What emotions are you experiencing? It is advisable, however, not to exaggerate the number of vulgarities, while it is always advisable to weigh the lexical choice (Douglas, 2019) (example 22).

22)   **Proposta didattica**

Titolo: La cinquecento e noi
Trama: Due amici di Roma partono con una vecchia cinquecento per andare a trovare un compagno di classe che vive a Bilbao. Il viaggio permetterà ai due amici di conoscersi di più e di affrontare nuove esilaranti avventure con sconosciuti.
Scena: Lungo la strada incontrano Filipe che a Nizza fa l'autostop. Quando i due amici si fermano, Filipe afferra lo zaino di uno di loro e fugge.
Compito: Crea delle battute che includono il prima, l'ora e il dopo del furto.

3. 11. Change of register

As we have seen previously with the scheme borrowed from Berrutto, lexicon and syntax, as well as the structure of a sentence, can change from one register to another. The change of register also entails a change from possible dysphemisms to euphemisms. In this regard, the Berruto scheme is taken up using three registers. Students can practise changing the register of some proposed phrases. It will then be interesting to see how the students have changed the sentences and compare them with each other (example 23).

23)

Standard letterario	Colloquiale	Gergale / trascurato
		Tom sta cazzeggiando come sempre.
		Ehi, bello! T'ho detto di non rompere le palle!
		Mi ha mandato a fanculo anche quel giorno!

The student here will be able to engage in a real linguistic exercise in which they will have to extract all their knowledge in order to sometimes use vocabulary and an adequate syntactic structure in the register. The teacher can, each time, choose whether to enter some vulgar or more 'nuanced' terms.

3. 12. Metaphor

Putting the metaphor into practice undoubtedly helps to play with the language by understanding its richness. Here one may propose some metaphors with the use of animals – given that they are widely used. First of all, there can be sentences or short dialogues, and students will reflect on the characteristics of the animal in relation to the content of the text itself. Sometimes, the same metaphor is also present in L1, and sometimes, however, it is completely different. The context should help to understand the metaphorical meaning to which it refers. It is also possible to present short comics with balloons. The use of images, as it is known, strengthens the text and sometimes works as a visual translator. If film clips are found, they are also very useful.

Here are some examples[10] (figures 2, a-h):

Due persone si lamentano della macchina davanti che va piano.

Una signora si sente piena dopo aver mangiato molto.

Un ragazzo non ha il coraggio di fare un tuffo in piscina perché soffre di vertigini.

Una ragazza riflette sul comportamento di un giovanotto.

---

[10] Illustrated (for this chapter) by Gaia Fredella.

Una donna si lamenta con la suocera.

Una ragazza si arrabbia con il fidanzato.

Un uomo mangia molto a una cerimonia.

Una mamma visita la stanza del figlio che studia in un'altra città.

Figure 8. 2. Metaphor

3. 13. Italian law: condemned, yes or no?

Going into the world of slander is also a way to enter the world of Italian law. A very useful research exercise is to understand if expressions have been condemned by the court as offensive and defamatory. There are several examples that students can find online.

In the cases presented here, the expression is seen in its connotative meaning. *Patata* and *finocchio* are two foods, but their dysphemistic connotation can refer to 1) a female genital organ or burning problem (as already seen) and, in the case of *finocchio,* 2) a homosexual person.

Example 1: Patata bollente

> Il Tribunale di Catania condanna a una multa di 11mila euro per diffamazione un giornalista per il suo articolo messo in prima pagina di Libero (10/2/2017) dal titolo 'Patata bollente' sulla sindaca di Roma[11].

Example 2: Finocchio

> La Corte Suprema di Cassazione, sentenza 4815 del 2019[12] condanna un dirigente per aver chiamato per anni *finocchio* un proprio dipendente[13].

On the other hand, Italian law has not condemned other terms and expressions, such as: *cazzate* (minor things) and *mi hai cagato il cazzo* (you're annoying).

Example 3: *Cazzate*

> La Cassazione con sentenza 49423/2009 assolve un trentunenne accusato di ingiuria per aver detto la frase *"Papa', andiamo via, abbiamo cose più importanti da fare che ascoltare le sue cazzate'* durante una riunione condominiale[14].

---

[11] Redazione ANSA (2021 October 5). Diffamazione Raggi, condannati a multe Feltri e Senaldi Sentenza del Tribunale di Catania, Pm aveva chiesto il carcere. Retrieved from https://www.ansa.it/sicilia/notizie/2021/10/05/diffamazione-raggi-condannati-a-multe-feltri-e-senaldi_61f84782-e203-4bc3-bf44-72b3de788b84.html

[12] La Corte Suprema di Cassazione – Sezione lavoro (2019 February 19). 04815/19. Retrieved from www.diritto-lavoro.com/wp-content/uploads/2019/02/sentenza-4815-del-2019.pdf

[13] Pietrobelli, G. (2019 February 21). Verona, chiamò per anni "finocchio" un dirigente del pastificio: condannato il figlio di Giovanni Rana, Il Fatto Quotidiano. Retrieved from https://www.ilfattoquotidiano.it/2019/02/21/verona-chiamo-per-anni-finocchio-un-dirigente-del-pastificio-condannato-il-figlio-di-giovanni-rana/4988360/

[14] Cataldi, R. (2009 December 13). Cassazione: via libera all'espressione "cazzate". E' volgare ma non offende. Retrievd from www.studiocataldi.it/articoli/7793-cassazione-via-libera-all-espressione-cazzate-e-volgare-ma-non-offende.asp

Example 4: *Mi hai cacato il cazzo*

> Con sentenza del giudice di pace di San Pietro Vernotico, in data 12 novembre 2012, G.V. era assolto dalle accuse di ingiuria, minaccia e danneggiamento in danno di M.A.M. , perché il fatto non sussiste, in relazione alla frase 'oggi mi hai cacato il cazzo, la prossima volta non suono più e rompo qualsiasi auto che trovo davanti' ed al danneggiamento dell'auto di proprietà della M. , avvenuto il giorno successivo[15].
>
> *Cassazione, sentenza n. 15710/2014*

One activity that can be proposed is the search for some expressions to understand if they have been condemned and why. The work could also take place in groups. Here is an example (24):

24)	Testo	Condanna: sì / no +	Motivo	Sentenza n.
	Mafioso			
	Puttaniere			
	Stato di merda			
	Leccaculo			

4. Conclusion

An important reflection is what teachers must do nowadays. Teaching, facilitating learning and acquiring a language in a university context is a task that requires skills but also the desire to get involved and explore, together with students, the richness of the Italian language. And that is without limits or prejudices.

A degree in philology, in the Italian language, in modern languages, in Italian Studies or in translation is the basis for several professional roles, such as teacher, researcher, translator, proof-reader, writer, and publisher, among others. Students reach an advanced level of Italian, usually a C1 or C2. Their knowledge, however, currently seems to be partly limited by the exclusion of a part of the Italian language: indecent language. Many of us might think it is

---

[15] La Corte Suprema di Cassazione – Sezione penale (2014 April 8). 15710/14. Retrieved from www.infocds.it/item.asp?IDArticolo=3239

right to leave this part of the language out. There are people who say: no, it is too strong, it is too daring! Others, on the other hand, will think that it is not morally correct.

The truth, however, is that we should see language for what it is. Language is a means. It is a means of communication. And in all this, the language, in its immense richness, operates in a different way.

Providing educational planning that respects the various levels, for example, of the *Common European Framework of Reference for Languages*, is a prerequisite for the student to progress to a higher level in the various semesters and academic years and to acquire more and more language skills. On the other hand, however, to omit an important linguistic part, especially because it is very frequent in speech and in the media and in cinema, means – in my opinion – to provide a language that is ideally clean but does not accurately reflect reality.

But to cover, cut and censor is a double-edged weapon that may seem salvific on one side and sharp on the other. Informing students about swear words does not mean teasing or taking offence during a lesson, but providing those useful tools for understanding, also independently, how to behave in the face of various events where such language will occur.

A translator who deals with subtitling will have more and more opportunities to encounter vulgar language. And the most difficult part will be to relate to these expressions and to think how best to be able to translate them in the correct way, when possible. But let us not forget the other areas, however, because, both as teachers and as educators, for example, but also simply in everyday life, when walking down a street at eleven in the evening, knowing how to recognise swearing words is not only a matter of knowing the language better and in more detail but also of being able to understand how to behave accordingly.

That said, I am aware that teaching indecent language is not always possible, depending on the sensitivity of the students and the teachers, the place, and the country, but also the pedagogical offer and the institution itself that requires mentors and teachers to propose an inclusive language. Ultimately, it is a linguistic, educational, cultural and social task of the language teacher, and he/she needs to be aware of this and decide whether and how to present it, always with the agreement of the university students and the institution.

References

Antonelli, G. (2014). *Comunque anche Leopardi diceva le parolacce. L'italiano come non ve l'hanno mai raccontato*. Mondadori.

Antonelli, G. (2019). *Volgare Eloquenza. Come le parole hanno paralizzato la politica*. Editori Laterza.

Azzaro, G., Cohen M., & Malavolti E. (2007). *Insulti e pregiudizi. Discriminazione etnica e turpiloquio in film, canzoni e giornali*. Roma: Aracne.

Bartezzaghi, S. (2010). *Non se ne può più*. Mondadori.

Bellonci, M. (1972). *Tu vipera gentile*. Mondadori.

Bertoluzzi, R. (2016). *Acqua in bocca*. Difusión.

Berruto, G. (1993). Le varietà del repertorio. In Sobrero, A. A. (Ed.), *Introduzione all'italiano contemporaneo*, (pp. 3–36). Laterza.

Biemmi, I. (2017). Il sessismo nella lingua e nei libri di testo: Una rassegna della letteratura pubblicata in Italia. In Biemmi, I. (Ed.), *Educazione sessista: Stereotipi di genere nei libri delle elementari*, (pp. 19–60). Torino: Rosenberg & Sellier.

Bonomi, I., & Maraschio, N. (2017). *L'Italiano. Conoscere e usare una lingua formidabile. Giornali, radio e tv: la lingua dei media*. Roma: GEDI, Gruppo Editoriale L'Espresso.

Caon, F. (2008). Potenzialità della canzone per l'insegnamento della lingua, della cultura e della letteratura italiana. *Cuadernos de italianistica cubana*, 9, 49–57.

Capotorto, C. (2019). *La strabiliante capacità di mandare tutto a puttane*, Youcanprint.

Capuano R. G. (2006). *Elogio del turpiloquio. Letteratura, politica e parolacce*. Stampa Alternativa.

Capuano R. G. (2007). *Turpia. Sociologia del turpiloquio e della bestemmia*. Costa & Nolan Edizione.

Capurso, A. (2014). *Offese, insulti e turpiloquio nella politica italiana da Cavour a Grillo*. Il settimo libro.

Cavallaro, E. (2019). *In culo alla mafia. Ignazio Cutrò, un testimone che ha cambiato le cose*. Caracò.

Claire, E. (1980). *A foreign student's guide to dangerous English*. Rochelle Park, NY: Eardley Publications.

Costamagna, L. (2010). *L'italiano con le canzoni*. Perugia: Guerra Edizioni.

Costantino, V. (2010). *Chi è senza peccato non ha un cazzo da raccontare*. Marcos y Marcos.

Cottarelli, M. (2018). *Parliamo di parolacce senza dire parolacce*. Pascal.

Council of Europe (2020). *Common European Framework of Reference for Languages: Learning, teaching, assessment – Companion volume*. Strasbourg: Council of Europe Publishing.

Crescenzi, R., & Cervigni, S. (2016). *Chimica Organica e Biochimica. Cheppalle!: Chi l'ha detto che studiare la chimica deve essere per forza palloso??*. CreateSpace Independent Publishing Platform.

De Francesco, A. (2012). *La palla al piede. Una storia del pregiudizio antimeridionale.* Feltrinelli.

De Giuli, A. Gustalla, C., & Naddeo, C. M. (2012): *Magari B1/C1.* Firenze: Alma Edizioni.

De Klerk, V. (1991). Expletives: Men only? *Communication Monographs,* 58, 156–169.

Dewaele, J. (2006). Expressing anger in multiple languages. In Pavlenko, A. (Ed.), *Bilingual Education and Bilingualism,* (pp. 118–151). Clevedon: Multilingual Matters LTD.

Di Leccese, A., & Cò, E. (2013). *La Costituzione italiana è una cagata pazzesca.* Sovera Edizioni.

Dougan, D. (2019). *Creative Writing 1 Scriptwriting.* Open College of the Arts.

Drozde, L., & Vogule, G. (2008). *Censorship in Translation of Taboo Words.* Leiden: Koninklijke Brill.

Finn, E. (2017). Swearing: The Good, the Bad & the Ugly. *ORTESOL Journal,* 34, 17–26.

Foote, R., Woodward, J. (1973). A preliminary investigation of obscene language. *Journal of Psychology,* 83, 263–275.

Gawinkowska, M., Paradowski, M. B., & Bilewicz M. (2013): Second Language as an Exemptor from Sociocultural Norms. Emotion-Related Language Choice Revisited. *Plos ONE,* 8 (12). Retrieved from https://journals.plos.org/plosone/article?id=10.1371/journal.pone.0081225

Gottfried, A. E. (1990). Academic intrinsic motivation in young elementary school children. *Journal of Educational Psychology,* 82(3), 525–538.

Horan, G. (2013). 'You taught me language; and my profit on't/Is, I know how to curse': cursing and swearing in foreign language learning. *Language and Intercultural Communication,* 13(3), 283–297. Retrieved from https://www.frontiersin.org/articles/10.3389/fpsyg.2015.00444/full

Husna, N. (2019). University Students' Perception in Using English Swear Words. *Advances in Social Science, Education and Humanities Research* - 2nd International Conference on Islam, Science and Technology (ICONIST 2019), 408, 29–34. Atlantis Press.

Jakobson, R. (1960): Linguistics and Poetics. in Sebeok T. (Ed.), *Style in Language,* (pp. 350–377). Cambridge, MA: M.I.T. Press.

Jalongo, M. & Bromley, K. (1984). Developing linguistic competence through song. *Reading Teacher,* 37(9), 840–845.

Janschewitz, K. (2008). Taboo, emotionally-valenced, and emotionally-neutral word norms. *Behaviour Research Methos, Instruments, & Computers,* 40, 1065–1074.

Jay, T. & Jay, K. (2013). A Child's Garden of Curses: A Gender, Historical, and Age-Related Evaluation of the Taboo Lexicon, *The American Journal of Psychology,* 126(4), 459–475.

Jay, T. (2000). *Why we course. A neuro-psycho-social theory of speech.* Philadelphia: John Benjamins.

Jay, T. (2005). American women, their coursing habits and religiosity. In Jule, A. (Ed.), *Women, religion, and language,* (pp. 63–84). New York: Palgrave-Macmillian.

Koolstra, C. M, Peeters, A. L., & Spinhof, H. (2002). The Pros and Cons of Dubbing and Subtitling. *European Journal of Communication.* 17(3), 325–354.

Lai, E. R. (2011). *Motivation: A Literature Review Research Report.* Pearson.

Lenel, O. (1907). *Edictum Perpetuum.* Leipzig: Verlag Von Bernhard Tauchnitz.

Lindquist, K. A., MacCormack, J. K., & Shablack, H. (2015). The role of language in emotion: predictions from psychological constructionism. *Frontiers in Psychology,* 6, 1–17.

Luyken, G. M., Reid, H., & Herbst, T. (1995). The semantics of audiovisual language transfer. in *Libri e riviste d'Italia. La traduzione. Saggi e documenti (II),* (pp. 267–279). Istituto poligrafico e Zecca dello Stato, Ministero per i beni culturali e ambientali.

Massei, G., & Bellagamba, R. (2017). *Nuovo Espresso 5.* Alma Edizioni.

Matura, A. (2008). Motivazioni storiche e socio-culturali dell'uso dei nomi degli animali domestici nelle espressioni italiane, francesi e spagnole che riguardano l'amore. *Romanica Cracoviensia,* 8 (1), 70–99.

McCarthy, W. (1985). Promoting language development through music. *Academic Therapy,* 21(2), 237–242.

McEnery, T. (2006). *Swearing in English: Bad language, purity and power from 1586 to the present.* New York, NY: Routledge.

McGuinness, R. (2013 April 2). Why the **** do we swear all the time? Metro. Associated Newspapers Limited. Retrieved from https://metro.co.uk/2013/04/02/you-why-the-do-we-swear-all-the-time-3563858/

Mercury, R. E. (1995). Swearing: A "bad" part of language; A good part of language learning. *TESL Canada Journal,* 13(1), 28–36.

Messina, S. (2017): Quando lo schermo racconta: rapporti linguistici tra cinema e televisione. In Rossi, F., & Patota G. (Ed.), *Lingue e linguaggi del cinema in Italia* (pp. 101–116). Aracne editrice.

Morozzi, G. (2018). *L'era del porco.* TEA.

Mugford, G. (2008). How rude! Teaching impoliteness in the second-language classroom. *ELT Journal,* 62(4), 375–384.

Ochs, E. (1979). Introduction: What Child Language Can Contribute to Pragmatics. In Ochs, E. & Schieffelin, B. B. (Eds), *Developmental Pragmatics.* New York: Academic Press.

Origi, E. (2019). *Partorire, porca miseria!* Hygeia Press.

Pavesi, M., & Malinverno, A. L. (2000). Usi del turpiloquio nella traduzione filmica. In Taylor C. (Ed.), *Tradurre il cinema. Atti Covegno* (Trieste, 29-30 novembre 1996), (pp. 75–90). Trieste: Dipartimento di Scienze del Linguaggio.

Pinker, S. (2007). *The staff of thought. Language as a window into human nature.* Viking Pinguin.

Pugliese, R., & Zanoni, G. (2015 November 12–13) Keynote addresses on La scortesia linguistica? Scelte didattiche in un approccio pragmatico all'italiano L2. Standard and variation in second language education: A cross-linguistic perspective Conference, Università di Roma Tre.

Regagliolo, A. (2022): *L'italiano indecente e colorito per studenti stranieri.* Torino: Ledizioni.

Sabatini, F. (1987). Più che una prefazione. In Sabatini, A. (Ed.), *Raccomandazioni per un uso non sessista della lingua italiana* (pp. 13-22). Roma, Presidenza del Consiglio dei Ministri.

Sanguineti, F. (2021). *Le parolacce di Dante Alighieri*. Tempesta Editore.

Shea, C. (2009). Using English songs: An enjoyable and effective approach to Elt. *English language teaching*, 2(1), 88–94.

Stamateas, B., & Marseguerra, C. (2014). *È facile liberarsi dei rompipalle*. TEA

Swan, M. (2005). *Practical English Usage* (3rd ed.). Oxford: Oxford University Press.

Tartamella, V. (2006). *Parolacce. Perché le diciamo, che cosa significano, quali effetti hanno.* Rizzoli.

Tosco, B. (2012). *Perché le donne credono nel colpo di fulmine, gli uomini nel colpo di culo.* Mondadori.

Vallortigara, G. (2005). *Cervello di gallina. Visite (guidate) tra etologia e neuroscienze*. Bollati Boringhieri Editore.

Varrone, A. (2002): *Erotica Pompeiana: Love Inscriptions on the Walls of Pompeii*. (Berg R. P. trans). Roma: «L'ERMA» Di Bretschneider.

Villaggio, P. (2002). *Vita, morte e miracoli di un pezzo di merda*. Mondadori.

Wedlock, J. (2020). Teaching about Taboo Language in EFL/ESL Classes: A Starting Point. *ORTESOL Journal*, 37, 33–47.

Williamsson, J. (2009): *How Brits Swear The use of swearwords in modern British English*. Mid Sweden University.

Zamora, P., Alessandro, A., Ioppoli, E., & Simone, F. (2006). *Hai voluto la bicicletta...: esercizi su fraseologia e segnali discorsivi per studenti di italiano LS/L2*. Guerra Edizioni.

Zangemeister, K., & Schöne, R. (Eds). (1871). *Corpus inscriptionum Latinarum Vol. 4: Inscriptiones parietariae Pompeianae*. Berolini: Apud Georgium Reimerum.

Zavalloni, G. (2015). *La pedagogia della lumaca. Per una scuola lenta e non violenta.* Emi Editore.

Web references

ADGBLOG Italiano L2 / Ls (2022). L'italiano con le parolacce. Retrieved January 15, 2022, from www.adgblog.it/2011/10/01/litaliano-con-le-parolacce/

Cataldi, R. (2009 December 13). Cassazione: via libera all'espressione "cazzate". E' volgare ma non offende. Retrievd from www.studiocataldi.it/articoli/7793-cassazione-via-libera-all-espressione-cazzate-e-volgare-ma-non-offende.asp

I magnetici anni (2018 February 20). 1981 Rai Rete 1 Sanremo 81 Luca Barbarossa (7 febbraio). Retrieved January 12, 2022, from www.youtube.com/watch?v=dSYDuJ5t6aI

IIF - Italian International Film (2015 February 9). Viva l'Italia, Scena divertente – Clip ufficiale. [Youtube video]. Retrieved January 15, 2022, from www.youtube.com/watch?v=roab3pmHgZo.

La Corte Suprema di Cassazione – Sezione lavoro (2019 February 19). 04815/19. Retrieved from www.diritto-lavoro.com/wp-content/uploads/2019/02/sentenza-4815-del-2019.pdf

La Corte Suprema di Cassazione – Sezione penale (2014 April 8). 15710/14. Retrieved from www.infocds.it/item.asp?IDArticolo=3239

Parolacce. Retreived 8 November, 2021, www.parolacce.org

Pietrobelli, G. (2019 February 21). Verona, chiamò per anni "finocchio" un dirigente del pastificio: condannato il figlio di Giovanni Rana, Il Fatto Quotidiano. Retrieved from https://www.ilfattoquotidiano.it/2019/02/21/verona-chiamo-per-anni-finocchio-un-dirigente-del-pastificio-condannato-il-figlio-di-giovanni-rana/4988360/

Rai (2018 February 18). Luciana Littizzetto - Il problema di spazzare e i nomi delle vie - Che tempo che fa. [Youtube video]. Retrieved January 15, 2022, from www.youtube.com/watch?v=jy5VXTTU-p8

Rai (2018 March 26). Il monologo di Paola Cortellesi - David di Donatello 2018. Retrieved January 15, 2022, from www.youtube.com/watch?v=4WjhLSkXqTk

Redazione ANSA (2021 October 5). Diffamazione Raggi, condannati a multe Feltri e Senaldi Sentenza del Tribunale di Catania, Pm aveva chiesto il carcere. Retrieved from https://www.ansa.it/sicilia/notizie/2021/10/05/diffamazione-raggi-condannati-a-multe-feltri-e-senaldi_61f84782-e203-4bc3-bf44-72b3de788b84.html

Teleambiente (2021 December 16). Zelig, Teresa Mannino: Quando a Natale scarti i regali ti ritrovi alle spalle un'isola di plastica. Retrieved January 15, 2022, from www.youtube.com/watch?v=xAQOJTkGO_s

TVblog (2012 May 19). Focus Ascolti – Amici vince perché è invecchiato il suo pubblico. Retrieved January 15, 2022, from www.tvblog.it/post/35947/focus-ascolti-amici-vince-perche-e-invecchiato-il-suo-pubblico

Part II.
Italian through projects and case-studies

Chapter 9

Teaching specialist language skills in Italian through History of Art

Cinzia Bacilieri
University of York

Abstract: The paper will describe the challenges of developing specialist language skills for students of History of Art and Italian language through Italian for Art Historians. The paper will illustrate the experimental initiatives that provide the key to facilitating the acquisition of specialist skills essential to the History of Art discipline for complete beginner-level students. The first part will illustrate the historical context of setting up this interdisciplinary content-based language module and the challenges faced by the language teacher when planning and delivering a course that has to be fully integrated into an undergraduate degree programme. The second part of the paper will present examples of selected case-studies, teaching material and classroom activities to illustrate the deep impact that the interdisciplinary nature of the courses has on the students' engagement and learning.

Keywords: History of Art, *Italian for Art Historians*, Italian, Teaching, Specialist language

***

1. Introduction

The study of foreign languages – taken as an elective or discovery module, or on an extra-curricular basis – has widely been recognised as one of the key subjects used to boost student's employability skills and enhance internationalisation programmes across the Higher Education sector in the UK (Corradini, Borthwick and Gallagher-Brett, 2016; University of York, 2020a and 2020b; University of York, 2020-2030). The 2019-2020 'Survey of Institution-Wide Language Provision in universities in the UK' (AULC-UCML, 2020) identifies that courses classified as 'Languages for Specific Purposes' (LSP) represent 30% of the language provision and approximately 10% of their student enrolments. In the context of the Institution-Wide Language Provision – also known in some British universities as Languages for All (LFA) – the majority of the LSP courses fall under distinctive key areas of expertise, such as 'skills-based and academic' (45%), 'discipline specific' (40%) and 'vocational' (28%), with some crossover between the three categories. They also seem to pivot around six disciplines, with Arts and Humanities (50%), Medicine (about 40%) and Business (33%) as the most predominant ones, followed by Social Sciences, Physical Sciences & Engineering and Law. It is important to note that the teaching of LSP-related skills also tends to be embedded into general language courses; therefore, bespoke courses focusing entirely on LSP represent a distinct minority.

For almost two decades, the Department of History of Art (HoA) at the University of York has been offering its students the opportunity to study Italian ab-initio through the media of Art by aiming to enhance students' academic and employability skills through LSP. The LSP programme in HoA started as an initial five-year-long trial period (2004-2009), where the department offered its students the possibility to take on an extracurricular basis *Italian, Reading Skills for Art Historians* (Bacilieri, 2014). The popularity of the course among students led to the decision to offer the course in 2010 as an accredited optional module embedded into the first year of the BA in History of Art. Reflecting on students' feedback analysis and teaching practices, at the time of the accreditation process, it was decided to transform the existing course into a newly designed pioneering four-skills LSP course called *Italian for Art Historians* (Bacilieri 2018). The latter is currently still offered as a 20-credit-bearing module by BA History of Art single- and joint-honours students (between 90-95% of the cohort) and on an extracurricular basis to other undergraduate or postgraduate students (approximately 5% of the cohort). As a matter of fact, it is important to add that during the trial period, French and German were also offered alongside Italian in the *Reading Skills for Art Historians* provision. However, during the accreditation process, it was decided to keep only Italian as the language, this being the highest recruiting LSP language in HoA.

Both *Italian Reading Skills for Art Historians* and *Italian for Art Historians* were created by the Department of Language and Linguistic Science (L&LS) and, respectively, were or are delivered through its LFA programme. The establishment and development of Art-related LSP courses in York are testimony of a long-lasting collaboration between the two departments and, in particular, the joint effort between art historians in HoA and an LSP specialist in L&LS with a background in Italian Art and Archaeology (Bacilieri, 2018; Bacilieri, in press). The continuing popularity of the module among HoA students over the years has been a contributing factor towards the proposal of a new joint-honours BA in Languages and History of Art between L&LS and HoA (which is due to start in the academic year 2023-2024). It is important to add that the popularity of Italian in HoA is extremely exceptional as Italian is by large not the most popular language of choice among modern foreign language students (Kelly, 2016; AULC-UCML, 2020; internal L&LS and LFA statistics 2012-2022).

2. Teaching Italian through History of Art

The common association between Italian language and Art and Humanities studies is well known and is primarily due to the fact that Italy – through its history, language and culture – has been strongly intertwined long relationship with the History of Art since 1400 when Florence was first described as 'the cradle of the Renaissance'. From the seventeenth to early nineteenth century, Italy was the key destination of the aristocracy's traditional trip through Europe called the 'Grand Tour', and the country is currently home to the largest number of UNESCO world heritage sites in the world (UNESCO 2022), to name a few.

Since its establishment in 2010, *Italian for Art Historians* has been consistently the language module choice of the majority (60-85%) of HoA undergraduates who chose to embed a language in their studies. The module also has a proven record of high 'End of the Year Module Evaluation' students' satisfaction scores, routinely ranging between 4.5-4.9 out of 5 (internal LFA statistics 2012-2022). One of the reasons for its success is undoubtedly the fact that, in addition to the proven correlation between the Italian language and culture and the History of Art as a discipline, a number of research staff in HoA specialise in Italian Art, and they are also fluent Italian speakers. As a result, the department is not only committed to embed languages into its programme to boost students' employability skills but also has a keen interest in LSP and Italian language to maximise students' engagement with other modules in the undergraduate and postgraduate studies. Furthermore, students in the BA can choose the pathway 'with a year abroad', with some of the most famous Italian 'Cities of Art' being, as expected, a very popular destinations for the placement.

Finally, the module has been created and developed by an Italian language specialist with first-hand research and professional experience in the LSP-related subject of the course, Art and Archaeology, and a proven record of publications in the field of LSP methodology in Art and Humanities. The background of expertise revolving around the curricula design of Italian for Art Historians is absolutely unique in the field of LSP teaching and represents one of the key factors of the effectiveness of the teaching and learning, as well as the popularity of the module (Bacilieri, 2018; Bacilieri, in press).

With regard to the *Italian for Art Historians* cohort, although the course is designed for complete ab-initio and, in particular first-time language learners, between 50-57% of the students enrolled on the course have previously studied a different language at GCSE or AS/A level. LFA Students' feedback analysis (2012–22) demonstrates that instead of furthering their existing foreign language skills by continuing to study the previous language, many students seem to have chosen to take up Italian purposely because of the specificity of the LSP nature of the course, thus its relation to the History of Art discipline.

Examples of recent undergraduate students' module evaluation feedback comments (2020 was not collected, due to the pandemic) highlight the value and enjoyment gained from the course:

- I have loved this course; I hope to carry on Italian for Art Historians 2 next year (2019).

- I think the bespoke nature of the course is great because we are Art Historians, so it is good to have this class directly involved with our other studies (2021).

- I actually like learning the language and want to continue it, which is very different to how I have felt learning languages before (2021).

- One part has lacked clarity from the HoA department; it is whether we will be able to continue this course next year, especially for those wanting to take a year abroad in the third year (2021).

- I have enjoyed learning Italian this year, and I found the involvement of art history very interesting and useful (2022).

It is important to note that, despite a consistent students module evaluation and satisfaction's high scores – with comments showing a grown interest in Italian and a willingness to deepen their knowledge of the language through a continuation course – only 30-40% of each *Italian for Art Historians* cohort usually enrol in the general *LFA Italian Level 2* course in the following year. At present, *Italian for Art Historians* is only offered at Level 1 for one year only, with no follow-up course at a higher level. Students' feedback comments have consistently shown that the LSP character of the course is at the core of their learning motivation factors because it is perceived as being extremely useful for further Art-related studies or for a future career as an art historian. As a result, it can be argued that the low intake of HoA students continuing to study Italian in York can be explained by the fact that general language courses are perceived by ex-LSP students as not as useful or career-driven.

Italian for Art Historians was purposely created and specifically developed for Year 1 undergraduates but in response to requests by HoA postgraduate students working on Italian Art studies, the course is currently offered to postgraduates on an extracurricular basis. The majority of postgraduates enrolled in the course tend to have prior knowledge of the Italian language, ranging from A1-A2, according to the language proficiency classification by the Council of Europe's Common European Framework (CEFR) (Council of Europe, 1998). This said, they still represent a distinctive minority in the cohort (5%). The low intake can probably be explained by the financial costs and the fact the course starts from an ab-initio level: postgraduates in HoA have to self-fund their studies and, due to its bespoke nature, *Italian for Art Historians* is considerably more expensive than general Italian language courses offered in the LFA provision.

Examples of recent postgraduate students' module evaluation feedback comments illustrating the usefulness of the course:

- I found all materials we used for this module were very close to the art history field, we used primary and secondary sources in relation to Italian arts (2018).

- My research focuses on Renaissance Italian art, and most of the reading materials were concentrated on old Italian masters' works, thus very useful for me (2018).

- I found the course useful because it clarified the pronunciation rules for the myriad art terms originating in Italian. It weighed on my application for summer volunteering at Castle Howard because the house owns a collection of Italian paintings from various eras and genres, as well as hardstone Italian cabinets and other furnishings. Visitors to the house come from all over the world, and it was important to describe exhibits with their proper names. Familiarity with the foundations of the language also encouraged me to approach resources in Italian in my own research. With its dual focus on linguistic and art-historical skills, I think the course could be successfully developed past stage one. (2021)

- I decided to take *Italian for Art Historians* on an extracurricular basis because I have always been interested in languages. During the seminars, we learned the most basic phrases and sentences that you would need for describing a piece of art; meanwhile, we also touched on similar important topics, such as ordering a coffee when you are on holiday in Italy! With the competence I have gained from the *Italian for Art Historians* language course, I am going to have an addition to my CV that will boost my employability and provide better prosperity when searching for a job. (2022)

3. Curricula design: embedding general language skills in a specialist language course

Published work on methodology related to the teaching of Italian through the media of Art has been surfacing only in the last decade or so (Gobbis and Paoli Legler, 2012; Bacilieri 2018; Bacilieri, in press) with also the appearance of purposely designed textbooks such as *L'Italiano attraverso la storia dell'arte* (Angelino and Ballarin, 2006), *Percorsi italiani: L'Italia dell'arte* (Magnatti and Massei, 2016), *L'italiano dell'arte* (Andriuzzi, 2017), *L'Italiano per L'arte* (Porreca, 2020), *Parliamo di arte* (Garelli, 2020), and comprehensive online teaching resources related to Italian through Art (Accademia del Giglio, 2013).

Most of the existing volumes are clearly meant to be used a) as a subsidiary material for general Italian language courses with an LSP component, or b) as a main resource for an Art and Humanities-related LSP course. Their target audience is that quite proficient users of the language, i.e. upper intermediate/advanced students ranging between B1-C1 CEFR. The same level of a student's language proficiency is expected for other existing online teaching material related to Italian through Art (Accademia del Giglio, 2013). In addition, the majority of the teaching material appears to focus almost entirely on a) the acquisition of specialist vocabulary (such as colours and shades, painting techniques etc.) or b) the development of reading comprehension skills through artist biographies or descriptions of the most famous artworks for each period. It is true that an experienced teacher could still make use of some of the material and adopt it for lower-level teaching, but classroom activities could not rely entirely on these sources for students below the B1 CEFR level. Furthermore, in most of the existing Art-related language teaching material, the very little emphasis seems to be placed on speaking and almost none on the listening component, resulting in very poor development of a student's communicative skills, a vital component of the language learning process for ab-initio students. This is no surprise if we consider that, historically, in LSP teaching, there has always been an emphasis or, at times, even a unique focus on the traditionally called 'passive skills, such as writing and reading, more than working on the development of an all-round set of language skills. This is particularly noticeable in subjects such as

English for academic purposes (Hutchinson and Waters, 1987; Hyland, 2002). It can be argued that a teaching approach focused on the enhancement of specific skills, such as, for instance, reading comprehension or translation, can be really effective in language learning at a proficiency level. However, such a methodology can be highly ineffective when teaching ab-initio students, as it would mean that they will not acquire all the language skills necessary to become 'functional' users of the target language.

In York, the issue of teaching a course whose syllabus was not conducive to the development of an all-round set of language skills was already felt during the first pilot *Italian Reading Skills for Art Historians*. As did many contemporary LSP courses, its syllabus focused primarily on exercises aiming to develop reading, translation and summarising skills on the topic of Italian History of Art. As a result, communicative competence was completely left out of the curriculum, on the principle that both speaking and listening were deemed as not as important for a career of an art historian as, at the time, the students' career-focus was totally biased towards History of Art and not modern languages. Consequently, students who completed the course developed excellent reading comprehension skills and an ability to identify cognates and specialist vocabulary at a high level. Yet, due to the selectiveness of the set of skills developed, they were unable to perform simple tasks such as ordering a coffee at the bar, asking for directions or buying tickets at the train station in Italy.

Reflecting on student's needs, it was felt that the acquisition of almost exclusively reading and writing skills was quite restrictive for ab-initio learners: because it would not provide the all-round language learning experience needed for students wanting to spend a year abroad or conducting research in Italy (Bacilieri, 2018; Bacilieri, in press). Furthermore, the course was specifically designed with a length of 19 weeks, and the lack of basic communicative skills represented a big barrier for students who wanted to improve their Italian further by switching to the general LFA Italian Level 2 course in the following year. Even though students' reading skills were noticeably higher (B1 CEFR) than those who had completed a general *LFA Italian Level 1* course (A1-A2 CEFR), their lack of speaking and listening skills would make the switch from a specialist to a general language course extremely disadvantageous.

During the process of designing the curriculum for *Italian for Art Historians*, particular attention was therefore given to the creation of a pioneering syllabus aimed at enabling future art historians to interact and communicate effectively in the target language (Bacilieri, 2018). For this reason, instead of focusing solely on Art-related written sources, emphasis was given to the development of language competences needed for a) carrying out research in

Italian archives, museums or art galleries, b) successfully applying for and completing a Year Abroad placement in Italy c) easily transitioning from a specialist language course into a general language course. Speaking and listening skills were therefore included alongside reading and writing skills, with also a distinctive split between specialist material relevant to the History of Art discipline and general material relevant to real-life in Italy for developing intercultural competences.

Finally, all the content-integrated and specialist component of *Italian for Art Historians* was designed to boost students' employability skills with practical exercise useful for a future career in a History of Art-related field. Even more, to maximise the accreditation, essential crossover points with the existing BA Programme were identified and included in the course. As a result, the new syllabus featured exercises pivoting around monuments and archaeological sites, artists' biographies and related artworks, translations and art critical analysis, which also appeared in other modules in the BA. This was achieved thanks to a collaborative approach between lecturers in HoA with native or near-native knowledge of Italian and the language specialist.

4. Applied teaching methodology

Italian for Art Historians is specifically designed for ab-initio students of Italian who might not be particularly strong linguists as their main academic discipline differs from language studies. In particular, the developed teaching methodology purposely aims to facilitate first-time language learners with the language acquisition process since they represent a high percentage of the cohort.

Despite the fact that the course's starting point is that of absolute beginners-level, from day one, teaching material pitched at a more advanced level is used for the specialist component. For this reason, an experimental LSP teaching methodology has been developed for the course pivoting between two key elements (Bacilieri 2018). On one side, general language teaching – with material from A1 CEFR upwards on a progressive path – and on the other, the acquisition of specialist language knowledge through material more suitable for an advanced level (B2-C1 CEFR). This is because the latter level is considered more similar to that of original sources and authentic material found in the History of Art, thus being more 'realistic'.

Although many classroom activities are purposely designed around material related to the History of Art to develop the four language skills (listening, writing, reading and speaking), in the first half of the course, there is a distinctive split between the class time spent on general language learning (30%) and specialist language learning (70%). At this stage, the specialist component revolves around the development of language skills similar to traditional LSP courses, i.e. the development of grammar knowledge, vocabulary and reading & writing skills (Fig. 9. 1.).

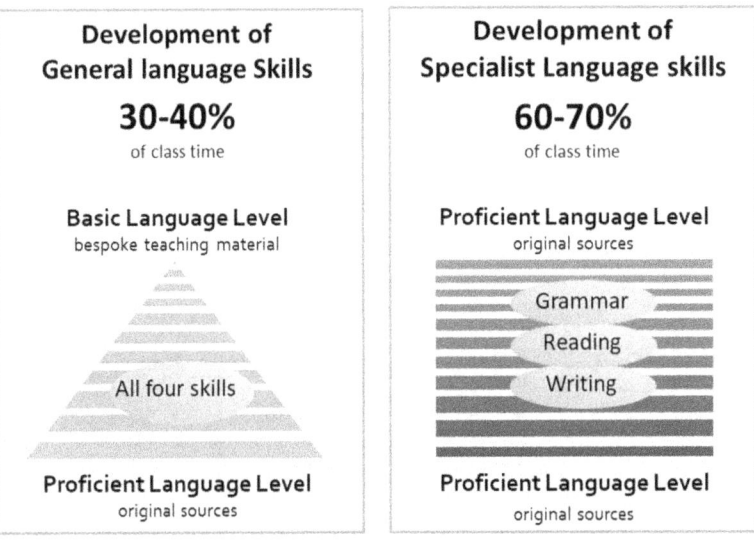

Figure 9. 1. The split between class time spent on the development of specialist and non-specialist language skills in the first half of the course

The time spent between specialist and non-specialist language skills can be adjusted depending on the lesson's needs and as the course progresses, as shown in Fig. 9. 2. In fact, as the students' language competence improves, the general language component embedded in each lesson gradually broadens and reaches 40-50% of the class time. This is because the lesson can now include activities revolving around topics such as ordering at the café of a museum or describing past activities done during a hypothetical trip to famous Italian cities of art. At the same time, the skill set of the specialist language component expands by adding speaking and listening skills with bespoke exercises aimed to boost employability skills, such as describing a work of art, as an art historian would do, or buying a ticket at an art gallery.

With regard to the teaching methodology, the progressive language-learning path (pitched at A1-A2 CEFR) for the development of general language structures and communication competence mirrors that of a general language course (Bacilieri, 2018). As noted above, in the first half of the course, the general language component covers not more than 30-40% of each class time and focuses primarily on the developing of communicative skills and intercultural competence in real-life situations (for instance, topics such as providing personal information, enquiring about jobs and occupations, describing the family etc.). This split between general language teaching and a core component of specialist language teaching is perceived as being extremely beneficial for the learner (Bacilieri, in press) (fig. 9. 2.).

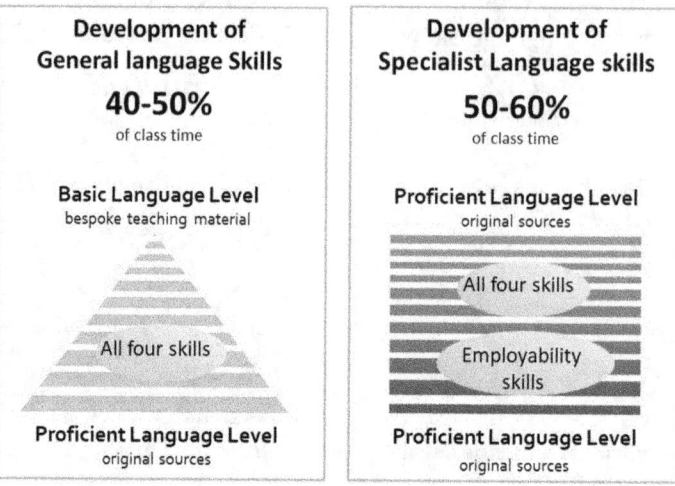

Figure 9. 2. Split between class time spent on development of specialist and non-specialist skills in the second part of the course

Undoubtedly, the progressive learning approach of the general language component, similar to that of a beginner-level Italian class, helps students to use the language in context actively and not focus only on more 'passive' activities, such as reading a biography of an artist. The analysis of students' feedback indicates that the development of general language skills seems to be consistently a pivotal motivation factor in the learning process. By gaining familiarity with a number of real-life scenarios that might be used during a trip to Italy, students learn to produce increasingly more elaborate conversation patterns as the course progresses. This progression in the development of intercultural competence and communication is a great tool to help students to recognise progress with their learning.

5. Examples of classroom activities

In the beginning, the majority of the teaching time is spent on developing specialist language skills through History of Art-related material. The general language teaching is based on material that progressively increases in complexity (A1-A2 CEFR), with a focus on communication, whilst the specialist component is deployed through original sources or advanced material from the outset, at B1-B2 CEFR from the start. However, descriptive critique of art and technical vocabulary skills are developed through purposely created material or original material used in the discipline. For instance, in the early stages, simple vocabulary, grammar and language patterns are used to encourage students to actively describe paintings such as *Il Compianto sul Cristo morto* by Giotto (Fig. 9. 3.).

Descrivere un dipinto

☐ *Writing, Speaking and vocabulary practice*

Search the following nouns and adjectives in the dictionary then choose the appropriate ones in relation to *Il Compianto sul Cristo morto* by Giotto.

1. Bidimensionale
2. Realismo
3. Architettura
4. Luce
5. Rilievo
6. Storicità
7. Tridimensionale
8. Fantasia
9. Bianco e nero

Now, using the characters below, create sentences to describe the painting by Giotto
Esempio: A *sinistra c'è Cristo.*
1. Cristo
2. La Madonna / la Vergine
3. Maria Maddalena
4. San Giovanni
5. Nicodemo e Giuseppe d'Arimatea
6. Angeli

Figure 9. 3. Example of exercises

It is important to note that in York, the unique collaboration between the LSP specialist and art historians with knowledge of the target language has led to the creation of extremely realistic (and appropriate to the 'real' work of an art historian) bespoke teaching material for the course. For instance, the process of designing activities is greatly facilitated by the art historians' input since they can demonstrate first-hand the language competence and skills needed in their research work on Italian Art: examples of translated texts, information for accessing monuments and archives in Italy, or when applying for or during their Year Abroad in Italy. This collaboration was a vital factor not only in identifying authentic material used for teaching but also in setting realistic targets for students based on art historians who use Italian in their line of work.

The course continues to develop reading skills following the same focus used for *Italian Reading Skills for Art Historians*. Students study biographies of the most important Italian artists and descriptions of their most famous masterpieces, primarily focusing on Medieval, Renaissance and Baroque Art and the most known artists such as Giotto, Raffaello, Michelangelo, Caravaggio, etc. They will read translations from famous original sources (such as Vasari's *Le Vite* and Palladio's *I quattro libri dell'architettura*) and use some of the most important websites used for History of Art (for instance, the official Ministero della Cultura's beniculturali.it). Reference is also made to Italian museum maps and information, as well as contemporary art critiques in Italian.

Most of the translation exercises are based on the real-life work of an art historian (for instance, translating an article from a publication on Italian Baroque Art written by one of the lectures in HoA). From a teacher's point of view, it is important to add that the development at a fast pace of specific language skills essential to the work of an art historian is vital in the course. For this reason, very early in the course, students develop the ability to extract key information from extremely elaborate art-related authentic descriptions and to confidently recognise and match old-style Italian (e. g. extracts from Palladio's work) to the official English translation.

In the context of LSP, it is important to say that students the analysis of students' feedback indicates that students find the advanced-level material much more authentic because of its similarities to those they may already have encountered in their art-related studies. Such material seems to motivate instead of discourage them, as it feels as if they are gaining familiarity with the History of Art discipline. From the very first day, this material can also be used to practice basic grammar structures with exercises that include asking students to recognise all the articles, feminine and masculine or plural nouns, combined propositions etc., in the biography of Raffaello Sanzio in *Italiano Attraverso la Storia dell'arte* (Angelino and Ballarin, 2006) which is pitched at B2-C1 CEFR. Such diversity in the applied classroom teaching material seems to be particularly effective in helping students to increase their self-confidence when they have approached original sources in Italian in other modules. In fact, it is particularly relevant to students who are planning to take other modules on Italian Art as part of their studies or plan to spend time in Italy as part of their Year Abroad or for their research. From an LSP teaching perspective, there is undoubtedly a big gap between a student's level of language proficiency needed to fully understand and make use of the material for the 'general language skills' component and the one for the LSP component in the course. It is important to say that the use of such advanced level material in an ab-initio environment might be perceived as a very daunting task for a non-LSP experienced teacher, whilst LSP students in *Italian for Art Historians* are able to integrate both levels in their learning.

As the course progresses, communicative skills related to the History of Art are progressively embedded into class activities whilst they are still taught at an appropriate level for that of a beginner's student (A1-A2 CEFR material). For instance, after students are taught numbers, dates and how to read the clock, as their language competence develops, class exercises can focus on role-plays such as 'Asking for opening and closing times at the Galleria dell'Accademia in Venezia' or enquiring about an artist's date of birth or death, as shown in Fig. 9. 4.

STUDENTE A
Speaking and Writing
Ask the correct questions to your colleague to fill the gaps with the missing dates.
Esempio di domande e risposte:
STUDENTE A: Che giorno è nato Michelangelo?
STUDENTE B: Michelangelo è nato il....................
STUDENTE B: Che giorno è morto Michelangelo?
STUDENTE A: Michelangelo è morto il..........................

Michelangelo di Lodovico Buonarroti Simoni ....– 18 febbraio 1564
Raffello Sanzio da Urbino 6 aprile or 28 marzo, 1483 –..
Leonardo di ser Piero da Vinci .... – 2 febbraio 1519
Giorgio Vasari 30 luglio 1511 – ....
Jacopo Comin detto Tintoretto .... – 31 maggio 1594
Michelangelo Merisi da Caravaggio detto il Caravaggio 29 settembre 1571 – ....

Figure 9. 4. Examples of History of Art-related exercises for students to practice numbers and dates.

Another example is shown in Fig. 9. 5. After learning how to introduce themselves and buy items at the market, students are invited to apply the same language competence to ask for information, buy a discounted ticket or to book a guided tour at a museum or art gallery.

Alla biglietteria del museo

❑ *Vocabulary*

Asking for tickets:

Un biglietto per favore *or* Vorrei due / tre/ quattro biglietti per …
- un biglietto   intero / ridotto   per la mostra   di Tiziano
                                                     temporanea
                                                     permanente

- due biglietti   interi   / ridotti   per il museo
                                                  per la visita guidata
                                                  per il tour della città
                                                  per la cripta

Enquiring about prices and discounts:

- Quanto costa   il biglietto?
                  l'entrata / l'ingresso?
- Ci sono sconti per studenti?
- Il biglietto è gratis per studenti di storia dell'arte?

Enquiring about opening and closing times:

- A che ora apre / chiude   la galleria d'arte?

Enquiring about guide tour

- C'è la vista guidata in inglese / italiano?
- Quanto costa la visita guidata?
- Quanto dura la visita guidata?

Cultura italiana: in Italia i musei sono generalmente chiusi il lunedì!

Figure 9. 5. Vocabulary used to prepare students for role-plays focusing on asking for a ticket or booking a guided tour in a museum in Italy

From the middle of the course onwards, particular attention is paid to illustrating the transferability of the acquired specialist skills (this is particularly important to demonstrate to the cohort that they can successfully enrol into general language courses in the future). Students first learn colours and the technical vocabulary to describe composition, background, clothing and characters' physical appearance visible in Piero della Francesca's *Il Battesimo di Cristo*. Following that, they are asked to apply the same language skills to describe a photo of their family and so use them in a much more contemporary context. The same process of transferability is also applied in the opposite way, from a non-specialist to a specialist context. As an example, after learning how to express a preference between food items on the menu of the historical Caffè Florian in Piazza San Marco or the bar inside Museo Correr in Venezia, students are taught to consolidate the previously learnt language skills to express their preference between *La Scuola di Atene* by Raffello and *La Vocazione di San Matteo* by Caravaggio. The continuous exchange from specialist-to-general and from general-to-specialist language teaching in class activities helps students to recognise the practical applications efficiently and consequently appreciate the usefulness of each newly acquired language pattern and grammar structure.

With regard to the LSP component, the final part of the course focuses primarily on art critic and boosting student's employability skills via exercises such as 'Giving or asking for directions' at the London National Gallery or Uffizi Museum (Fig. 9. 6.). By the end of the course students can successfully give directions to tourists in Italian and British museums, or present a guided tour in Italian on famous Italian artworks such as *La Nascita di Venere* by Botticelli or *Il Compianto sul Cristo morto* by Giotto) or even make a comparison between the various *Annunciazioni* by Beato Angelico.

Finally, the course also uses technology-enhanced teaching and learning (e.g. online personal portfolios, audio and video material) to enrich students' engagement with the LSP component, art-related activities, student-teacher interaction, and for monitoring students' progress. For instance, one of the tasks of the end of the year's Summative Assessment Oral Exam includes the creation of student-led video presentations where students have to describe two Italian masterpieces – e.g. *La Primavera* by Botticelli and *Bacchino Malato* by Caravaggio – using technical vocabulary appropriate to that of an art historian to explain the composition, theme, character description, shades and colours, background etc. Videos produced by students as part of their formative assessment portfolio are also used as a marketing tool for both departments and demonstrate the importance of modern foreign languages in the academic curricula. Furthermore, the opportunity to watch videos created by previous students who attended the same course is perceived as encouraging by prospective students. This is also confirmed by the students' response to the 'LFA Programme Introductory Talk' at the beginning of each academic year. Transformed into an asynchronous online activity as a result of the pandemic, the module introduction video features existing students' videos and each year, after watching it, a number of Y1 students in HoA ask to change their module choice so as to enrol on *Italian for Art Historians*.

Lavorare al museo in Inghilterra
Speaking practice
Al telefono
You are working at the National Gallery in London. Looking at the map (website - the National Gallery) and giving directions over the phone to Italian visitors who have arrived at the following underground stations and want to reach the National Gallery entrance.
Give the tourists directions from:
Leicester Square
Charing Cross

Remember to start the conversation with:
Pronto, NATIONAL GALLERY?
Pronto, scusi.... per venire alla National Gallery?

All'ingresso
You are working at the National Gallery in London. Italian visitors arrive at the following entrances and would like to visit some of the highlights in the collection. Consult the plan, and room numbers and give them directions accordingly.
Portico Entrance
Getty Entrance
Education Centre Entrance
Sainsbury Wing Entrance

Figure 9. 6. Example of speaking practice

6. Conclusions

The success and popularity of *Italian for Art Historians* in HoA and of Italian as an LSP discipline in the context of the History of Art is primarily due to its specialist language-related content-integrated nature. This is immediately followed by the fact that the course a) is purposely tailored to the needs of future art historians working in the History of Art field, and b) helps students to gain proficiency in the four language skills, as they would meet in a general language course. Even though Italian as a general subject is without a doubt in decline in the UK (Kelly, 2016; AULC, 2020; internal L&LS and LFA statistics 2019-2022), the popularity of Italian in the LSP context is instead on the rise. In York, HoA students clearly seem to appreciate the crossovers between Italian for Art Historians and other modules in the HoA's UG and PG programme, the specialised nature of the course and also the level of language competence that they can reach. Through LSP, students can become more engaged in both disciplines, and the bespoke pioneering applied teaching methodology specifically designed for this course enables particularly committed students to reach B1 CEFR (above the competence reached by students in general LFA Level 1 language course part of the same L&LS provision). This is particularly relevant to students who are taking the course because they are planning to focus their future studies on Italian Art or are considering applying for post-graduate employment in Italy as they would like to spend some time living and working in Italy.

References

Accademia Del Giglio (2013). *L'italiano con la storia dell'arte: 32 esercizi e comprensioni per studenti stranieri B1/B2*. Retrieved 29 Aprile 2022 from www.adgblog.it/2013/12/23/litaliano-con-la-storia-dellarte-2/

Andriuzzi, R. (2017). *L'italiano dell'arte. Corso di lingua italiana*. Hoepli.

Angelino, M., & Ballarin, E. (2006). *L'Italiano attraverso la storia dell'arte*. Guerra Edizioni.

AULC-UCML (2020). *Survey of Institution-Wide Language Provision in universities in the UK: 2019-2020*. Retrieved 29 April 2022 from https://aulc.org/wp-content/uploads/2021/07/AULC-UCML-survey-of-Institution-Wide-Language-Provision-in-universities-in-the-UK-2019-2020.pdf

Bacilieri, C. (2014). Italian for Art Historians: Learning Italian at the University of York through a specialist language course. *Association for Art Historians Bulletin (AAH)*, 117, 5.

Bacilieri, C. (2018). Italian through History of Art: delivering interdisciplinary content-based language modules in Higher Education context. In *Scientific Journal of Teaching English for Specific and Academic Purposes, Special issue: Languages for Specific Purposes in Higher Education*, 6(2), Special Issue. Edited by LSPHE, 53–63.

Bacilieri, C. (in press). Developing speaking skills in Italian for Art Historians. In *New Trends in Learning and Teaching Speaking Skills*. Cambridge Scholars Publishing.

Corradini, E., Borthwick, K., & Gallagher-Bret, A. (2016). Introduction to languages and employability skills. *Employability for languages: a handbook*, (pp. 1–8). Dublin: Research-publishing.net.

Council of Europe (1998). *Modern languages: learning, teaching assessment. A common European framework of reference*. Strasbourg: Council of Europe.

Garelli, G. (2020). *Parliamo di arte*. Loescher Coedizioni.

Gobbis, A., & Paoli Legler, M. (2012). Come l'arte può motivare l'interesse per apprendenti di lingua italiana L2". *Italiano LinguaDue* 3(2).

Hutchinson, T., & Waters, A. (1987). *English for Specific Purposes: A learning-centred approach*. Cambridge: CUP.

Hyland, K. (2002). Specificity revisited: how far should we go now? *English for Specific Purposes*, 21(4), 385–395.

Kelly, M. (2016). Foreword. In Corradini E., Borthwick, K., & Gallagher-Brett, A. (Eds.), *Employability for languages: a handbook*, (pp. xix–xx). Singapore: SG. Research-publishing.net.

Magnatti, M., & Massei, G. (2016). *Percorsi italiani: L'Italia dell'arte*. ELI.

Marshall, K. (2001). *Survey of less specialist language learning in UK universities 1998-1999*. Centre for Languages Linguistics and Area Studies. Retrieved 29 April 2022 from www.llas.ac.uk/resources/614.html

Porreca, S. (2020). *L'italiano per l'arte*. Alma edizioni.

University of York (2020a). *International Strategy 2017 – 2020*. Retrieved 29 April 2022 from www.york.ac.uk/about/mission-strategies

University of York (2020b). *Learning and Teaching Strategy 2015 – 2020*. Retrieved 29 Aprile 2022 from www.york.ac.uk/about/mission-strategies

University of York 2020-2030. *University Strategy 2020 – 2030*. Retrieved 29 April 2022 from www.york.ac.uk/about/mission-strategies

UNESCO (2022). Commissione Nazionale Italiana per l'Unesco. Retrieved 29 April 2022 from www.unesco.it

Chapter 10

For an interdisciplinary approach in language learning: exploring the use of subtitling in the Italian language classroom

Rosalba Biasini
University of Liverpool

Francesca Raffi[1]
University of Macerata

Abstract: This contribution discusses a research-led learning and teaching project, *Learn Italian with Subtitles*, created via a collaboration between the Universities of Macerata (Italy) and Liverpool (UK). The project, which merges audiovisual (henceforth AVT) studies and foreign language (henceforth FL) pedagogy, is focused on the use of interlingual subtitling for learning Italian as a FL.

After a theoretical introduction on FL learning and teaching through interlingual subtitling, followed by a description of the project and an analysis of students' response, the authors argue that the advantages of using subtitling activities in language education are numerous: first, students adopt an active role during these activities, which increases motivation toward their broader learning experience. Also, by actively producing subtitles (i.e., tangible outputs), they become aware of and make decisions about communication, sociolinguistics, and pragmatics aspects, developing advanced language and language-related skills as well as soft skills and digital fluency.

Keywords: Subtitling, Audiovisual, Interlingual, Interdisciplinary, English, Italian

***

---

[1] The authors made equal contributions to the conception and writing of this chapter. In particular, Rosalba Biasini is responsible for Sections 3 and 4; Francesca Raffi for Sections 1, 2, and 5.

1. Introduction

In the 1990s, audiovisual translation became a recognised academic discipline, mainly concerned with "the transfer of multimodal and multimedia speech (dialogue, monologue, comments, etc.) into another language/culture" (Gambier, 2013: 45). Scholars have produced a wealth of material on AVT over the last decades, especially with regard to subtitling, which is the most widely used form of AVT. Subtitles can be either interlingual or intralingual, depending on the linguistic transfer. Interlingual subtitling has been defined as "a rendition in writing of the translation into a TL [target language] of the original dialogue exchanges uttered by the different speakers, as well as of all other verbal information that is transmitted visually (letters, banners, inserts) or aurally (lyrics, voices off)" (Díaz-Cintas, 2019: 212). Thus, subtitles in this context present a translation of the source language soundtrack into a different language, generally aimed at FL viewers but also, and most interestingly for the purposes of the present essay, useful for language learners (Díaz-Cintas, 2001; 2006).

Intralingual subtitling is a practice that "consists of presenting on screen a written text accounting for the dialogue, music, sounds and noises contained in the soundtrack for the benefit of audiences with hearing impairments" (Díaz-Cintas, 2019: 212). This implies maintaining the language of the original soundtrack but adding relevant auditory details (i.e., linguistic and paralinguistic features) that are important for understanding the story line. Interestingly, with the first studies of audiovisual materials and their applications in formal language learning contexts, only intralingual subtitles for deaf and hard-of-hearing learners were seen as effective pedagogical tools (see Davila, 1972), and this attitude remained prevalent in the 1980s (see Caldwell, 1973; Baker and Damper, 1986; among others). However, in the same decade, scholars also started to investigate the effectiveness of subtitling for hearing learners (see Lambert, Boehler and Sidoti, 1981; among others), thanks to developments in cognitive psychology which offered a more solid starting point for exploring new tools able to facilitate cognitive processes in the FL classroom. A key turning point was the publication of Paivio's (1986) dual coding theory (DCT), according to which multiple representations (i.e., both verbal and non-verbal) of the same information help to improve memory and learning.

Although some scholars have evaluated the direct experience of using AVT techniques in the classroom since the late 1970s (Wegner, 1977), further reflection is needed on the successful implementation of subtitling activities in FL learning and teaching and on how the use of subtitles should be implemented more regularly and consistently in language education. With all this in mind, this chapter discusses a research-led learning and teaching experience at the University of Liverpool (henceforth UoL), focused on the use of AVT, specifically interlingual subtitling (FL > L1), in a final year module of Italian as a FL. To the best of our knowledge, the project is the first to centre on Italian as a FL at the undergraduate level in a UK-based university.

After this introductory section, Section 2 discusses a number of studies and projects which have demonstrated the benefits of interlingual subtitling in the FL classroom since the early 1990s. Then, after a description of the *Learn Italian with Subtitles* project (Section 3) briefly outlined above, the preliminary results are discussed in Section 4[2]. Finally, some conclusions are drawn (Section 5).

2. FL teaching and learning through interlingual subtitling

In the 1990s, several scholars in the field of FL teaching and learning investigated the effectiveness of both intra- and interlingual subtitling. Danan (1992) conducted research on interlingual subtitling[3], using Paivio's (1986) dual coding theory to demonstrate the usefulness of interlingual subtitling for FL acquisition among beginner and intermediate learners. He explained its success by the multiple memory paths created by the visual and bilingual input.

Moving from the 1990s to the 2000s, one of the most prolific scholars of this decade in the field of subtitling applied to language learning and teaching was Caimi (2002, 2005; among others), who strongly advocated the use of subtitles to stimulate students in their learning development in terms of phonetics, vocabulary, grammar, and pragmatic competence, by focusing on multiple channels of communication (both verbal and nonverbal), and behaviour patterns, thus exposing students not only to the target language but also to the target culture characteristic of another community.

In line with Caimi's (2008) study, Borghetti (2011) discussed the ways in which the active creation of interlingual subtitles can be used to promote better the development of students' intercultural awareness in the FL classroom; in particular, helping the students to reflect on their own role as mediators between two different cultures. For example, students can be asked

---

[2] It must be noted that this project and the corresponding research are still in the initiation phase: the results collected so far and presented here are therefore partial, hence the project description outline should be considered the basis for a more extended analysis that will follow in a further study.

[3] In the present section, the focus is on interlingual studies, projects, and experiments, in line with the characteristics and nature of the *Learn Italian with Subtitles* project at the University of Liverpool (UK). Intralingual subtitling (or captioning) has also been extensively investigated and used in the FL classroom. For further references, see Bibliography: Intralingual Subtitles (Captions) and Foreign/Second Language Acquisition, available at: www.fremdsprachee-und-spielfilm.de/Captions.htm.

to choose between strategies of foreignisation or domestication (Venuti, 1995) when making translation choices to deal with cultural references, encouraging them to reflect on their responsibility to the target audience.

A few years later, Baños Piñero and Sokoli (2015) presented ClipFlair, a European-funded project aimed at providing an easily accessible online platform for FL learners with activities which included subtitling. According to the results of student surveys, subtitling activities created an interactive and entertaining learning environment, which increased student motivation and independence, and provided exposure to non-verbal cultural elements, as well as authentic linguistic and cultural aspects of communication in context. Interestingly, the two authors also shed light on the potential of subtitling to promote "transferable skills" (ibid., p. 204), which are indeed expected to grow exponentially in the coming years (see Section 3), "thus demanding a set of add-on skills that higher education institutions will have to include in their existing curricula in order to boost graduates' employability" (Díaz Cintas and Remael, 2021: 62).

More recently, Lertola (2019) has offered a systematic review of the empirically-based experimental studies conducted in the last 20 years that have foregrounded the positive links between subtitling tasks and FL learning. Positive learning outcomes are reported on incidental vocabulary acquisition, idiomatic expression retention, development of pragmatic awareness, listening comprehension skills, and writing and translation skills.

As far as the teaching of Italian is concerned, few studies and projects have been carried out so far, despite the bulk of research conducted over the years and despite the growing interest related to the use of interlingual subtitling in the FL classroom. Among the few studies that have been published, Lertola (2013) described an experiment involving undergraduate students of Italian as a FL, mainly with English as their first language, at the National University of Ireland, Galway (levels A1-A2). It was demonstrated that subtitling promotes the incidental acquisition of new word meanings in terms of productive recall.

Moving from linguistic to cultural competence, Borghetti and Lertola (2014) further expanded Lertola's (2013) experiment by focusing on A2/B1-level students of Italian; findings confirmed that the use of subtitling tasks helps students better develop intercultural skills. Incalcaterra McLoughlin and Lertola (2014) discussed the introduction of subtitling activities as a regular part of Italian language courses, in this case at the B1-B2 level, and also reported on students' feedback on their subtitling experience. According to students' responses, subtitling improved their motivation to learn Italian. Most interestingly, their opinions on subtitling and translation as language learning tools were different and tended to be more positive in relation to subtitling (see Section 4).

More recently, Beltramello (2019) explored the combination of subtitling and other AVT tasks in a class of Italian learners (B2 level) in their fourth and final year of their bachelor's degree, once again at the National University of Ireland, to help students develop an awareness of pragmatic features of conversation and the dynamics of face-to-face interaction (i.e., pragmatic and sociolinguistic competence). The subtitling tasks proved to be effective in guiding students to question the meaning of certain utterances, the intention behind a speaker's utterance, and social relationships between interlocutors.

According to the information we have, the only project conducted outside Ireland and related to English as L1 and Italian as a FL is the one discussed in McKenzie (2018) and conducted at Victoria University of Wellington, New Zealand. The project involved undergraduate students of Italian (A2-B1 level) who were asked to subtitle the Italian comedy classic *Il secondo tragico Fantozzi* into English. The same sample of students also answered a survey to reflect on the overall effectiveness of the project. Positive results confirmed the effectiveness of subtitling as a language learning tool, both in terms of linguistic/cultural competence and motivation/enjoyment.

Therefore, previous studies and experiments conducted outside the UK have demonstrated that the advantages of using subtitling activities in language education are numerous, by virtue of their capacity to enhance both language and cultural skills, capitalising on the richness (thanks to the multi-semiotic reception of the stimuli presented) and authenticity (authentic audio-visual language inputs) of audiovisual texts, as well as the enjoyment offered by learning tasks related to subtitling. Such tasks enable students to practise listening, reading, and writing skills through entertainment and exercises using authentic materials, i.e., samples of language produced by a real user of that language for a real audience, thus developing idiomatic competence since the language is contextualised through real-life situations. In fact, in a subtitling task, the communicative reason for performing the activity is immediately evident, giving a clear purpose and a functional dimension to the new text and, consequently, to the tasks performed by students. As Talaván (2006: 327) puts it, a subtitling task "has a sense of purpose in itself [...] and the accompanying tasks also look for a sense of communicative achievement that can allow learners to transfer these performance-oriented learning experiences to real-life business situations in which they take part". This motivates learners to keep on practising and encourages them to extend their intake of the language.

Subtitling also offers the opportunity to develop learner-centred tasks based on interactive activities, which can be performed both individually and in groups. This can be done under the guidance of the teacher or independently to promote autonomous and cooperative language learning, which enhances student motivation and proves to be fundamental in situations in which teaching is carried out remotely, as further discussed in the following sections.

3. The project

Following a fortunate encounter between the two authors of this study – Dr Rosalba Biasini, an Italian language practitioner based at UoL, and Dr Raffi, an academic specialising in (AVT) Translation Studies (University of Macerata, Italy) and a professional audiovisual translator – via an Erasmus+ partner institution, a series of workshops on subtitling in language education was organised at the UoL, including teachers' development days and the Annual 2019 Translation Lecture, which Dr Raffi delivered. These initial contacts inspired the creation of a subtitling course which has become integrated into one final year Italian language module. The learning and teaching aims of this project are primarily linguistic and cultural, as well as interlinguistic and intercultural, as it is essentially part of a language module in which translation activities are included (Borghetti, 2011; Borghetti and Lertola, 2014), as further discussed in the following sections.

3. 1. The Italian programme at the University of Liverpool

At UoL, learners of Italian language can start a course as absolute beginners or at the intermediate level, identified in some UK institutions as 'advanced' (CEFR level B1/B2). After a biennium where the two cohorts follow different pathways, based on four weekly hours of contact time for beginners and three for intermediate learners, students generally spend their third year abroad. On their return, both sets of students are merged for the final year module, which, in line with the national Subject Benchmark Statement for Languages, Cultures and Societies, prepares students to reach a level of proficient linguistic and cultural competence of at least [CEFR] C1 (AQA, 2019: 18).

The Italian programme, which combines language modules with 'content' modules taught in English, develops a broad range of Italian language skills from linguistic competence – through historical, cultural, and transnational studies (including literature and film) – to practical, digital, and mediation skills (UoL, n.d.). The whole language programme includes elements of translation in both directions (FL (IT)>L1 (EN); L1 (IT)>FL (EN)): didactic exercises to enhance language acquisition are introduced early with lower-level learners, and from Year Two elements of translation and interpreting are incorporated into language modules to develop linguistic awareness as well as mediation and intercultural skills.

It must be emphasised that the aims of the programme are those of a language and culture undergraduate university course, which means that it includes an introduction to a variety of employability skills, with a specific focus, for the language component, on translation and interpreting, but the course is not designed to train professionals in this field – only to provide basic competence and knowledge in the translation sector, while the main objective remains language education.

Italian classes for finalist undergraduates at LCF include, on average, 9-15 students per year, and because of their relatively small size, relations among peers, as well as between learners and tutors, are generally amicable and collaborative. This furnishes an appropriate background for teaching innovation and data analysis, and for these reasons, it was possible to launch this project. Most students who take part have English as their first or main language, with rare exceptions, and it is very common for participants to study at least one other language, in which they tend to be more proficient.

In their final year, students are not directly taught grammar in dedicated sessions, and classes do not focus mainly on specific skills, e.g., writing and reading or speaking and listening. Instead, module components are based on short 'projects' aimed at developing a combination of competence, skills, and knowledge[4]. The module also includes a weekly class dedicated to translation, and in the second semester, the subtitling class is replaced by interpreting practice. The following section gives an outline of the learning and teaching aims of the *Learn Italian with Subtitles* project.

3. 2. Project structure and activities

As anticipated, the project activities, which include classwork and independent practice, cover different steps of the subtitling process. First of all, it must be noted that at this pilot stage of the project, a decision was made not to work with reversed subtitling but only in the direction of Italian (FL) > English (L1)[5]. The benefits of using any form of translation in language education have been widely investigated and, especially in the field of Italian language pedagogy, several studies have affirmed and reinforced a full 'rehabilitation' of translation techniques in language education after decades of 'ostracism'

---

[4] In the first semester, one of these projects, for instance, explores the language of literature, and students work toward writing a literary review. In the second semester, the focus is on the language of advertising, and via the creation of an advertisement, students develop not only language and cultural competencies, but also soft skills, related for instance to digital fluency and communication.

[5] Reverse subtitling is the kind of subtitling in which the soundtrack/audio language and the subtitle language are different, but in this case the former is the L1, and the latter is L2. For instance, the soundtrack language is English, and the subtitle language is Italian for viewers whose L1 is English.

(Balboni, 2010)[6]. For this specific project, it was agreed to use FL > L1 activities for three main pedagogical reasons. First of all, finalists in Italian mainly start as beginners, and at the end of the programme, their linguistic competence, as well as their confidence, is still developing. Additionally, the translation class, a component of the same language module, in the first semester is taught in the opposite direction (L1 > FL). Finally, in the second semester, the translation class 'changes direction' (FL > L1), while the subtitling sessions are replaced by interpreting classes. Therefore, a variety of translation tasks and activities are offered in both directions, which helps to make student performance more balanced.

Choosing this direction of translation (FL > L1) also offers many advantages: when students 'read' in their language of study an authentic text (in the case of AVT resources, this could be a clip, a video, or a podcast), they can learn to appreciate the complexity of both the linguistic content and the cultural system in which it is embedded. Furthermore, the exercise of creating a target text in the form of English subtitles strengthens linguistic and interlinguistic competence among students, even in their first or stronger language (Lertola, 2015). This allows them to better focus on: comprehension of the source text with all its nuances; the process of translating a text, which includes evaluating meaning and expression, negotiating choices, and finding solutions; and the subtitling task, thereby learning new skills which enhance digital fluency.

The Semester 1 final year Italian course lasts for 12 weeks, with three contact hours per week (and a total of 150 hours of study time per module, including classwork and independent study time), one of which is dedicated to subtitling. Each class includes a theoretical part focused on subtitling rules and guidelines as well as practice. The first classes focus on establishing the basis of the subtitling process, providing students with information about the sector and possible career opportunities in line with the institution's recommendations. In addition to Dr Raffi's support both as an academic specialising in (AVT) Translation Studies, and as a professional audiovisual translator, at UoL, we also benefit from the support of a technician with expertise in subtitling software, video-making, and both Mac and MS operating systems: being able to rely on separate training, especially on the use of the selected software and technical problem solving, in the form of *ad hoc* video tutorials created by our technician, allowed us to free up more class time to focus on the actual activity of subtitling.

In the first pilot year of the project, once the chosen guidelines were agreed upon and basic rules established, students were introduced to subtitling

---

[6] For a summary of this theoretical discussion, see Biasini (2016).

software. We opted for a free, easy-to-use software, Subtitle Edit, which was downloaded onto all machines in an equipped language laboratory on campus. However, since not all operating systems support this software, when classes moved online in 2020-21, during the COVID-19 pandemic, we introduced a second subtitling tool, Aegisub, which helped us cater for all students. Switching to online classes meant that students had to ensure that they had to download and to install the software onto their personal computers at home. This was also an opportunity for students to refresh and expand their digital skills and learn how to access and run new programmes while keeping their machines 'healthy' and up-to-date.

The project activities cover all aspects of the subtitling process, and classes generally follow the pattern inspired by the learning unit (LU) model *globalising/analysing/synthesising/reflecting* formalised for Italian by Balboni[7]. The activity starts with 'reading' an audiovisual text: a variety of sources are used, including movie and documentary trailers, web series, and social media clips[8]. Given the learners' proficiency level, it was decided not to provide subtitles (neither in English nor in Italian). After an initial viewing, followed by a discussion (based on comprehension, analysis of linguistic and cultural traits, and the identification of potential challenges), students are provided with the full transcript: this allows the tutor to choose a more complex text, which can, for instance, highlight linguistic variations, use of jargon, idiomatic expressions, and irony. Then, a sequence of the text is assigned to the class for independent (or group, in some cases) subtitling practice; this is the 'reacting' stage: students use the software to create subtitles for the chosen extract. At the end of the class, a student is asked to share their attempt: this can be done anonymously by sending the task to the tutor, or, if appropriate, the student can share their screen (working online has eased this procedure). The class is asked to comment on the translation choices made, offer alternatives, and eventually negotiate a final proposal as a group. Finally, at home, students continue to subtitle the weekly set video or work on a new clip that the tutor has previously selected and shared via the institutional VLE, and the completed task is emailed to the tutor. Feedback is sent back via email and can also be used as a starting point for the next class.

---

[7] In English, see e.g., Balboni, 2007, especially 39–52.
[8] Over the years, varied materials were chosen to offer a broad range of cultural and linguistic resources. We used a variety of clips including trailers for the documentary *Come il peso dell'acqua* (Segre, 2014) and the film *Domani è un altro giorno* (Spada, 2019), as well as humoristic short videos by Italian comic group The Jackal. Some of these samples also involved off-screen voices, which helped introduce new elements to the subtitling task.

It must also be noted, although a deeper analysis of this topic would require a more extensive discussion, that students undergo a summative assessment on completion of a subtitling test, which currently constitutes 30% of the final module mark. The hard task for the test is similar to those used for class practice, and in the weeks running up to the assessment, a mock test is set to help students become accustomed to exam conditions (see Appendix for an example of a summative assessment task). The tasks used over the years in the subtitling tests constitute a form of authentic assessment that, while appropriately reflecting the knowledge and skills that need to be tested, mirror authentic tasks that students can expect to undertake outside of academia and that require the real-life thinking processes that experts use to solve the problem in a real context (Gielen et al., 2003; Gulikers et al., 2004).

4. Preliminary results

We are in the early stages of examining our results, and data collection and analysis are still in progress, which means that it is not yet possible to present a final evaluation of the project. These preliminary reflections are intended to comment on the evolution of the project so far, including students' performance and satisfaction, as well as tutors' feedback. A survey will be used to test the hypothesis above, and students' results will be studied diachronically and also in comparison with former laboratory tests, as well as other assessments (e.g., speaking tests) to determine whether introducing subtitling tasks has had a substantial and consistent impact over the years.

Informal data, which include the initial reading of students' module feedback and performance, seem to point positively toward the direction outlined above. The numerous advantages of using subtitling activities in language education, suggested by previous studies, experiments, and projects (see Section 2), seems, in fact, to have been confirmed by the class practice. It has been noted that students have adopted a more active role during the set tasks and in their learning experience, with increased motivation enhanced by opportunities to practise in their independent learning time and to receive timely feedback. Moreover, subtitles and captions are nowadays largely available and observable in everyday life. Since out-of-class exposure to subtitled AVT products assists FL learning (Lindgren and Muñoz, 2013; Peters et al., 2018), this authentic experience has offered students a fresh perspective on the practical application of their learning, as well as a continuous and varied source of stimuli and inputs.

It must be noticed that, as with all innovations, especially those with a digital focus, the integration of subtitling tasks into the language course also presented some challenges. First of all, tutors need to be trained: the level of expertise required clearly depends on the course learning outcomes that are set in the first place. Investments must be made, especially in terms of time for training and technical equipment. As stated previously, this specific project has greatly benefited from external expertise regarding the theoretical framework and professional advice, as well as internal support, thanks to a patient and reliable technician: institutions willing to introduce such innovations must be aware of these needs and their implications.

Finally, it must also be acknowledged that, especially at the beginning, the setting of subtitling tasks can be time-consuming: as with all text-based activities, material selection requires time, and in the case of these tasks, it can also involve additional video-cutting and conversion, while transcripts need to be searched for or typed and drafted. Factoring in time is the case for marking assessment as well, whether formative or summative, as providing accurate feedback involves not only linguistic, cultural, and mediation skills, but also digital and sector competence, supported by the appropriate technical equipment and the assistance of a tutor whose first language is English, given the direction of the translation. Needless to say, large cohorts can therefore generate a discouraging workload.

However, the tutors' evaluation of the project so far is highly favourable: on top of the positive outcomes suggested above, students have shown an increased level of collaboration, supporting each other with technical hiccups or linguistic queries, sharing linguistic resources, and slowly gaining increased confidence. Although the disruption caused by the national and local lockdowns in England between 2020 and 2021, which affected two out of the three cohorts that have taken part in the *Learn Italian with Subtitles* project so far, this opportunity to learn new skills and delve deeper into Italian language and culture has given students a more optimistic view on their learning and on their future as linguists, which has also created a palpable sense of achievement and progress within the class.

5. Conclusion

Since the 1970s, AVT modalities have attracted considerable attention in the field of FL learning and teaching. The first studies were considered pioneering in their successful efforts to provide students with new tools and learning experiences, but these researchers interestingly viewed interlingual subtitles as obstacles to language learning and teaching (see Wegner, 1977). This attitude changed in the 1980s when the potential of interlingual subtitling as an additional language learning tool was fully discovered and applied in FL classrooms (see Section 2).

A subtitled product is the result of the interplay of "the original spoken/ written word, the original image and the added subtitles" (Díaz Cintas, 2010:

344), and this calls for a variety of skills, which can be taught and improved through well-planned activities covering the different steps of the subtitling process. In the communicative context created by the audiovisual product, different signifying codes "operate simultaneously to produce meaning" (Chaume, 2012: 100), and a translator must understand the functioning of these codes to convey the equivalent message in the target language, taking into account the various components which can be acoustic-verbal (dialogue), acoustic-non verbal (score, sounds), visual-non verbal (image), and visual-verbal (subtitles). The need for synchrony between these components, along with the change of mode from oral to written, imposes both temporal and spatial constraints, which make a literal, word-for-word translation impossible, necessitating the use of condensation and reformulation strategies (Díaz Cintas and Remael, 2021). The visual context is explicit and needs to be taken into consideration in the translation process, together with cultural and intercultural issues and pragmatic aspects of communication. Therefore, subtitling offers the opportunity to negotiate meaning and to work simultaneously on multiple aspects of a given language. Hence, subtitling can be considered an effective language learning tool that can be integrated into FL study to help students develop competence in these different areas, and its potential has recently increased even more. As O'Sullivan (2013: 2) remarks, " [t]ranslation is usually thought of as being about the printed word, but in today's multimodal environment, translators must take account of other signifying elements too".

As the preliminary results of our project demonstrate (see Section 4), by actively producing subtitles, i.e., tangible outputs, students become aware of and make decisions about communicative, sociolinguistic, and pragmatic aspects of both languages while also learning a variety of transferable and soft skills which enhance their employability, particularly in the audiovisual and translation fields (Díaz Cintas and Remael, 2021: 62). In addition, introducing subtitling tasks to a language class helps develop translation and mediation skills with a special focus on digital awareness and fluency (Ávila-Cabrera and Corral Esteban, 2021). Incidentally, due to the unfortunate outbreak of the COVID-19 pandemic, followed by several national and local lockdowns that imposed remote learning, students had to rely even further on their digital skills.

To conclude, with this chapter, we hope to have increased awareness of the advantages of applying AVT modalities to the learning and teaching of Italian as a FL. The project we have presented, which is still running and expanding, could pave the way to a better understanding of the benefits and good practices of AVT in FL teaching and learning at LCF and other universities.

References

AQA (2019). *Subject Benchmark Statement: Languages, Cultures and Societies.* Retrieved 28 April, 2022, from https://www.qaa.ac.uk/docs/qaa/subject-benchmark-statements/subject-benchmark-statement-languages-cultures-and-societies.pdf

Ávila-Cabrera, J. J., & Corral Esteban, A. (2021.) The project SubESPSKills: Subtitling tasks for students of business English to improve written production skills. *English for Specific Purposes*, 63, 33–44. Retrieved from https://doi.org/10.1016/j.esp.2021.02.004

Baker, R. G., & Damper, R. I. (1986). Educational aspects of television subtitling in deaf education. *Behaviour & Information Technology*, 5, 227–236.

Baños Piñero, R., & Sokoli, S. (2015). Learning foreign languages with ClipFlair: Using captioning and revoicing activities to increase students' motivation and engagement. In Borthwick, K., Corradini, E., & Dickens, A. (Eds), *10 years of the LLAS elearning symposium: Case studies in good practice*, (pp. 203–213). Dublin: Research-publishing.net

Beltramello, A. (2019). Exploring the Combination of Subtitling and Revoicing Tasks: A Proposal for Maximising Learning Opportunities in the Italian Language. *International Journal of Language Translation and Intercultural Communication*, 8 (April), 93–109. Retrieved from https://doi.org/10.12681/ijltic.20279

Biasini, R. (2016). Per una rivalutazione del ruolo della traduzione nella didattica dell'Italiano LS. In Mazzotta, P., & Abbaticchio, R. (Eds.), *XXI Congress AIPI Associazione Internazionale Professori di Italiano Vol. L'insegnamento dell'italiano dentro e fuori d'Italia*, (pp. 37–50). Florence: Franco Cesati Editore.

Borghetti, C. (2011). Intercultural learning through subtitling: The cultural studies approach. In Incalcaterra McLoughlin, L., Biscio, M., & Mhainnín, M. A. (Eds.) *Audiovisual Translation Subtitles and Subtitling: Theory and Practice*, (pp. 111–137). Oxford: Peter Lang.

Borghetti, C. & Lertola, J. (2014). Interlingual subtitling for intercultural language education: a case study. *Language and Intercultural Communication*, 14(4), 423–440. Retrieved from https://doi.org/10.1080/14708477.2014.934380

Caimi, A. (2002). Cinema: Paradiso delle lingue. I sottotitoli nell'apprendimento linguistico. In *Rassegna Italiana di Linguistica Applicata (RILA)*, 34, 1-2 (pp. 19-51). Roma: Bulzoni.

Caimi, A. (2005). Subtitling in a cognitive perspective to encourage second language learning. In Sanderson, J. D. (Ed.), *Research on Translation for Subtitling in Spain and Italy*, (pp. 65–77). Alicante: University of Alicante.

Caimi, A. (2008) Subtitling: Language Learners' Needs vs. Audiovisual Market Needs'. In Anderman, G., & Díaz Cintas, J. (Eds.), *Audiovisual Translation. Language Transfer on Screen* (pp. 240–251). London: Palgrave Macmillan.

Caldwell, D. C. (1973). Use of graded captions with instructional television for deaf learners. *American Annals of the Deaf*, 118, 500–507.

Chaume, F. (2012). *Audiovisual translation: dubbing*. Manchester: St. Jerome Publishing.

Danan, M. (1992). Reversed subtitling and dual coding theory: New directions for foreign language instruction. *Language Learning*, 42(4), 497–527. Retrieved from https://doi.org/10.1111/j.1467-1770.1992.tb01042

Davila, R. R. (1972). *Effect of changes in visual information patterns on student achievement using a captioned film and specially adapted still pictures.* PhD thesis, Syracuse University: Syracuse.

Díaz Cintas, J. (2001). *La traducción audiovisual: el subtitulado.* Salamanca: Ediciones Almar.

Díaz Cintas, J. (2006). La subtitulación y el mundo académico: perspectivas de estudio e investigación. In Perdu, N. A., Garcia, F. I., Ortega, E., & M. A. Garcia (Eds.), *Inmigración, cultura y traducción: reflexiones interdisciplinares*, (pp. 693–706). Tarrasa: Editorial Bahai.

Díaz Cintas, J. (2010). Subtitling. In Gambier, Y., & van Doorslaer, L. (Eds.), *Handbook of Translation Studies*, Volume 1, (pp. 344–349). Amsterdam: John Benjamins.

Díaz Cintas, J. (2019). Audiovisual Translation. In Angelone, E., Ehrensberger-Dow, M., & Massey, G. (Eds.), *The Bloomsbury Companion to Language Industry Studies*, (pp. 209–230). London: Bloomsbury.

Díaz Cintas, J., & Remael, A. (2021). *Subtitling: concepts and practices.* New York: Routledge.

Gambier, Y. (2013). The position of audiovisual translation studies. In Millán, C., & Bartrina, F. (Eds.), *The Routledge Handbook of Translation Studies*, (pp. 45–59). Abingdon: Routledge.

Gielen, S., Dochy, F., & Dierick, S. (2003). Evaluating the consequential validity of new modes of assessment: The influence of assessment on learning, including pre-, post- and true assessment effects. In Dochy, F., Segers, M., & Cascallar, E. (Eds.), *Optimising new modes of assessment: In search of quality and standards*, (pp. 37–54). Dordrecht: Kluwer Academic Publishers.

Gulikers, J. T. M., Bastiaens, T., & Kirschner, P. (2004). A five-dimensional framework for authentic assessment. *Educational Technology Research and Development* 52, 67–85.

Incalcaterra McLoughlin, L., & Lertola, J. (2014). Audiovisual translation in second language acquisition: Integrating subtitling in the foreign language curriculum. *The Interpreter and Translator Trainer* 8(1), 70–83.

Lambert, W. E., Boehler, I., & Sidoti, N. (1981). Choosing the languages of subtitles and spoken dialogues for media presentations: Implications for second language education. *Applied Psycholinguistics* 2 (2), 133–148. Retrieved from https://doi.org/10.1017/S0142716400000904

Lertola, J. (2013). *Subtitling new media: Audiovisual translation and second language vocabulary acquisition.* Galway: National University of Ireland.

Lertola, J. (2015). Subtitling in language teaching: suggestions for language teachers. In Gambier Y., Caimi, A., & Mariotti, C. (Eds.), *Subtitles and language learning*, (pp. 245–267). Bern: Peter Lang.

Lertola, J. (2019). *Audiovisual translation in the foreign language classroom: applications in the teaching of English and other foreign languages.* Voillans: Research-publishing.net.

Lindgren, E., & Muñoz, C. (2013), The influence of exposure, parents, and linguistic distance on young European learners' foreign language comprehension. *International Journal of Multilingualism* 10, 105–129.

McKenzie, R. (2018). Subtitling in the classroom: Il secondo tragico Fantozzi (1976)', *Neke - The New Zealand Journal of Translation Studies*, 1(1). Retrieved from https://doi.org/10.26686/neke.v1i1.5160

O'Sullivan, C. (2013), Introduction: Multimodality as Challenge and Resource for Translation. *Journal of Specialised Translation* 20, 2–14.

Paivio, A. (1986). *Mental representations: a dual coding approach.* New York: Oxford University Press.

Peters, E., & Webb, S. (2018). Incidental vocabulary acquisition through viewing L2 television and factors that affect learning', *Studies in Second Language Acquisition* 40 (3), 551–577. Retreived from https://doi.org/10.1017/S027226 3117000407

Talaván, N. (2006). Using the technique of subtitling to improve business communicative skills. *RLFE, Revista de Lenguas Para Fines Específicos* 11(12), 313–346.

Venuti, L. (1995). *The translator's invisibility: a history of translation.* London: Routledge.

Wegner, H. (1977). *Teaching with film.* Bloomington: Phi Delta Kappa.

Web References

Raiplay. Genitori vs figli. L'eccelsamico. Retrieved 4 May, 2022, from https://www.raiplay.it/video/2016/02/Genitori-Vs-Figli---Laposeccelsamico-3d06ce8c-fd02-4ad3-ba0a-f9d336ff886d.html.

Appendix: an example of subtitling task for summative assessment

Marking criteria and instructions were shared via the institutional VLE with the students at the beginning of the Semester as follow:

MARKING CRITERIA AND INSTRUCTIONS FOR THE SUBTITLING TEST
The subtitling test will take place during our normal class time in Week 12. It will be preceded by a mock test in Week 10, also during class time.
For the subtitling test, you will have 50 minutes to subtitle at least 1 minute of video (TBC, depending on the source). At the end of the test, you will need to submit your task on Canvas > Assignments > Audio-Visual Text Entry Assessment > link named "ITAL311 Audio Visual Assessment".

Marking criteria:
60% TRANSLATION: you will translate from Italian into English. You will be assessed on:
1) comprehension of the source text (e.g., meaning, pertinence, omissions)
2) linguistic accuracy (e.g., register, style)
3) ability to convey a cohesive and coherent message
4) production of a functional and effective text
5) ability to transfer cultural and connotative aspects of the source text

40% TASK: you will need to complete at least 1 minute of a given audio-text (TBC, see above). You will be assessed on:
1) temporal dimension (e.g., time-in/time-out, synchronisation, scene changed, line numbers)
2) punctuation and other conventions (e.g., punctuation, dialogues dash, use of Italics)
3) segmentation (e.g., line breaks within subtitles, line breaks across subtitles)
4) linguistic/translation issues (e.g., condensation, omissions, reduction)

Notes: use of dictionaries and linguistic supports IS allowed for this test. Use of machine translation systems (Google Translate and similar) IS NOT allowed and will be verified.
You will have the script in Italian.

On the day of the test, conducted online in the last two academic years, the task is released on the VLE. It consists of an mp4 in VLC format, supported by the subtitling software in use, and the clip transcript, with a brief synopsis and – if appropriate – explanatory notes.

For an interdisciplinary approach in language learning 249

An example is below – the clip can be watched at this weblink, from minute 01:48: https://www.raiplay.it/video/2016/02/Genitori-Vs-Figli---Laposeccelsamico-3d06ce8c-fd02-4ad3-ba0a-f9d336ff886d.html.

GENITORI VS FIGLI [1]
This web series was created by a screenwriting workshop of the Centro Sperimentale di Cinematografia (Experimental Centre of Cinematography) and is focused on the theme of the relationship between parents and their teenage children. The series comprises twelve 2-3-minute episodes about what parents do in their relationship with their children, which always seems ridiculous, shocking, pathetic, absurd, nostalgic to the teenagers.

L'ECCELSAMICO [2]
Guido: Eh no, vedi, Napoleone è morto nel '21.
Ragazzo: Lui è Guido, IL MIO ECCELSAMICO. [3]
Madre: Ragazzi, vi ho portato un po' di pane e cioccolata.
Guido: Ah, grazie!
Madre: Ma guarda che meraviglia! Guarda che quaderno tutto ordinato!
Ragazzo: Tutti ne hanno uno in classe, è la storia più antica del mondo. Avete presente, no? Bene contro male.
Madre: Guarda qua! Tutto una cancellatura.
Ragazzo: Ma io sono mancino, ci passo sopra con la mano.
Guido: Ma non ti devi preoccupare... anche a me succedeva sempre... poi ho imparato a scrivere con la destra e adesso sono ambidestro, insomma...
Madre: Senti Guido, ma perché non ti fermi con noi a pranzo?
Ragazzo: Pure a pranzo?! Senti mamma, ma forse è occupato.
Guido: Veramente...
Ragazzo: Hai visto?
Guido: No, veramente no, ecco. Solo... non vorrei disturbare.
Madre: Ma stai scherzando? Ma ci fa un enorme piacere.
Guido: Quindi arriviamo davanti alla porta però c'è una trave che la blocca. Mi guardo dietro e... ci sono le fiamme ovunque... quindi, prendo la nonna me la carico sulle spalle e... mi butto fuori dalla finestra! Esattamente prima che... che l'incendio divampasse.
Ragazza: Volevo vedere te in una situazione del genere... allo spiedo, la nonna!
Guido: Ti posso assicurare che non sarebbe stata una bella esperienza.
Ragazzo: Caffè per tutti?
Padre: Nonononono!
Ragazza: Ma sai Guido, lui ha paura persino dei fiammiferi. E ha anche

paura dei cani, de... delle cavallette. E degli aghi!
Ragazzo A: Eh, può bastare, eh? Ha capito. Eccolo che arriva, eccolo che arriva, il momento del finto modesto. Tre, due, uno...
Guido: Ecco diciamo che forse sono stato avvantaggiato dal fatto di aver fatto servizio sull'ambulanza, ecco. Lì impari a tenere i nervi saldi, insomma.
Padre: Cioè con tutti i compiti che vi danno, trovi anche il tempo di fare dello sport?
Guido: Mah, correrò un paio di volte al mese, sono pigrissimo!
Ragazza: Ma dai! Sembrate la pubblicità del fitness: prima... e dopo!
Guido: Ecco, non mi alleno granché. Sarà per via del lavoro...
Madre: Lavori?!
Guido: Mah sì, lavoro... nel senso... do un po' di ripetizioni: fisica, algebra...
Padre: Per cortesia non tocchiamo il tasto algebra.
Madre: Ma non è che tu potresti dargli una mano?
Ragazzo: No...
Guido: Sì, certo, tanto di algebra ho finito il programma!
Padre: Ci faresti un favore enorme!
Guido: Ma volentieri!
Ragazzo: No, no, no! Questo no!
Padre: E Guido? Le ripetizioni? A che ora viene?
Ragazzo: Non viene, mi ha picchiato.
Padre: Oh Signore! Fa vedere... Mamma mia che roba! Metti questa, su.
Ragazzo: Ah!
Padre: Però, che destro Guido, eh?

---

[1] Create a subtitle for this title.
[2] You do not need to create a subtitle for this title. See note no.3.
[3] This is a pun between the adjective "eccelso" and the noun "amico". Propose your own translation and write the word (and the article and/or the possessive adjective, if you are using any of these) in capital letters, as this is also the title of the episode.

Chapter 11

Embodied and experiential immersion into transculturality: learning Italian through ethnography and translation

Eliana Maestri
University of Exeter

Abstract: How can educators contribute to heightening the understanding of Italian culture? How can they improve the students' acquisition of the Italian language? How can they increase opportunities for experiential learning? This chapter aims to answer these questions by discussing a project undertaken by students and educators at the University of Exeter as a case study. It also aims to bring to the fore strategies devised to incorporate the interplay between ethnography and translation in the multilingual classroom. Special emphasis is placed on the importance of working collaboratively with local communities and, at the same time, turning community engagement into an opportunity for in-class and out-of-class reflection on the making of cultures, the production of knowledge and the translator's role. Critical attention is devoted to translation as a method for embodied, experiential learning within the broader framework of Modern Languages as a multidiscipline.

Keywords: Transculturality, Ethnography, Translation, Italian, Learning

***

1. Introduction

Published in 2019 by a pool of UK researchers at the intersection of Modern Languages and ethnography[1], the article 'Ethnography and Modern Languages'

---

[1] The new Subject Benchmarking Statement (2022) refers to the discipline as 'Languages, Cultures and Societies' rather than 'Modern Languages', which makes the need for ethnographic work even clearer.

remains inspirational and forward-looking. It illustrates the transformative potential of ethnographic research within Modern Languages as a multidiscipline by outlining interdisciplinary outcomes and benefits for present and future linguists, researchers and undergraduate curricula. Ethnographic theories and methods have informed approaches to the practice of language teaching and learning for decades, but, as these researchers claim, they should be applied more consciously and fully by Modern Languages educators and students. Practising ethnography in Modern Languages teaching and learning allows the discipline to broaden its horizons by encompassing the observation and the study of linguistic and cultural co-creations beyond "forms of print" and within "more ephemeral forms of performance which require us to travel to them" (Wells et al., 2019: 6). Intended as "participatory and collaborative models of engagement" with a real-life scenario (Wells et al., 2019: 1), ethnography enables students and researchers to interact with actors and agents of linguistic and cultural co-production within, outside or at the geopolitical margins of national identity and communities. It also enables them to tap into and replicate modes of individual and group negotiation of meaning and performance while refining their sensitivity to cultural diversity, polylingual encounters, transcultural interactions and, above all, experiential and embodied learning experiences (Wells et al., 2019: 3).

Naomi Wells et al. (2019: 3-4) maintain that the British Year Abroad programme, whereby Modern Languages students spend one year of their degree working abroad or studying at a partner institution in a country other than the UK, is a perfect example. While improving their language skills, undergraduate students have the opportunity to practice "emplaced and embodied forms of language and cultural learning which are less easily replicated in the student's home context" (Wells et al., 2019: 3-4). However, despite its significance, Year Abroad programmes in British institutions are not the only 'perfect' example of the extent to which ethnographic immersion in the country of study can enrich and enhance students' experiential learning. For instance, Wells et al. (2019) mention translation as a way of practising language and cultural encounters. However, despite this, they do not offer specific examples of it or of how curricular activities could benefit from it.

The present chapter aims to offer an example of how translation and ethnography can be practised within and outside the classroom while drawing on an innovative and pioneering optional course as a case study. The course, designed to deepen the University of Exeter students' knowledge of languages, among which Italian, and cultural reality, will be used here to reflect on how translation and ethnography could be incorporated into the classroom. Following Wells et al.'s (2019) recommendations, this chapter also aims to bring to the fore the strengths of translation as a method and framework in embodied and experiential learning and language acquisition. Finally, it aims to respond to the call to afford Modern Languages greater visibility as an interdisciplinary subject and platform used to heighten students' employability skills. As Wells et al. (2019: 7) maintain, "Modern Languages has remained largely invisible and seemingly failed to capitalize on the opportunity to share our unique expertise on the subjects of working across multiple languages in the analysis of cultural texts and materials". A way out of invisibility would be, I believe, to empower practices of translation and reflections upon translation in Higher Education. Therefore, the results discussed below seek to offer an insight into practices of translation performed by students-ethnographers and advice on how Higher Education institutions and educators could capitalize on them. These capitalizations would encourage the 'ethnographic turn' in Modern Languages acquisition as a complement or supplement to Study Abroad programmes. Within this framework, Italian Studies is seen as a subdiscipline in constant dialogue with and informed by Modern Languages as a whole. A reflection on the aims and essence of Italian Studies abroad can be found in the conclusive remarks.

2. Translation and ethnography: a composite, long-standing interrelationship

Translation Studies and ethnography have long shared common research methods, objects of study, frameworks and goals (Buzelin, 2022). As Hélène Buzelin maintains, translation has appropriated ethnography as a methodology to "document and analyse translation and interpreting events in context" and "to solve translation problems" (2022: 32). Thanks to its polymorphic and empirical nature, ethnography has lent itself to various applications and research methodologies, including translation. As early as 1945, American linguist Eugene Nida, for example, proposed biblical translations based on a dynamic-equivalence theory designed to respond to the cultural needs of specific audiences, audiences who had to be ethnographically observed and framed (Wolf, 2002: 185; Buzelin, 2022: 32; see also Gentzler, 2001: 32-34; Munday, 2016: 62–70). On the other hand, translation has offered ethnography food for thought, warranting serious consideration for the work and research carried out by cultural anthropologists in multilingual and multicultural settings (Wolf, 2002; Buzelin, 2022). Translation has also been used by cultural anthropologists to reflect on their linguistic experiences and on how translation, interpreting and intercultural mediation can be benefitted from in ethnographic research (Wells et al., 2019: 7).

Translation Studies as a discipline has been slow in adopting ethnographic research and methodologies, despite initial attempts carried out by some of the fathers of the discipline (see Nida above). As Buzelin (2022) explains, the reduced pace was tied to a particular moment in the development of Translation Studies, namely the implementation of descriptive approaches to translation by Israeli translation scholar Gideon Toury. These approaches were imbued with positivistic biases and were based on scientific, systematic and objective observation of reality in translation (Buzelin, 2022: 36–37; see also Munday, 2016: 174–185). Within it, not much space was left for ethnography, including subjective and intersubjective approaches to cultural translation. Today, and especially after the 'sociological turn' in Translation Studies aimed to study translation as a network of agents and agencies responsible for the production, reception and consumption of translation (Wolf and Fukari, 2007; Buzelin and Baraldi, 2016), ethnography has gained considerable ground in translation (Buzelin, 2022: 37, 40).

Prominent Translation Studies scholars have devoted attention to the intersections between translation and ethnography, devising practical strategies and methods aimed at assisting practitioners and researchers in the study of translation from an experiential and subjective standpoint (Wolf, 2002; Hubscher-Davidson, 2011; Saldanha and O'Brien, 2013). In particular, as Buzelin (2022: 38-39) also claims, Michaela Wolf (2002) and Séverine Hubscher-Davidson (2011) have proved to be useful in pushing the boundaries of ethnography in translation by placing special emphasis on the intersubjective construction of cultural translation and the significance of intersubjective reflection upon it. Even if they situate their analysis of the interlinks between ethnography and translation within different theoretical and pragmatic stances – whereas the discussion of the former is based on translation products and the making of cultures through translation, the discussion of the latter is based on translation processes and specifically Think Aloud Protocols (TAPs) and interview-TAPS – their reflections are useful in discussing specific approaches to embodied and experiential teaching and learning. In particular, the theoretical underpinnings outlined by Wolf (2002) and Hubscher-Davidson (2011) have framed the design of a fourth-year undergraduate course in Modern Languages at the University of Exeter. These underpinnings will be used below to shed light on the innovative aspects of this course, whose strengths lie at the intersection between translation and ethnography in Modern Languages acquisition. For the purpose of this volume, special attention will be devoted to the acquisition of the Italian language and the refinement of the student's knowledge of Italian culture and identity.

3. Translation and ethnography: teaching and learning migratory contexts

Driven by the need to enable students to *feel* what it means to speak a second language and to use their senses, bodies and brains to appreciate the usefulness of intersubjective negotiations between multilingual and multicultural speakers, University of Exeter colleagues and I have designed and refined 'Transcultural Devon', a fourth-year module in the Department of Languages, Cultures and Visual Studies. The module, which aims to collect stories of migration to Exeter, stems from two initial projects, the first called 'Italians in Exeter' and the second 'Transcultural Devon', carried out by Danielle Hipkins, Professor of Italian Studies and Film, Alice Farris, Lecturer in Italian, and Valentina Todino, Italian Cultural Association Event Organizer, Drop-in Coordinator for Refugees Support Devon and Honorary Research Fellow at Exeter. Hipkins suggested the project become a Modern Languages and Cultures 'content' module in 2020, drawing on the expertise of Alice Farris, who led its integration into the curriculum with funding from the Exeter Education Incubator, Susana Afonso, Senior Lecturer in Portuguese with research interests in language and self-narratives of migration, David Salas, an internationally award-winning filmmaker and Lecturer in Film Practice and Exhibition, and Eliana Maestri, Senior Lecturer in Translation Studies, researching the interlinks between migration and translation. The module continues to benefit from the contribution offered by Valentina Todino, who acts as Community Liaison Officer to provide precious links with the Devon community, share valuable examples of ethnographic research and guarantee the success of the module. In order to complete this module, students are required to interview members of the migrant community in Devon via Zoom in their first language (including Italian)[2], video-record their interviews, subtitle their recorded video-interview in English, and upload their subtitled interviews to our 'Transcultural Devon' digital archive website bearing testimony to the migration to Devon (https://transculturaldevon.exeter.ac.uk/)[3]. As the website claims, the "videos offer the opportunity to observe how a personal story is told, and how it is shaped or

---

[2] It should be noted that different groups of students interview different groups of migrants every academic year.

[3] When the module was created, students chose to record their interviews using audio-recorders or video-cameras. During the Covid-19 pandemic, in-person interviews were not allowed and students were required to interact with interviewees only via Zoom. During the period of transition to a post-Covid-19 pandemic, online activities (such as students' interviews) were maintained in place as safe measures. This chapter has been written in the midst of hybrid approaches to teaching and learning (allowing combinations of in-person and online activities). Online interviews have been maintained because they are less time-consuming and practical. They allow students to establish good working relations with interviewees, while maintaining safety and the comfort of everyone's personal space. They also allow students to video-record their interviews using digital devices, which are more efficient to use than video-cameras (often requiring training). Comparing the effectiveness of in-person ethnography *versus* virtual ethnography is beyond the scope of this study. For more information regarding virtual and hybrid ethnographies, see Liz Przybylski (2021).

influenced by the way we translate ourselves from one culture to another". In addition to this, interviews are conducted "in each person's mother tongue to facilitate the expression of personal feelings and recognize polylingual Devon" (Ibid.). As demonstrated by the recordings that populate the abovementioned website, not only do the interviews show the student's engagement with the migrant community in Devon in the first languages (other than English) spoken by its members, but they also demonstrate the development of their understanding of migration to Devon and the composite, transcultural nature of language communities in the UK.

As implied by the module aims and objectives, undergraduate students are required to act as linguists as well as ethnographers interacting with and collecting qualitative data from selected members of the local community. In other words, their acts are informed by the distinctive features of ethnography, which, as summarized by Saldanha and O'Brien, include the "'engagement with the object of study – going into the field – and a willingness to learn from those who inhabit the culture' (Koskinen, 2008: 37) as well as a focus on the researcher's personal involvement with the data" (quoted in Buzelin, 2022: 39). Acting as ethnographers, the students develop links with the local community in Devon, raise awareness of key issues surrounding migration across the wider student community and online and reflect on the dynamics of writing history through the production of a historical video-archive. In addition to this, acting as ethnographers, the students are required not only to engage with the Other (the migrant at the periphery of culture and society) in their source languages but also to subtitle their source languages into English as the target language of the 'Transcultural Devon' video-archive. As Hubscher-Davidson maintains: "They [ethnographers] represent society and cultures through the act of writing, thereby performing and constructing ethnography through translation processes" (2011: 3). Sensitive to the production and consumption of cultures outside national borders, students are exposed to personal stories of migration and the importance of retaining their distinctiveness and uniqueness. The need to subtitle videos obliges students to think more thoroughly about the nuances of specific word choices, i.e. language in context. This need encourages students to do justice to the stories and, more generally, to contribute to the advancement of British culture and society. Presentations, currently being given in local secondary schools in Devon, on the value of 'Transcultural Devon' showcase not only the students' linguistic abilities but their empathic skills in teasing out the migrants' solidarity and positive involvement with the local community. Finally, the online publication of the interviews offers students the unique opportunity to demonstrate their acquired language skills and cultural competences to the public, generating a lasting legacy for future students and providing a model for collaboration and memory.

Links between translation and migration have been discussed at length by various Translation Studies scholars, among whom Wolf (2022), Michael Cronin (2003; 2009; 2013) and Loredana Polezzi (2006; 2009; 2012). In particular, as Polezzi argues, the etymology of 'translation' captures and reveals, at the same time, aspects of mobility and movement encapsulated and generated by the very act of translation, unveiling translation as "the movement or transfer of objects and people across space" as well as "a form of transportation or appropriation of the foreign within the language and culture of the nation" (2009: 172). Migratory contexts, such as Devon, bring about, as Paul Bandia puts it, "intersection or encounter between disparate cultures" (2014: 273). Devon, a British county situated in the South West of the United Kingdom, hosts migrants from European and non-European countries, fostering the interaction between and among a diversity of languages and communities whose centres and cultural associations are right in the heart of the region: Exeter. Due to the cultural and linguistic pluralism characterizing, solely from a touristic perspective, one of the most attractive regions in the UK, the Devon migrant communities depend heavily on translation and, in particular, self-translation expressing themselves in English as their 'second' language. In light of this, it was deemed important to develop a project and a module that could enable Higher Education students to use their language skills and become more knowledgeable about the demographic and linguistic complexity of the South West of England. The project and the module also wanted to counteract the need for migrants always to express themselves in a second language, giving them the chance to present themselves in the language with which they are most comfortable and familiar.

According to the Migration Observatory at the University of Oxford (https://migrationobservatory.ox.ac.uk), which has released online a wide-ranging demographic analysis of the South West based on the 2011 UK census, the racial composition and complexity of the South West, including Devon, remains undoubtedly attractive. The South West has "one of the smallest foreign-born populations of any of the ten regions of England and Wales" (Ibid.), but, despite this, it has attracted particular attention due to a population increment of 62 per cent between 2001 and 2011. The increment, unevenly spread from a geographical viewpoint, has affected such areas as Bristol and Bournemouth, which have seen "the foreign-born population increase by more than 100 per cent" (Ibid.). The number of foreign-born residents in the South West, as illustrated by the Migration Observatory website, has continued to grow, reaching in 2017 "a total of 513,000 people born in other countries", namely "an estimated 9.4% of the South West's population of 5,448,000" (Ibid.). Italy continues to remain among the top ten countries of origin for the UK, and the South West hosts 2 per cent of the UK's Italian-born residents. Many of these Italian migrants display a strong sense of national identity, cherishing, as our 'Transcultural Devon' website bears testimony, their 'foreign' language skills. They apply what Cronin would call "translator-nomad" strategies – typical of travellers (Cronin, 2013: 194) – resisting the "homogeneity" of languages and displaying "different accents, lexical variations, dissimilar patterns of language usage" along with "lexical exoticisms and the invocation of translation as intertextual presence" (Cronin, 2013: 195). While refining the 'Transcultural Devon' project, it was deemed imperative to give Italian language students the opportunity to devote time, energy and attention to the linguistic and cultural exploration of 'transcultural Italies' and Italian communities, communities scattered around Great Britain and, as *Transnational Italian Studies* also discusses, the globe.

4. Translation and ethnography: towards an embodied and experiential immersion in language acquisition

As one of our fourth-year Italian language students states: "There is no doubt that the 'Transcultural Devon' module gave me a chance to use theories of applied linguistics and translation that are studied on the compulsory advanced language modules, in a context that is real and meaningful"[4]. Therefore, what translation strategies do students display and enact? What does it mean for them to do ethnography in/and translation? And, specifically, what do they discover about Italy? What heightens their understanding of Italy outside of Italy? I will answer these questions by analysing some of the video-interviews that populate our 'Transcultural Devon' video-archive published online. The following analysis aims to shed light on the strengths of this project as well as its innovative aspects, in the hope that it can offer educators new ideas and strategies for teaching Italian in a contextual and meaningful environment.

The first discovery that the 'Transcultural Devon' project allows students to make is related to the asymmetries of power relations between cultural stances. Wolf, for instance, states that "it should be stressed in this context that ethnography, as well as translation, are inevitably positioned between systems of meaning which are marked by power relations" (2002: 183). "Relat[ing] this *dépaysement* through the eyes of different migrants with stories that should be told to the greater public"[5] encourages in-class reflection on the position of minorities in the world, including Italian migrants. It also encourages in-class reflection on the active use of linguistic choices to redress power imbalances or address "culturally constructed senses

---

[4] Email correspondence with a student of Italian, 1 May 2022.
[5] Email correspondence with a student of Italian, 1 May 2022, italics in original.

of belonging"⁶ with care. Students, who, throughout the module, become familiar with Wolf (2002), Hubscher-Davidson (2011) and Shu-Hsin Chen (2011), learn that the "interviewer is more likely to have more power than the interviewee" (Chen, 2011: 120) and that, in any face-to-face communication, power means manipulation, control and influence. Being in a teaching and learning environment, they become mindful of the fact that their aim for good grades or their fear of failure could lead them sub/consciously to exercise more or less power over their interviewees. They also learn that linguistic imperfections in the practice of a second language are not symptoms of weakness to be ashamed of but signs of strength as "being a non-native interviewer [...] makes it easier to elicit information from native interviewees" (Chen, 2011: 119). They, therefore, learn to experience their linguistic limitations as an advantage and a golden opportunity to devise suitable strategies for data collection and production in ethnographic research (Chen, 2011: 132). Their enacted experiential learning leads them to embrace alterity, disempowered by socio-cultural normative discourses and dynamics, including old-fashioned ways of conducting ethnographic research (Buzelin, 2022; Wolf, 2002: 184). The power they would usually have as British natives are taken away and balanced out by them being non-native speakers of the language used for the interview. Speaking the language of their interviewees enables students to overthrow binary oppositions and "feel equally one of many people that have become culturally adopted and accepted in and outside of Italy [and] as someone *touched* by Italy"⁷.

Students are encouraged to conduct semi-structured interviews despite and because of their linguistic limitations. Syntax and registers are explored fluently and dynamically, serving as tools to rephrase or retranslate information about key linguistic and cultural concepts to be grasped in conversation. What could be seen as a cultural gap or, simply, a doubt in conversation triggers the desire to seek explanations or retranslations for the sake of "harmony" (Chen, 2011: 126) or empathy, which allow for the refinement of students' linguistic skills. Due to limitations of space, the interviews discussed below represent a limited – even if enlightening – set of examples. More can be found by consulting the 'Transcultural Devon' website, which hosts new video-recordings continually. The student interviewing Valentina (who migrated to Devon in 2012 from the North-East of Italy, https://transculturaldevon.exeter.ac.uk/), for example, displays excellent translation skills, which enable her to ask questions or rephrase statements when needed. For example, the student corrects her translated Italian with no hesitation, rewording sections of her questions and

---

⁶ Email correspondence with a student of Italian, 1 May 2022.
⁷ Email correspondence with a student of Italian, 1 May 2022, italics in original.

stressing, in one instance, the last vowel ending the adjective 'semplici' to mark her awareness of correct gender agreements: "Il fatto che non sei più legata all'Italia ti ha reso le cose più semplice ... o più semplici" (00:20:58-00:21:05). The student also shows excellent retranslation techniques not only when she corrects linguistic errors but also when she tries to enhance cohesion in conversation, clarifying possible misunderstandings. While discussing the reasons for Valentina's moving to Devon, the student reiterates, summarizes and retranslates Valentina's argument well before asking her following question: "È vero, Exeter è una piccola città ma bellissima ma per tante persone che si trasferiscono in Inghilterra la scelta più ovvia, come hai detto tu, è Londra o Manchester" (00:14:21-00:14:40). This well-phrased observation, however, is followed by a faulty question (probably due to the fact that more complex syntactic structures – for example, comparatives – should have been used) which makes the student's information-seeking probe unclear: "Era più difficile che Exeter è una città piccola, è una piccola città?" (00:14:40-00:14:51). The variation of the position of the adjective 'piccola' hints at a possible desire to rephrase or expand the student's question beyond its limitations, which remain apparent. The student is, in fact, able to reply to the interviewee's need for clarification ("In termini di lavoro o di integrazione?" [00:14:52-00:14:59]) with confidence, linking the information offered previously by the interviewee and the current one in a cohesive manner: "Le due" (00:14:57).

Semi-structured interviews are conducted without the use of prearranged scripts or questions but with the freedom for the interviewer to adapt and respond to the interviewee's reactions and sensorial observations. Linguistic interaction, whose major components are improvisation and the reading of corporeal gestures, thus gains ground, establishing itself as the key mode of communication. In these instances, translations happen across sensory borders, enriching the student's experiential learning event. When Valentina, for example, explains the challenges that the Italian job market poses, she accompanies her statement ("La situazione lavorativa in Italia è molto difficile. [...] Anche volendo trovare un lavoro normale ... non si trova" [00:23:22-00:23:34]) with a typical Italian gesture shaking her thumb and index finger up in the air. Seeing the lack of appropriate response from the student, Valentina translates her gesture into words, an interlingual translation, into English, of her bodily posture: "This means: you can't find it... there's no luck" (00:23:36-00:23:40). Words and languages fluctuate from Italian to English and vice versa[8] and oscillate between the physical and the verbal domain, adding complexity to the meaning-making exercise between Valentina and the Exeter student.

---

[8] Interviewees do not often switch to English, but they sometimes do, demonstrating the rich linguistic repertoires of the speakers.

Photographs are shown as objects of cultural memory (00:5:06), "function[ing] metonymically to afford presence to a home experience in a distant place" (Burns, 2020: 182). They elicit the imagination – as interviews are conducted online – of a tactile and affective dimension key to ethnographic research (Hubscher-Davidson, 2011: 2), stimulating the student's visual experience and sustaining the pace of the ethnographic interview. Like Valentina, participants are often asked to bring to their interview meaningful objects that would serve as a prompt and metaphor for feelings and emotions attached to their migration experience. While securing a sensory experience, objects contribute to the transcending of possible barriers erected by the computer screen. In other words, they contribute to what Koskinen calls "contextualised and situated observing" (quoted in Hubsher-Davidson, 2011: 5), which is an essential practice in ethnographic research. In this light, video-interviews, therefore, do not represent a limitation to ethnographic fieldwork but a potential. They become a means to "better tap less tangible aspects of the translation process, such as visualisations or emotional and intuitive behaviours", to use Hubscher-Davidson's words (2011: 2).

When the conversation pertains exclusively to verbalization, code-switching and translanguaging, performed by the interviewee, add an extra layer of complexity to Valentina's interlingual translations. Valentina often punctuates her explanations in Italian with short and punchy phrases in English. These phrases supplement Italian expressions, such as 'fare un catch up' or 'work-in-progress', translate interlingually what Valentina expresses in Italian, such as 'la vita di paese' along with 'village life' or 'oddio' along with 'God forbid', complementing her argument with a plurality of languages. Unsurprisingly, the student does not react to any of them. She nods by welcoming Valentina's urge to translate, retranslate and back translate, in and out of English as well as in and out of Italian. In short, this video-interview is testament to the fact that ethnography, namely the required core activity of the 'Transcultural Devon' project and module, helps students to appreciate the fluidity of languages and the unavoidable construction of identity and culture through translation. The translation is not an easy task here. It does not entail any 'direct' rendering of messages from language A into language B by falling back on idealistic or untenable symmetries between systems of signs and symbols. It is instead a multidirectional transfer of images, meanings, values, beliefs, intentions and emotions across boundaries on the move, shifting negotiations of meaning and the centres of culture continuously. As eloquently explained by Polezzi quoting Asad:

> If we assume that the translator/ethnographer can treat an entire culture as a self-contained text and "translate" it by "matching written sentences in two languages, such that the second set of sentences

becomes the 'real meaning' of the first", then the results of that translation process will only reinforce unequal relationships of power between those who translate and those who are translated. (2012: 104)

What other translation strategies do students learn? How do they engage with in-class discussions pertaining to Italian culture, language acquisition and knowledge production? By default, the Devon-based Italians interviewed by the students are prismatic characters to tap into: polyglots travelling between languages and cultures in a permanent flux of self-translation and subverting hierarchies of source texts and target texts. Within these contexts, notions of fidelity and equivalence in the translation are questioned, overthrown and, eventually, blown apart, making video-subtitling challenging (even if stimulating). Students learn that translation does not happen between monolingual realms but rather within monolingual realms, as Reine Meylaerts teaches them (2013). How do students subtitle the co-presence of two or more languages in conversation? Do they understand their significance? Do they want to disclose to their audience (the viewers of the 'Transcultural Devon' website) the linguistic complexity constituting the beauty and the foundation of these multicultural speakers' language abilities? As educators, we encourage them to give visibility, when possible, to the linguistic plurality that characterizes these instances of transcultural Italies and that enriches the linguistic landscape of such a small South West region of England. We encourage them to challenge viewers' expectations and translation 'norms' (Wolf, 2002), running counter to national requirements of social and linguistic cohesion and assimilation into one language, one nation and one culture. As Bandia maintains: "Migrants are expected to negate or minimize their own history in order to fit better into the sociohistorical context of the host country in a way evocative of an ethics of domesticating or assimilationist translation" (2014: 275). Bandia raises students' awareness of the ideological risks of subtitling interviewees' speeches into homogenizing, standardizing and normalizing English.

Students' reflections on foreignizing *versus* domesticating strategies of translation and subtitling are also informed by Cronin's recommendations: "In the context of powerful, hegemonic cultures, to advocate a foreignizing, refractory or abusive approach to translation could be seen as a subversive, progressive practice which undermines the homogenizing pretensions of the dominant languages and cultures" (Cronin, 2009: 170). Cronin's recommendations are often applied to the translation of Italian speakers that draw from multiple linguistic repertoires (dialect and regional Italian), such as Claudia, who left Florence for Exeter more than 7 years ago. This justifies why Claudia's playful use of the Italian regional adjective 'sudicio' to describe her moka coffee pot is not 'formally' translated or domesticated in her video-interview (00:26:06) but retained and framed by inverted commas. The Italian adjective is also preceded by the English 'a bit dirty' and then explained/translated by the student's added comment 'as we say in Florence...'. This polylingual form of writing and translating aims to provide special value to an Italian object that, as Claudia says, is not just a cliché, being one of the most popular Italian icons, but the symbol of her cultural memories of migration. It also aims to introduce Anglophone viewers to Claudia's rich linguistic repertoire and multiple regional, national and international linguistic identities, which, as she maintains, are situated partially here (Devon) and partially there (Italy and the specificity of her region) (00:22:14). Finally, it aims to translate into words Claudia's resistance to Brexit and her disappointment from an unexpected 'low blow' (00:14:47), which has shaken her sense of belonging to the UK. In this light, the student's foreignizing strategy of translation aligns with Cronin's interpretation of translation as a form of resistance:

> For political or other reasons speakers of minority languages may have a perfectly good knowledge of a dominant language (Catalans knowing Spanish) but still insist on translation from and into that language. Translation in this instance is not about making communication possible but about establishing identity or enacting a form of resistance to the claims of the hegemonic language. (2009: 171)

Claudia's interview is used in class as a prompt for further discussion and reflection. In it, students see an attempt to maximize the singularity of the participant's voice as well as that of the student interviewer.

5. Translation and ethnography in the classroom as the Third Space

As discussed above, translation takes place at various levels in the Transcultural Devon project. Students are exposed to an array of emotions, values and beliefs translated into words by the interviewees and retranslated into subtitles by the students. Because of this, students are given the space and time to co-reflect on their own emotions and affective engagement with the Other. As Hubscher-Davidson claims: "It can be a challenging task to shed light on often confusing, contradictory or seemingly nonsensical data" (2011: 5). No immediate answer can be produced, and for that, they, once again, act as 'professional' ethnographers. Wolf reminds us of Margaret Mead's argument in favour of lengthy reflections in anthropology: "I should like to be able to interpose between my statement and the reader's consideration of that statement a *pause*, a realization not of what authoritative right I have to make the statement I make, but instead of how it was arrived at, of what the anthropological process is" (2002: 187, my italics). Time and reflexivity are therefore factored into the classroom, in line with ethnographic requirements, as Hubscher-Davidson explains: "Ethnography recognizes the importance of reflexivity and the researcher's role as a participant in the research process" (2011: 7). Following Hubscher-Davidson's recommendations, the student-researchers reflection on the study "forms part of the collected data and is an integral part of the analytical process" (2011: 7).

Explorations of the data and the student's intersubjective relation with them take place both in students' reflective written statements and in the classroom. The majority of the module classes and workshops are designed to reflect on translation. Students express the need to be faithful to their data, especially in subtitling, demonstrating respect for their interviewees' values and displaying ethical responsibilities towards their anglophone audience (see Pym, 2012). They are undoubtedly driven by the ambition to obtain a good mark and impress their assessors, but they are also motivated by genuine ethical principles. Students often problematize subtitling techniques which, in order to comply with audio-visual constraints, require summarizations or crystallizations of messages by falling back on "omission or simplification"[9]. Students question the practicality and the effectiveness of subtitling techniques or 'etiquette' at the expense of the interviewees' authenticity and voice. They want "to balance the demands of linguistic and emotional implications of conveying an accurate transcript of what the interviewee offered in the medium of" their first language[10]. Through subtitling, students experience one of the most prominent challenges met by translation and ethnography: "The persistence of an ideology claiming transparency of representation and immediacy of experience" (Clifford quoted in Wolf, 2002: 185). Wolf's assertion that "Meanings are no longer perceived as being roughly the same across different cultures, but as something to be represented in codes and symbols linked to the translator's and the ethnographer's subjectivity and background" (2002: 185) acquires weight in language acquisition classes such as 'Transcultural Devon'. Critical thinking is applied by students in the module who enrich their language acquisition by raising crucial questions. They concur with Husbsher-Davidson, who claims that "institutional patterns of behaviour become practices that organize discourse, and convert it into another discourse during which the participant loses his [sic] voice" (2011: 9).

The classroom becomes a valuable forum hosting students' reflections on the interpretation of the ethnographic data and strategies of translation. It can be equated to Wolf's (2002) and Shirley Jordan's (2002) appropriation of Homi Bhabha's Third Space, namely a fertile in-between space where constant

---

[9] Email correspondence with a student of Italian, 1 May 2022.
[10] Email correspondence with a student of Italian, 1 May 2022.

linguistic negotiations are at play. Wolf (2002) and Jordan (2002) give prominence to a space that is neither of the Other nor the Self, but rather an in-between space overflowing with infinite possibilities, combinations and interaction, "the site of the encounter between different cultures" (Wolf, 2002: 188). "This negotiation" – Wolf (2002: 189) continues – "has been interpreted as a synonym for translation, inasmuch as the effort to translate demands the negotiation of cultural contradictions and misapprehension". In the classroom, students assess, evaluate, adapt, adopt and/or discard various translation solutions enhancing their in-betweenness and liminality in a productive way. These negotiations are possible not only because they are required to subtitle European or non-European languages interviews into English but also because they are required to attend non-language specific classes and workshops, where a plurality of languages and cultures are at work. Linguistic performances are compared, confronted, and continuously translated in and out of English and between any language combination. Latin and non-Latin languages are compared, and specific applications are contextually explained so that students learn from one another, moving from one linguistic domain to the other in a fluid way. An issue which is frequently raised in the classroom relates to how interviewers address their interviewees in terms of register and style. Students of Italian discuss various grammatical scenarios (the Lei form or the subjunctive used as imperative) which support the formality and the respect paid to interviewees. In this context, translation is not just a pedagogical exercise to facilitate students' language acquisition. It becomes 'the' language that students use to communicate and reflect. Thus, centre stage is afforded to translation as well as moments of translation. These precious moments raise students' awareness of translation as a visible practice and of translators as agents of change and cultural negotiation.

6. Conclusion

This chapter presents the positive outcomes of a project and an undergraduate experimental module that place intercultural contacts and negotiations at the centre of the learning and teaching experience. It gives prominence to the learning objectives of a module that excites students and educators at the University of Exeter. Following in the footsteps of Wells et al., the convenors and tutors of 'Transcultural Devon' draw on the fruitful interplay between translation and ethnography to welcome alterity in the classroom and on the screen. Testament to transculturality as a value is the 'Transcultural Devon' short film[11] produced by Todino, Farris, Hipkins, Salas

---

[11] 'Transcultural Devon' (7 December 2021). Transcultural Devon - Displaced Belonging. Retrieved May 2, 2022, from www.youtube.com/watch?v=MhoFHugs4Ws.

and the University of Exeter students at the end of the 2021 academic year with a 2020-21 Education Incubator award. Set in Devon, the film stages a polyphony of European voices which escape confinement and restrictive labels. As this film demonstrates, the course provides valuable opportunities for the students to engage with the migrant community in Devon and to do justice to it. Students' ethnographic data (video-interviews) populate a long-lasting video-archive which amplifies the voice of the migrants through the powerful medium of their first languages. It enables students to reflect on and better understand what it means to be a language specialist in the post-Brexit era and to develop first-hand experience with modern language speakers (including Italian) at a time when contacts are limited and regulated by social distancing and preventative measures for Covid-19. Keen to respond to students' requirements, the project empowers students allowing them to develop employability skills and, as a student of Italian states, "to express our passion of languages in an industry setting (language services and community engagement)"[12]. It also enables students to become independent learners and reflective agents in charge of their own linguistic choices and co-responsible for the making of cultures as well as the setting of the module syllabus. Themes explored to date vary according to interviewees' backgrounds and the student's interests and include: cultural belonging, affiliations to cultural groups and communities, language practices, uprooting, homing, gender issues in migration, and so on.

The 'Transcultural Devon' project and module are the outcomes of a concerted effort of a number of Exeter educators (*in primis* Todino, to whom I am indebted) who believe in people as resources to be cherished, maximized and represented in long-lasting memories of migration. These educators and I wanted to respond to the students' need to "engage with members of the community that valorised our attainment of a language and put its use into the application of intercultural communication"[13]. The approach that I have developed here to explain this project reflects my own research interest (translation, migration and ethnography), contribution, and take on the module. The module could, however, lend itself to other narratives, analyses and perspectives. Equal contribution is provided by my colleagues researching adjacent disciplines and would deserve further attention and discussion. For example, Hipkins provides valuable input on the significance of digital archives in modern society and oral history as knowledge production, Todino on cultural memories of migration and liaison with the Devon community, Salas on filming and production, Afonso on self-narratives

---

[12] Email correspondence, 1 May 2022.
[13] Email correspondence with student of Italian, 1 May 2022.

of migration and Farris on subtitling. In this chapter, not sufficient attention has been devoted to a number of these aspects, which would deserve the contribution of these scholars to come to light. I, therefore, invite them to respond to this chapter and continue to participate in intellectual debates on 'Transcultural Devon' while improving the academic objectives of this project.

Finally, the module is situated within a new tradition of 'transnational' studies, including transnational Italian Studies celebrated by Charles Burdett and Polezzi (2020a). This tradition aims to broaden the horizons of a discipline which, by responding to globalization and social mobility, encompasses the study of transcultural phenomena and transnational productions across Italian borders. We, therefore, aim to respond to some of the higher education-related questions raised by Burdett and Polezzi, animating the field of Italian Studies to date: "What does 'Italian studies' stand for in this transforming world? What does it mean to 'study Italian' in today's academic context? And how can we define 'transnational Italian studies'?" (2020b: 1). Burdett and Polezzi (2020b: 2) note that studying Italian at University level implies the acquisition not only of language skills but also of translation skills, which equip students with the ability to travel across borders and move between languages and cultures. 'Transcultural Devon' aims to do this. It aims to satisfy the students' curiosity for the world, a world in which Italians play a fundamental role, and to "promote the discovery of unique experiences through ethnography or in general through cultural exposure"[14]. The course is modelled on paradigms that situate the study of the Italian language and culture within a broader context of transnational migration wherein the local is as important as the global, and the circulation of hybridized texts, people and objects is the norm. By raising awareness of the Italian culture outside its geopolitical borders, the module also finds its place within a broader multidiscipline, namely Modern Languages, which, in the words of Burdett and Polezzi, "promotes a model of Modern Languages not as the inquiry into separate national traditions, but as the study of languages, cultures and their interactions" (2020b: 0). In this light, the module does not want to rule out any opportunity to investigate first-hand experiences with cultural products generated in Italy. Objects of studies, in fact, incorporate those whose lives and values are continuously informed by a more or less strong bond with Italy as their country of origin. Conversely, the module considers ties, connections and associations between Italy and other European and non-European group identities as a possible corpus of study, celebrating singularities and transnational contributions to local communities, including the South West of England.

---

[14] Email correspondence with student of Italian, 1 May 2022.

Acknowledgement

I would like to express my sincere gratitude to my University of Exeter colleagues and especially: Danielle Hikpins, Alice Farris, Valentina Todino, David Salas and Susana Afonso, for involving me in this project and for allowing me to contribute to it by enhancing every possible link with translation. I cherish our collaboration and all the work that we have done and that we will continue to do with our students. I would also like to thank other colleagues in the Department of Languages, Cultures and Visual Studies – Katie Brown, Alice Farris and Adam Horsley – for reading my chapter and giving me invaluable feedback.

References

Bandia, P. F. (2014). Translocation: Translation, Migration, and the Relocation of Cultures. In Bermann, S., & Porter, C. (Eds.), *A Companion to Translation Studies*, (pp. 271–284). Chichester, West Sussex: Wiley Blackwell.

Burdett, C., & Polezzi, L. (Eds.), (2020a). *Transnational Italian Studies*. Liverpool: Liverpool University Press.

Burdett, C., & Polezzi, L. (2020b). Introduction. *Transnational Italian Studies*, (pp. 1-24). Liverpool: Liverpool University Press.

Burns, J. (2020). Mobile Homes: Transnational Subjects and the (Re)Creation of Home Spaces. In Burdett, C., & Polezzi, L. (Eds.), *Transnational Italian Studies*, (pp. 177–194). Liverpool: Liverpool University Press.

Buzelin, H. (2022). Ethnography in Translation Studies: An Object and a Research Methodology. *Slovo.ru: Baltic accent*, 13(1), 32–47.

Buzelin, H., & Baraldi, C. (2016). Sociology and Translation Studies: Two Disciplines Meeting. In Gambier, Y., & van Doorslaer, L. (Eds.), *Border Crossings: Translation Studies and Other Disciplines*, (pp. 117–139). Amsterdam and Philadelphia: John Benjamins.

Cronin, M. (2003). *Translation and Globalization*. London: Routledge.

Cronin, M. (2009). Minority. In Baker, M., & Saldanha, G. (Eds.), *The Routledge Encyclopedia of Translation Studies*, (pp. 169–172). London and New York: Routledge.

Cronin, M. (2013). Travel and Translation. In Gambier, Y., & van Doorslaer, L. (Eds.), *Handbook of Translation Studies*. Volume 4, (pp. 194–199). Amsterdam and Philadelphia: John Benjamins.

Chen, S-H. (2011). Power Relations between the Researcher and the Researched: An Analysis of Native and Nonnative Ethnographic Interviews. *Field Methods*, 23(2), 119–135.

Gentzler, E. (2001). *Contemporary Translation Theories*. Clevedon: Multilingual Matters.

Hubscher-Davidson, S. (2011). A Discussion of Ethnographic Research Methods and their Relevance for Translation Process Research. *Across Languages and Cultures*, 12(1), 1–18.

Jordan, S. A. (2002). Ethnographic Encounters: The Processes of Cultural Translation. *Language and Intercultural Communication*, 2(2), 96–110. DOI: 10.1080/14708470208668079

Meylaerts, R. (2013). Multilingualism as a Challenge for Translation Studies. In Millán, C., & Bartrina, F., (Eds.), *The Routledge Handbook of Translation Studies*, (pp. 519–533). London and New York: Routledge.

Migration Observatory. The University of Oxford. Retrieved 2 May 2022, from https://migrationobservatory.ox.ac.uk.

Munday, J. (2016). *Introducing Translation Studies: Theories and Applications*. London: Routledge.

Polezzi, L. (2006). Translation, Travel, Migration. *The Translator*, 12(2), 169–188. DOI: 10.1080/13556509.2006.10799214

Polezzi, L. (2009). Mobility. In Baker, M., & Saldanha, G. (Eds.), *The Routledge Encyclopedia of Translation Studies*, (pp. 172–178). London and New York: Routledge.

Polezzi, L. (2012). Translation and Mobility. In Gambier, Y., & van Doorslaer, L. (Eds.), *Handbook of Translation Studies*. Volume 3, (pp. 102–107). Amsterdam and Philadelphia: John Benjamins.

Przybylski, L. (2021). *Hybrid Ethnography: Online, Offline, and In Between*. Volume 58. London: Sage.

Pym, A. (2012). *On Translator Ethics: Principles for Mediation between Cultures*. Amsterdam: John Benjamins.

Saldanha, G., & O'Brien, S. (2013). *Research Methodologies in Translation Studies*. London; New York: Routledge.

The Quality Assurance Agency for Higher Education. (2022). *Subject Benchmark Statement. Languages, Cultures and Societies*. Fifth Edition, Version for Consultation. Gloucester. Retrieved 15 November 2022, from www.qaa.ac.uk.

Wells, N., Forsdick, C., Bradley, J., Burdett, C., Burns, J., Demossier, M., Hills de Zárate, M., Huc-Hepher, S., Jordan, S., Pitman, T., & Wall, G. (2019). Ethnography and Modern Languages. *Modern Languages Open*, 1(1), 1–16.

Wolf, M. (2002). Culture as Translation – and Beyond. Ethnographic Models of Representation in Translation Studies. In Hermans, T. (Ed.), *Crosscultural Transgressions: Research Methods in Translation Studies II. Historical and Ideological Issues*, (pp. 180-192). Manchester: St Jerome.

Wolf, M., & Fukari, A. (Eds.), (2007). *Constructing a Sociology of Translation*. Amsterdam: Philadelphia: John Benjamins.

Web references

'Transcultural Devon' Stories of migration and language. Interview with Claudia. The University of Exeter. Retrieved 2 May 2022, from https://transculturaldevon.exeter.ac.uk/items/show/27

'Transcultural Devon' Stories of migration and language. Interview with Valentina. The University of Exeter. Retrieved 2 May 2022, from https://transculturaldevon.exeter.ac.uk/items/show/19

'Transcultural Devon' Stories of migration and language. The University of Exeter. Retrieved 2 May 2022, from https://transculturaldevon.exeter.ac.uk/

'Transcultural Devon' (7 December 2021). Transcultural Devon - Displaced Belonging. Retrieved 2 May 2022, from www.youtube.com/watch?v=MhoFHugs4Ws.

Chapter 12

Learning Italian with cartoons

Stefano Maranzana
Emory University

Abstract: This chapter discusses the use of captioned video cartoons in the Italian language classroom at the university level. A brief introduction considers first the use of captioned videos in general and cartoons in particular to enhance second language acquisition. Owing to their slow speech rate, the authentic interpersonal dialogues, and the numerous lexical repetitions, cartoons, especially those created for young children, allow for authentic language exposure that can engage and motivate learners while at the same time developing their listening comprehension skills and vocabulary acquisition. The chapter next focuses on the importance of humour in the classroom as it provides teachers and students with a respite from formal assignments, affording a change of pace that may contribute to lowering the affective filter experienced by learners (Bell, 2009). In the end, I present a part that focuses on a methodology for the use of *Peppa Pig* at the university level.

Kwywords: Cartoons, Peppa Pig, Italian, Humor, Authentic language

***

1. Introduction

The sociocultural understanding of second language acquisition (SLA) favours the contextual and social character of language, and it is characterized by a deviation from the traditional teacher-oriented grammar-based second language (L2) instruction (Pavlenko and Lantolf, 2000). From a sociocultural perspective, L2 learning goes beyond the skill of how to construct grammatically correct sentences and entails also learning to use language in the proper social context to engage in meaningful interactions in everyday life settings (Garrett, 2008). Introducing authentic video materials such as animated cartoons in the language classroom offers learners an opportunity to experience the dynamics of daily-life conversation and acquire new vocabulary and idiomatic expressions within a highly contextual environment.

Indeed, children's cartoons can be regarded as a pragmatic resource because they provide well-illustrated situational frames which contain the same time context and language (Nightingale, 2014). As maintained by the literature, exposing learners to materials that are not intended for language learning provides them with richer samples of the target language that allow them to discern the dynamics of authentic communication where the emphasis is on message and not on language *per se* (Ciccone, 1995; Herron et al., 1995; Gilmore 2007; Pilz, 2008; Torregrosa Benaven and Sánchez-Reyes Peñamaría, 2011; Maranzana, 2022a).

This chapter discusses the use of captioned video cartoons in the Italian language classroom at the university level. A brief introduction considers first the use of captioned videos in general and cartoons in particular to enhance L2 acquisition. Owing to their slow speech rate, the authentic interpersonal dialogues, and the numerous lexical repetitions, cartoons, especially those created for young children, allow for authentic language exposure that can engage and motivate learners while at the same time developing their listening comprehension skills and vocabulary acquisition. Indeed, cartoons as authentic audio-visual material enable teachers to involve learners, attract their attention and, importantly, establish a non-threatening atmosphere for presenting the information.

The chapter next focuses on the importance of humour in the classroom as it provides teachers and students with a respite from formal assignments, affording a change of pace that may contribute to lowering the affective filter experienced by learners (Bell, 2009). I conclude with a section that focuses on a potential methodology for the use of *Peppa Pig* with same-language captions for first and second-semester university-level students.

2. Captioned video

Captions are the synchronised juxtaposition of text, superimposed at the bottom of the screen, that replicates verbatim the speech event occurring in a video. While *subtitles* designate the written translation of the speech in a language other than the one spoken on video (i.e., speech in one language and text in another) and will not be discussed in this study, captions are intralingual, i.e., the word-by-word transcription within the same language. Although the primary purpose of captioning is to act as a visual cue for the Deaf, textual aids in the form of captioned audio-visuals have been used in second language (L2) pedagogical situations and have been studied to assess their efficacy (Vanderplank, 2016; 2019).

Research into captioning's effectiveness as a tool for L2 development began already in the early 1980s (Taylor, 2005). In one of the earliest investigations to assess captioning's influence on comprehension, Price (1983) found that the 450 participants improved their understanding when the video was accompanied by captions. Subsequent studies have reinforced the opinion that using captioned videos in L2 instruction advances learner's comprehension (Chai and Erlam, 2008; Danan, 2004; Montero Perez et al., 2014; Vanderplank, 2010; Winke, Gass, and Sydorenko, 2010; 2013). Danan (2004), in her meta-analysis of research focusing on captioned video, offers a wide-ranging synopsis of the advantages as well as the limitations of captions that have been recognized by researchers. As for the limitations, captioning may be unfitting for lower-level learners or learners with low reading proficiency (Danan, 2004). The relationship between the effectiveness of captions and students' proficiency levels has been explored by Taylor (2005), who reports that captions aided third-year college students better than first-year students. The latter found the real-time presentation of sound, image, and caption to be distracting. Interestingly, also the learners' cultural background has been noticed to have an impact on how they perceive the utility of captions for L2 understanding. As noted by Bravo (2008), all the participants in her longitudinal study who at first found captions vexing or distracting were from Italy or Spain, two countries with a practice of dubbing foreign media rather than subtitling (Vandreplank, 2016). Thus, for learners who are not used to consuming videos with superimposed textual aids, captions may be a nuisance rather than a support.

Although studies tend to suggest that captions can be useful in vocabulary recall and acquisition (Bird and Williams, 2002; Gambier, 2007), Vandergrift (2007) points out that relying on captions may, in fact, hinder the development of important compensatory listening strategies, i.e., the ability of learners to infer and fill the gaps where words are not entirely understood (see also Vanderplank, 2010). In this view, a captioned video might delay language acquisition, as it fails to simulate a real-life setting where the listener is unable to rely on the contiguous display of word-by-word text and is thus stimulated to pursue alternative strategies to reach comprehension. Indeed, Pujolá (2002) and King (2002) have argued that the presence of captions makes it difficult to determine with certainty whether comprehension scores given in the literature to validate the helpfulness of captions reflect participants' listening or, rather, their reading skills.

Nevertheless, Danan (2004) shows that the benefits associated with the occurrence of captioning with audio-visuals include improvements in language production, increased word identification and vocabulary-building skills, greater ability to detect nuances in speech, and the diminution of learners' anxiety. Overall, the literature also suggests that captions may indeed offer more gains than shortcomings, especially due to the bimodal reinforcement of *sound*

+ *text* (Vanderplank, 2010): the redundancy generated by the matching auditory and visual stimuli thus functions as a catalyst to learning. Winke, Gass, and Sydorenko (2010) submitted that captions could improve learners' attention and advance their learning achievements by forming a connection with their prior knowledge. The elevated amount of conscious attention exerted by learners to language use while reading the captions, submits Vanderplank (1990), is, in itself, a crucial element in terms of language acquisition. In other words, conscious language learning, that is, the learner's effort to read captioned video, as opposed to simply watching the video, produces significant language improvements (Vanderplank, 1990; 2016).

Captions can support learners to isolate and notice lexical elements, hence clarifying a potentially unclear input and enabling word/phrase recall with more accuracy (Chai and Erlam, 2008; Montero Perez et al., 2014; Winke, Gass and Sydorenko, 2010). As a result, by promoting form-meaning mapping, a central process for L2 development, captioning helps learners process and decode what they hear through visualization and the identification of word boundaries (Winke, Gass and Sydorenko, 2013). In Maranzana (2022b), participants reported being able to 'see' what was said in real-time and identify what, during a first viewing, seemed like an indistinct string of sounds. Not only could they parse the sentence, but they could also discriminate the boundaries between each word. Hence, captions helped learners to isolate and notice lexical components, thus clarifying what was at first an indistinct input and enabling word/phrase recall with more precision.

Noticing unknown words in the input is the first step in the acquisition process (Huckin and Coady, 1999; Hulstijn, 2001), and the vital role of attention is also at the basis of Vanderplank's (1990; 2016) model on language learning via captioned video. Vanderplank (1990) identifies attention as a conscious process of selection centred on 'noting and gathering' information systematically and on a reflective constituent in which learners notice a gap while comparing their L2 competency with the input they perceive in the captioned video (p. 229).

In order to determine how learners absorbed captions, Chai and Erlam (2008) asked 10 Chinese learners of L2 English who were presented with a captioned video in English whether they paid attention mostly to the captions, the sound, or the onscreen images. Participants stated that they fixated more on the captions. They also reported that occasionally they were incapable of reading and listening at the same time, while others indicated that they could effortlessly alternate reading the captions and paying attention to what was unfolding on the screen. The authors determined that while watching the captioned video, learners tend to prioritize reading over listening, which may prevent them from processing the audio and thus pay less attention to the information delivered by the aural stream and contextual clues. Chai and Erlam (2008) conclude by suggesting that learners ought to be exposed to both captioned and non-captioned videos, following the learning goals. Syderenko (2010) draws similar conclusions: alternating captioned and non-captioned audio-visuals would allow students to focus on vocabulary acquisition (captioned) as well as on listening strategies (non-captioned).

In a recent study, Vanderplank (2019) details the qualitative findings of the EURECAP Project, in which 36 learners of French, German, Italian and Spanish at the intermediate level and above in a large university in the UK were able to choose from various films on DVD with optional captions and watched them under their control in their own time. The article reports that while there were participants that became quite 'caption-dependent' and focused on reading to the exclusion of listening, it appears that it was the case with particular films that were especially challenging in terms of content, rapid speech or dialect. 'For the most part,' says Vanderplank (2019), "participants were able to make flexible and dynamic use of the captions to maximise enjoyment, enhance their understanding and develop their vocabulary knowledge and listening skills'" (p. 421).

In sum, captioning may act as a useful scaffolding device, furthering learners' comprehension and reinforcing acquisition, especially when the audio stream is particularly challenging, as is often the case with authentic materials (Vandreplank, 2016). One authentic type of audio-visual that can be used in L2 classrooms that might be somewhat less difficult for beginners is children's animated cartoons.

3. Animated Cartoons in L2 Instruction: *Peppa Pig*

There is a relatively small yet growing body of literature that focuses on the use of animated cartoons for the development of adult learners' L2 acquisition (Clark 2000; Bahrani and Soltani 2011; Bahrani and Sim 2012; Bahrani 2014; Bahrani, Tam and Zuraidah 2014; Saeedi and Biri 2016; Vulchanova et al. 2015; Maranzana, 2022a, Maranzana, 2021b). According to Bahrani (2014), the advantages of employing cartoons for L2 pedagogy are the following: (1) cartoons often grab the viewer-learner's attention, (2) they display a strong picture-to-word connection, (3) dialogues are simple, (4) with numerous repetitions, and (5) the rate of speech is often relatively low, depending on the cartoon. Moreover, video cartoons, particularly those that are created for young children, often involve more distinctly articulated speech in standard L2 accents (Vulchanova et al., 2015). Describing his pedagogical strategies, Clark (2000) suggests that cartoons display information in a non-threatening manner and have the potential to support thinking processes and discussions. Indeed, characteristically, cartoons tend to exaggerate and emphasize a particular cultural feature or behaviour that can be used in the classroom as a topic for discussion and/or social analysis (Bahrani and Soltani, 2011). Furthermore, cartoons allow learners to be exposed to authentic language in different contextual situations (Abuzahra, Farrah, and Zalloum, 2016).

Inquiring into the effectiveness of exposure to three different types of original videos (news, cartoons, and films), Bahrani and Sim (2012) implemented a 10-week study comprising 60 low-level learners of English. The news programs were CNN, BBC, Press TV and CBS News on the economy, politics, society and science. Participants were allocated into 3 groups: the first group was exposed to news, the second to cartoons, and the third to feature films. The results of the post-test suggest that the first group (news) did not improve language proficiency overall, while the other two groups (cartoons and film) gained significant competence, specifically, the group that watched cartoons. Low gains were found in the group who watched newscasts, possibly because of the degree of specialized terminology present in this type of media.

Saeedi and Biri (2016) sought to assess the benefits of animated cartoons for grammar instruction. Twelve episodes of the animated cartoon *The Looney Tunes Show* were imparted to English as a Foreign Language (EFL) Turkish and Persian students' during a six-session treatment. This study used a pretest/post-test design and was concerned with the acquisition of one specific English grammar construction on conditional sentences. It aimed at comparing the performance of two groups of learners exposed to two different approaches to teaching this form. 17 participants in the control group (without video) were exposed to explicit grammar instruction, while the 17 participants in the experimental group received instruction through the use of the animated cartoon. Each time a conditional sentence was used by one of the characters in the cartoon, the instructor paused and replayed the clip, drawing the participants' attention to that specific sentence. The results of the post-test showed that the overall learning of the conditional sentences by the participants of the experimental group improved significantly ($p=$ .003), and they exhibited a gain in knowledge, the researchers claim, because they were exposed to the animated cartoon. Additionally, the majority of the participants in this study revealed in succeeding interviews positive attitudes towards the use of animated cartoons and saw it as an effective and helpful resource for learning the conditional form.

Vulchanova et al. (2015), who looked at the effect of captions and subtitles using video cartoons on English comprehension and acquisition in a group of 114 Norwegian High School students, mention that they selected the American animated cartoon series *Family Guy* because the researchers judged that it was more likely to be understood by the participants, both in terms of language and plot. Maranzana (2022a) investigated the attitudes of university-level students toward the use of the children's cartoon *Peppa Pig*. The participants were both Italian L2 novice and intermediate-level students, and most of them regarded the cartoon as an engaging and valuable activity for language acquisition. Humour was reported to have rendered the endeavour less stressful, engaging the students while giving them a respite from the traditional textbook-oriented activities. Furthermore, being exposed to Italian idioms in context, together with the instructor's explanations, was often mentioned in the data as a helpful dynamic of the in-class discussions as they recognized that the type of language occurring in the cartoon is not usually taught in formal L2 classrooms Maranzana (2022a). Indeed, as indicated by Nigmatullayevna (2022), students can effortlessly assign the linguistic content of the cartoon to the appropriate setting within real-life communication, developing their ability to understand contextual language and employ pragmatic use in everyday situations.

The cartoon brought to the classroom authentic material that presented language in context, an aspect that was regarded favourably by participants Maranzana (2022b). They acknowledged that behind a 'silly' and comical children's cartoon lay rich and authentic everyday L2 speech that is seldom represented in the traditional textbook.

4. The Role of Humour to Stimulate L2 Learning

Considering Krashen's (1982) affective filter hypothesis and the importance of maintaining a low affective filter (i.e., facilitating a relaxed learning environment), it may be argued that language educators should always attempt to reduce the tensions or anxieties that permeate classrooms with a healthy and balanced injection of humour in their pedagogy. This can bring about the students' psychological comfort leading to a productive learning environment. Yet, what is humour exactly, and how can it be integrated into the language classroom?

Humour is regarded as a universal type of discourse and a strategy for social interaction. Indeed, humour is intimately related to human nature and permeates discourse and communication on a daily basis (Schmitz, 2002), becoming a sort of 'social lubricant' (Reilly, 2006: 151). Humour is an inseparable part of the human experience and, therefore, an essential aspect of humanity's remarkable capacity for language. In fact, it stands as one of the few universals applicable to all societies and all languages throughout the world (Kruger, 1996; Trachtenberg, 1979). Humour is part of nearly all social encounters; indeed, humour is a central part of sociolinguistic competence in any culture (Medgyes, 2002; Vaid, 2006; Bilokcuoglu and Debreli (2018). The aim of this section is to foster awareness towards the implications of pedagogical humour, as well as classroom humour in general, for learning a second language.

As in other acts of communication, humour encompasses several variables. It involves past experiences, skills, moods, information, and beliefs. A certain degree of sophistication and cognitive complexity is required to connect these features and to convey and understand humorous implications. In other words, humour is highly arbitrary and difficult to define with precision. The work by Gardner and colleagues has played a significant role in drawing attention to socio-affective factors and the importance of positive attitudes in language learning (Gardner and Lambert, 1972; Gardner, 1985; 2010). As Deneire (1995) discusses at length, the L2 language classroom presents high levels of tension/anxiety for the learner. Not only do students strive to communicate in a new and unfamiliar tongue, but they are also required to do so in front of peers. This triggers a distinctively tense/anxious learning atmosphere – if compared with other instructional settings – because the student is divested of his or her L1 language expertise and, consequently, also of part of his or her personal and cultural identity (Deneire, 1995; Askildson, 2005). Language teachers are conscious of the importance of diffusing that tension in the classroom and of how the L2 learning process is supported, not only through a variety of effective pedagogies but also by nurturing the positive emotions which are essential for the long-term undertaking of language learning (MacIntyre and Mercer, 2014). However, '[w]e still live,' argues Watson (2013), "with the outdated idea that learning must be hard work, and must NOT be fun" (p. 2, emphasis in the original). Indeed, Berk (2003) mentions three reasons why instructors at higher education institutions are disinclined to use humour in their courses. First, humour is not an integral part of any formal syllabus; second, the mistaken assumption that to integrate humour in the class, the teacher needs the talents of a consummate comedian; third – and perhaps more importantly –, the conviction among many educators that teaching is a *serious* profession and the inclusion of humour in teaching is regarded as indecorous and frivolous.

Still, humour provides teachers and students with an occasion for a respite from the formal and 'serious' assigned material, affording a change of pace that may contribute to lowering the tension that many learners experience during the learning process. Humour is, in fact, regarded as a valuable medium for students to learn the vocabulary, syntax, semantics, and conventions of the language they are studying, as well as to achieve a better understanding of its culture (Bell, 2009; Askildson, 2005).

Psychologically, humour infuses a positive emotional and social environment in the classroom, thus allowing the learners to be more receptive to the information that they are exposed to and that is being submitted by the instructor (Askildson, 2005; Bell, 2009; Garner, 2006) as well as boosting alertness which ultimately prompts greater information acquisition (Zillmann et al., 1980). Wandersee (1982) showcases the many benefits of introducing humour in the classroom. These include relief in teaching sensitive subjects, fostering togetherness, keeping students lively and attentive, enhancing the function of students' mental faculties, lowering tension in the classroom, making instruction easier to understand, making learning a more personable and enjoyable endeavour, and in general creating a more effective learning ambience. An interesting theory recently put forth by Wanzer, Frymier, and Irwin (2009), the *Instructional Humour Processing Theory* (IHP), stresses that the humorous messages used by teachers should increase student motivation and alertness and lead to the creation of a positive environment.

Humour in the form of language play, argues Forman (2011), "is a form of verbal art which emerges from creativity, and shades into wit, into intelligence, all of which are dimensions of daily language use; and so the experiences afforded by humour may indeed represent a valuable resource for second language classrooms" (pp. 563-564). Bell (2009) suggests that humorous language play may support the acquisition of L2 vocabulary, especially by letting lexical items be processed more deeply, rendering them more memorable.

Of course, humour can be a double-edged sword, and it needs to be handled with care Pomerantz and Bell (2011). A mismanaged sense of humour, says to Morrison (2008), may offend, lead to embarrassment or to a ruinous drop in students' self-esteem. Consequently, taking into consideration the likelihood that humour may harm, it is vital that there be strategies and restraint with regard to the employment of humour in the classroom. Indeed, Berk (2003) recommends not to use what she refers to as 'high risk' humour, that is, references that make fun of people or sensitive issues such as race, gender, religion, etc., as this kind of humour "shuts down communication and erects a barrier to learning" (p. 23). Instead, the author suggests the use of 'low-risk' humour; one does not run the risk of offending the students. Admittedly, it may be argued that it becomes somewhat difficult to determine with precision whether we are using 'high risk' or 'low risk' humour. Hence, the use of an animated cartoon for young children, such as *Peppa Pig*, may infuse a reasonable dose of 'low risk' humour and would be a safer choice than, for example, *Family Guy* or *South Park*, which are notoriously thorny in matters of political correctness (Sienkiewicz and Marx, 2009).

5. *Peppa Pig* for 1st and 2nd semester university-level Italian classes

What follows are a series of suggestions on how to employ *Peppa Pig* with the same language captions in the L2 Italian classroom. Although the cartoon could be successfully used in third-semester courses – perhaps focusing more on advanced grammar and discussion – I will discuss the potential use of Peppa Pig for first- and second-semester learners here. Without much prior organization, this cartoon can be used, for example, at the beginning of class, to start off on a humorous and stress-free note. A humorous moment fosters a reduction of anxiety on intellectually demanding tasks, and the positive atmosphere established at the onset of class can help students to relax (Pomerantz and Bell, 2011). I will, however, propose a more structured way to use *Peppa Pig*, in which the instructor could take advantage of the 5-minute episode for a full one-hour class time.

5. 1. Choosing the right episode

An initial step is to determine which episode will be employed. In this regard, it is important to ensure that the episode has a certain bearing on the vocabulary and/or the grammatical structures covered in the textbook. Consequently, the instructor should perform comprehensive online research to select an episode (or more) relevant to the programme. Although quite time-consuming, it can be easily done by searching on the YouTube platform. It suffices to either execute a search on YouTube with the wording 'peppa pig italiano' to find a wide array of episodes or by accessing the official YouTube channel *https://www.youtube.com/user/CanaleUfficialePeppa/videos*. The downside of this process is that frequently on YouTube, many episodes are grouped together (about 50), so it may become rather wearisome to locate a specific one. Moreover, captions are often autogenerated and thus contain abundant inaccuracies. Alternative ways are to search on YouTube for already captioned videos (i.e., "peppa pig in italiano con sottotitoli") or download an episode in Italian with a YouTube downloader program website and manually add the captions in a .rtf file. Although this procedure is more time-consuming, it may yield a better result in the end as the instructor is in control of the accuracy of the captions and full transcript. If, when the chosen moment to use the cartoon, the chapter in the textbook features vocabulary about food and grocery shopping, the instructor could show the episode entitled *La spesa (Shopping* – Season 1, Episode 49), which can be accessed on YouTube by following this link: www.youtube.com/watch?v=hJcESYiBz-A. In this episode, Peppa's family go to the grocers to buy food, and thus the vocabulary involves, among others, fruits and vegetables.

Before each episode screening, the title of the episode should be introduced, along with 4 to 6 key vocabulary terms and expressions, on a PowerPoint presentation projected on the classroom screen. These introductions serve as *advance organizers*, i.e., scaffolding strategies meant to activate the learners' prior knowledge and thus bridge the gap between unfamiliar information and previously known information. Presenting advance organizers before video viewing is recognized in SLA as an important device to help L2 learners understand its contents (Herron, 1994; Herron et al., 1995; Yang, 2014). The vocabulary presented in the PowerPoint should include terms that would help students in the comprehension of the plot: different terms may be tested in subsequent vocabulary tasks if the instructor chooses to do so.

5. 2. First and second screenings of the episode

I suggest screening the episode of *Peppa Pig* twice: once without captions and once with captions. During the viewing of the first episodes, students can concentrate on the plot and on trying to understand the gist of the speeches through prior knowledge and abundant paralinguistic cues. During the second screening, captions should be turned on to allow the students to increase their comprehension by seeing the speech instead of just hearing it in real-time.

As discussed earlier, other than the use of captions to render the audiovisual more accessible to learners, it could be beneficial to provide a printed text with the full transcript of the speech. The difficulty of comprehending an audiovisual in an L2 is engendered by the fact that the flow of information on the screen is rapid and promptly gone (Kaiser, 2011). Moreover, offering a transcription, as maintained in Paesani, Allen and Dupuy (2014), facilitates language and content processing by affording learners greater control over the received information, allowing them to reread passages if needed and more time to dwell on the information. It could be beneficial for the student to be provided with a full transcript of the episode after the first two screenings and during the discussion in order to maximize exposure, repetition and comprehension.

5. 3. Discussion

After watching the episode twice, the rest of the class time could be used for an instructor-facilitated discussion in either English or Italian, depending on the level and involving the entire class. They can be conceived to foster whole-class participation and allow students to acquire language in a setting where tension is minimal, as there are no specific questions to answer individually or grades to worry about. The discussion may involve, on the one hand, pointing out any relevant lexical or grammatical features appearing in the episode and responding to questions posed by the students – this would entail watching some excepts a third time; alternatively, the discussions can be aimed at eliciting students' language production and promote active engagement of critical thinking from the entire class, drawing attention to the link between the language used in the specific episode and attitudes, values, conventions, ideals and beliefs (Kern, 2000, p. 17).

The episodes can foster discussions on language by hearing the dialogues and viewing the captions and drawing the attention of the learner to key vocabulary, and making them aware of how in some cases, they were able to infer the meaning of a certain word by extrapolating it from the context (Dupuy and Krashen,1993; Loewen, Erlam and Ellis, 2009; Mohebbi, 2013). The simplicity of the *Peppa Pig* episodes in terms of plots and language, as well as the repetitive quality of this genre of animated cartoons, grants the students a certain degree of learning autonomy that leads them to capitalize upon their prior knowledge, cement it, and create new knowledge. Instead of trying to acquire new words by means of vocabulary lists that are devoid of any meaningful immediate context, learners have the opportunity to hear and see the words within a familiar context, thus increasing the probability that the term be assimilated. In other words, simply presenting to a student that the word *occhiali* is the Italian word for 'eyeglasses' is less salient than if the learner were exposed to an event (in real life or in the video) in which, for instance, an individual finds her glasses and utters the sentence "Finalmente ho trovato i miei occhiali" ('I finally found my glasses') while picking them up wearing them, as occurring in Season 1, Episode 9, *Papà Pig perde i suoi occhiali* (*Daddy Loses his Glasses*). The few terms included in the PowerPoint presentation are intended as advance organisers to aid students' overall comprehension of the plot by introducing key vocabulary terms. Learners are thus not explicitly instructed about the meaning of all the words word featured in the episode, and they are not asked to make a deliberate effort to commit lexical items to memory. Instead, through contextualized exposure, they are able to construct and internalize the meaning by inference and prior knowledge.

However, the incidental acquisition of new words is not the only potential benefit of this activity. As they replicate real-life situations, these cartoons showcase such a diversity of grammar use that can be expedient to demonstrate to students that grammar is not merely a set of rules to memorize and apply but functional meaning-making building blocks. Being exposed to the dialogues in the show gives learners the opportunity to notice the use of L2 grammatical patterns they have been formally taught in class, albeit this time framed within a meaningful context, and thus acquire or reinforce previously taught grammatical patterns. Even though the *Peppa Pig* cartoons are intended for an audience of pre-schoolers and the plots are exceedingly simple, a close look at the grammar employed by the characters and the narrator reveals considerable complexity. For instance, in just 5 minutes of running time, the episode *La macchina nuova* (*The New Car*, Season 1, Episode 23) features dialogues comprising the use of 1) the present tense, 2) the past tense (both the *passato prossimo* and the *imperfetto*); 3) the subjunctive; 4) the future tense, and 5) both the direct and indirect object pronouns (i.e., *him* vs *to him*, which in Italian are very frequent and are particularly challenging to acquire for an L2 Italian learner). The first few minutes of the in-class discussions can be devoted to playing back a selection of speech samples that showcase representative grammatical illustrations to draw the student's attention to their application for meaning-making, and not just as to complete a cloze exercise in a worksheet dedicated exclusively to, say, the present tense.

In a constructivist classroom setting, students are supported to develop critical thinking towards the learning material rather than limiting the learning setting to the teacher's demonstrative endeavours. The traditional language lesson plans are often based on oral instruction or visual demonstrations of the learning content, which is generally followed by learners' practice sessions. Conversely, a constructivist approach affords the learners the opportunity to discover knowledge, albeit with the teacher's support. Students can be stimulated to debate in the classroom by asking proactive questions and interacting until they produce their own knowledge and share their ideas with the classroom. During this process, the instructor acts as a facilitator and aims at stimulating students' thoughts, reflection, ideas and acquisition of knowledge on language and through language.

The instructor should also aim at interpreting the videotext while nurturing critical awareness of the relationship between spoken, written, visual and audio-visual texts, discourse practices, and social and cultural contexts (Dupuy, 2011). As we have seen, the episodes of the cartoon can also be used as a springboard for instructor-facilitated whole-classroom discussions on language use, but also on cultural and social contexts using the target language. The episodes of *Peppa Pig* generally revolve around a definite theme, i.e., recycling, exercising, going on a trip, etc. These focused and familiar storylines can give the opportunity to engage in discussions in Italian about everyday activities.

6. Conclusion

In this chapter, I argue that children's animated cartoons, and especially *Peppa Pig*, are a precious resource to be employed effectively, not exclusively, but as a complement to more traditional methods as argued by other scholars (Bahrani and Sim, 2012; Bahrani and Soltani, 2011; Bahrani, Tam and Zuraidah, 2014; Ecke, 2015; Saeedi and Biri, 2016; Vulchanova et al., 2015; Maranzana, 2022a; 2022b). Because of its accessibility, owing to the somewhat slower speech rate, the simplicity of the plots and the high word-image correlation, this cartoon is more accessible than other, more age-appropriate videos and can be introduced in novice classes as well (Maranzana, 2021). The brevity of each episode of *Peppa Pig*, clocking at around five minutes, is also a valuable trait. Each episode offers a complete story while extracting a video clip from a longer audiovisual (e.g., a film), decontextualizes the narrative and some interpretive meaning might be lost (Kaiser, 2011). The rich contextual and paralinguistic clues provide sufficient support to the learner to allow them to at least follow along with the episode and understand the gist of the story. Furthermore, the humorous nature of the episodes lends itself to a non-threatening learning environment that can both engage the students and give them relief from the typically stressful conditions of the classroom setting. Humorous discourse is extremely complex in its forms and functions (Bell, 2009); because of its cultural basis, it may be very difficult for a language learner to grasp the subtleties and facets of humour expressed in the L2 (Deneire, 1995).

The humour present in a children's cartoon such as *Peppa Pig* is more accessible across cultures because the cultural aspects in it are highly stylized. Once students are familiarized with listening to authentic L2 material that is designed for children, they may feel more confident to be exposed to content that is more age-appropriate and cater for their individual interests. Cartoons such as *Peppa Pig* feature comical scenarios and scripts that may invite students' attention and keep them alert and engaged throughout the learning moments. Cartoons can be a viable tool to teach students various kinds of social perspectives and behavioural perceptions just by noticing body language. In other words, cartoons have dual learning functions; they enable understanding of concrete or intangible concepts and encourage learners to analyse linguistic and bodily messages from characters' behaviours or by appraising their emotions in contexts. The very nature of a video cartoon can fuse formal and informal learning because it is principally focused on everyday situations that involve characters performing typical daily life activities.

References

Abuzahra, N., Farrah, M.A.H., & Zalloum, S. (2016). Using cartoon in language classroom from a constructivist point of view. *Arab World English Journal (AWEJ) Special Issue on CALL*, (3).

Atkinson, D. (2002). Toward a sociocognitive approach to second language acquisition. *The Modern Language Journal*, 86(4), 525–545.

Askildson, L. (2005). Effects of humor in the language classroom: Humor as a pedagogical tool in theory and practice. *Arizona Working Papers in SLAT*, 12, 45–61.

Bahrani, T. (2014). An overview on the effectiveness of watching cartoons as authentic language input for language learning development. *International Journal of Language Learning and Applied Linguistics World (IJLLALW)*, 5(2), 550–556.

Bahrani, T., & Sim, T. S. (2012). Audiovisual News, Cartoons, and Films as Sources of Authentic Language Input and Language Proficiency Enhancement. *Turkish Online Journal of Educational Technology*, 11(4), 56–64.

Bahrani, T., & Soltani, R. (2012). The pedagogical values of cartoons. *Research on Humanities and Social Sciences*, 1(4), 19–22.

Bahrani, T., Tam, S. S., & Zuraidah, M. D. (2014). Authentic language input through audiovisual technology and second language acquisition. *SAGE Open*, 4(3), 1–8.

Bell, N. D. (2009). Learning about and through humor in the second language classroom. *Language Teaching Research*, 13(3), 241–258.

Berk, R. A. (2003). *Professors Are from Mars, Students Are from Snickers: How to Write and Deliver Humor in the Classroom and in Professional Presentations.* Sterling, Virginia: Stylus Publishing.

Bilokcuoglu, H., & Debreli, E. (2018). Use of humour in language classes: an effective 'filter' or affective filter? *Journal of language and linguistic studies*, 14(3), 347–359.

Bird, S., & Williams, J. (2002). The effect of bimodal input on implicit and explicit memory: An investigation into the benefits of within-language subtitling. *Applied Psycholinguistics*, 23(4), 509–533.

Bravo, M. C. C. (2008). *Putting the reader in the picture: Screen translation and foreign language learning.* Unpublished doctoral dissertation, Universitat Rovira i Virgili, Tarragona, Spain. Retrieved from https://www.tdx.cat/bitstream/handle/10803/8771/Condhino.pdf?sequence=1&isAllowed=y

Chai, J., & Erlam, R. (2008). The effect and the influence of the use of video and captions on second language learning. *New Zealand Studies in Applied Linguistics*, 14(2), 25–45.

Ciccone, A. A. (1995). Teaching with original video: Theory and practice. In Eckman, F. R., Highland, D., Lee, P. W., Mileham, J., & Weber, R. R. (Eds.), *Second language acquisition theory and pedagogy* (pp. 203-215). Mahwah, NJ: Erlbaum.

Clark, C. (2000). Innovative strategy: Concept cartoons. *Instructional and learning strategies*, 12, 34–45.

Danan, M. (2004). Captioning and subtitling: Undervalued language learning strategies. *Meta: Journal Des Traducteurs/Translators' Journal*, 49(1), 67–77.

Deneire, M. (1995). Humor and foreign language teaching. *Humor: International Journal of Humor Research*, 8(3), 285–299.

Dupuy, B., & Krashen, S. D. (1993). Incidental Vocabulary Acquisition in French as a Foreign Language. *Applied Language Learning*, 4, 55–63.

Dupuy, B. (2011). CLIL: Achieving its goals through a multiliteracies framework. *Latin American Journal of Content & Language Integrated Learning*, 4(2), 21–32.

Forman, R. (2011). Humorous Language Play in a Thai EFL Classroom. *Applied linguistics*, 32(5), 541–565.

Gambier, Y. (2007). Sous-titrage et apprentissage des langues. *Linguistica Antverpiensia*, 6, 97–113.

Gardner, R. C., & Lambert, W. E. (1972). *Attitudes and motivation in second language learning*. Rowley, MA: Newbury House.

Gardner, R. C. (1985). *Social psychology and second language learning: The role of attitudes and motivation*. London, England: Edward Arnold.

Gardner, R. C. (2010). *Motivation and second language acquisition: The socio educational model*. New York, NY: Peter Lang.

Garrett P. B. (2008) Researching Language Socialization. In Hornberger, N. H. (Ed.) Encyclopedia of Language and Education. Springer, Boston, MA. Retrieved from https://doi.org/10.1007/978-0-387-30424-3_254

Gilmore, A. (2007). Authentic materials and authenticity in foreign language learning. *Language Teaching*, 40(2), 97–118.

Heidari-Shahreza, M. A. (2021). Humor in the language classroom: Pedagogical benefits and practical considerations. *TESOL Journal*, 12(2).

Herron, C. (1994). An investigation of the effectiveness of using an advance organizer to introduce video in the foreign language classroom. *The Modern Language Journal*, 78(2), 190–198.

Herron, C., Morris, M., Secules, T., & Curtis, L. (1995). A comparison study of the effects of video-based versus text-based instruction in the foreign language classroom. *French Review*, 68(5), 775–795.

Huckin, T., & Coady, J. (1999). Incidental vocabulary acquisition in a second language. *Studies in Second Language Acquisition*, 21(2), 181–193.

Hulstijn, J. H. (2001). Intentional and incidental second language vocabulary learning: A reappraisal of elaboration, rehearsal and automaticity. In Robinson, P. (Ed.), *Cognition and second language instruction*, (pp. 258–286). Cambridge, England: Cambridge University Press.

Kaiser, M. (2011). New approaches to exploiting film in the foreign language classroom. *L2 Journal*, 3(2), 232–249.

Kern, R. (2000). *Literacy and language teaching*. Oxford, England: Oxford University Press.

King, J. (2002). Using DVD feature films in the EFL classroom. *Computer Assisted Language Learning*, 15(5), 509–523.

Krashen, S. (1982). *Principles and practice in second language learning and acquisition*. Oxford: Pergamon.

Kruger, A. (1996). The nature of humor in human nature: Cross-cultural commonalities. *Counseling Psychology Quarterly*, 9(3), 235–241.

Loewen, S., Erlam, R., & Ellis, R. (2009). The incidental acquisition of third person-s as implicit and explicit knowledge. In Singleton, D. (Ed.), *Implicit and explicit knowledge in second language learning, testing and teaching*, (pp. 262–280). Bristol, England: Multilingual Matters.

MacIntyre, P. D., & Mercer, S. (2014). Introducing positive psychology to SLA. *Studies in Second Language Learning and Teaching*, 4(2), 153–172.

Maranzana, S. (2021). Imparare l'italiano L2 con i cartoni animati sottotitolati: Attitudini degli studenti universitari in USA. *Cultura & Comunicazione* 9(19).

Maranzana, S. (2022a). Intermediate Learner Opinions on Captioned Video Cartoons for Language Acquisition. In Bin, Z., Thomas, M., Barr, D. &, Jia, W. (Eds.), *Emerging Concepts in Technology-Enhanced Language Teaching and Learning* (pp. 232–252). IGI Global.

Maranzana, S., (2022b). Animated Cartoons to Promote 'Real Language' Learning: Attitudes of Undergraduate Students of Italian. In Scala C. (Ed.) *How to Engage Today's Learners in Language Classes.* Wilmington, Delaware: Vernon Press.

Medgyes, P. (2002). *Laughing matters: Humour in the language classroom.* Cambridge University Press.

Mohebbi, H. (2013). Investigating Vocabulary Learning in Second Language Classroom context: Recent Findings, Future Outlook. *Advances in Asian Social Science* (AASS), 4(3), 882–886.

Montero Perez, M., Peters, E., & Desmet, P. (2014). Is less more? Effectiveness and perceived usefulness of keyword and full captioned video for L2 listening comprehension. *ReCALL,* 26(01), 21–43.

Morrison, M. K. (2008). *Using humor to maximize learning: The links between positive emotions and education.* Lanham, MD: Rowman & Littlefield Education.

Nightingale, R. (2014). Well I Never!: Formulaic Language as a Pragmatic Resource in Child Entertainment Media. In Gabryś-Barker, D. (Ed.), *Studying Second Language Acquisition from a Qualitative Perspective* (pp. 203–218). Cham, Switzerland: Springer International Publishing.

Nigmatullayevna, A. U. (2022). Using Cartoons to Develop Learners Speaking Skills. *Uzbek Scholar Journal,* 3, 1–3.

Paesani, K., Allen, H. W., & Dupuy, B. (2014). *A Multiliteracies Framework for Collegiate Foreign Language Teaching.* Upper Saddle River, NJ: Pearson.

Pavlenko, A., & Lantolf, J. P. (2000). Second language learning as participation and the (re) construction of selves. In Lantolf, J. P. (Ed.), *Sociocultural theory and second language learning* (pp. 155–177). Oxford, England: Oxford University Press.

Pilz, K. (2008). Italian Language and Culture in Close-Up: Using Film at All Levels of Proficiency. In Occhipinti, E. (Ed.), *New Approaches to Teaching Italian Language and Culture: Case Studies from an International Perspective,* (pp. 468–497). Newcastle Upon Tyne, England: Cambridge Scholars Publishing.

Pomerantz, A., & Bell, N. D. (2011). Humor as safe house in the foreign language classroom. *The Modern Language Journal,* 95, 148–161.

Price, K. (1983). Closed-captioned TV: An untapped resource. *Matsol Newsletter,* 12(2), 1–8.

Pujolá, J. T. (2002). CALLing for help: Researching language learning strategies using help facilities in a web-based multimedia program. *ReCALL,* 14(2), 235–262.

Reilly, R.C. (2006). Humor as a Social Lubricant in an Expert Thinking System. *The International Journal of Learning,* 13(2), 149–158

Saeedi, Z., & Biri, A. (2016). The Application of Technology in Teaching Grammar to EFL Learners: The Role of Animated Sitcoms. *Teaching English with Technology*, 16(2), 18–39.

Schmitz, J. R. (2002). Humor as a pedagogical tool in foreign language and translation courses. 15(1), 89–113.

Sienkiewicz, M., & Marx, N. (2009). Beyond a cutout world: Ethnic humor and discursive integration in South Park. *Journal of Film and Video*, 61(2), 5–18.

Sydorenko, T. (2010). Modality of input and vocabulary acquisition. *Language Learning and Technology*, 14, 50–73.

Taylor, G. (2005). Perceived processing strategies of students watching captioned video. *Foreign Language Annals*, 38(3), 422–427.

Trachtenberg, S. (1979). Joke telling as a tool in ESL. *TESOL Quarterly*, 13, 89–99.

Torregrosa Benavent, G., & Sánchez-Reyes Peñamaría, S. (2011). Use of authentic materials in the ESP classroom. *Encuentro* 20, 89–94.

Vaid, J. (2006). Joking across languages: Perspectives on humor, emotion, and bilingualism. *Bilingual Education and Bilingualism*, 56, 152.

Vanderplank, R. (1990). Paying attention to the words: Practical and theoretical problems in watching television programmes with uni-lingual (CEEFAX) subtitles. *System*, 18(2), 221–234.

Vandergrift, L. (2007). Recent developments in second and foreign language listening comprehension research. *Language Teaching*, 40, 191–210.

Vanderplank, R. (2010). Déjà vu? A decade of research on language laboratories, television and video in language learning. *Language teaching*, 43(01), 1–37.

Vanderplank, R. (2016). *Captioned media in foreign language learning and teaching: Subtitles for the deaf and hard-of-hearing as tools for language learning.* London, England: Palgrave Macmillan.

Vanderplank, R. (2019). 'Gist watching can only take you so far': attitudes, strategies and changes in behaviour in watching films with captions. *The Language Learning Journal*, 47(4), 407–423.

Vulchanova, M., Aurstad, L. M., Kvitnes, I. E., & Eshuis, H. (2015). As naturalistic as it gets: subtitles in the English classroom in Norway. *Frontiers in psychology*, 5, 1510.

Wandersee, J. H. (1982). Humor as a teaching strategy. *American Biology Teacher*, 44(4), 212–18.

Wanzer, M. B., Frymier, A. B., & Irwin, B. (2009). *An explanation of the relationship between teacher humor and student learning: Instructional humor processing theory.* Paper presented at the annual meeting of the Eastern Communication Association.

Watson, E. C. (2013). Teaching Italian with the Virtual Reality of Video. *AISHE-J: The All Ireland Journal of Teaching and Learning in Higher Education*, 5(2).

Winke, P., Gass, S., & Sydorenko, T. (2010). The effects of captioning videos used for foreign language listening activities. *Language Learning & Technology*, 14(1), 65–86.

Winke, P., Gass, S., & Sydorenko, T., 2013. Factors Influencing the Use of Captions by Foreign Language Learners: An Eye-Tracking Study. *The Modern Language Journal*, 97(1), 254–275.

Yang, H. Y. (2014). The Effects of Advance Organizers and Subtitles on EFL Learners' Listening Comprehension Skills. *CALICO Journal*, 31(3).

Zillmann, D., Williams, B. R., Bryant, J., Boynton, K. R., & Wolf, M. A. (1980). Acquisition of information from educational television programs as a function of differently paced humorous inserts. *Journal of Educational Psychology*, 72(2), 170–180.

Chapter 13

Italian through geography at university level

Leonardo Masi
Cardinal Stefan Wyszyński University in Warsaw

Abstract: The chapter addresses the issue of teaching Italian geography in the context of Italian studies at the university level. In the first part, the author discusses the importance of this subject for the understanding of the culture of the peninsula and tries to indicate the most correct denomination for it. The second part lists some of the resources that the teacher has available for this subject. The third part focuses on the relationship between language teaching and geography teaching, on the one hand referring to concepts such as the Direct Method, the Adjunct Model and the division between Content-Driven and Language-Driven programs, and on the other hand to the direct experience of the courses that the author taught for beginners in the degree course in Italian Studies at a Polish university.

Keywords: Geography, Regions, Italy, Italian, Teaching

***

1. Introduction

The great differences between the various regions of Italy are known to many, but certainly not to all those who approach the study of language. Still, more than a century and a half after the unification of Italy, the perception of Italy fluctuates between the image of a cohesive country (on a cultural, economic, and political level) and that of a country made up of hundreds of small homelands, each with its own dialect and traditions. Foreigners often perceive only a vague dualism between the North and the South of the peninsula; sometimes, they identify with the entire country elements that are actually linked to a single city (Neapolitan songs and Venetian gondolas outside of Italy become simply Italian). The scholar Luca Serianni (1997: 474) noted how, historically, foreigners' perception of unity, which is not so obvious to Italians, concerns language (dialects are not perceived at all), geography and culture tout court. This happens

> because of historical influences (the image of Italy was sufficiently clear and cohesive as a repository of ancient memories and, in a modern way, because of its literary, artistic and musical life); geographical influences (the undeniable unity of the *bel paese ch'Appennin parte, e 'l mar circonda e l'Alpe*); and, above all, literary influences: the Italian learned at home was very often that of books, especially poetry books and libretti for music.

It is of little importance that the distance in kilometres between Turin and Brussels is the same as that between Turin and Bari and that if a traveller were to be suddenly teleported to the three cities, one after the other, he might have trouble telling whether Turin belongs to the same country as Bari or to that of Brussels.

Now, whether we see the issue from the point of view of the environmental hypothesis (language is influenced by the context in which it is spoken) or whether we start from the Sapir-Whorf hypothesis (it is our mother tongue that influences the way we see the world), the importance of the environment in relation to language does not change. It is, therefore, necessary to give a geographical context as precise as possible to those who approach the study of a language like Italian.

The reflections I would like to present in this chapter concern the possibility and the modalities of teaching Italian geography within a university curriculum in Italian studies. On the topic of content-based instruction, that is, language learning through the study of a content area (could be geography as well as history, or science, for instance), there are many relevant studies. In part, I will refer to them, in part to considerations that came from my experience as a university teacher of Italian Geography.

The idea of geography that can be most easily applied to the context of foreign language teaching is, in my opinion, the one that follows a traditional definition, such as the one proposed by Domenico Ruocco (1968: 5):

> geography studies the different distribution and combination on the earth's surface of the phenomena that modify its physiognomic characters and influence at the same time the working life of man, examines the associations of objects and phenomena that constitute the landscapes, describes the organic units in which it appears divided, as a result of an incessant process of spatial differentiation (regions),

and analyzes the territorial ensembles, the result of joint actions of natural forces and human interventions.

Of course, this is the definition of a scholar who leads us into territories of a discipline that would be too distant for language students, who are non-specialists in the subject. But it contains two elements that are of great interest to us, namely the idea of the interaction between the environment and the man who inhabits it, as well as the division of a territory into regions on the basis of certain characteristics. However, for my purposes, it needs some adjustments, i.e. it should be integrated with basic information about the cultural characteristics of the various regions: cinema, literature, music, cuisine, etc. We could therefore speak of *cultural geography*, but cultural geography is something else, a separate discipline defined in recent decades by the work of various scholars such as Paul Claval, Mike Crang, Giuliana Andreotti, Adalberto Vallega, Boris Grésillon, Don Mitchell, etc. Thus, thinking in terms of teaching that should be included in the university curriculum of Italian studies, it would be better, for the choice of the name, to limit ourselves to a more neutral 'Italian Geography' or 'Geography and Culture of Italy'. Of course, each language will translate the name of the subject based on a number of criteria. In the Sorbonne program, for instance, the three-year degree in LLCER (*langues, littératures et civilisations étrangères et régionales*) includes the subject *Culture Générale géographique et historique* in the first semester and *Culture Générale artistique et littéraire* in the second semester. At the University of Warsaw the subject was called *Współczesne Włochy – Geografia, społeczeństwo, polityka* (Contemporary Italy: Geography, Society, Politics); at the University of Salamanca it's simply *Geografía de Italia*. In fact, Ruocco (1979: 7) argued that

> many products of human genius and collective experience, like environmental assets in the broadest sense, are elements of geographical space and factors of its transformation, and therefore fall within the domain of geography, which has in the territorial realities organized and felt by men one of the main objects of study, of its specific competence.

From this point of view, every adjective may become superfluous, and 'geography' can be intended as an umbrella term, which includes concepts such as geopoetics (thus shifting the centre of gravity towards literature) or take us into the territories of the geography of tourism, to give just two examples.

The duration of a geography course should obviously be adapted to the needs and rules of the university systems of individual countries. In Polish universities, for example, where courses are generally 30 hours divided into 15 lessons of 90 minutes each (including the eventual final test), it's difficult to fit even a superficial treatment of the twenty Italian regions into a single semester. In these cases, it is possible, as in the above-mentioned program of Sorbonne University, to divide the material between more strictly geographical topics in the first module and general artistic and literary culture in the second. Or have recourse to a further in-depth course according to the level of study, leaving the second module as an optional course of choice. The important thing is that the contents of the course are not limited to repeating universally known information about Italy (if anything, it can be used to disprove stereotypes that are in part false!), but can be an opportunity to learn about aspects of the landscape and culture that are not normally part of the mainstream image of the Peninsula.

The problem that I would keep as central in this subject is the denomination and characterization of the respective areas of the Italian territory: regions, cities, rivers, mountains, lakes, seas, national parks, and monuments (What-Where?). According to the time available, the list can be extended to food and wine products, the characterization of the inhabitants of a city or a region, famous people (Who-Where-What?), and so on. In requiring skills from the student, the teacher must take care to establish a balance between hard and soft data.

2. Resources

The issue of the teaching materials is interrelated with the language in which the subject should be taught and – if it is taught in Italian – with the level of language proficiency required.

Speaking of didactic materials, a first substantial division can be made between publications entirely dedicated to Italian geography for foreigners and publications in which geography is only one element among many others. As far as the first type of publications is concerned, therefore excluding online resources, the only books I am going to analyze are the manual by Paolo Balboni and Maria Voltolina entitled *Geografia d'Italia per stranieri* (2005), written in Italian that I think can be approached from a pre-intermediate level, and *Explore Italy and its regions/Esplora l'Italia e le sue regioni* (2013), a bilingual Italian-English publication where the parts in Italian are divided into two modules on two levels of difficulty, for beginners and advanced. Paolo Balboni published another book in 2022 entitled *Italian Geography for Foreigners B2-C2*, which I will not dwell on; however, both in terms of language and content, it is too advanced. Indeed it seems to me that this book could be intended for Italian students at a high school level. Nor will I dwell on the 2005 publication *Benvenuti in Italia*, even if this interesting textbook deserves a few more words. It is divided into three sections:

Geografia – Storia – Civiltà. The interesting element in this text is, in my opinion, the division of the material not by regions but by thematic areas, emphasising above all the man-environment and man-territory dynamics rather than the artistic and cultural heritage: "a geography that is concerned not so much with the description of the world, as it is, but with its interpretation, with why it is the way it is" (2005: 6)

Balboni and Voltolina's book (2005) is divided into three parts. First, there are some overviews of Europe and Italy (2005: 9–23). In the end, we find a glossary and a crossword puzzle which tests both knowledge of geographical terminology and the names of Italy's main mountains, rivers, etc. The second section (2005: 29–116) is the largest, containing twenty subchapters, each dedicated to a region; the subchapters are, in turn, divided into several parts: an initial table that collects basic information about the territory, then a few paragraphs on cities, economy, communication routes, languages are spoken in those areas, etc.; then, depending on the region, there are more specific paragraphs on aspects that most characterize certain places, sometimes with the inclusion of literary texts or songs. The last section (2005: 117–142) is divided into two parts that the authors define as "economic geography" and "cultural geography": the first is represented by some pages on transport, industry, and agriculture, the "made in Italy" brand and tourism; the second is dedicated to some of the most representative personalities of culture, which are presented in relation to places in the peninsula. For example, in the section entitled *La geografia dei musicisti classici*, each composer or performer is matched to his place of origin: Giuseppe Verdi to Parma, Vincenzo Bellini to Catania, Gaetano Donizetti to Bergamo, Luciano Pavarotti to Modena, etc.

Compared with the book by Balboni and Voltolina (2005), which contains many images and much text, *Explore Italy and its regions* (2013) present a much more minimalist approach. Here, too, the division into chapters respects that of the twenty regions, but only essential information is given about each one: to make a quantitative comparison, the chapter on Piedmont in Balboni and Voltolina (2005) contains about 1,500 words, while *Explore Italy* (2013) it contains only 364! In module 1 (two pages), first, there is a list of the provinces that make up the region; other geographical notions are also given through fixed formulas such as *il capoluogo, il fiume più lungo, il monte più alto*, etc. Then there are some general phrases that characterize the region and three illustrated words (for example, in the case of Valle d'Aosta, we find *il camoscio, lo stambecco, l'aquila reale*; in the case of Piedmont, there are *riso, granoturco, frumento*. Module 2 (one page) presents a more advanced reading, but still very brief. There are then some follow-up questions, sometimes riddles.

But geography is a very present theme in almost all Italian language courses for foreigners, even if in different proportions. I would like to briefly review some of the most popular courses, premising that there is no space here for in-depth analysis: my examination was limited to four commercially available courses covering levels A1-B2: *Un nuovo giorno in Italia* (2015; 2016; 2017; 2019), *Spazio Italia* (2013a; 2013b; 2013c; 2014), *Nuovissimo Progetto Italiano* (2019; 2020) e *Via del Corso* (2017; 2018; 2019; 2021).

Un nuovo giorno in Italia (2015; 2016; 2017; 2019) is a four-volume course (level A1-B2) whose chapters are linked by the narrative path of a train trip from Northern to Southern Italy, which allows showing a cross-section of the Country and its cities. It is not surprising, then, that many chapters present Italian places and dwell on the aspects that characterize them. The approach is comparable to that of *Via del Corso*, in which the story that holds the protagonists together takes place in four different Italian cities, one for each of the four volumes: Rome, Florence, Venice and Naples. Therefore, the environmental context is intertwined with the plot, even if, compared to *Un nuovo giorno in Italia*, in *Via del Corso*, it rarely comes in the foreground. In *Nuovissimo Progetto Italiano*, apart from the map that we find in the first volume (2019: 27), only in the second volume/B1-B2 do we have a teaching unit focused on Italian cities (2020: 39-54); *Spazio Italia* dedicates even fewer pages to geography, for example, in volume 2/A2 there is only one section expressly dedicated to Italian cities and monuments (2013b: 34-35) and in volume 3/B1 only in one unit are there a few pages dedicated to Bologna (2013c: 25-28, 40); but in volume 1/A1 Italian (2013a) geography is dealt with mainly in the sections *L'Italia in video* and *L'Italia in internet* at the end of the individual chapters.

The design of a geography course at the university level should therefore be tied to and subordinate to the choice of textbook for teaching the practical language if such a choice is planned. If practical language courses are thrifty in providing information about the Italian geographic and cultural environment, one will consequently have to provide this information in a separate course. Conversely, the choice of a book such as *Un nuovo giorno in Italia* should, in theory, allow the geography teacher to be able to focus on new aspects beyond those presented in the textbook. He could even borrow from the textbook some pages and develop himself with the students, creating thus a better synergy between the two subjects.

The materials mentioned above are all in the scope of the didactics of the Italian language, but any other text, even if it was not originally intended for didactic purposes, can, of course, be used, as long as – in the case we are using materials in Italian – it is of a linguistic level suitable for the level of the students for whom it is intended. There is no shortage of resources (especially books and newspaper or magazine articles, but also blogs) originally written in the student's mother tongue or translated; even video materials about Italy (documentaries at a more or less amateur level) are abundantly present on platforms like YouTube in various languages.

In the case of students who are not able to read entire chapters or monographs in Italian, the teacher will have to do a survey of what is available in the student's mother tongue and propose a bibliography of reference. In this case, the course can also be an opportunity to approach those literary classics in which the Italian landscape is the main character. To give the most obvious examples, we can cite Goethe's *Italienische Reise* or Pavel Muratov's *Obrazy Italii*, but perhaps more interesting for students might be works of Italian literature seen in a geopoetic key: Bassani's novels set in Ferrara, Svevo's in Trieste, Erri de Luca's or Elena Ferrante's in Naples, Vasco Pratolini's in Florence, Giuseppe Berto's in Venice, Pasolini's in Rome, Lampedusa's, Sciascia's, Brancati's in Sicily, and again *Cristo si è fermato a Eboli* by Carlo Levi for the Lucania – the list would be very long, also considering how in recent years the characterization of geographical space has become, together with that of culinary culture, a topos of much literature, especially noir. Many works of Italian literature have been translated into many languages, and therefore they should not be difficult to find. I would suggest, however, that students be given a list of works from which to choose a reading that they could then briefly refer to in plenary.

If we are looking for a literary work that presents a detailed picture of the whole of Italy, I think that *Viaggio in Italia* by Guido Piovene is unsurpassed. In this volume, born from a series of reportages carried out for RAI between 1953 and 1956, therefore in an Italy that was in some ways completely different (between the ruins of the Second World War and the economic boom), the writer succeeds in capturing, almost with the gaze of the anthropologist, the characteristic traits of the regions and cities visited, providing a series of very vivid and current portraits of the landscape and its inhabitants, that are still very relevant today. But other interesting ideas could also come from the anthology *Scrittori italiani di viaggio*, edited by Luca Clerici (2008).

I would tend instead to avoid publications that go so far as to make personal evaluations of contemporary Italy, not for an excessive caution related to political correctness, but because I believe that, especially when approaching a country and a culture that are substantially unknown for them, students should have the time to form their own opinions. Beyond the rightness of the judgment, the risk is, therefore, that of approaching Italy through a ready-made ideology, which does nothing but reinforces stereotypes that we would prefer to avoid, especially with regard to very thorny issues, such as populism, the role of the Church, emigration, etc., that are often divisive. It is better, in my opinion, to keep neutral information. Pure factual knowledge, even if today it is no longer fashionable in didactics, has the merit of being little subject to change: the river of Florence will always be the Arno, and the Adriatic Sea will hardly change its name. We should always keep in mind that the main objective of the average student is still to learn the language: of course, some may consider it as a vehicle to learn about literary and artistic culture, but for others, it will be a way to deepen political issues, it is better, however, to leave the reading of in-depth texts about to individual initiative and limit the geography course to simpler concepts (all the more so if these are to be delivered in Italian).

3. Geography and Language Learning

The use of geography as a tool for language learning has been convincingly described by Diane Larsen-Freeman in the chapter on the Direct Method contained in *Techniques and Principles in Language Teaching* (2000: 23–34). In this method, meaning must be conveyed directly in the target language through the use of demonstrations and visual aids. Larsen-Freeman explains how geography can be used as a means of language teaching and reports the experience of an English class in an Italian *scuola media*, where the teacher avoided the native language while the class took dictation on the geography of the United States, labelled blank maps with previously reviewed geographic features, practised the pronunciation of words such as 'river', and so on. Geography can actually be easily taught through visuals, but in the long term, the Direct Method doesn't allow great insight, and it is not exactly what we will use in an Italian Geography academic course. Anyway, curiously sharing Ruocco's opinion quoted earlier in this chapter but from an opposite angle, Larsen-Freeman (2000: 26) writes that a principle of the Direct Method is that "culture consists of more than the fine arts (e.g., students study geography and cultural attitudes)".

When we talk about teaching Italian geography to Italian studies students, we are also talking about content-based teaching of language, but the fundamental point remains in what percentage should the linguistic element prevail over the cultural element in the broad sense, how strong should the emphasis on one or the other element. There are different models of content-based instruction: some of them tend to be "content-driven language programs", and others are more "language-driven programs". Myriam Met (1999) effectively sums up the characteristics of both: in the Content-Driven, content is taught in L2, content learning is the priority, language learning is secondary, content objectives are determined by course goals or curriculum, teachers must select language objectives, students evaluated on content mastery; in the Language-Driven, content is used to learn L2, language learning is the priority, content learning is incidental, language objectives determined by L2 course goals or curriculum, students evaluated on content to be integrated, students evaluated on language skills/proficiency. However, we must remember that, in our case, we are not describing a stand-alone language course but a course embedded within a curriculum with many other subjects. In a Content-Driven program, content must not necessarily be taught in a non-native language (immersion). In a university context, what seems to fit well is the Adjunct Model described among others by Snow (2001: 308), in which students are concurrently enrolled in a language class and a content course. A key feature of this model is the coordination of objectives and assignments between language and content instructors. I had already mentioned the importance of a synergy between the language teacher and Geography teacher when I analysed the available books from which to choose for the course eventually. Content instructors who want to use a second language can use a variety of techniques to make the message more comprehensible to beginners. But first of all, also depending on the strategy of the curriculum coordinator, it will be necessary for the teacher to decide whether it is preferable to give up some of the content (the students will get then only the simplest information so that they can learn the language through it), or whether the primary issue of the course has to be the presentation of notions as clearly as possible to the students, even in their native language, relegating the teaching of the language during the course to only a few moments. In short, as Myriam Met (1998) explained, language proficiency influences the selection of content, but at the same time, content influences the language skills students will develop. Considering the above, I see three possible approaches for a semester-long geography course involving 30 hours of instruction for three different levels of Italian proficiency: advanced, intermediate and beginner.

Having the possibility to choose, I would tend to place such a course at the beginning of the curriculum. In any case, whatever the level, the structure of the lesson can follow a similar pattern for all three types of approach: the basic language used to communicate will, of course, change. At an advanced level, the class will be held only in Italian, and the teacher may ask students to read texts or watch audiovisual material in Italian at home. In a course for pre-intermediate or intermediate-level students, the teacher can avoid the use of the first language as much as possible. The materials (written texts, audiovisuals, etc.) will be submitted to the students in Italian if the language level is within their reach. The balance between content and language is up to the teacher to manage. Materials in the second language can be previously adjusted by the teacher or even translated (by the teacher or by the students). At this level, in my opinion, comprehension exercises can be best carried out. One type of test could be the following: after a listening exercise, the student has to insert names on a map with geographical features unnamed (the so-called 'cartina muta'). Now I would rather like to focus on the possibilities of a geography course for beginners in which the teacher will introduce the second language gradually.

4. An approach for beginners

The following considerations are based in part on my experience between 2015 and 2021 as a teacher of Italian cultural geography as well as an author of the Italian studies program at Cardinal Stefan Wyszynski University in Warsaw. The subject was intended for first-semester students. Italian geography for beginners was intended to be taught mostly in the first language, and the course was possibly open also to students of other disciplines. Although the primary goal of the course was not the learning of the language, it can be assumed that at the end of the course, the students, in addition to about 50 words of geographic vocabulary, have learned to use the names of places studied in the second language, so it was required for example, the use of the form 'Mare Adriatico' instead of the various 'Adriatic Sea', or 'Morze Adriatyckie'. Furthermore, the students learnt not only single terms but also simple phrases related to places and inhabitants of Italy: *Piemontese falso e cortese, Veneziani gran signori, Padovani gran dottori, Veronesi tutti matti, Vicentini mangiagatti, Se Parigi avesse il mare, sarebbe una piccolo Bari*, etc. A geography course placed at the beginning of the curriculum was intender rather as a kind of viaticum to the study of language and culture that was particularly effective since the teaching of this subject – unlike other more abstract subjects, which require readings and class discussions – allows for a greater presence of visuals and hands-on experience. (Met, 1998: 58)

During the semester, students prepared short reports in which each of them presented, in their first language, a chosen place on the peninsula or related cultural aspects. The stress of expressing oneself in the second language was almost absent: as far as the linguistic part was concerned, the teacher corrected pronunciation and small inaccuracies. But we must consider that lower proficiency levels in such content-based instruction will tend to focus more on understanding the input content than on the linguistic form (Kowal and Swain, 1997; Williams, 2001).

Assuming 15 lessons (which in the case of introductory lesson and test could be reduced), the distribution of topics can be done as follows: two lessons on the general geography of the peninsula (mountains, seas, rivers, lakes, roads, regions and their capitals, the system of provinces and municipalities, languages and dialects, ethnic minorities, etc.); then a series of lectures in which individual regions are examined successively (the proportions will have to be well calibrated, and probably for some regions it will be necessary to dedicate an entire lesson – probably this will be necessary for Lombardy, Tuscany, Latium and Campania, for different reasons). A concluding lesson may possibly re-propose the material done previously from the point of view of the geography of the most important personalities of culture and science on the model of Balboni and Voltolina.

At the beginning of the course, each student may be assigned a region or city. Then, a calendar will be agreed upon according to which each student will expose in a multimedia presentation his or her research in plenum. The internal organization of the single lessons dedicated to the Italian regions can then follow this general scheme:

1. Introduction by the teacher who briefly presents the region(s) to be discussed.

2. Presentation by the student (which should not exceed 10 minutes).

3. Discussion of both content and language issues and development of some concepts contained in the presentation; the teacher may integrate them with the notions that he/she considers fundamental and that were not included in the presentation or may repeat and underline some information. Depending on the direction of the discussion, the personal interests of the students, or other elements that are difficult to predict, the teacher may show short videos or assign students 'mini-papers' that will be presented at the beginning of the next lesson (about 3 minutes, no multimedia presentation required). These 'mini-papers' can be about the biography of a character, the history of a place, a monument, a museum, the plot of a film, an Italian dialect, an ethnic minority, etc.

4. Conclusion and summary of key points to remember about the region(s) discussed.

By assigning each student a paper and at least one 'mini-paper', the lessons acquire a more lively and less monotonous character, as well as an element of greater elasticity. They also allow for a brief return to the previous lesson's themes at the beginning of a lesson, thus picking up on the key points before continuing with the discussion of the new regions.

5. Conclusion

The knowledge of geography, today more than ever, is a fundamental way to know and understand the world around us, its changes, and its major problems. It can also open new perspectives in the world of work, giving language students means and skills. It is difficult to imagine a study of the Italian language that does not also include a study of the geography of Italy. Within a university curriculum, a course in Italian geography can pay off even at the very beginning. I hope that these notes of mine can contribute to the emergence of new perspectives on teaching this subject.

References

Balboni, P. E., & Voltolina, M. (2005). *Geografia d'Italia per stranieri*. Perugia: Guerra.

Balboni, P. E. (2022). *Geografia italiana per stranieri B2-C2*. Roma: Edilingua.

Chiappini, L., & De Filippo, N. (2015). *Un nuovo giorno in Italia. Percorso narrativo di italiano per stranieri*. Livello A1. Torino: Bonacci.

Chiappini, L., & De Filippo, N. (2016). *Un nuovo giorno in Italia. Percorso narrativo di italiano per stranieri*. Livello A2. Torino: Bonacci.

Chiappini, L., & De Filippo, N. (2017). *Un nuovo giorno in Italia. Percorso narrativo di italiano per stranieri*. Livello B1. Torino: Bonacci.

Chiappini, L., & De Filippo, N. (2019). *Un nuovo giorno in Italia. Percorso narrativo di italiano per stranieri*. Livello B2. Torino: Bonacci.

Clerici, L. (Ed.) (2008). *Scrittori italiani di viaggio*. Mondadori.

Explore Italy and its regions. Esplora l'Italia e le sue regioni. (2013). Long Bridge Publishing.

Kowal, M., & Swain, M. (1997). *From Semantic to Syntactic Processing*. In Johnson, K. & Swain, M., (Eds.), *Immersion education: international perspectives*, (pp. 284–309). Cambridge: Cambridge University Press.

Larsen-Freeman, D. (2000). *Techniques and principles in language teaching* (2nd Edition). Oxford: Oxford University Press.

Marin, T., & Diadori, P. (2017). *Via del Corso. Corso di italiano per stranieri*. A1. Roma: Edilingua.

Marin, T., & Diadori, P. (2018). *Via del Corso. Corso di italiano per stranieri*. A2. Roma: Edilingua.

Marin, T., & Diadori, P. (2019). *Via del Corso. Corso di italiano per stranieri*. B1. Roma: Edilingua.

Marin, T., & Diadori, P. (2021). *Via del Corso. Corso di italiano per stranieri*. B2. Roma: Edilingua.

Marin, T. (2019). *Nuovissimo Progetto Italiano. Corso di lingua e civiltà italiana 1*. Roma: Edilingua.

Marin, T. (2020). *Nuovissimo Progetto Italiano. Corso di lingua e civiltà italiana 2*. Roma: Edilingua.

Met, M. (1998). Curriculum Decision-making in Content-based Language Teaching. In Cenoz, J., & Genezee, F. (Eds.), *Beyond Bilingualism*, (pp. 35–63). *Multilingualism and Multilingual Education*.

Met, M. (1999). *Content-Based Instruction. Defining Terms, Making Decisions*. Washington: The National Foreign Language Center.

Ruocco, D. (1968). *Orientamenti e compiti della geografia moderna*. Napoli: L.S.E.

Ruocco, D. (1979). Beni culturali e geografia. *Studi e ricerche di geografia, 1*.

Ruocco, D. (1979). Beni culturali e geografia. In *Studi e Ricerche di Geografia*, (pp. 1, 1–16). Genova.

Serianni, L. (1997). Percezione di lingua e dialetto nei viaggiatori in Italia tra Sette e Ottocento. *Italianistica: Rivista di letteratura italiana*, 26(3), 471–490.

Silvestrini, M., & Novembri, G., & Ceccanibbi A.M., & Paradisi, R., (2005). *Benvenuti in Italia, volume 1*. Perugia: Guerra.

Snow, M. A. (2001). Content-based and Immersion Models for Second and Foreign Language Teachings. In Celce-Murcia, M. (Ed.), *Teaching English as a Second of Foreign Language* (3rd Edition), (pp. 303–318). Boston: Heinle & Heinle.

Tommasini, M. G., & Diaco, F. M. (2013a). *Spazio Italia. Corso di italiano per stranieri 1*. Torino: Loescher.

Tommasini, M. G., & Diaco, F. M. (2013b). *Spazio Italia. Corso di italiano per stranieri 2*. Torino: Loescher.

Tommasini, M. G., & Diaco, F. M. (2013c). *Spazio Italia. Corso di italiano per stranieri 3*. Torino: Loescher.

Tommasini, M. G., & Diaco, F. M. (2014). *Spazio Italia. Corso di italiano per stranieri 4*. Torino: Loescher.

Williams, J. (2001). The effectiveness of spontaneous attention to form. *System, 29*, 325–40.

Web references

Grado en Estudios Italianos por la Universidad de Salamanca. Plan de Estudios (2022). Retrieved 30 April, 2022, from www.usal.es/files/grados/planes/plan_estudios_estud_italianos_abril2022.pdf.

Licence LLCER Italien (no date). Retrieved 30 April, 2022, from https://formations-lettres.sorbonne-universite.fr/fr/index/licence-XA/arts-lettres-langues-ALL/licence-llcer-italien-LLLCR1L_606.html

Współczesne Włochy – geografia, społeczeństwo, polityka (no date). Retrieved 30 April, 2022, from https://usosweb.uw.edu.pl/kontroler.php?_action=actionx:katalog2/przedmioty/pokazPrzedmiot(prz_kod:3223-WW-OG).

Chapter 14

The teaching of Italian through *Process Drama*

Ilaria Salonna

University of Warsaw

Abstract: Given the importance of affective and aesthetic dimensions in second language acquisition, the chapter discusses the didactics of Process Drama in relation to teaching the Italian language in higher education. As a teacher-artist with a theatrical background, the author presents her personal idea of teaching Italian through improvisation and diction training, within the creative atmosphere of the theatre laboratory, without aiming at staging a performance. This proposition is compared with the principles of Process Drama didactics in teaching Italian as a second language, where the artistic creation of a scenario offers room for improvisation and various dramatic actions. The creative phase is then followed by a meta-reflection under the teacher's guidance so that students can inductively confront themselves with the learning content of their own experience. This teaching method in higher education enhances sociocultural skills, such as non-verbal and intercultural communication, which are relevant to second language acquisition at advanced and proficiency levels.

Keywords: *Process Drama*, Theatre, Intercultural, Non-verbal, Communication, Italian

***

1. Introduction

In my personal practice as a theatre artist and Italian L2 teacher with undergraduates at University, I could see that the application of dramatic techniques to didactics could lead to the development of metacognitive skills, such as emotional intelligence, social behaviour, creativity and critical thinking. All these aspects, which are responsible for the affective involvement of the learners within an artistic experience, are leading students to consolidate their learning in a very living way.

The aesthetic involvement in an artistic process affects individual experience (Dewey, 1934). Results of applying the model of 'embodied cognition' (Gallese, 2005) in education show the deep relationship between engaging the body and enhancing learning and memory. Specifically, within the differentiation between learning and acquisition of a second language, Krashen theorizes the 'affective filter hypothesis', which intervenes on three levels: (1) motivation, (2) self-confidence, and (3) anxiety (Krashen, 1982). These three levels are responsible for the process leading to a successful acquisition and competence in a new language. It has been proven that teaching methods directly lowering the 'affective filter' are effective in second language acquisition.

In the learning process through drama, students can develop higher communication skills while training their knowledge of Italian as a second/foreign language, previously acquired in more classical structured courses. In my view, these Italian/Theatre classes should be considered necessary training for university students to test and verify, through an inductive approach, what, in theory, has already been studied in other specific courses such as Italian Grammar or Literature.

Among all the didactic methods involving theatre art, I would like to discuss here *Process Drama*, in particular in the context of advanced learning, such as at university, where speaking and conversational abilities are trained at a higher level of education. It is quite broad to talk about theatre art without specifying the many different techniques and multiple contexts, such as rehearsals, text analysis, improvisation exercises, physical scores, and performances on stage, in which the teaching of Italian as a foreign language could be involved. Relying on my own experience as a theatre artist, *Process Drama* appears closer to my idea of theatre training and requires creative work from the teacher's side.

Krashen underlines that the affective filter hypothesis defines the language teacher in a 'new way'. I think that this statement is coherent with *Process Drama*'s central idea of a 'teacher-artist' fully involved in students' activity during the lessons. I consider *Process Drama* a great opportunity to explore the teaching profession from an artistic perspective. *Process Drama* approach requires that teachers have theatrical skills. For this reason, in *Process Drama* didactics, it is legitimate to talk about 'teacher artistry' (Piazzoli, 2018).

Far from the idea of theatre staging, which is often multiplying anxiety and fear of acting in front of an audience, rather than calming it, the laboratory frame of *Process Drama* provides instead the best environment for lowering the 'affective filter' and enhancing an honest and playful engagement. The creation of a playful atmosphere that develops creativity and freedom is effective in developing motivation and self-confidence.

Due to the personal nature of this teaching approach, in this chapter, I will present my own perspective on theatre training and teaching. I would like to encourage everyone, no matter if with or without an artistic background, to try the *Process Drama*. This method sees the teacher as a leader participating from within the student's learning process rather than outside of it. After the lived experience of the play, the teacher is then bringing the student to reflect upon what was enacted in order to extract, in an inductive way, all the linguistic aspects explored.

2. Process Drama *in Glottodidactics*

University students are already adults, and they can easily handle multiple varieties of situations where the second language they are learning could be applied. For these reasons, University classes are the ideal context for *Process Drama*. A teacher could choose to utilize this methodology for a short part of a long course or propose an entire cycle of meetings during a semester having the characteristic of a theatre laboratory.

According to *Process Drama* methodology, as explained by Heathcote D. and Bolton G. (1994) and introduced in second language education by Kao S. M. and O'Neill C. (1998), the theatrical work is conceived as a closed laboratory, where the focus is not on the rehearsal of a performance to be presented to an audience. On the contrary, this would mean shifting the aim of the laboratory from didactics to performance erroneously.

There are three phases in the didactics of *Process Drama*: the initial phase is related to the definition of the *pre-text* from which it is then possible to create a dramaturgical idea. This can be anything that can give an impulse to create a story in which to start to play different roles: it could be a picture, an article or a film. The teacher's role relates to the pre-text. The teacher-artist is the one starting to play in the context in order to engage the other participants in creating episodes connected to it.

The phase of the 'dramatic experience' starts mainly with the use of the technique of improvisation, following the instructions given by the teacher along the path. After this experiential phase, there is a third and fundamental one based on the reflection upon what occurred during the improvisations. Only after this reflective phase is it possible to consolidate the 'dramatic experience' into new linguistic competencies.

Process Drama is pursuing only a didactic aim: in this context, the aim is teaching and learning a second language on multiple levels. Thanks to the alternative use of the tools of improvisation and reflection, *Process Drama* is operating on an intercultural level, thus offering a type of learning that it is truly embracing all the various aspects of a language, as well as creating a bridge towards the personal relationship that each student has with the foreign language. The use of the acting technique of improvisation involves an aesthetic and sensory level: one thing is to talk about an experience, and another thing is to embody the circumstances that are leading towards the happening of that experience. Another level is then the affective one because there is an impact that any acting exercise of improvisation leaves behind in the memory of the doers.

The 'reflection in action' (O'Mara, 2006) is a fundamental ability for *Process Drama* teachers. The teacher-artist has a maieutic approach, and the theatre pedagogue in a traditional theatre laboratory. Through precise questions, the teacher aims to stimulate students' creativity and the ability to reflect upon the experience, always bearing in mind the didactic aim. By constantly keeping the pre-text on which the fictional world is built, the teacher stimulates participants always to use vehicular language.

Process Drama is already a quite known method in glottodidactics, so it is possible to define learning objectives according to the didactic strategies applied. The variety of exercises that can be proposed with *Process Drama* is quite wide so that the teacher can adapt the lessons and the course accordingly to the different linguistic competencies that the students must acquire. As a method focused on student's active participation, motivation is more easily leading towards attention, which is essential for a concrete engagement in the learning process (Diadori, 2001).

In glottodidactics, *Process Drama* reveals itself as an effective tool for engaging participants in searching for a more authentic language. This allows us to explore linguistic aspects that are sometimes difficult to learn when studied in a too abstract way, such as phraseologies and discourse makers, often present in conversational language.

3. The importance of atmosphere and the balance between risk and safety in the dimension of playing

More often than we think, the knowledge of a language (grammar, vocabulary, syntax) is not directly proportional to the ability to communicate in that language. Therefore, it is fundamental to create a learning environment in which anyone can feel safe to make mistakes and to take risks in communicating with others, finding oneself directly involved in situations that are – as in a role-play – reminding the real life. When we face the need to communicate in a foreign language, we do it regardless of the difficult circumstances in which we may find ourselves in daily life. Not often it occurs to be in such extreme situations as, for example, calling an ambulance after an accident or explaining ourselves in a shop where nobody speaks our language. The ideal "as if" that helps actors work with circumstances could help a student train her/his communication skills in a foreign language. The rehearsal room provides the best atmosphere that allows such work with the circumstances in a playful way, enhancing creativity and exploring different solutions. In this sense, the theatrical experience, while reproducing and reminding the real life, reveals itself as more rich and instructive.

Atmosphere is a category that should be considered when leading and evaluating best practices in learning and education. For that, "a single lesson consists of a vast amount of relevant variables that constitute an atmosphere, such as number, age, and sex of the pupils, their culture, ethnic, and social origin, their educational background, individual mood, and the combined impact of different characters" (Wolf, 2019: 48). Also, other elements are directly affecting the atmospheres of learning: "they surround us in an invisible manner, containing a little moisture, some gases, particulate matter, particular smells, and perhaps also some components we may never know of. In an educational context, it is a mixture of emotions, moods, embodied stirrings, weather conditions, architectonic design, pretensions, memories, and some rather mysterious components." (Wolf, 2019: 164).

As much as for the actor's work, conceived in its dimension of trial and learning, also in an imaginary classroom, the atmosphere is an important aspect to take care of. From the perspective of using theatre techniques for teaching Italian as a second/foreign language, it is, therefore, fundamental to take care of the space and the relations between participants.

When talking about space in relation to atmosphere, one shall consider both architectural (e.g. if we are working in an old or modern building, the materials used for building it, the colours of the wall and pavements, the distribution of windows and doors) and weather like aspects (light and temperature of the place, smells), i.e. all elements that – as the etymology of the word atmosphere (*athmos*, to breath) says – involve air. Is it a comfortable space, inspiring calm, familiarity, and trust? Is it a place where I would like to come back and where I can communicate about myself with confidence and mutual understanding? Also, the way the space is organized can influence the atmosphere. For example, it is important to understand how to sit down. Should chairs be placed in a circle or along the walls? With which distance? Where is the teacher positioned? Are the learners alone or in pairs or groups? There is no correct answer to these questions. It is important to pay attention to these aspects because the theatre laboratory established for learning purposes must also be organized through formal and structural elements. Creating the best conditions for the exercise of theatre art is essential for using it as a tool for teaching and learning content. These aspects appear so much important, especially when such conditions are not the best for starting a theatre laboratory. The teacher, well trained in learning atmospheres, should be able to adapt and be flexible in order to create, each time, the most effective environment for helping learners in taking action.

The technical aspect of a good atmosphere is fundamental for creating the best climate and enhancing creative freedom. All the relations among the participants to the theatre laboratory relate to the atmosphere according to a mutual influence, in which the space disposition and the physical characteristics of the place can affect the quality of the presence and the well-being.

This becomes more evident when using improvisation as a theatrical method because, in this case, the environment should allow and inspire playfulness. One should feel a natural tendency to take risks as normally any game requires, but at the same time, the confidence of being comfortable and safe also in making mistakes.

There must be a fundamental distinction between the space of normal life and the rehearsal room or the classroom. In the rehearsals room, but ideally, any learner in a classroom feels free to be oneself, without the fear of being judged or unsuccessful: 'Love your mistakes' is the motto of such laboratory and its special atmosphere.

Atmosphere as a special role in acting technique on two main levels: on the one hand, the level of discipline in the creative work; on the other hand, one of the plays itself, the situations, the character, and the plot that has to be enacted on the scenic space (rehearsals room or stage). A good working atmosphere is fundamental for keeping working on a creative level when it comes to artistic work and also in a pedagogical context.

4. Playing with the stereotypical theatricality of the Italian language: Improvisation and Diction

Learning a language is not a mechanical process. Moreover, it is unrealistic to not consider the inherently complex characteristics of a natural language, with its pragmatics and its meta-linguistic system of values, ideas, relations, and styles, which have an impact on the aesthetic of the communication itself. For this reason, thinking about the Italian language, I am choosing to start from a stereotype, which is the supposed theatricality and special musicality of the Italian language.

Ask anyone not a native Italian speaker to make a parody of someone speaking in Italian, and you will have a character of someone almost singing while talking with a loud voice and performing very wide and open gestures:

almost like an opera singer. However, I am far from being ironic here. I do think there is a deep truth in stereotypes because they are also bringing a paradigmatic value as an expression of specific cultural references. In the case of the supposed theatricality of the Italian language, the cultural references are the *Commedia dell'arte*, a form of theatre based on improvisation technique, and the Medieval Italian poetry of *Dolce Stil Novo* and beyond, in which sound and phonetics are so much related to the meaning conveyed by the words.

Commedia dell'arte, as a theatre genre, has strong historical roots, thus representing a traditional form of theatre, codified and taught by generations of families of artists since the late twenty-first century. It is widespread in Europe, from Italy, reaching crowds from common people to monarchs. It brought Italian culture outside the peninsula by the initiative of nomad actors, most of the time rejected by the rest of society in their own town of origin. The main characteristics of *Commedia dell'arte* is the presence of typical characters, most of the time played with Masks, and the repetition of stories, mostly known from the main cultural repertoire, around strong, fixed structural patterns. This set of rigid rules is in *Commedia dell'arte* the *conditio sine qua non* that is allowing improvisation. That is why in this context, we often meet the word *canovaccio*, which means a sketch of a text, in which it is noted how the different characters interact in each act of the play, following a set of situations and events.

Commedia dell'arte artists are most of the time playing the same characters (one or two) all throughout their lives. The life of an actor at that time corresponded more or less with his/her own career. It means that they lived all the time as nomads and artists; their home was the caravan, where they lived, travelled, loved and played. However, when considered outside its historical context according to an anthropological perspective, *Commedia dell'arte* has become a well-established technique transversally crossing all the theatre genres so that we can find elements of it also in contemporary theatre.

I personally trained a lot in the use of improvisation as rehearsing technique. I am Italian by birth and had a theatrical education in the frame of Italian classical theatre academy tradition. I specialized myself with the Russian director Anatoli Vassiliev, who belongs to Stanislavski's legacy, as like Mikhail Chekhov's work on physical actions (Chekhov, 1991), and above all, Marja Knebel (Knebel, 1959). In the frame of this pedagogical tradition in theatre, the acting technique of improvisation became my main practice.

An intuitive understanding of improvisation brings out the concepts of spontaneity and freedom. Nevertheless, practising improvisation requires the respect of a complex set of rules and relations, both structural and compositional, which are coming straightforward from the text of the play, in a balance between the strict respect of the rules of the play and the 'anarchic' strength of creativity (Lupo, 2006).

This improvisational practice is called *etjud*. As a rehearsing technique, *etjud* practice proceeds by making different trials on the same scene, or monological line of a character, so that it is possible, layer by layer, to enact the whole dramaturgical complexity of the play. The aim is to reach a sort of translation, in the literal sense of a passage, from the written text of the play to the scenic enacted one of the performances.

Another way to define *etjud* practice is 'to read the text with your own feet'. Priorly the text is analysed, and then, thanks to the *etjud*, actors try through their improvisation if the analysis is correct, i.e. corresponds with the dramatic action. This practice starts from the fundamental assumption that there is a literary text, i.e. the one written on the page, and the scenic text, i.e. the one realized by actors. That is why Marja Knebel, a theoretician-practitioner of such rehearsing methodology, defined it as 'action-analysis', i.e. analysis *for* the action and *through* the action. This definition clarifies better the distinction between a literal, philological analysis of the text of a theatre play and the analysis that is useful for the actor in order to gather the impulses for improvising during the *etjud* (Knebel, 1959). Before starting an improvisation, the actors-students have to go through a very precise analysis of the play, according to the 'action-analysis' methodology, which is meant to offer actors the 'tools' they need for improvising.

Another aspect of the stereotypical image of the Italian language is its musicality and the importance of sound and intonation in this language. It is emblematic that even Dante chose to define Tuscany with an audial and phonetical association: *la terra dove il sì suona*. It is also remarkable that, as an acting student at the theatre academy, I rediscovered Dante's *Divina Commedia* in a richer and deeper way than I did previously as an Italian high school student. *Divina Commedia* is compulsory reading in Italian high schools, so I did know these verses before being accepted at the theatre academy. However, I believe that my true first encounter with this text happened during the classes I had at the *Accademia dei Filodrammatici* of Milan with my teacher Teresita Fabris, a former actress who worked very young also with Vittorio Gassman and Orazio Costa. She later established with Toni Comello the *Trebbo* Theatre in Milan, acting and creating performances also with the participation of important Italian poets and Nobel laureates such as Eugenio Montale and Salvatore Quasimodo. Studying Italian diction, especially working on masterpieces of Italian literature, is undoubtfully a very enriching learning experience. If, with improvisation techniques, it is possible to explore in a surprising way the pragmatics of the language, with diction training, as well as the study of the right pronunciation and intonation of words and sentences in Italian, it is possible to reach even a deeper level in this language through the tool of theatre art. The Italian language also has lots of homograph words that allow, for example, the comedy of equivoques. Sometimes homographs are not homophones, like, for example, the word "botte", in which the vowel 'o' can be pronounced differently and change the meaning of the word. These cases are often ground for playful interactions based on equivoques and comic misunderstandings.

The comedy of equivoques is so widespread in Italian comic tradition that we can see it in Pirandello's play but also widely used in the filming productions with Totò. This brings actors to play on a level that is just suggested by words and their meanings, but it involves a wider semantic horizon, thus creating playful situations for both actors and spectators.

5. Practical indications for a Theatre-Italian laboratory

The working material to be played by students should be structured in a way that can keep a good 'dramatic tension' (Piazzoli, 2018). Any text, or *canovaccio*, even if very short and simple, should have some basic structure that could be enacted in a theatrical scene. In other words, there must be a beginning in which certain circumstances are set, the atmosphere, the characters with their aim, the conflict, the situation with some events that can change it, and the final resolution.

Haseman and O'Toole (1986) are formulating a model with the following dramatic elements: (1) situation, (2) role, and (3) relationships, driven by (4) dramatic tension, directed by (5) focus, made explicit in (6) place and (7) time through (8) language and (9) movement, to create (10) mood and (11) symbol which all together create the experience of (12) dramatic meaning. These elements are discussed in detail by Piazzoli (2014).

The teacher creates a situation where the students can easily play, so it is preferable to know who they are, which is the relation with the language they are learning, for which purposes they are attending these classes at university, what is their personal life situation, age and life objectives, etc.

Unlikely an actor, a student of Italian L2 is not probably in search of the spontaneity of the action on stage. However, similarly to an actor, a second language learner is keen to train the ability to be oneself in extraneous situations. We can maybe make a comparison here between the foreign reality of the fictional world of the play and the foreign language within the world explored through fictional situations. Therefore, we can see that learning to speak another language means as well to train spontaneity and freedom as much as it is for an actor.

The comparison between an actor and a student of Italian L2 can show how advantageous it can be to try the approach of theatre improvisation as it is conceived in actor's training for learning Italian as a foreign language. The pedagogue's task is to lead the student towards the discovery of oneself as a speaker of Italian without enacting characters or stereotypes. According to the grammar of acting, in order to refuse something in a performative way, one must start to play with the object that must be rejected, as much as we do with a ball that finally we throw away.

Game and playfulness are the working rules for this didactic methodology. Each student should finally get to his own true and natural way of expressing oneself. It is a process, and it requires time and multi-layered work that goes along with the ability to use the language and also for expressing emotions and elaborated thoughts. It is also recommended to propose multiple sets of training exercises on the textual material and not just the rehearsals of the scenes. Scenes are the artistic outcome, in a way, something that can be shown to an audience. The laboratory also consists of the preparation for acting the scenes through the special material given by the teacher.

I am proposing to divide the space and the time of the session into two parts: firstly, a part of active-reading of dramaturgy; secondly, the time for showing enacted scenes and micro-scenes to other participants. Given this division of the working session, I suggest focusing on the following elements:

1. **Space**: The working place appears firstly centred around the work on the text so that we can find a space organized around a big table or an empty area closed by a circle of chairs. The teacher is sitting together with others, and everyone can have papers and take notes. In the second part of the session, there is empty space offered for the performance.

2. **Movement** and physical actions: Characters' physical definition will help in finding their communicative style. It is very intuitive to search for the inner tempo-rhythm of a character through the work on his/her bodily movements and gestures, his/her behaviours. Language and its intonation are also directly connected to these non-verbal elements of communication.

3. **Meeting** the Other: As underlined by E. Lévinas, meeting with the other is a process of transforming and discovering oneself. In particular, acknowledging the other makes the self human (Lévinas, 1982). The performance consists of meeting with the Other one and the Unknown, if we consider that a character

and a play correspond to another individual and a new world with different values than ours. Whenever learning a new language, we face meeting with another culture and civilization, different ways to construct our thinking and different styles of communication. Therefore, by considering language in its performative aspect, it is also allowing an experience that is unpredictable and unprecedented as much as the type of involvement of a performer in action.

4. **Dramaturgy**: To have a written text is always helping, even in the case of very simple scenes invented by participants and even if in the form of a *canovaccio*.

Although in *Process Drama,* there is not a fixed text to start from, the teacher cooperating together with the participants in creating and exploring a theatrical path that starts from a *canovaccio* or, otherwise said, a pre-text. A good pre-text can allow many improvisation exercises and different possibilities of playing within a fictional situation or setting. In second language classes conducted through the art of theatre, the text works as a fundamental tool of study and not only a learning material: students could work on the difference between direct and indirect speech, the variety of linguistic styles employed in describing a situation or an environment and in daily conversations. With the improvement in mastering the language, more nuances and levels will naturally appear. There can be different approaches according to the different starting levels. If we are improvising, it is not recommended to learn a text by heart, and actors have to find their own words in order to play according to their tasks and aim for the action. However, sometimes it could be useful, especially for beginners, to learn short texts and dialogues by heart in order to play and enact some communicative formulas often used in simple situations. At the A1 of the *Common European Framework of References for Languages* level, for example, learners can understand and use very basic expressions to satisfy concrete needs; they can introduce themselves and others, ask and answer questions about personal details, such as where they live, people they know and things they do every day; they can interact as long as the other person speaks slowly and clearly. On an A1 level, it would be discouraging to work on too complex texts, and it is then fundamental for the teacher to be ready to adapt them to make tasks easier in the execution. It is preferred as an approach that creates a certain familiarity with the material through repetition, coordination of voice and movement, interaction and rhythm. Therefore, texts on this level are based on short dialogues in simple situations, similar to those we can find in a first-level book. The difference is that students will be compelled to act on certain characters, and they will have to use their acting skills in order to add an emotional experience to what they are doing.

To train the ability to read through exercises of correct pronunciation and diction could be an opportunity not only to learn Italian in a playful way but also to explore its pragmatics, focusing on its linguistic performativity (Austin, 1962). The teacher working with beginners, and lower intermediate students, could take inspiration from some Italian humoristic literature such as, for example, Achille Campanile's *Tragedie in due battute* (Campanile, 1931). An example of a good working material for exercising diction for beginners is also Gianni Rodari's poems for children, which are suitable for being learned easily by heart because of their rhythmical structure.

In the context of teaching Italian as a second language could be useful to invite students to do reading exercises, always bearing in mind the context of *Process Drama*. For example, while having defined the pre-text for the group of students, the teacher could propose improvisations based on role-play interactions and exercises involving writing and reading: like a poet making a performance commemorating a historical event, or a journalist reading a statement in front of an audience, someone receiving a love letter quoting concrete pieces of literature and reading it out loud or dedicating them to someone, etc. It is important that all the creative propositions are inserted in the general fictional set invented by the teacher.

These practical indications for a Theatre-Italian session are suitable for applying the didactics of *Process Drama*. Any artistic work is perfectionated by the practice; however, I recommend to teachers interested in acting techniques the most known works by Stanislavski, such as the classic American edition *An actor prepares* (Stanislavski, 1936) and the overmentioned Knebel (1959). For a general view of acting techniques through the lenses of theatre anthropology, I recommend Eugenio Barba's writings (2015, 2010).

A good knowledge of the syllabuses for the teaching of Italian as a second and foreign language for all the different levels is also recommended in order to choose the right texts suitable for the actual competencies that students will acquire during the course.

6. Conclusion

The research on *Process Drama* for teaching Italian as a second/foreign language is currently ongoing, and new publications are constantly appearing. The fascinating role played by the teacher within this methodology represents a learning perspective in itself for Italian language students at university. In *Process Drama*, the pedagogical relation is student-centred, and the teacher needs to display true artistry in leading and creating the theatrical path allowing students' active participation. If we consider academic education also as a preparation for professional life, students could specialise through this methodology, with the intention of building expertise as teacher-artists by profession.

The task of assuming a different role in order to play and co-create with other participants a collective theatrical experience has great value for intercultural competencies, which are also part of the acquisition of a foreign language. The linguistic engagement enhanced by *Process Drama* didactics occurs on different dimensions, including cognitive, affective and social ones (Svalberg, 2009). Learning Italian through theatre is configuring itself as a sociocultural process (Van Lier, 2000) and a remarkable experience in students' personal life.

More and more importance is given to sociocultural competence in communication, and this aspect should also be considered in the linguistic didactics at University. As underlined by Balboni, despite the awareness of the evolution of the model of communicative competence in academic programs, there is still not enough attention given to non-verbal and intercultural communication (Balboni, 2012: 83). Thinking about an academic perspective of research, but also University teaching, it is, therefore, important to strengthen the presence of didactic methodologies, such as *Process Drama*, that are enhancing such neglected aspects, which are instead relevant in second language acquisition.

References

Austin J. L. (1962). *How to do things with words*. Clarendon Press: Oxford.
Balboni P. E. (2012). Sapere una lingua: dall'idea intuitiva al significato scientifico. In Balboni, P. E., & Daloiso, M. (Eds.), *La formazione linguistica all'Università*, (pp. 75-116). Venezia: Edizioni Ca' Foscari.
Barba, E., & Savarese, N. (2015). *I cinque continenti del teatro. Fatti e leggende della cultura materiale dell'attore*. Bari: Edizioni Di Pagina.
Barba, E. (2010). *On Directing and Dramaturgy*. London-New York: Routledge.
Campanile, A. (1931). *Teatro completo*. Milano: Treves.
Chekhov, M. (1991). *On the technique of acting*. New York: Harper Collins.
Dewey, J. (1937). *Art as experience*. Harvard University Press.
Diadori, P. (2001). *Insegnare l'Italiano agli Stranieri*. Milano: Mondadori Education.
Gallese, V. (2005). Embodied simulation: From neurons to phenomenal experience. *Phenomenology and Cognitive Science*, 4 (1), 23–48.
Haseman, B., & O'Toole J. (1986). *Dramawise: An introduction to the elements of drama*. Melbourne: Heinemann.
Heathcote, D., & Bolton, G. (1994). *Drama for learning: an account of Heathcote mantle of expert approaches to education*. Portsmouth: Heinemann.

Kao, S. M., & O'Neill, C. (1998). *Words into worlds: Learning a Second Language through Process Drama*. London: Ablex Publishing Corporation.

Knebel, M. (1959). O deïstvennom analize piesy i roli, Iskusstvo, Moskva. Edizione Italiana a cura di A. Bergamo, L'analisi della pièce e del ruolo mediante l'azione. Bulzoni, 2009: Roma.

Krashen, S. (1982). *Principles and Practices in Second Language Acquisition*. University of Southern California.

Lévinas, E. (1982). *Éthique et infini: Dialogues avec Philippe Nemo*. Paris: LGF/ Le Livre de Poche.

Lupo, S. (2006). *Anatoli Vassiliev. Au coeur de la pedagogie theatrale. Riguer et anarchie*. Paris: L'Entretemps.

O'Mara, J. (2006). Capturing the ephemeral: reflection-in-action as research. *Drama Australia Journal*, 30 (2), 41–50.

Piazzoli, E. (2014). Engagement as perception. *International Journal of Language Studies*, 8(2), 91–116.

Piazzoli, E. (2018). *Embodying language in action: The artistry of process drama in second language education*. London: Palgrave MacMillan Publisher.

Stanislavski, K. S. (1936). *An actor prepares*. London-New York: Routledge.

Svalberg, A. M. (2009). Engagement with language: Interrogating a construct. *Language Awareness*, 18 (3-4), 242–258.

Van Lier, L. (2000). *The ecology and semiotics of language learning. A sociocultural perspective*. Massachusetts: Kluwer Academic Publishers Norwell.

Wolf, B. (2019). *Atmospheres of learning*. Milan: Mimesis International.

Suggested readings

Marini-Maio, N., & Ryan-Scheutz, C. (Eds.). (2010). *Set the Stage!: Teaching Italian through Theater*. Yale University Press.

Chapter 15

Learning from the essay

Valentina Tibaldo
University of Oxford

Abstract: According to Theodor Adorno, "the way the essay appropriates concepts can best be compared to the behaviour of someone in a foreign country" (Adorno, 1958). The present contribution expands on this comparison between the essay as a literary genre and the challenges of learning a foreign language by exploring both its theoretical implications and its application to students of Italian at a university level. The essay, which literally means 'attempt', as it is conceived by Adorno and Lukács (1911), entails a kind of knowledge characterised by incompleteness and tentativeness, grounded in experience, focused on details but aiming at all-encompassing observations. Analysing essays written in Italian and experimenting with this literary form represent for the students an unparalleled opportunity not only to improve their reading comprehension and writing skills but also to familiarise themselves with the notion of intercultural communication as it is developed by Balboni (2019) and Piller (2011).

Keywords: Essay, Italian, Literary genre, Creative writing

***

1. Introduction

Looking at the essays he has just finished writing, Georg Lukács wonders whether they can constitute a book; the matter at stake is not the concern, common among writers, about the coherence and consistency of their works, especially in the case of collections of different pieces, but rather the more general question about the nature of the essay, the possibility of considering it a literary genre. For his pieces to compose a book, Lukács needs to identify some sort of unity that makes them a "literary form of its own" (1974: 1). Many scholars have explored the same issue, scrutinising his and other works, but defining this literary form has proven to be an arduous task. This may not come as a surprise for a genre whose first and foremost characteristic is elusiveness; for Berardinelli (2002: 17) the essay is "il più mutevole e inafferrabile dei generi", while Boetcher Joeres (1993: 152) defines it as a "boundary form". "What the essay is, has never been precisely determined", we read in the *Dictionary of World Literary Terms* (Shipley, 1970), so instead of a definition, we are provided with a description which touches upon some common elements; "in general, it is a composition, usually in prose, of moderate length and on a restricted topic", characterised by "concern for, or excellence in, manner of expression" (Shipley, 1970: 106). Incompleteness and tentativeness are further distinctive features which trace back to the first use of the word *essais*, attempts, the "wonderfully elegant and apt title" Montaigne chose in 1580 for his trials (Lukács, 1974: 9). However, essayists can be found before the sixteenth century, despite the fact that Plato, Seneca or Marcus Aurelius would not call themselves in this way; more recent examples, instead, usually include Kierkegaard, Woolf, Musil, Weil, Benjamin among many others. Essay is a word that is used very often in Anglo-American universities to label assignments which, however, are not expected to be elaborate in style and limited in range to express a subjective point of view or display an incomplete nature. As Landrum-Geyer (2015: 2) points out, "what most teachers call essays in the classroom are more accurately labelled as articles or themes, or at the very least a specific essay subgenre – the academic essay". The same can be said when the word is employed in the context of foreign language classes which are often organised around the four skills; students are asked to write an even wider range of texts, letters, postcards, recipes, reviews, summaries, and short stories but not attempts.

The present contribution explores precisely the potential pedagogical value of using the essay as a literary form in teaching Italian at the university level. It draws on three-year experimentation held at the University of Oxford and provides both theoretical insights and practical applications. It sets to demonstrate that the essay can represent a useful resource to help students not only to improve their reading comprehension and writing skills but also to develop intercultural competencies, as well as awareness of their writing practices in their first language.

2. Developing self-awareness through the essay

For three years, I have taught an essay class at the University of Oxford in which about ten first-year students with an intermediate level of Italian were asked to engage with the essay as a literary genre. The class ran for the whole academic year with sessions every two weeks and included theoretical insights on the debate around the form of the essay, discussions of examples by Italian writers, and exercises of composition. Typically, students had to submit their essays a week before the class to then focus on an excerpt from a theoretical text and answer some questions in preparation for the upcoming session. These passages were taken from Lukács (1974), Adorno (1991), Boetcher Joeres (1993), Woolf (2003), and D'Agata (2009), among others, and usually given in English. The questions students had to submit two days before the class were meant to help them to navigate these often quite dense texts and, more importantly, to offer them an opportunity to self-reflection on their assumptions about how we know, why we engage with literary texts, what we learn when we study a foreign language. Indeed, the selected excepts all explored the idea that the essay as a form entails a distinctive experience, asks the works of art very important questions, and pursues a specific kind of understanding. Adorno, for example, states that the essay is dismissed in academic contexts as it questions the equation of knowledge with organised science; "the essay reflects what is loved and hated instead of presenting the mind as creation *ex nihilo* on the model of an unrestrained work ethic", he writes, "luck and play are essential to it. It starts not with Adam and Eve but with what it wants to talk about; it says what occurs to it in that context and stops when it feels finished rather than when there is nothing to say. Hence it is classified as a trivial endeavour" (1991: 4). For him, the value of the essay lies precisely in that it forces us to consider what it is usually dismissed, the fragmentary and the contingent, and to ask ourselves whether totality, objectivity or eternity are ever at reach.

Woolf agrees with Adorno that this literary form is not afraid of showing that its findings are grounded in an embodied experience and further distinguishes between subjective and personal self-awareness and the automatic validation of any thoughts just because they are ours. The essay, for her, is fundamentally about the pleasure of writing, the delight great works of literature bring us, and the joy of commenting on them, and this pleasure is an extremely serious matter. "We must be sure that we are not praising the famous because they have been praised already and the dead because we shall never meet them wearing spats in Piccadilly", she writes, inviting us not to be intimidated by celebrated writers but also to be precise in discussing their works; "we must know what we mean when we say that they can write and give us pleasure. We must compare them; we must bring out the quality. We must point to this and say it is good because it is exact, truthful, and imaginative" (2003: 262). Not only the essay acknowledges that thoughts and opinions are not created *ex nihilo*, but it also deals with works of art, ideas or events that are historically situated. According to Lukács, "it is part of its essence that it does not draw something new out of an empty vacuum but only gives a new order to such things as once lived. And because he only newly orders them, not forming something new out of the formless, he is bound to them" (1974: 10). This bound implies honesty and precision, as Woolf underlines, and also a sort of ironic modesty; indeed, this literary form is, on the one hand, deeply aware of its limits and constraints and, on the other, addresses broad and ambitious questions. For Lukács, one of the reasons why the essay can explore such issues is that it does not interrogate life directly but the form it has assumed through the mediation of literature and art. The fact that essayists focus so intensively on the style of both the works they discuss and of their own writing is grounded in the idea that form can be "a world-view, a stand-point, an attitude vis-à-vis the life from which it sprags: a possibility of reshaping it, of creating it anew" (1974: 8). At the same time these writers are always aware that their knowledge is derivative, and if sometimes they believe they have "come close to the ultimate", they inevitably realise that after all, they have "no more to offer than explanations of the poems of others" or at best their own ideas (1974: 9).

3. Emotions and intercultural competence

Thanks to these and similar theoretical insights, students were invited to reflect on the characteristics associated with the essay, asking themselves whether emotions affect understanding, what kind of knowledge a subjective point of view may offer, and whether play and luck ever granted them any discovery. More importantly, they were encouraged to consider whether their own experience as learners of one or more foreign languages resonates with this literary form. "The way the essay appropriates concepts can best be compared to the behaviour of someone in a foreign country", Adorno states, as in such a situation, one has to deal with the complex and challenging nature of language, not the simplified description drawn by coursebooks, ascertaining the meaning of a word from its different contexts instead of looking up dictionary's entries. "This kind of learning remains vulnerable to error, as does the essay as form; it has to pay for its affinity with open intellectual experience with a lack of security that the norm of established thought fears like death" (1991: 13). The lack of security does scare not only the norm of established thought but also learners who, on the one hand, need generalisations in order to navigate complex language systems and, on the other, keep encountering exceptions to rules. The way in which the essay scrutinises details in order to answer a broad and general question without assuming that a definitive answer exists can help students to deal with the unpredictable, peculiar aspects of a language. The discomfort they can feel in relation to the arbitrariness of meanings and usages may be similar to the uneasiness provoked by the essays they are asked to read, which tend not to go straight to the point. Furthermore, by considering the role played by emotions in shaping our response to intricate, complex subject matters, learners can better understand their response to the challenges of encountering a different language and culture.

In this respect, the essay is a particular apt form to develop intercultural competences. In *La comunicazione interculturale*, Balboni and Caon underline that mastering a language alone does not guarantee an effective communication with someone with a different culture as assumptions, fear, difficulty to decipher attitudes and values of the Other can lead to misunderstandings. "Avere consapevolezza del punto da cui si osserva e allenarsi a cambiare il punto d'osservazione attraverso il decentramento e lo straniamento", they state "diventano i presupposti fondamentali per comunicare con interlocutori di altra cultura e ridurre il rischio di giudicare sulla base di pregiudizi e stereotipi" (pp. 148-149). According to them, the learner of a foreign language along with linguistic skills, should develop relational ones which they define as "saper osservare (decentrarsi e straniarsi), saper relativizzare, saper sospendere il giudizio, saper ascoltare attivamente, saper comprendere emotivamente (empatizzare ed extopizzare), saper negoziare i significati" (2015: 147). Essayists, in a way, are very familiar with these skills; they constantly acknowledge that the understanding they offer is the result of a given experience and specific point of view which, for this reason, often produce an estrangement-effect. They carefully scrutinise a subject matter, a work of art, an event conscious that this would lead them to revise their own categories, face conflicts, experience insightful intuitions and the discomfort of insecurity. It is precisely the awareness that any encounter is an opportunity to become aware of one's own assumptions, as well as of those of the Other that makes the essay a valuable source to explore the idea of intercultural communication. "Accorgerci di noi stessi mentre comunichiamo con gli altri, dei nostri paradigmi che diamo spesso per scontati (e spesso per aprioristicamente giusti o gli unici possibili)" is one of the experiences that the learner of a foreign language should be familiar with according to Balboni and Caon (2015: 157), and at the same time is one of the aims of the fragmentary, incomplete, extremely self-aware form that is the essay. Furthermore, both this literary genre and the intercultural approach underline the crucial role played by language in shaping meaning. The essay explores its questions by focusing on style, in a foreign language class, it is precisely through the language that students are given accesses to a different culture.

4. Essay classes. Two pedagogical applications

These questions about knowledge, this literary form, and the experience of learning a foreign language were the background of the classes I taught, while the sessions consisted of reading and discussing examples of essays written in Italian. These texts were approximately 400 words long and were chosen to explore a specific aspect of the genre, expanding the discussion started by the preparatory reading, but also in relation to the authors students were reading for the literature courses; Calvino, Ortese, Scego, Ginzburg, among others. The texts were provided with some contextual information, a list of vocabulary and some notes explaining the cultural references; they were divided into two parts, so students were asked to read and discuss 200 words at a time, and they were free to use both English and Italian. For example, the first session was dedicated to introducing the essay as a literary genre and the notion of intercultural communication. The entry 'essay' in the *Dictionary of World Literary Terms* and the list of relational skills compiled by Balboni and Caon (2015) constituted the preparatory readings, while in class, we discussed the portrait of Montale given by Sereni in *Ognuno riconosce i suoi*. Montale was one of the set authors for first-year students of Italian; therefore, they were familiar with his figure, and they could also compare the style of Sereni's text with that of the academic essays they had to read for the literature course.

> Ho incontrato Montale per la prima volta nel maggio del '38, durante una breve sosta a Firenze di ritorno da Roma. Dove, naturalmente, se non a un tavolo delle Giubbe Rosse? Credo di aver capito fin da allora che portava su di sé con fastidio quel doppione di sé stesso che si forma via via con la fama. C'è un'arte anche nel gestire, nell'amministrare il doppione di sé. Credo che Montale abbia sempre rifiutato quest'arte, convinto, come credo sia, che la poesia è la radiazione di un uomo e non qualcosa di professionale e che, almeno per quanto lo riguarda, la dissacrazione della poesia è già avvenuta in lui sin dai primissimi versi. («Ma assaggi un po' di queste cipolline, di questi meravigliosi sottaceti» era il suo modo di dirottare chi cercava di coinvolgerlo in discorsi sulla poesia quando mezza Italia cominciava a parlare di lui). Adesso Montale stava lì a due passi da me, seduto in silenzio in mezzo alla mia generazione, con l'aria di uno che aspetta qualcosa e magari è disposto ad alzarsi per incontrarla a metà strada. Infatti si alzò di scatto, scusandosi appena: «Adesso devo andare, è tardi» («tardi, sempre più tardi» gli facevo eco dentro di me). Questo era, più o meno, il tempo delle Occasioni.

The passage is taken from Sereni (2013: 1009-1010) but edited to be suitable for an Intermediate level. After a brief introduction about the course, the author and the context from which the excerpt is taken, students were asked to read it and familiarise themselves with style, eventually asking questions about expressions or phrases that were unclear. They had to choose among a list of adjectives the ones that better describe the figure of Montale as it emerges from this text, *cupo, solare, schivo, serioso, ironico, estroverso, disponibile, burbero, affabile* etc. They were invited to motivate their choices, pointing out specific passages and discussing their overall impressions. Then,

I would introduce the notion of the subjective point of view as a fundamental element of the form of the essay and discuss with the students the ways in which it informs the text and the representation of Montale. In particular, they were encouraged to consider the imbalance between the two poets, the role played by fame in determining their relationship and what Sereni can grasp of Montale.

> Questo non è un ricordo, è un sogno, recente. Siamo a un funerale, tra molte facce note. C'è anche Montale, a due passi da me. Noto che C., uno scrittore di età intermedia tra Montale e me, è molto invecchiato: «una foresta di capelli interamente bianchi, e una barba bianca come quella che la neve fa alle statue». Non le parole esatte, ma la sensazione è nitida nel sogno. Montale no, sembra persino ringiovanito, riposato e pimpante. Al termine, uscendo, mi chiede che cosa penso della messa in italiano. Gli rispondo che mi aspettavo di peggio, che così il testo torna a imporre il suo significato, che prima era disperso in una litania che di impressionante aveva solo l'accento. «Sì,» dice «ma allora bisognerebbe confrontare punto per punto, coi testi alla mano.» E poi, col passaggio repentino di tono che gli è proprio, come affastellando le parole: «Preferivo la messa in latino, era una specie di *forfait* con l'Eterno: questa no, è un impegnativo contratto, un duro contratto» ridacchia. (Sereni 2013: 1012-1013)

By describing a dream, this second passage makes the subjective nature of Montale's description even more explicit and offered the opportunity to develop further the discussion around the understanding that a subjective point of view may offer. Indeed, if at the *Giubbe Rosse*, Montale eludes any questions by underlining the quality of the pickles and pickling onions, and Sereni is unable to speak to him despite their proximity, in the dream, they are able to have a conversation. Students were invited to notice the differences in both Sereni's and Montale's attitudes in the two excerpts and compare the adjectives they chose for the first passage with those they could find in the second one, *ringiovanito, riposato, pimpante*. Furthermore, this text offered the opportunity of discussing the tentative and a-systemic attitude of the essay, evident in a sentence like "non le parole esatte, ma la sensazione è nitida nel sogno" and in the discussion around the mass in Latin. Sereni and Montale's exchange allowed me to touch upon the consequences on Italian society of the Second Vatican Council and to bring attention to the problem of language, whether meaning is a forever given or something that needs to be constantly negotiated. In the last part of the session, students were invited to discuss whether their experience of learning foreign languages could resonate with the way in which Sereni portray Montale, sharing, if they wanted to, how they feel when they speak the various languages they know, whether they are more or less confident, more or less aware of their way of thinking, of what they manage to communicate. For the following week, they were asked to write a 400-word-long essay portraying a fictional or real person through their actions, tics, and habits. They could experiment with some of the techniques employed by Sereni, for example employing the 'presente narrativo' or 'storico'.

"And the irony I mean consists in the critic always speaking about the ultimate problems of life, but in a tone which implies that he is only discussing pictures and books, only the inessential and pretty ornaments of real life – and even then not their innermost substance but only their beautiful and useless surface" writes Lukács (1974: 9) in a page that has been the starting point for a session dedicated to the questions we try to answer when we discuss works of art. The text we discussed in relation to this issue was Primo Levi's *Tradurre Kafka*, a quite intense piece of writing which was presented towards the end of the academic year and was chosen because the students were familiar with the work of its author and usually actively engage with it.

> Amo e ammiro Kafka perché scrive in un modo che mi è totalmente precluso. Nel mio scrivere, nel bene e nel male, sapendolo o no, ho sempre teso a un trapasso dall'oscuro al chiaro, come (mi pare lo abbia detto Pirandello, non ricordo più dove) potrebbe fare una pompa-filtro, che aspira acqua torbida e la espelle decantata: magari sterile. Kafka batte il cammino opposto: dipana senza fine le allucinazioni che attinge da falde incredibilmente profonde, e non le filtra mai. Il lettore le sente pullulare di germi e spore: sono gravide di significati scottanti, ma non è mai aiutato a rompere il velo o ad aggirarlo per andare a vedere cosa esso nasconde. Kafka non tocca mai terra, non accondiscende mai a darti il bandolo del filo di Arianna.
>
> Ma questo mio amore è ambivalente, vicino allo spavento e al rifiuto: è simile al sentimento che si prova per una persona cara che soffre e ti chiede un aiuto che non le puoi dare. Non credo molto al riso di cui parla Brod: forse Kafka rideva raccontando agli amici, al tavolo della birreria, perché non si è sempre uguali a sé stessi, ma certo non rideva scrivendo. La sua sofferenza è genuina e continua, ti assale e non ti lascia più: ti senti come i suoi personaggi, condannato da un tribunale abietto e imperscrutabile, tentacolare, che invade la città e il mondo, annidato in soffitte lerce ma anche nella solennità oscura del duomo; o trasformato in un insetto goffo e ingombrante, inviso a tutti, disperatamente solo, ottuso, incapace di comunicare e di pensare, capace ormai soltanto di soffrire. (adapted from Levi, 2017: 939)

Also, in this case, the text has been edited in order to preserve its meaning despite the abridged form. By the time it was presented to the students, they had become quite familiar with the style and posture of the essay. After being briefly introduced to the topic of the session and the work of Kafka, they would usually identify quite readily the subjective point of view and comment on a statement like "mi pare lo abbia detto Pirandello, non ricordo più dove". In analysing this passage, particular attention was paid to the use of metaphors which required some time to be deciphered, also because of the difficulty of the lexicon. In order to facilitate their understanding, I showed them some images and a short video in the case of the *pompa-filtro*. Students were encouraged to reflect on Levi's use of such metaphors to mark the difference between Kafka's writing and his own but also underline that such a difference is connoted. Emotions, indeed, play a crucial role in Levi's ambiguous relationship with Kafka's work, and as the text progresses, it becomes clear that the divergent ways the two writers take to portray evil in literature touch upon ethical and existential problems.

> La famosa e commentatissima frase che chiude il libro come una pietra tombale («… e fu come se la vergogna gli dovesse sopravvivere») non mi pare affatto enigmatica. Di cosa si deve vergognare Josef K., quello stesso che aveva deciso di combattere fino alla morte, e che in tutte le svolte del libro si proclama innocente? Si vergogna di moltissime cose contraddittorie, perché non è coerente, e la sua essenza (come quella di quasi tutti) consiste nell'essere incoerente, non uguale a sé stesso nel corso del tempo, instabile, erratico, o anche diviso nello stesso istante, spaccato in due o più individualità che non combaciano.
>
> Si vergogna di aver conteso con il tribunale del duomo, e insieme di non aver resistito con energia sufficiente al tribunale delle soffitte. Di aver sprecato la vita in meschine gelosie d'ufficio, in falsi amori, in timidezze malate, in adempimenti statici e ossessivi. Di esistere quando ormai non avrebbe più dovuto esistere: di non aver trovato la forza di sopprimersi di sua mano quando tutto era perduto, prima che i due goffi portatori di morte lo visitassero. Ma sento, in questa vergogna, un'altra componente che conosco: Josef K., alla fine del suo angoscioso itinerario, prova vergogna perché esiste questo tribunale occulto e corrotto, che pervade tutto quanto lo circonda. È finalmente un tribunale umano, non divino: è fatto di uomini e dagli uomini, e Josef, col coltello già piantato nel cuore, prova vergogna di essere uomo. (Levi, 2017: 940)

The second passage aimed to underline that Levi's different view on the role and style of literature does not prevent him from a deep understanding of certain aspects of Kafka's work. By focusing on statements like "la famosa e commentatissima frase [...] non mi pare affatto enigmatica" and "ma sento, in questa vergogna, un'altra componente che conosco", students could reflect once more on the way in which the essay treats complex subject matters and the emotional response they provoke; the contradictory nature of shame but also the fact that Levi's personal experience is that of a concentration camp survivor. Students were invited to analyse the shift in Levi's attitude towards Kafka but also the reader by focusing on the style of the text. For this purpose, they were split into two groups, each analysing one passage, assessing the rhetorical strategies, for example the tendency of organising words in pairs in the first one ("amo e ammiro", "nel bene e nel male", "sapendolo o no", "germe e spore", "la città e il mondo", "spavento e rifiuto") and of structuring the second excerpts through repetition and climax ("si vergogna di aver conteso", "e insieme di non aver resistito", "di aver sprecato la vita", "di esistere", "di essere uomo"). The assignment for the following week was to write a 500-word-long text about a book, a movie or a videogame they thought it stated something true about life and should include observations, analysis, as well as the emotional response.

5. Conclusion

The overall response of the students to the class was positive, especially in relation to the assignments. These included narrative as well as reflective pieces, letters, and dialogues, all forms that the elusive genre of the essay experiments. For example, after having discussed Calvino's analysis of the power dynamics in *I promessi sposi*, students were asked to imagine the relationship between the protagonists of a picture of their choice; when we read two excerpts of *Piccolo e segreto* by Ortese, they had to write about the shift in our relation with the environment discussing Bocca's statement that "tutte le cose che oggi ci appaiono orrende, allora ci apparivano bellissime" (Bocca, 1980: 97). Other assignments involved writing a letter to a friend addressing a conflict, continuing a story when the first lines were provided or starting it in case it was the conclusion that was given. One out of four sessions was left open for students to share their writings, discuss the ways in which they developed the assignments and reflect on what they were learning. As Scheg (2015: 24) shows, introducing short creative writing tasks in academic contexts is a useful tool to help students "to enjoy writing and associate writing with positive elements of themselves". According to her, the benefit is two-fold; on the one hand, "students become more trusting of the classroom environment" and, on the other, their "confidence that their thoughts and abilities to write are welcome and respected" increases (2015: 27). Her reflections are part of a debate around the purpose of academic composition in L1 inaugurated by Bishop (1990) to which, I believe, research on foreign language writing could give an important contribution; essay classes can represent a space where students explore the complex and broad implications of learning to write, are presented with different styles and writing tasks, and build confidence in themselves.

Furthermore, these classes make a strong case for adopting a multilingual approach to writing pedagogy also at the university level when students are expected to write both in their first or second language and in one or more foreign ones. Recently, Forbes (2020) has analysed the phenomenon of cross-linguistic transfer of writing skills in schools, in particular from the foreign language to the first one, "if the use of writing strategies is explicitly developed within the FL classroom (where students are arguably more explicitly aware of themselves as *language* learners)", Forbes states, "then it seems logical that this knowledge could not only benefit FL writing tasks but might also positively affect L1 writing" (2020: 3). Because of its focus on the form, the essay can be a useful tool to facilitate the cross-linguistic transfer within university curricula.

Finally, the essay can offer an important contribution also within the field of foreign language education if we understand its aim as that of 'developing a better cognitive understanding of "self" and "other" and a more refined affective capacity for a desirable relationship to "otherness"' (Byram, 2008: 145). In his work, Byram challenges the idea that a learner should be considered "as one who is 'almost' a native speaker" and suggest instead to conceive them "as a 'complete' individual" (2008: 58). He too stresses the importance of developing intercultural competences which partially overlap with those indicated by Balboni and Caon (2015); "readiness to suspend disbelief about other cultures and belief about one's own", knowledge of "societal and individual interaction", "the ability to interpret a document or event from another culture, to explain it and relate it to documents from one's own", the capacity of "interpret and relate" (2008: 230-232). However, his approach distinguishes itself for the idea that foreign language teaching is a political action and among the intercultural competencies should develop a "critical cultural awareness", "an ability to evaluate critically and on the basis of explicit criteria perspectives, practices and products in one's own and other cultures and countries" (2008: 233). Not only do essays often explicitly address political issues, but the unsettling nature of its form may represent a particularly helpful resources in the education for intercultural citizenship envisaged by Byram. As Adorno points out, the essay ultimately "shakes off the illusion of a simple and fundamentally logical world, an illusion well suited to the defence of the status quo" (1991: 15).

References

Adorno, T. W. (1991). The Essay as Form. In Tiedemann, R. (Ed.), Nicholsen S. W. (Trans.), *Notes to Literature Vol I*, (pp. 3–23). New York: Columbia University Press.

Balboni, P. E., & Caon, F. (2015). *La comunicazione interculturale*. Venice: Marsilio.

Berardinelli, A. (2002). *La forma del saggio. Definizione e attualità di un genere letterario*. Venice: Marsilio.

Bishop, W. (1990). *Released Into Language. Options for Teaching Creative Writing*. Urbana: National Council of Teachers of English.

Bocca, G. (1980). *Miracolo all'italiana*. Milan: Feltrinelli.

Boetcher Joeres, R. (1993). The passionate essay. Radical feminist essayists. In Boetcher Joeres, R. & Mittman, E. (Eds.), *Politics of the Essay*, (pp. 151–171). Indianapolis: Indiana University Press.

Byram, M. (2008). *From Foreign Language Education to Education for Intercultural Citizenship. Essays and Reflections*. Blue Ridge Summit, PA: Multilingual Matters.

D'Agata, J. (Ed.), (2009). *The Lost Origins of the Essay*. Saint Paul, Minn.: Graywolf Press.

Forbes, K. (2020). *Cross-Linguistic Transfer of Writing Strategies. Interactions between Foreign Language and First Language Classrooms*. Blue Ridge Summit, PA: Multilingual Matters.

Landrum-Geyer, D. (2015). Essaying. In Berg, D. & May, L. A. (Eds), *Creative Composition. Inspiration and Techniques for Writing Instruction*, (pp. 1–9). Blue Ridge Summit, PA: Multilingual Matters.

Levi, P. (2017). Tradurre Kafka. In Belpoliti, M. (Ed), *Opere complete vol. II*, (pp. 939–940). Turin: Einaudi.

Lukács, G. (1974). On the Nature and Form of the Essay. A Letter to Leo Popper. In Bostock A. (trans.), *Soul and Form*, (pp. 1-18). Cambridge, MA: The Mit Press.

Scheg, A. B. (2015). Give it a Taste. Serving Creative Writing in Small Doses. In Berg, D. & May, L. A. (Eds.), *Creative Composition. Inspiration and Techniques for Writing Instruction*, (pp. 24–29). Blue Ridge Summit, PA: Multilingual Matters.

Sereni, V. (2013). Ognuno riconosce i suoi. In Raboni, G. (Ed.), *Poesie e prose*, (pp. 1006–1014). Milan: Mondadori.

Shipley, J. T. (1970). 'Essay' in *Dictionary of world literary terms. Forms, techniques, criticism*. London: Allen & Unwin.

Woolf, V. (2003). The Modern Essay. In McNeillie, A. (Ed.), *The Common Reader, Vol 1*, (pp. 247–262). London: Vintage, vol. I.

Index

A

academic; 3; 7; 16; 32; 46; 48; 49; 94; 97; 99; 106; 115; 207; 216; 217; 221; 222; 229; 230; 234; 238; 240; 248; 255; 266; 267; 298; 317; 320; 321; 324; 326; 328; 329
Accademia dei Filodrammatici; 312
Accademia della Crusca; 16; 28
acquisition; 3; 6; 7; 29; 38; 106; 119; 126; 194; 215; 220; 221; 222; 235; 236; 238; 251; 253; 254; 258; 262; 264; 265; 267; 271; 272; 273; 274; 275; 276; 277; 279; 282; 283; 305; 306; 317
Adorno; 319; 320; 321; 329
Adriatic Sea; 298; 300
aesthetic; 60; 74; 80; 305; 306; 308; 310
affixation; 108
Anna Maria Barbera; 193
anthropology; 263; 316
anxiety; 273; 278; 280; 306
Archaeology; 216; 217
Arno; 298
articulation; 3; 4; 8; 10; 11
artist; 76; 97; 220; 224; 305; 306; 307; 308
Arts; 27; 31; 69; 216; 219; 298
assessment; 15; 18; 30; 31; 92; 93; 96; 229; 242; 243; 248
Atlante lessicale toscano; 23
atmosphere; 139; 272; 278; 280; 305; 307; 308; 309; 310; 313
autonomy; 38; 47; 48; 49; 98; 127; 178; 282

B

Bacchino Malato; 229
Bacilieri; 62; 81; 216; 217; 220; 221; 222; 223; 224
Balboni; 99; 100; 240; 241; 254; 255; 301; 302; 317; 320; 323; 324; 329
balloon; 60; 63; 65; 67; 70; 71; 72; 77; 80; 203
BBC; 276
Beato Angelico; 229
Bertinetto; 8; 134
Biasini; 233; 238; 240
bilingualism; 22
Blanco; 194
blasfemia; 168
blasphemy; 187
Boccaccio; 18; 183; 188
Bologna Declaration; 95
Borotalco; 192; 193
Botticelli; 229
British; 81; 216; 229; 252; 256; 257; 259
Buster Brown; 80

C

Calvino; 324
Canepari; 9; 10
canovaccio; 311; 313; 315
Caon; 194; 323; 324; 329
caption/s; 63; 65; 67; 70; 71; 72; 73; 80; 235; 242; 272; 273; 274; 275; 276; 280; 281; 282
Capuano; 130; 182
Caravaggio; 226; 227; 229

Cardinaletti; 129
Carlo Levi; 297
Carlo Magno; 18
Carlo Verdone; 192
Carta dei dialetti d'Italia; 22
cartoon/s; 59; 61; 62; 70; 71; 271; 272; 275; 276; 277; 279; 280; 282; 283; 284
Castaldi; 75; 80
cazzo; 169; 170; 177; 179; 182; 183; 192; 194; 196; 205; 206
CEFIRE; xix
CEFR; X, 87; 89; 92; 93; 96; 99; 219; 220; 221; 222; 223; 224; 226; 227; 231; 238
character; 8; 22; 23; 31; 35; 99; 4; 14; 21
Checco Zelone; 193
Chiapello; 38; 44
children; 80; 82; 167; 249; 271; 272; 275; 277; 283; 284; 316
Chomsky; 5
classroom; 6; 7; 13; 40; 41; 43; 48; 54; 68; 69; 88; 98; 166; 167; 180; 181; 192; 216; 220; 222; 224; 226; 233; 234; 235; 236; 251; 252; 263; 264; 265; 271; 272; 273; 277; 278; 279; 280; 283; 284; 309; 310; 320; 328; 325
CNN; 276
code-switching; 22; 261
coglione; 166
colorito; 168; 182; 187
comic strips; 60; 61; 62; 70; 71; 73; 79; 80
comics; 59; 60; 61; 62; 63; 64; 65; 66; 67; 68; 69; 70; 71; 72; 73; 74; 75; 77; 78; 79; 80; 81; 82; 83; 203
Commedia dell'arte; 311
Common European Framework of Reference for Language; 180

communication; 37; 41; 45; 46; 48; 53; 60; 66; 87; 88; 90; 91; 92; 93; 97; 99; 100; 130; 168; 171; 186; 187; 199; 207; 223; 224; 233; 235; 236; 239; 244; 259; 260; 263; 266; 272; 277; 278; 279; 295; 305; 306; 309; 310; 314; 315; 315; 317; 319; 323; 324
competence; 39; 42; 88; 92; 93; 95; 96; 97; 99; 100; 105; 135; 137; 140; 220; 221; 223; 224; 225; 227; 228; 231; 235; 236; 237; 238; 239; 240; 243; 244; 276; 277; 293; 306; 317; 372
composition; 60; 66; 229; 259; 320; 329
compound/s; 123; 124; 125; 126; 127
comprehension; 46; 48; 55; 94; 95; 132; 199; 220; 221; 236; 240; 241; 248; 271; 272; 273; 275; 276; 281; 282; 299; 319; 320
Computer-Assisted Language Learning; XI, 40, 45, 48
Conative; 171
connotative; 174; 175; 180; 204; 248
constructivism; 38
cooperation; 43
CORINÉI; 45; 49; 53; 54
Corriere della Sera; 88; 99
Corte di Cassazione; 185
Cortelazzo; 23; 136; 138
Corto Maltese; 74
Costamagna; 194
Council of Europe; 38; 39; 88; 95; 180; 219
COVID; 241; 244; 255; 266
Criminal Code; 180
Cristo si è fermato a Eboli; 297
cultural translation; 254

culture; 4; 5; 6; 45; 59; 60; 63; 69; 71; 81; 82; 100; 169; 186; 217; 234; 235; 238; 243; 251; 254; 256; 257; 261; 262; 267; 277; 278; 291; 292; 293; 294; 295; 297; 298; 300; 301; 309; 311; 315; 322; 323; 329

Cursing; 168; 169; 170; 171; 174; 175; 176; 180; 181; 184; 186; 188; 189; 199

D

Dante; 18; 129; 138; 182; 183; 188; 312
David di Donatello; 200
De vulgari eloquentia; 129; 138
deductive approach; 76
denotative; 174; 175
deverbal nouns; 109; 110
Devon; 255; 256; 257; 258; 259; 260; 261; 262; 263; 264; 265; 266; 267
Dewaele; 168; 180
Diabolik; 62; 74; 81
diachronic; 17; 148; 149; 150; 151; 154; 173
dialectology; 15; 17; 21; 22; 23; 30; 31; 129; 130; 135; 137; 138; 148; 154; 155
dialettologia; 15; 22; 23
diamesic; 173
diastratic; 173
diatopic; 173
didascalia; 63; 65
diglossia; 22; 23; 129; 136
Direct Method; 291; 298
Diritto Penale; 180
Disney; 70; 73; 81; 82
Divina Commedia; 312
Dolce Stil Novo; 311
dramaturgy; 314; 315
Dylan Dog; 62; 74; 81; 82

Dysphemism; 170; 173

E

Emanata; 63; 65; 67
Emotive; 92; 171
Erri de Luca; 297
ethnographers; 253; 256; 263
ethnography; 251; 252; 253; 254; 255; 256; 258; 261; 263; 264; 265; 266; 267
Euphemism; 170; 192
extracurricular; 216; 219

F

Fabio Volo; 183
Fabri Fibra; 194
Family Guy; 276; 279
fanculo; 166; 202
Fantozzi; 237
fashion; 60; 78; 99; 118
Fatto Quotidiano; 190
feedback; 31; 42; 43; 46; 47; 216; 218; 219; 224; 226; 236; 241; 242; 243; 268
FL; 38; 43; 45; 57; 60; 62; 66; 68; 69; 78; 233; 234; 235; 236; 237; 238; 239; 240; 242; 243; 244; 329
Florence; 130; 217; 262; 263; 296; 297; 298
fluency; 71; 105; 106; 107; 108; 234; 239; 240; 244
fluidity; 261
foreign language; 6; 7; 38; 45; 46; 48; 55; 60; 68; 69; 71; 91; 92; 95; 96; 97; 98; 109; 126; 130; 132; 139; 180; 182; 185; 186; 187; 217; 218; 233; 258; 276; 292; 306; 308; 309; 313; 314; 316; 317; 319; 320; 321; 323; 329
formale aulico; 172; 173

Francesco Sabatini; 16
Francoprovençal; 151
Fumetto; 75; 77; 78, 79

G

Galician; 153
Gallese; 306
Game; 174; 310; 314
Gardner; 278
gender; 110; 113; 123; 150; 260; 266; 279
geography; 22; 291; 292; 293; 294; 295; 296; 298; 299; 300; 301; 302
Georg Lukács; 320
Gianni De Luca; 68
Gianni Rodari; 316
Ginzburg; 324
Giotto; 225; 226; 229
Giovenale; 188
Giubbe Rosse; 324; 325
Giuseppe Verdi; 295
globalization; 297
glottodidactics; 307; 308
Goethe; 297
Goldoni; 131; 137
grammar; 3; 5; 19; 27; 28; 45; 60; 66; 68; 70; 76; 106; 151; 155; 176; 179; 186; 223; 225; 226; 229; 235; 239; 271; 276; 280; 282; 306; 308; 314
Grammatica storica; 20; 27; 28
graphic novels; 60; 62; 67; 70; 73; 74; 75; 81; 82
Guido Piovene; 297
Gutter; 63; 65; 68

H

harassment; 187
Herron; 272; 281

higher education; 13; 45; 59; 66; 77; 89; 95; 96; 100; 215; 236; 253; 257; 267; 278; 305
history; 15; 17; 18; 19; 20; 21; 24; 25; 26; 28; 30; 31; 32; 62; 75; 80; 81; 82; 83; 130; 137; 148; 183; 215; 216; 217; 218; 219; 221; 222; 224; 226; 227; 231; 256; 262; 266; 292; 301
History of Art; 215; 216; 217; 218; 221; 222; 224; 226; 227; 230; 231
History of the Italian Language; 15; 17; 18; 21; 30; 31
human speech; 3; 4
Humanism; 18
Humanities; 216; 217; 220
Humboldt-Universität; 5
humour; 61; 169; 271; 272; 277; 278; 279; 284
hypertextuality; 90

I

Iacopone da Todi; 131
identity; 116; 171; 178; 252; 254; 258; 261; 263; 278
Il Compianto sul Cristo morto; 229
immersion; 7; 37; 43; 251; 252; 258; 299
inductive approach; 76; 306
innovation; 38; 45; 80; 90; 239
Instructional Humour Processing Theory; 279
intercultural; 37; 38; 39; 45; 46; 48; 49; 54; 55; 56; 87; 88; 92; 93; 96; 100; 222; 223; 224; 235; 236; 238; 244; 253; 265; 266; 305; 308; 317; 319; 320; 322; 323; 324; 329
interdiction; 170
interdisciplinary; 16; 45; 59; 75; 216; 234; 252; 253
Internazionale; 190

Italian language; 4; 5; 8; 15; 17; 18; 21; 29; 30; 31; 59; 60; 69; 87; 88; 97; 98; 99; 100; 110; 117; 124; 126; 165; 167; 168; 180; 181; 183; 185; 186; 206; 216; 217; 219; 220; 234; 236; 238; 239; 243; 251; 254; 258; 267; 272; 296; 302; 306; 310; 311; 312; 313; 316

Italian Studies; 3; 4; 5; 6; 7; 13; 15; 16; 18; 24; 29; 31; 32; 89; 137; 154; 206; 253; 255; 258; 267; 291; 292; 293; 298; 300

italiani regionali; 129; 130; 137; 154

italiano burocratico; 172; 173

italiano colloquiale; 172

italiano gergale; 172; 173

italiano regionale popolare; 172

Italo-Romance; 142; 148; 149; 150; 152; 154

Italy; 15; 17; 18; 19; 20; 21; 22; 23; 27; 30; 31; 32; 33; 45; 46; 54; 55; 75; 79; 80; 81; 82; 83; 129; 130; 131; 135; 136; 137; 141; 142; 147; 149; 152; 154; 186; 190; 217; 220; 221; 222; 224; 225; 226; 228; 231; 233; 238; 257; 258; 259; 263; 267; 273; 291; 292; 293; 294; 295; 296; 297; 300; 302; 311

J

Jay; 169; 170; 171
Jespersen's Cycle; 141; 142

K

Kafka; 326; 327; 328
Krashen; 282; 306

L

l'albo a fumetti; 61

L2; 3; 4; 5; 6; 7; 8; 9; 10; 11; 13; 71; 94; 95; 181; 194; 197; 239; 271; 272; 273; 274; 275; 277; 278; 279; 280; 281; 282; 283; 284; 298; 299; 305; 313; 314

La Primavera; 229

La Repubblica; 88; 190

La Scuola di Atene; 229

La strada verso casa; 183

La Vocazione di San Matteo; 229

language acquisition; 3; 6; 29; 38; 106; 126; 222; 235; 238; 253; 258; 262; 264; 265; 271; 273; 274; 277; 284; 305; 306; 317

Languages for Specific Purposes; 87; 97; 99; 215

Latin; 18; 19; 24; 25; 26; 27; 30; 116; 117; 118; 121; 122; 129; 141; 145; 149; 188; 265; 325

Laura Pausini; 189

learners; 13; 37; 44; 45; 46; 47; 49; 57; 66; 67; 87; 88; 89; 91; 92; 93; 94; 95; 98; 99; 100; 105; 106; 111; 114; 115; 117; 126; 142; 181; 218; 221; 222; 234; 235; 236; 237; 238; 239; 241; 266; 271; 272; 273; 274; 275; 276; 278280; 281; 282; 283; 284; 306; 309; 310; 315; 322; 329

learning process; 95; 97; 126; 140; 220; 224; 278; 306; 307; 308

Ledgeway; 21; 26; 27; 130; 133; 134; 135; 138; 143; 146; 149; 152; 153

Leo Ortolani; 61; 62

Leonese; 153

Lessico Etimologico Italiano digitale; 23

Lexicalizations; 146; 147

LiceoStabili; 39; 40; 41; 42; 44; 53

lingua franca; 46; 97
linguistic transfer; 234; 329
linguistics; 3; 4; 5; 6; 7; 13; 15; 16; 17; 18; 19; 20; 21; 23; 24; 25; 27; 28; 29; 30; 31; 32; 40; 89; 96; 115; 137; 148; 168; 183; 258
literacy; 59; 60; 66; 67; 76; 81; 82; 110; 130
Little Nemo; 80
London National Gallery; 229
Loporcaro; 8; 135; 138; 149; 153
Loredana Bertè; 195
Luca Barbarossa; 195
Luca Serianni; 292
Luciano Pavarotti; 292
Lucio Dalla; 194

M

Mahmood; 194
Maiden; 23; 24; 26; 27; 130; 135; 138
Måneskin; 196
Marazzini; 21; 137
Marcus Aurelius; 320
Mare Adriatico; 300
Martin Mystère; 62; 74; 81
Massimiliano Bruno; 165; 167
merda; 166; 168; 176; 177; 182; 183; 188; 191; 201; 206
metafora; 63; 65
Metalinguistic; 3; 6; 7; 10; 12; 43; 46; 47; 106; 111; 171; 185
Metaphor/s; 175; 176; 183; 185; 190; 202; 203; 204; 261; 327
Michelangelo; 226; 227
Migliorini; 21; 131
Migration Observatory; 257
Mobile-Assisted Language Learning; 40
Modern Languages; 44; 206; 221; 251; 252; 253; 254; 255; 267

Molinelli; 142
monolingual; 7; 32; 262
Montale; 312; 324; 325
morpheme; 108
morphosyntax; 138; 141; 143
motivation/s; 38; 87; 148; 187; 218; 224; 233; 236; 237; 238; 242; 279; 306; 307; 307
multilingual; 39; 46; 47; 48; 55; 66; 67; 129; 251; 253; 254
multimodal; 58; 60; 66; 67; 68; 234; 244
Museo Correr; 229

N

neo-standard; 135; 172; 173
Nunan; 42; 47

O

obscenity; 187; 188
onomatopea; 63; 65
Orbis Latinus; 27
Ortese; 131; 300; 324; 328

P

Palladio; 226
Paola Cortellesi; 200
paralinguistic; 234; 281; 284
parasynthesis; 109; 118
parolacce; 166; 168; 182; 183
part of speech; 108; 109; 115; 127
Patota; 20; 21
pedagogy; 29; 66; 93; 233; 239; 275; 277; 329
Peppa Pig; 271; 272; 275; 277; 279; 280; 281; 282; 283; 284
Phatic; 171
philology; 17; 184; 186; 187; 206

Index

Phonetics; 3; 4; 5; 6; 7; 8; 10; 11; 13; 186; 235; 311
phonology; 4; 5; 10; 13; 19; 20; 22; 27; 107; 109; 121; 138; 143
Piccolo e segreto; 328
Piero della Francesca; 229
Pietro Aretino; 189
Pirandello; 183; 313; 326; 327
Placito capuano; 130
Plato; 320
Poetic; 70; 71; 171; 194; 197
Polezzi; 257; 261; 267
politics; 22; 97; 99; 276; 293
Pompeii; 167; 188
Porreca; 220
Portuguese; 39; 153; 255
Process Drama; 305; 306; 307; 308; 315; 316; 317

Q

questione della lingua; 131; 137

R

Raffaello; 226
Raiplay; 249
Referential; 171
Rinascimento; 19; 21
Roberto Benigni; 193
Rohlfs; 27; 138; 143; 145; 146; 147
role-play; 227; 228; 308; 316
Roman Jakobson; 171

S

Sannicandrese; 148
Sanremo; 194; 195; 196
Sanskrit; 107
sarcasm; 169
Sardinian; 25; 116; 138; 150; 151; 153

Satire; 81; 188
Sciascia; 297
second language; 7; 29; 38; 105; 106; 126; 182; 235; 254; 257; 259; 272; 278; 279; 299; 300; 305; 306; 307; 313; 315; 316; 317
Second World War; 297
semantics; 106; 107; 118; 278
Seneca; 320
Sereni; 324; 325; 326
sexist; 181; 187; 200; 201
Sio; 61; 62; 73
skills; 3; 4; 7; 11; 29; 38; 45; 48; 71; 72; 75; 76; 81; 87; 93; 94; 95; 97; 182; 198; 206; 207; 215; 216; 217; 218; 219; 220; 221; 222; 223; 224; 225; 226; 228; 231; 233; 236; 237; 238; 239; 240; 241; 242; 243; 244; 252; 254; 256; 257; 258; 259; 266; 267; 271; 272; 273; 275; 278; 294; 299; 302; 305; 306; 309; 316; 319; 320; 323; 324; 329
SLA; 38; 44; 272; 281
Sobrero; 23; 99
Sorbonne; 43; 46; 54; 293; 294
sottocodici; 99
South Park; 279
speech; 3; 4; 5; 7; 8; 12; 63; 65; 67; 70; 71; 73; 80; 90; 94; 95; 105; 106; 108; 109; 115; 127; 130; 137; 142; 167; 168; 173; 179; 182; 186; 193; 194; 197; 207; 234; 272; 273; 275; 277; 281; 283; 284; 315
standard letterario; 172; 173; 185; 202
storytelling; 71
subtitling; 181; 198; 233; 234; 235; 236; 237; 238; 239; 240; 241; 242; 243; 244; 248; 262; 264; 267; 273
suffix; 108; 109; 110; 111; 112; 113; 114; 115; 116; 117; 118; 119; 120; 121; 127

suppletion; 120
Svevo; 297
syntax; 19; 20; 22; 25; 29; 31; 107; 133; 135; 174; 202; 259; 278; 308

T

tabù; 168
Tartamella; 182
tecnico-scientifico; 172; 173
teletandem; 38; 39; 42; 44; 46; 47; 48; 49; 53; 54; 55; 56
Telmon; 129
Teresa Mannino; 193
Tex; 62; 74; 81;
textbook; 4; 92; 277; 280; 294; 296
The Godfather; 197
The Kennedy Center; 69
The Looney Tunes Show; 276
theatre; 171; 193; 201; 305; 306; 307; 308; 309; 310; 311; 312; 313; 314; 315; 316; 317
Tintoretto; 227
Topolino; 61; 62; 70; 81
Totò; 313
transcript; 241; 248; 264; 280; 281
translator; 181; 186; 203; 206; 207; 238; 240; 244; 258; 261
Tre Corone; 131; 137
Tre uomini e una gamba; 198
Treccani; 28
Tuscan; 31; 129; 130; 131; 132; 133; 134; 135; 138; 151

U

Uffizi; 229
undergraduate; 5; 6; 132; 215; 216; 217; 218; 235; 236; 237; 238; 252; 254; 256; 265
UNESCO; 38; 217
UNIBO-Lyon; 39; 40; 41; 42; 47; 56
UNIRoma3-GU; 39; 40; 41; 42; 43; 47; 56
UniTO-UMCS; 39; 40; 42; 43; 45; 56
Universal Grammar; 151
University of Oxford; 257; 320

V

Vanderplank; 272; 273; 274; 275
Varrone; 167
Vasari; 227
Vasco Pratolini; 297
Vasco Rossi; 196
Venice; 296; 297
Viaggio in Italia; 297
vignetta; 61; 62; 64; 65
vilification; 187; 190
Vincenzo Bellini; 295
Viterbese; 148
Viva l'Italia; 165
vocabulary; 3; 59; 69; 70; 71; 74; 92; 105; 106; 107; 121; 123; 126; 127; 174; 180; 186; 187; 190; 199; 202; 220; 221; 223; 225; 228; 229; 235; 236; 271; 272; 273; 275; 278; 279; 280; 281; 282; 300; 308; 324
vulgar; 18; 30; 165; 167; 168; 169; 171; 173; 174; 176; 177; 179; 180; 181; 183; 185; 186; 187; 188; 191; 192; 193; 194; 197; 198; 200; 202; 207

W

W.I.T.C.H; 74
WebQuests; 98; 100
Wedlock; 184; 188
Winsor McCay; 80
word-formation; 105; 106; 107; 108; 109; 126; 127

Z

Zerocalcare; 62; 81

www.ingramcontent.com/pod-product-compliance
Lightning Source LLC
Chambersburg PA
CBHW072120290426
44111CB00012B/1716